THE ULTIMATE ENCYCLOPEDIA OF
CRICKET

THIS IS A CARLTON BOOK

First published in 1997 by
Carlton Books Limited
20 St Anne's Court
Wardour Street
London W1V 3AW

10 9 8 7 6 5 4 3 2 1

A CIP catalogue record for this book is available from the British Library

ISBN 1 85868 418 8

Project Editor: Martin Corteel
Editorial Assistant: Roland Hall
Project Art Direction: Diane Klein
Picture Research: Lorna Ainger
Production: Garry Lewis
Design: Steve Wilson

Printed and bound in Dubai

ACKNOWLEDGEMENTS
All the first-class statistics comply with the Match Guides issued by the Association of Cricket Statistics. The assistance of Philip Bailey is acknowledged in the compilation of career records. The secretarial services of Lyn Steel proved invaluable. The authors are also grateful for the help rendered by David Lemmon.

(OPPOSITE) FUN TIME *West Indian fans*
(OVERLEAF) KNOCKING FOR SIX *Graham Thorpe*

THE ULTIMATE ENCYCLOPEDIA OF CRICKET

The definitive illustrated guide to World Cricket

Peter Arnold and Peter Wynne-Thomas

CARLTON

CORNHILL
CORNHILL
CORNHILL

CONTENTS

PAUL ADAMS At the World Cup 1996

501 NOT OUT Brian Lara's record-breaker

CASTLE LAGER

INTRODUCTION

It used to be said of cricket that it was played in those countries which at one time made up the British Empire. That this is no longer true can be seen from the chapter in this book dealing with cricket around the world. But it cannot be pretended that cricket has ever threatened to challenge for popularity the sport of association football, which is now played in practically every country that exists.

However, where cricket can make a plea for supremacy over most games is in the deep affection it inspires in its followers. Cricket has its aficionados like bullfighting, although it would be hard to find two more different recreations. This love of the game partly comes from its complexity and variety. There are so many angles from which the game can be appreciated and discussed. This in turn has given cricket the best literature of any sport. Such writers as John Arlott, Neville Cardus, C.L.R. James, R.C. Robertson-Glasgow, Alan Ross and Francis Thompson have written memorably about the game. Cricket is, or at least was, a game which goes with an ambience, an atmosphere, an attitude, a way of life, perhaps most commemorated in the phrase "It's not cricket", meaning something which is not in the highest traditions of fairness, sportsmanship and "playing the game". However, as with many things relating to cricket, this phrase may not be all it seems. In quoting it in *Encyclopaedia of Word and Phrase Origins* (Fact on File Publications, New York and Oxford, 1987), Robert Hendrickson suggests that the phrase was possibly first used when villagers of Boxgrove, near Winchester, were prosecuted for playing the game of cricket on a Sunday in 1622, and defended themselves by claiming "It's not cricket", thus hoping to avoid paying their proper fines for breaking the law. If this were true, then the phrase should not represent an aspiration to the highest levels of behaviour at all but a mean way of avoiding punishment by lying.

The idea that cricket is a byword of honesty and fair play is a comparatively recent one. Sir Henry Newbolt's poem 'Vitai Lampada', extolling the sense of honour and bravery which the schoolboy cricketer "bears through life like a torch in flame", having felt his Captain's hand on his shoulder and his orders to "play up! play up! and play the game!" was published only in 1897, during what is now called cricket's "Golden Age".

As the chapter in this book on the origins of cricket relates, cricket had been played for hundreds of years before this, and in the eighteenth century in England was a prime form of betting for high stakes, and no doubt attracted many of the same rogues more usually associated with the equally ancient and aristocratic sport of horse-racing. Bets were struck not only on the outcome of matches but on how many runs individual batsmen would make and attendant bookmakers would change the odds about events as play progressed. Of course this led to bribery, with William Lambert of Surrey, the leading professional all-rounder of his day, being banned from Lord's after allegedly fixing the England v Nottingham match in 1817. And as the chapter on Test cricket in this book describes, two members of the English touring party in Australia in 1881–82 took bribes to lose a match and were denounced when they failed to bribe a third player, who was beaten up for reporting them. A far cry from "playing the game".

In the first half of the twentieth century the idea that people might bet on cricket would have seemed sacrilege to 99 per cent of its followers. Yet with legal restrictions lifted from betting in England in the 1960s, it was not long before bookmakers had offices or tents in the major cricket grounds and even that pillar of the establishment and conservatism, the BBC's "Test Match Special", began telling listeners the current betting odds as Test match fortunes fluctuated. Ironically it was in 1981, 100 years after the betting scandal in Australia, that the Australian players Dennis Lillee and Rodney Marsh placed bets on England to win the Test at Headingley when the bookmakers were offering odds of 500–1 against. That Lillee and Marsh were playing and collected some very nice winnings was regarded only with amusement by cricket fans. There was rightly no suggestion of any impropriety on the part of the Australians, only admiration tinged with envy for their good judgement.

Cricket is a game which is ever changing, usually, according to its fans, for the worse, but, as with the gambling, what is unthinkable one day often becomes the acceptable norm the next. Sunday cricket is an example. The law banning it back in the seventeenth century did not survive long, but it was only during the Second World War that club cricket became common on Sundays in England, and it was not until 1966 that professional cricket was played on a Sunday, and even then it was still illegal to charge for admission. The Sunday League began in 1969, and the first Sunday play in a Test match occurred as late as 1981.

One-day international cricket began in Australia in 1970–71, and there is now so much of it that for space reasons this book has dealt fully only with the apex of it, the four-yearly World Cup.

Cricket fatalists are always claiming that cricket is on its deathbed. One fear is that because of the attractions of more 'instant' diversions there are not enough boys playing it in schools, which anyway lack the equipment and playing fields. Another fear is that the attention span of the average fan in today's rush of a world grows shorter and shorter and will soon be unable to cope with a game which might last for days. And the cricket fan himself is changing, to the annoyance, for example, of the typical MCC member, who likes to sit wearing his bacon-and-egg tie in the womanless pavilion at Lord's and tut at the behaviour of the bare-chested or weirdly dressed in the popular stands, especially those who chant 'England's barmy army', a recent addition to the equally mindless 'Mexican wave'.

Cricket has always embraced a wide variety of fans and, indeed, players. It was only a few years ago that the announcement of 'F.J. Titmus' as the batsman going out to bat at Lord's was changed as he approached the wicket to 'Titmus, F.J.', he being a professional, not an amateur. He was luckier than the turn of the century professional, who would not have his initials at all on the scorecard, while the amateur would also have the prefix 'Mr'. Thus the England openers against the Australians at the Oval were "Mr. F.S. Jackson and Hayward". The Australians, being a sort of half-and-half, were allowed their initials but not the 'Mr.', as in M.A. Noble.

It is hoped that this book will appeal to the Lords, the Misters, and those whose initials come front or back. As many aspects of the game as possible are covered. Details of the early history of the game are constantly being discovered, and the chapter covering cricket's origins contains the latest research. The spread of cricket around the world is recorded in a summary of the state of the game in those countries where it is at all organized. The Test cricket chapter attempts to give a summary of the sway of fortunes in the series of games between each pair of the nine Test-playing countries. The World Cup, thrillingly won in 1996 by one of the latest entrants to Test cricket, Sri Lanka, is covered by a chapter which describes all six competitions to date. The players are dealt with in two sections, the larger containing biographies and career figures of some 200 or so of the best cricketers in the history of the game. A separate section deals with the legends of the game and gives fuller details of 12 of the giants who have strode the cricket stage, from W.G. Grace to Brian Lara.

There are separate chapters on the famous grounds, on the administration and structure of the game, on the history of the Laws, on equipment, on culture, and on scandals and controversies. There is a short records and statistics section and a chronology, although the book is not meant to be a statistical tome – *Wisden* can supply all the figures – but more one to be read for enjoyment and used as a reminder and reference.

All those casual unsung scorers in club matches all over the world, who each week have to call out 'bowler's name?' when the opposition make a bowling change, will be amused to hear of the cry when Glamorgan visited Cambridge University in 1996, and Glamorgan's Test bowler Steve Watkin was unlucky enough to have had his wallet stolen (at Cambridge? It's not cricket). When going out to field he asked a member of the press to cancel his credit cards for him. An enquiry from one of the issuing companies led to a yelled request from the pavilion: 'bowler's mother's maiden name?'

THE OPENERS COME OUT *The South Africans at Lord's in 1994.*

THE EARLY HISTORY OF CRICKET

The game of cricket began in the Weald in south-east England. The landed gentry of the area adapted the game, took it to the great public schools and to Oxford and Cambridge Universities. Thence the schoolboys and students took it back to their estates. In Nottinghamshire and Yorkshire in particular the game rapidly gained popularity. Through the army, cricket was introduced across the British Empire.

The search for when and where cricket started has occupied historians since the Reverend James Pycroft made the first attempt at tracing the story of the game in 1851.

A single statement by a witness in a court case in Guildford in 1598 contains the first definite mention of cricket. John Derrick, aged 59, stated that at the time he was a schoolboy at the Free School in Guildford he and his friends played "creckett" on a disputed piece of land in Holy Trinity Parish in Guildford.

Cricket was therefore being played by boys in Guildford around 1550. In 1541 an Act of Parliament aimed at stimulating the practice of archery among the populace banned people from playing and wasting their time on a great list of common games, but cricket was not one of those. Clearly cricket at that point was confined to boys in a relatively small area of south-east England and not worthy of mention.

The second definite mention of the game again comes from the Guildford area, from the hamlet of Wanborough. Here in 1613 a person was hit by another using a "cricket staff". Nine years later an ecclesiastical court in Chichester had before it five youths accused of playing cricket in the churchyard at Boxgrove, a village near Chichester, on a Sunday. In 1624 a coroner's jury at West Hoathly in Sussex listened to a case in which a man accidentally hit and killed a fellow player with a small staff called a "cricket batt". These two men were part of a group playing cricket on Horsted Green.

Five years later came the case of the curate of Ruckinge near Maidstone being heard in the Archdeacons Court. The curate was playing at "cricketts" with some of his parishioners after divine service on a Sunday.

These stray references to cricket continue on through the seventeenth century. Plotting them on a map of the British Isles reveals that they are all confined to the south-east corner of England and form a rough crescent, from Chichester in the south-west up to Surrey and across to the south-west area of Kent. The crescent neatly encloses the Weald – that part between the North and South Downs, which in Tudor times was the Black Country of England. Some 80 iron and glass foundries flourished in the region, using the ample iron ore deposits and, for fuel, the charcoal which could be easily produced from the abundant supply of wood from the Ashdown and St Leonards forests.

It has been suggested by some historians that cricket as an organized game began among the shepherds on the Downs, the theory being that the shepherd's crook could be a bat and the wicket gate used for sheep pens could have been the stumps; in addition the pasture grazed by the sheep would have been an ideal surface on which to play. However, the first references to a cricket bat all note it to have been a small batten or staff, whereas a shepherd's crook was six or more feet in length. The sheep certainly grazed the pasture, but generally on the considerable slopes of the Downs, rather than on the flatter land which would be more useful for arable crops. The other argument against shepherds being the instigators of cricket is that looking after sheep is normally a rather solitary occupation.

It is far more likely that ironworkers and those involved in the trades connected with the iron industry were the ones playing cricket.

Whichever theory one accepts, cricket certainly became popular in the Weald, which was itself a rather enclosed community. The game therefore took many years to emerge from the south-east corner of England. In any case most other regions had their own games

CRICKET IN THE VICTORIAN ERA *An illustration from* Every Boy's Book *by Edmund Routledge (1868).*

involving balls being hit with sticks: Yorkshire had knurr and spell, Gloucestershire had stoolball, Scotland had golf, and Ireland had hurling.

In the second half of the seventeenth century cricket began to attract spectators and gamblers. In 1668 there comes a mention of men selling drink at a cricket match near Maidstone and later the accounts of two landed gentry show money being paid for cricketing purposes, especially by the Earl of Sussex who resided at Herstmonceux Castle in East Sussex, and by Sir John Pelham, who lived at Halland, north-east of Lewes.

In 1700 a series of matches was played on Clapham Common with the players each betting £10, and in 1705 there is a mention of cricket being played on Walworth Common. Cricket was about to take London by storm. The first reference to a team styled "London" comes in a newspaper notice of 1707, when there were two "great matches" between London and Croydon, one in Croydon, the other in Holborn. The days were now clearly gone when the landed gentry and the people of the capital had no knowledge of cricket. A political pamphlet of 1712 attacking the Duke of Marlborough and Lord Townshend features the two playing cricket supposedly near Fern-hill in Windsor Forest for 20 guineas.

That match may be fanciful, but cricket was certainly established at Trinity College, Cambridge, before then – Thomas Blomer, a fellow of the college, wrote in 1710 that the undergraduates were eating their meals too fast, in order to go out and play cricket.

The first detailed description of a cricket match was published in 1706 in London. The author was William Goldwin, who was educated at Eton and King's College, Cambridge, and had gone up to the university in 1700. The description was written in Latin but a translation shows that the game Goldwin described would be easily recognizable as the game played today, with stumps and bails, a level pitch, two umpires and batsmen being dismissed bowled or caught, and the scoring of runs, which were recorded by a scorer.

With cricket now a common game among the landed gentry, as well as among the general public (a diary kept by Thomas Marchant, of Hurstpierpoint in Sussex, makes frequent references to inter-village matches in the locality), and with considerable sums of money being wagered on games, there must have been an agreed set of laws. It is most frustrating for historians that the earliest set extant date only from 1744, though it has been proved fairly conclusively that the 1744 version is a revision of an earlier code.

Several of the great landowners in the south-east were no longer content to go to matches and simply place their bets. They decided to form their own cricket teams and challenge each other. A letter of 1725 reveals that such challenges were taking place between the Duke of Richmond and his side from Goodwood, near Chichester, and Sir William Gage's side from Firle near Seaford. A third challenger was Edwin Stead of Kent. These challenges were usually played on the country estates of the patrons involved, but by 1730 a major enclosed ground in London was in use – the Artillery Ground, which still exists in City Road,

THE DUKE OF RICHMOND *one of cricket's early patrons.*

generated and the vast sums wagered, the laws of the game were redrafted. James Love was commissioned to write a heroic poem describing the match which was published a month after the game. Love, whose real name was Dance, was the son of the architect of the Mansion House in the City.

Over the next decade cricket matches were increasingly reported in the press, though not the detailed scores, only the results and team totals. The crowds became more unruly; an indication of the social standing of cricket in the 1740s is the position in the game of Robert Colchin. He was one of the best batsmen of the London Club and at the same time a major figure in the criminal underworld of the period. The point was reached where respectable people did not attend matches and eventually the Honourable Artillery Company, owners of the Artillery Ground, stopped the playing of public matches there. At the public schools and at Oxford and Cambridge the authorities tended to discourage cricket – as late as 1796 the Eton headmaster flogged the Eton team for playing a match against his wishes.

In 1751, the dissolute Prince of Wales died, in some reports as a result of being hit in the chest by a cricket ball. The other cricket patrons of the period faded away, and what major matches there were tended to be played back on the country estates, rather than in London.

FROM HAMBLEDON TO MARYLEBONE

A combination of apparently unrelated events, however, rescued cricket from the mire and took the game to new heights. Richard Nyren, whose uncles had been part of an outstanding team raised by

Moorfields. The landlord of the public house on the corner of the ground had a wall built round it and in the 1740s is recorded as charging spectators to watch the cricket.

At the same time as spectators began to be charged, cricket's first professional players were emerging. The Duke of Richmond and other members of the upper class who raised teams were employing men who were good cricketers as grooms, bailiffs and the like on their estate. One of the first such was Thomas Waymark, who is mentioned several times in contemporary reports. He was employed by Richmond.

Aside from the teams raised by Richmond, Gage and Stead, the principal side of the 1730s was the London Club whose home venue was the Artillery Ground. A report of 1732 ends with the comment: "This is the thirteenth match the London gamesters have played this year and not lost one match."

The stakes for matches were now reported to be £100 – a vast sum at that time. Frederick Louis, Prince of Wales, the eldest son of George II, had not long come from Hanover to England when he discovered that cricket was an ideal game for betting purposes. In 1733 he had picked a side and challenged Edwin Stead's Kent team for £30. In 1735 the stakes had risen to £1,000 and the Prince's opponent was the Earl of Middlesex, eldest son of the Duke of Dorset.

It need hardly be said that the major cricket matches in London soon began to attract every rogue and vagabond in the metropolis, as well as many from outside.

"THE GREATEST CRICKET MATCH EVER KNOWN"

It had been the habit of aspiring teams to challenge the London Club, but in 1744 Kent, raised by the Sackville family at Sevenoaks, challenged the rest of England. Played on the Artillery Ground, the game was described in the press as "the greatest Cricket Match ever known". The Prince of Wales, the Duke of Cumberland, the Duke of Richmond and many other notables attended the game. Kent won by one wicket and this is the first major match whose detailed score survives.

Because of the enormous interest

PRINCE FREDERICK ADOLPHUS *with a cricket bat (late seventeenth century).*

PRECURSOR TO LORD'S *Cricket played near White Conduit House, 1787.*

the Duke of Richmond and centred on the village of Slindon on the Goodwood Estate, became the landlord of an inn in the Hampshire village of Hambledon. The Reverend Charles Powlett, son of the Duke of Bolton and educated at Westminster and Trinity, Cambridge, was a curate of Itchen Abbas from 1763; his family home was near Basingstoke. Both men were passionately fond of cricket. The meeting of Nyren, Powlett and other interested parties resulted in the creation of the Hambledon Cricket Club some time in the mid-1760s. The club struggled for some years before it really took off around 1772. Through the decade which followed, the Hambledon Club built up a Hampshire side, capable of taking on and often beating the rest of England.

Richard Nyren captained the side, which was normally an all-professional eleven. Several players came from Hambledon itself but others came from places a good few miles distant, such as Noah Mann from Northchapel and later William Beldham from Wrecclesham.

Many of the gentry whom Powlett persuaded to join the club also took part in the social life of London and met at the Star and Garter Tavern in Pall Mall, which had been the unofficial headquarters of cricket and horse-racing for many years. The Jockey Club had been founded there and the laws of cricket revised there. In the 1780s the members of the Star and Garter played cricket among themselves on White Conduit Fields in Islington. They decided that they would like a private ground, rather than using White Conduit Fields to which the public had access.

In 1786, two members of the Star and Garter, the Earl of Winchelsea and Colonel Lennox, the son of the Duke of Richmond, asked Thomas Lord, who was paid to help with the matches on White Conduit Fields, if he would find a suitable piece of land and set out a private ground. Winchelsea and Lennox promised Lord their full support and Lord created what was to become known as Lord's Cricket Ground in Marylebone. The first matches were played there in 1787. The cricket club of the Star and Garter, which was also described as the White Conduit Club, soon became known as the Marylebone Cricket Club. The club itself can be traced back to the earliest known revision of the laws in 1744.

Owing to building development and the building of the Regent's Canal, Lord twice moved his ground and the present Lord's was established in 1814. The Marylebone Club attracted most of the wealthy supporters of cricket, particularly those educated at the major public schools and Oxford or Cambridge. The club continued to be the forum for the revision of the laws and was the most opulent cricket club in the British Isles. Its position as the world's premier club has remained unchallenged since it was established.

CRICKET CONQUERS THE WORLD

Cricket as a popular game was spread from its south-east England birthplace throughout the British Isles by the landed gentry. In some places, such as Leicester, Nottingham and Sheffield, it was soon adopted by the locals. In others, Ireland being an extreme example, the game scarcely moved outside the landowners' parks.

During the Napoleonic Wars, soldiers in some regiments were encouraged to play cricket – Colonel Lennox, for instance, organized inter-militia matches in the 1790s and a game of cricket was played prior to the Battle of Waterloo.

As the British Empire grew, the army garrisons stationed in its various outposts took cricket with them. On the continent of Europe, British residents in Paris, Rome and other cities played the game, though the local inhabitants, whether part of the Empire or not, initially paid little attention to this strange British ritual. North America, with its large number of residents of British descent,was the only part of the world outside the British Isles where cricket became established in the eighteenth century.

The American War of Independence caused a hiccup in the game's development in what was to become the United States, but cricket recovered and the first-ever English touring team overseas went to Canada and the United States in 1859: this was an all-professional side and the trip was profitable. The first genuine international match – the United States versus Canada had taken place 15 years earlier, in 1844.

The American Civil War brought a temporary end to matches between the States and Canada, put a stop to possible visits by an England team and found the embryonic game of baseball an easier game to play in wartime conditions. From the time the war ended, baseball grew in stature at the same speed as cricket languished. From the 1870s the only stronghold of cricket was in the Philadelphia area.

So cricket was to remain a minority sport in North America, but across the world in Australia the game grew as the number of emigrants from Britain increased. The development of Australia into its various colonies – Van Diemens Land (Tasmania), New South Wales, Victoria, South Australia, Queensland and Western Australia – led to cricketing rivalry between those colonies. The first inter-colonial game was between Tasmania and Victoria in 1850–51, then came the matches between Victoria and New South Wales, which were regarded as the great contests of the season until overshadowed by Test cricket. With an England side unable to go to America in the early 1860s because of the Civil War and its aftermath, it was a fortunate coincidence that an entrepreneur decided to arrange for an England team to tour Australia. The leading England players refused to go, but an England "Second" Twelve went and were highly successful financially, even though no team in Australia was capable of opposing them evenhanded (in most matches 22 Australians played 11 of England).

The first people of non-British stock to take to cricket in an organized fashion were the Parsee community of Bombay. They began playing in the 1840s and by the 1880s were sending touring teams to England. From the Parsees, cricket spread to the other Indian communities and what developed was the great Bombay Tournament between Europeans, Parsees, Hindus and Muslims. Until the Ranji Trophy (the Indian equivalent of the County Championship) was founded in the 1930s, the Bombay Tournament was the major cricket contest in India.

Development of cricket in both the West Indies and South Africa was initially through the military personnel stationed in those territories. In South America, especially the Argentine, the game was well established, but only among the English communities.

The first team to come to England on a cricket tour was in fact a side of Australian Aborigines in 1868. The team was not of first-class standard, but opposed local club sides in an over-ambitious programme of 47 two- and three-day games. The side was captained by the former Surrey county cricketer, Charles Lawrence. It was an experiment not repeated (at least until the 1990s).

FIRST TESTS *The Australian touring team of 1882.*

SWEET SUMMER SCENE *A cricket field at Bourneville, Birmingham, where recreational facilities were supplied by Cadbury's for their employees.*

The legalisation of over-arm bowling in 1864 is generally considered to be the starting point of 'modern' cricket. In the following years the immortal W.G. Grace began his career and created many of his records which succeeding generations aimed to equal or beat. By that date first-class cricket was being played in Australia, in New Zealand, where inter-provincial games had commenced in the 1860s, in the West Indies, where the first inter-colonial game was staged also in the 1860s, and of course in England, where the modern County Championship had begun with a match between Sussex and Kent in 1825. The first recognized first-class game in the United States was played in 1878 when Australia opposed Philadelphia. Some 10 years later, the match between England and South Africa at Port Elizabeth marks the start of South African first-class cricket, whilst 1891–92 saw the first-class England tour to India and the first first-class match between Europeans and Parsees. Cricket flourished in many of the British colonies and in particular in Fiji – the Fijian touring side to New Zealand was ranked first-class in 1894–95. But outside the Empire and isolated pockets such as Philadelphia, cricket remained a mystery!

PIONEERS OF CRICKET

ROBERT COLCHIN
(1713–1750)

The most famous professional of the 1740s, but it is believed that he was also a figure noted in the underworld, particularly for smuggling.

JOHN MINSHULL
(1741–1793)

Employed by the Duke of Dorset because of his batsmanship, he was the first player to score a century, in August 1769.

RICHARD NYREN
(1734–1797)

Landlord of the Bat and Ball Inn, Hambledon and captain of the famous side organized by the Hambledon Club in the 1760s and 1770s.

DAVID HARRIS
(1755–1803)

A fast under-arm bowler and the greatest bowler for the Hambledon Club. Much troubled by gout, he came to some matches on crutches, but still played.

9TH EARL OF WINCHELSEA
(1752–1826)

A notable patron who persuaded Thomas Lord to open his first ground. Lord Winchelsea was a talented player and staged many matches at Burley, his Rutland country seat.

4TH DUKE OF RICHMOND
(1764–1819)

His grandfather, the 2nd Duke had organized many matches in the 1720s and 1730s; Goodwood, the family seat in Sussex, was a major centre of cricket. The 4th Duke continued the tradition and played at Lord's from its foundation.

3RD DUKE OF DORSET
(1745–1799)

Promoted many matches at Sevenoaks and as Ambassador to France was partially responsible for the English cricket tour to Paris in 1789 (aborted due to the Revolution).

NOAH MANN
(1756–1789)

He came from North Chapel in Sussex, but played for the Hambledon Club as a good all-rounder. He came to a sad end by going to sleep in front of a fire. His clothes caught alight and he died from burns.

CRICKET AROUND THE WORLD

Wherever English people settled, cricket went with them. English soldiers, merchants and missionaries played the game in most countries of the world. In Europe the locals ignored the strange rituals as did the Chinese and Japanese in the Far East, but in India, Pakistan, Ceylon (now Sri Lanka) and the West Indies things were different.

ENGLAND

The owners of the great estates in the south-east of England, when they became involved in cricket and staged matches against each other, named the sides they raised after the county in which they resided. At the same time, a town side opposing another, but from a different county, often entitled the match as one between two counties, rather than two towns, in order to bolster the standing of the match. The fashion of using county titles therefore was established long before such organizations as county clubs existed. With large sums wagered on these county matches, rules were established as regards the status of players qualified to play – *bona fide* resident or born inside the county boundaries was the usual agreed condition.

Following the famous Kent versus England match in 1744, county patrons' ultimate ambition for their team was to beat the rest of England. Surrey, Sussex, Kent and Hampshire all aspired to this great achievement; so much so that in the first two decades of the nineteenth century a county versus the rest was virtually the only major county contest – actual inter-county games were unfashionable.

In the early 1820s, however, James Ireland took over the old Brighton cricket ground, which had been laid out for the Prince of Wales (later George IV). He believed that money could be made staging matches between Sussex and Kent and, after much disappointment, he managed to set up home and away fixtures in 1825. With the Hambledon Club having folded in the 1790s and the famous cricketers who made up that club's Hampshire team all gone, and with Surrey lacking any central organization, Sussex and Kent were the only major cricketing counties which could field good-class teams. So Ireland's idea caught on and

ORIGINALS *The Nottinghamshire Eleven of 1884.*

WILLIAM CLARKE *founder of Trent Bridge and of the All England Eleven.*

each season from 1825, Sussex and Kent battled it out for the county championship.

In the 1830s the Nottingham team, which had beaten every side in the Midlands, joined the inter-county contest by challenging Sussex. In 1845, Surrey finally got its act together, formed a county club and established its home at Kennington Oval. Sussex had become a county club in 1839 and Nottingham's county club first emerged in 1841. Thus individual patrons raising and running county sides had given way to groups of subscribers putting up money to pay for players and their expenses for away games. The extensive space the newspapers of the 1830s and 1840s devoted to these inter-county games gives an indication of their importance.

In 1846, however, William Clarke, captain of Nottinghamshire, and founder of Trent Bridge, engaged the leading players of the day for a side which was to become known as the All England Eleven. At a stroke, he deprived the major counties of their "stars" and within a year or two had built up a full fixture list for his England team, playing what amounted to exhibition matches in whatever town would pay his expenses. The star players preferred Clarke's team to their county side simply because Clarke offered full-time employment through the summer, whereas the county teams only arranged a handful of games.

It took a dozen or so years for the craze of what were called wandering professional elevens (there were in time rivals to Clarke's outfit) to reach its peak. Then inter-county cricket not only re-emerged but increased rapidly. The 1860s saw the creation of clubs for Glamorgan, Gloucestershire, Lancashire, Middlesex, Somerset, Worcestershire and Yorkshire (of the present day first-class counties) as well as a goodly number of clubs among the lesser counties.

Not that all the seven listed suddenly began to challenge Kent, Nottinghamshire, Surrey and Sussex for the title of "champion county" – only Lancashire, Middlesex and Yorkshire rose to first-class rank immediately on the creation of a county organization. The romanticism surrounding Hampshire, fuelled by tales of the great Hambledon days, meant that various patrons and groups made attempts to raise Hampshire sides, but usually with dire results. Derbyshire was created as a county club in 1871, but struggled to produce a worthwhile side; in contrast, Cambridgeshire had a worthwhile team in the 1860s, but failed to create a satisfactory county club.

With all these sides, it became impractical to decide which county was the best on a challenge basis so the press began making up crude league tables.

COUNTY CRICKET

Since cricket at this time was the only popular team ball game with nationally, indeed internationally, recognized laws and in England was the major participatory game, both for playing and watching, the general public had an enormous interest in which county, in each season, was the best. In 1873, after some years of dispute, it was decided to lay down clearly the qualification rules for county cricketers; players had been taking advantage of the loose rule that they could play for county of residence or of birth and had in some cases played for both in the same season. This duality was stopped and a more careful record kept to see that players genuinely resided in a county.

In the same year, the MCC decided to stage a knockout county competition. Only one match was played, however, before the scheme collapsed. The two main reasons for its failure were, first that all matches were fixed to be played at Lord's and, second, that by the very nature of a knockout competition players would not know whether they were required on a given match day until each round had been played. Most professional players had signed agreements with local clubs which meant they could not be released willy-nilly to play for other teams, but only for set county and major matches on dates that were fixed.

The press continued to decide on the county champion and on how the league tables were presented each year, through the 1870s and into the 1880s. The situation was not very satisfactory, especially since there was no hard and fast rule as to which counties were included in the results as shown in a league table of top teams. Somerset, Hampshire and Derbyshire were the three sides which caused the press most problems.

In 1887, the editor of *Wisden's Cricketers' Almanack* decided to take a firm line. He cut out the three counties noted above and formulated a new "points" system. To his embarrassment, in 1889 his system resulted in a three-way tie at the head of a table which contained just eight counties: Gloucestershire, Kent, Lancashire, Middlesex, Nottinghamshire, Surrey, Sussex and Yorkshire. The counties themselves decided to act and for 1890 devised a new "points" system, though they kept to the eight-county league. Somerset were particularly upset at being excluded; and the following year simply forced their way into the league by arranging matches with the top counties.

The *Wisden* editor then came up with the idea of creating three leagues of eight teams each with promotion and relegation, but any hope of this sensible arrangement collapsed in 1895 when Derbyshire, Essex, Hampshire, Leicestershire and Warwickshire were all given a place in the "County Championship". All the other counties with teams that wanted to play competitive county cricket then joined together to form a separate Minor Counties' Cricket Association. The architect of this plan was the Worcestershire Secretary, P.H. Foley, and it began in 1895.

In effect, this pattern of county cricket – First Class County Championship and Minor Counties Championship – has remained unaltered ever since. No county has ever been demoted from first-class to minor, but Worcestershire (1899), Northamptonshire (1905), Glamorgan (1921) and Durham (1992) have joined the top grade.

For the first two decades of inter-county games, which involved only Kent, Nottinghamshire and Sussex, Kent was the predominant shire. Kent supporters had persuaded the greatest batsman of the day, Fuller Pilch, to move from his native East Anglia and play for his adopted county. In the 1820s, bowling style switched from under-arm to round-arm and Pilch was the first batsman to master thoroughly the new style. "His style of batting was very commanding, extremely forward, and he seemed to crush the best bowling by his long forward plunge before it had time to shoot, or rise, or do mischief by catches" – thus Pilch's success was described shortly after he retired. Kent also possessed Alfred Mynn: "it was considered one of the grandest sights at cricket to see Mynn advance and deliver the ball". Sussex's answer to these two great players was William Lillywhite, uncle of the first England Test captain. Lillywhite was 30 years old before he came into his own as slow medium round-arm bowler – and he was 60 when he played his final game for his county. Nottinghamshire had their cunning under-arm bowler, William Clarke, and an elegant batsman in Joe Guy, but they were no match for the Kent side.

A combination of events in 1844 and 1845 led first to the conversion of a market garden into the Kennington Oval Cricket Ground and then to the formation of Surrey County Cricket Club. Within a few years, this new club had thoroughly shaken the three senior counties and the decade of the 1850s belonged to Surrey.

This Championship side was characterized by its all-round strength, rather than reliance on one or two stars. Tom Lockyer kept wicket, William Caffyn was the great all-rounder and Julius Caesar of Godalming the principal batsman. Heathfield Stephenson, the captain of the first side to Australia, was another all-rounder, whilst George Griffiths was the tearaway fast bowler who hit sixes.

In 1864 Surrey won six of their eight championship games and drew the other two. No one seeing the side that year could dream that 23 years would elapse before Surrey could claim the title again.

Next it was the turn of Nottinghamshire to hold centre stage. Between 1865 and 1886, the midland county were champions 14 times. In Alfred Shaw and Fred Morley they possessed the finest pair of bowlers in England; Billy Barnes and Wilfred Flowers were two all-rounders, both of whom played Test cricket – Flowers the first pro to achieve the "double" of 1,000 runs and 100 wickets in the same season. A succession of brilliant batsmen headed the run-getting. George Parr of Radcliffe-on-Trent succeeded Fuller Pilch as the best professional batsman in England, then Richard Daft, born in Nottingham, took over the crown from Parr, to be followed in his turn by Arthur Shrewsbury, who was to become the first man to reach 1,000 Test runs. Rather like the Surrey side of 1864, the Nottinghamshire team of 1886, having won the championship, faded away and, apart from the infamous triple tie of 1889, Nottinghamshire had to wait until 1907 for their next success.

THE THREE GRACES

In covering briefly the 20 years from 1865 onwards, one fact has been omitted and it is an Everest of an omission. A 16-year-old youth named William Gilbert Grace appeared in his first first-class match in 1865 – by the 1880s he was to vie with W.E. Gladstone as the best-known Englishman.

Born in a village near Bristol, he effectively belonged to no major county – Gloucestershire did not really exist in cricketing terms in 1865. His family remedied this shortcoming by single-handedly creating Gloucestershire County Cricket Club. Grace had two brothers, E.M. and G.F., both by any standards brilliant cricketers, but both operating in the shadow of W.G. – as did everyone. Gloucestershire played their first first-class, inter-county game in 1870; in 1873 they were acclaimed as the joint champions with Nottinghamshire. The county of the Graces, as they were quickly christened, retained the title in 1874, lost it to Nottinghamshire in 1875, but regained it in 1876 and 1877. Too much depended on W.G. Grace and, though he continued to lead the county until deposed in 1899, Gloucestershire never again ended a season at the head of the table. A peculiarity of the Gloucestershire side of the 1870s was that it contained only amateurs whereas Nottinghamshire generally fielded a side made up of all-professional players.

Throughout this period, Sussex and Kent, the oldest counties, went through some hard times; Yorkshire could field a good side, but their professionals were a wayward lot; Lancashire tied for the title with Nottinghamshire in 1879 and captured it in their own right in 1881, when most of the major Nottinghamshire professionals were on strike; Middlesex, through their London connections, had some fine amateurs qualified by residence or birth, but rarely managed to field a full-strength side; Derbyshire and Hampshire flirted on the fringes, without causing the top counties much trouble.

The closing years of the 1880s saw Surrey with a rebuilt eleven. The Ovalites were the champions 1887 to 1895, except for 1893. Walter Read and Maurice Read, unrelated, were Surrey's principal middle-order batsmen; the diminutive Bobby Abel opened the innings. George Lohmann, an outstanding medium-fast bowler, had Bill Lockwood as his partner.

The championship, especially in the years when Australia did not come to England, drew enormous crowds for the top matches. The tradition of Lancashire playing Yorkshire and of Nottinghamshire playing Surrey on the Whitsun and August Bank Holidays was established at this time.

THE SLEEPING GIANT WAKES

The decade of the 1890s saw the sleeping giant of cricket finally realize its potential. Yorkshire had found in Lord Hawke a leader who was capable of instilling some discipline into the professional ranks – one or two notable players were warned and then consigned to the scrapheap, but Yorkshire had ample reserves. Although, like all teams, the White Rose County had its less successful summers, for the next 70 years Yorkshire was the one side that was always feared.

During the Edwardian era, Yorkshire's power base was founded on twin all-rounders: two complementary characters whose records, when their careers finally closed, were the equal of anyone (except of course W.G.) who had participated in the game of cricket. George Hirst of Kirkheaton is the only man to score 2,000 runs and take 200 wickets in a single summer – when asked what he felt like, having reached this peak, he is reported as saying "tired". Wilfred Rhodes, Hirst's partner, and fellow left-arm bowler, is the only man to take more than 4,000 first-class wickets. He also hailed from Kirkheaton and his batting was almost as impressive with 39,969 runs. It hardly needs adding that he achieved the "double" 16 times (Hirst managed a total of 14). Not satisfied with two outstanding all-rounders, the county possessed a third in the amateur F.S. Jackson, but business commitments and his service in the Boer War meant that Jackson was not always available for his county. Jackson captained

England to the Ashes victory in 1905, but, with Lord Hawke in office, was never Yorkshire's official leader.

In the period up to 1914, despite Yorkshire's great superiority, the county did not take the title in the way Nottinghamshire and Surrey had earlier. Lancashire and Middlesex were allowed their turn and Nottinghamshire won in 1907. Even Warwickshire took a turn in 1911, but the strongest rival to Yorkshire in the years leading up to the First World War was Kent.

Lord Harris, one of the greatest figures in English cricket, had devoted himself to the revival of Kent cricket and his very long and arduous task finally bore fruit. Such cricketers as Blythe and Woolley made the Hop County once more a stronghold of the game. A comment must be made on Warwickshire's single success, due almost entirely to the single enigmatic figure of Frank Foster – he topped both batting and bowling tables and also captained the side.

YORKSHIRE'S OPENERS *Herbert Sutcliffe and Percy Holmes scored over 100 runs for the first wicket no less than 69 times.*

The 21 years between the wars might, in general, be described as a second War of the Roses; 12 championships to Yorkshire, five to Lancashire. That didn't leave many seasons for the other 15 teams: Middlesex won twice, Nottinghamshire and Derbyshire once each. In contrast, Northamptonshire came bottom eight times and for three successive summers failed to win a single game.

Yorkshire's championship wins were thanks to a team of stars, from Herbert Sutcliffe and Percy Holmes as opening batsmen through to such names as Hedley Verity and Bill Bowes. In the later 1930s came Len Hutton and Ellis Robinson. Lancashire had Ernest Tyldesley as their batting stalwart, Dick Tyldesley as the principal slow bowler, as well as such notables as Eddie Paynter and later Cyril Washbrook.

Middlesex's years were 1920 and 1921, with Patsy Hendren and Jack Hearne; Nottinghamshire, always a formidable batting side, won in 1929 when Harold Larwood and Bill Voce were at the top.

Derbyshire also owed their championship to the emergence of some sharp bowlers, Bill Copson and Alf Pope in particular. When cricket returned to normal after the Second World War, Yorkshire were again champions, but, after years of modest returns, Surrey came back with a vengeance. Led by the inspiring Stuart Surridge, the county had a perfect attack. In 1953, for example, the four Surrey bowlers, Alec Bedser, Peter Loader, Jim Laker and Tony Lock, were all in the top 10 in the English bowling averages. Laker (off spin) and Lock (left arm) were the slower bowlers, whilst Bedser and Loader opened. Surrey shared the title with Lancashire in 1950, then won it outright for seven successive summers commencing 1952.

Yorkshire climbed back in 1959

and gained seven titles between that year and 1968. In those 20 or so post-war years, three of the former also-rans had their moments of glory: Glamorgan won in 1948 and 1969, Hampshire in 1961 and Worcestershire in 1964 and 1965.

With county cricket in a parlous state financially in the late 1950s and early 1960s, the time had come for change. After years of discussion, a one-day limited-overs knockout competition for the counties finally emerged in 1963 – the Gillette Cup: in 1969 it was joined by a 40-overs-a-side Sunday League, sponsored by John Player, and yet a third limited-overs contest arrived in 1972, sponsored by Benson & Hedges.

In 1968 the authorities broke with tradition by allowing counties to play overseas Test cricketers without them having to qualify by residence. The immediate effect of this was that the domination by the counties with large populations was broken. Yorkshire alone decided to stick with players born within the county boundary: they soon felt the effect of this decision, though it was not until 1983 that they ended with the wooden spoon.

Essex and Middlesex came to the fore in the 1970s. The former, led by Keith Fletcher, possessed a fine attack, with John Lever and Neil Foster the principal seam bowlers and Ray East and David Acfield as spinners. The batting line-up included the captain and Graham Gooch and Ken McEwan, whilst Derek Pringle was the main all-rounder. Middlesex were led by the most talented captain of the day, Mike Brearley. Their spin attack revolved around John Emburey and Phil Edmonds, the West Indian Wayne Daniel opened the bowling, and Mike Gatting, who succeeded Brearley as captain, was the leading run-getter.

In a golden period in the late 1970s and 1980s, Middlesex won the County Championship seven times and gained seven one-day trophies, while Essex won a total of 11 titles.

With counties fielding overseas players and with the movement of players between counties on the increase, the spread of trophies was greater than in the past. Aside from Essex and Middlesex, who won more than any other side, seven counties – Hampshire, Kent, Lancashire, Nottinghamshire, Somerset, Warwickshire and Worcestershire – could all claim at least five titles and, other than Durham, all the rest could at least claim one. Warwickshire, with the services of Brian Lara in 1994 and Allan Donald in 1995, won the championship both seasons, and in 1994 also gained the Sunday League and Benson & Hedges titles. This was the season in which Lara recorded the first championship innings over 500 – 501 not out against luckless Durham at Edgbaston. Durham, who joined the first-class counties in 1992, have struggled to achieve the standard set by the other counties, remaining at or near the foot of the table each year.

ESSEX'S GREAT BATSMAN *Graham Gooch, who has hit 1,000 runs in a season 20 times.*

BREARLEY *an astute post-war captain.*

COUNTY CHAMPIONS SINCE 1864

1864	Surrey
1865	Nottinghamshire
1866	Middlesex
1867	Yorkshire
1868	Nottinghamshire
1869	Nottinghamshire, Yorkshire
1870	Yorkshire
1871	Nottinghamshire
1872	Nottinghamshire
1873	Gloucestershire, Nottinghamshire
1874	Gloucestershire
1875	Nottinghamshire
1876	Gloucestershire
1877	Gloucestershire
1878	Undecided
1879	Nottinghamshire, Lancashire
1880	Nottinghamshire
1881	Lancashire
1882	Nottinghamshire, Lancashire
1883	Nottinghamshire
1884	Nottinghamshire
1885	Nottinghamshire
1886	Surrey
1887	Surrey
1888	Surrey
1889	Surrey, Lancashire, Nottinghamshire
1890	Surrey
1891	Surrey
1892	Surrey
1893	Yorkshire
1894	Surrey
1895	Surrey
1896	Yorkshire
1897	Lancashire
1898	Yorkshire
1899	Surrey
1900	Yorkshire
1901	Yorkshire
1902	Yorkshire
1903	Middlesex
1904	Lancashire
1905	Yorkshire
1906	Kent
1907	Nottinghamshire
1908	Yorkshire
1909	Kent
1910	Kent
1911	Warwickshire
1912	Yorkshire
1913	Kent
1914	Surrey
1919	Yorkshire
1920	Middlesex
1921	Middlesex
1922	Yorkshire
1923	Yorkshire
1924	Yorkshire
1925	Yorkshire
1926	Lancashire
1927	Lancashire
1928	Lancashire
1929	Nottinghamshire
1930	Lancashire
1931	Yorkshire
1932	Yorkshire
1933	Yorkshire
1934	Lancashire
1935	Yorkshire
1936	Derby
1937	Yorkshire
1938	Yorkshire
1939	Yorkshire
1946	Yorkshire
1947	Middlesex
1948	Glamorgan
1949	Middlesex, Yorkshire
1950	Lancashire, Surrey
1951	Warwickshire
1952	Surrey
1953	Surrey
1954	Surrey
1955	Surrey
1956	Surrey
1957	Surrey
1958	Surrey
1959	Yorkshire
1960	Yorkshire
1961	Hampshire
1962	Yorkshire
1963	Yorkshire
1964	Worcestershire
1965	Worcestershire
1966	Yorkshire
1967	Yorkshire
1968	Yorkshire
1969	Glamorgan
1970	Kent
1971	Surrey
1972	Warwickshire
1973	Hampshire
1974	Worcestershire
1975	Leicestershire
1976	Middlesex
1977	Kent, Middlesex
1978	Kent
1979	Essex
1980	Middlesex
1981	Nottinghamshire
1982	Middlesex
1983	Essex
1984	Essex
1985	Middlesex
1986	Essex
1987	Nottinghamshire
1988	Worcestershire
1989	Worcestershire
1990	Middlesex
1991	Essex
1992	Essex
1993	Middlesex
1994	Warwickshire
1995	Warwickshire
1996	Leicestershire

GILLETTE/NATWEST TROPHY

GILLETTE CUP

1963 Sussex 168 (60.2 overs) beat Worcestershire 154 (63.2 overs) by 14 runs

1964 Sussex 131–2 (43 overs) beat Warwickshire 127 (48 overs) by 8 wkts

1965 Yorkshire 317–4 (60 overs) beat Surrey 142 (40.4 overs) by 175 runs

1966 Warwickshire 159–5 (56.4 overs) beat Worcestershire 155–8 (60 overs) by 5 wkts

1967 Kent 193 (59.4 overs) beat Somerset 161 (54.5 overs) by 32 runs

1968 Warwickshire 215–6 (57 overs) beat Sussex 214–7 (60 overs) by 4 wkts

1969 Yorkshire 219–8 (60 overs) beat Derbyshire 150 (54.4 overs) by 69 runs

1970 Lancashire 185–4 (55.1 overs) beat Sussex 184–9 (60 overs) by 6 wkts

1971 Lancashire 224–7 (60 overs) beat Kent 200 (56.2 overs) by 24 runs

1972 Lancashire 235–6 (56.4 overs) beat Warwickshire 234–9 (60 overs) by 4 wkts

1973 Gloucestershire 248–8 (60 overs) beat Sussex 208 (56.5 overs) by 40 runs

1974 Kent 122–6 (56.4 overs) beat Lancashire 118 (60 overs) by 4 wkts

1975 Lancashire 182–3 (57 overs) beat Middlesex 180–8 (60 overs) by 7 wkts

1976 Northamptonshire 199–6 (58.1 overs) beat Lancashire 195–7 (60 overs) by 4 wkts

1977 Middlesex 178–5 (55.4 overs) beat Glamorgan 177–9 (60 overs) by 5 wkts

1978 Sussex 211–5 (53.1 overs) beat Somerset 207–7 (60 overs) by 5 wkts

1979 Somerset 269–8 (60 overs) beat Northamptonshire 224 (56.3 overs) by 45 runs

1980 Middlesex 202–3 (53.5 overs) beat Surrey 201 (60 overs) by 7 wkts

NATIONAL WESTMINSTER BANK TROPHY

1981 Derbyshire 235–6 (60 overs) beat Northamptonshire 235–9 (60 overs) by losing fewer wkts

1982 Surrey 159–1 (34.4 overs) beat Warwickshire 158 (57.2 overs) by 9 wkts

1983 Somerset 193–9 (50 overs) beat Kent 169 (47.1 overs) by 24 runs

1984 Middlesex 236–6 (60 overs) beat Kent 232–6 (60 overs) by 4 wkts

1985 Essex 280–2 (60 overs) beat Nottinghamshire 279–5 (60 overs) by 1 run

1986 Sussex 243–3 (58.2 overs) beat Lancashire 242–8 (60 overs) by 7 wkts

1987 Nottinghamshire 231–7 (49.3 overs) beat Northamptonshire 228–3 (50 overs) by 3 wkts

1988 Middlesex 162–7 (55.3 overs) beat Worcestershire 161–9 (60 overs) by 3 wkts

1989 Warwickshire 211–6 (59.4 overs) beat Middlesex 210–5 (60 overs) by 4 wkts

1990 Lancashire 173–3 (45.4 overs) beat Northamptonshire 171 (60 overs) by 7 wkts

1991 Hampshire 243–6 (59.4 overs) beat Surrey 240–5 (60 overs) by 4 wkts

1992 Northamptonshire 211–2 (49.4 overs) beat Leicestershire 208–7 (60 overs) by 8 wkts

1993 Warwickshire 322–5 (60 overs) beat Sussex 321–6 (60 overs) by 5 wkts

1994 Worcestershire 227–2 (49.1 overs) beat Warwickshire 223–9 (60 overs) by 8 wkts

1995 Warwickshire 203–6 (58.5 overs) beat Northamptonshire 200 (59.5 overs) by 4 wkts

1996 Lancashire 186 (60 overs) beat Essex 57 (27.2 overs) by 129 runs

MINOR COUNTIES CHAMPIONS

1895	Norfolk–Durham–Worcestershire
1896	Worcestershire
1897	Worcestershire
1898	Worcestershire
1899	Northamptonshire–Buckinghamshire
1900	Glamorgan–Durham–Northamptonshire
1901	Durham
1902	Wiltshire
1903	Northamptonshire
1904	Northamptonshire
1905	Norfolk
1906	Staffordshire
1907	Lancashire II
1908	Staffordshire
1909	Wiltshire
1910	Norfolk
1911	Staffordshire
1912	In abeyance
1913	Norfolk
1914	Staffordshire
1920	Staffordshire
1921	Staffordshire
1922	Buckinghamshire
1923	Buckinghamshire
1924	Berkshire
1925	Buckinghamshire
1926	Durham
1927	Staffordshire
1928	Berkshire
1929	Oxfordshire
1930	Durham
1931	Leicestershire II
1932	Buckinghamshire
1933	Undecided
1934	Lancashire II
1935	Middlesex II
1936	Hertfordshire
1937	Lancashire II
1938	Buckinghamshire
1939	Surrey II
1946	Suffolk
1947	Yorkshire II
1948	Lancashire II
1949	Lancashire II
1950	Surrey II
1951	Kent II
1952	Buckinghamshire
1953	Berkshire
1954	Surrey II
1955	Surrey II
1956	Kent II
1957	Yorkshire II
1958	Yorkshire II
1959	Warwickshire II
1960	Lancashire II
1961	Somerset II
1962	Warwickshire II
1963	Cambridgeshire
1964	Lancashire II
1965	Somerset II
1966	Lincolnshire
1967	Cheshire
1968	Yorkshire II
1969	Buckinghamshire
1970	Bedfordshire
1971	Yorkshire II
1972	Bedfordshire
1973	Shropshire
1974	Oxfordshire
1975	Hertfordshire
1976	Durham
1977	Suffolk
1978	Devon
1979	Suffolk
1980	Durham
1981	Durham
1982	Oxfordshire
1983	Hertfordshire
1984	Durham
1985	Cheshire
1986	Cumberland
1987	Buckinghamshire
1988	Cheshire
1989	Oxfordshire
1990	Hertfordshire
1991	Staffordshire
1992	Staffordshire
1993	Staffordshire
1994	Devon
1995	Devon
1996	Devon

BENSON & HEDGES CUP

1972	Leicestershire 140–5 (46.5 overs)beat Yorkshire 136–9 (55 overs) 5 wkts
1973	Kent 225–7 (55 overs) beat Worcestershire 186 (51.4 overs) by 39 runs
1974	Surrey 170 (54.1 overs) beat Leicestershire 143 (54 overs) by 27 runs
1975	Leicestershire 150–5 (51.2 overs) beat Middlesex 146 (54.2overs) by 5 wkts
1976	Kent 236–7 (55 overs) beat Worcestershire 193 (52.4 overs) by 43 runs
1977	Gloucestershire 237–6 (55 overs) beat Kent 173 (47.3 overs) by 64 runs
1978	Kent 151–4 (41.4 overs) beat Derbyshire 147 (54.5 overs) by 6 wkts
1979	Essex 290–6 (55 overs) beat Surrey 255 (51.4overs) by 35 runs
1980	Northamptonshire 209 (54.5 overs) beat Essex 203–8 (55 overs) by 6 runs
1981	Somerset 197–3 (44.3 overs) beat Surrey 194–8 (55 overs) by 7 wkts
1982	Somerset 132–1 (33.1 overs) beat Nottinghamshire 130 (50.1 overs) by 9 wkts
1983	Middlesex 196–8 (55 overs) beat Essex 192 (54.1 overs) by 4 runs
1984	Lancashire 140–4 (42.4 overs) beat Warwickshire 139 (50.4 overs) by 6 wkts
1985	Leicestershire 215–5 (52 overs) beat Essex 213–8 (55 overs) by 5 wkts
1986	Middlesex 199–7 (55 overs) beat Kent 197–8 (55 overs) by2 runs
1987	Yorkshire 244–6 (55 overs) beat Northamptonshire 244–7 (55 overs) by losing fewer wkts
1988	Hampshire 118–3 (31.5 overs) beat Derbyshire 117 (46.3 overs) by 7 wkts
1989	Nottinghamshire 244–7 (55 overs) beat Essex 243–7 (55 overs) by 3 wkts
1990	Lancashire 241–8 (55 overs) beat Worcestershire 172 (54 overs) by 69 runs
1991	Worcestershire 236–8 (55 overs) beat Lancashire 171 (47.2 overs) by 65 runs
1992	Hampshire 253–5 (55 overs) beat Kent 212 (52.3 overs) by 41 runs
1993	Derbyshire 252–6 (55 overs) beat Lancashire 246–7 (55 overs) by 6 runs
1994	Warwickshire 172–4 (44.2 overs) beat Worcestershire 170 (55 overs) by 6 wkts
1995	Lancashire 274–7 (55 overs) beat Kent 239 (52.1 overs) by 35 runs
1996	Lancashire 245–9 (50 overs) beat Northamptonshire 214 (48.3 overs) by 31 runs

SECOND XI CHAMPIONS

1959	Gloucestershire
1960	Northamptonshire
1961	Kent
1962	Worcestershire
1963	Worcestershire
1964	Lancashire
1965	Glamorgan
1966	Surrey
1967	Hampshire
1968	Surrey
1969	Kent
1970	Kent
1971	Hampshire
1972	Nottinghamshire
1973	Essex
1974	Middlesex
1975	Surrey
1976	Kent
1977	Yorkshire
1978	Sussex
1979	Warwickshire
1980	Glamorgan
1981	Hampshire
1982	Worcestershire
1983	Leicestershire
1984	Yorkshire
1985	Nottinghamshire
1986	Lancashire
1987	Kent, Yorkshire
1988	Surrey
1989	Middlesex
1990	Sussex
1991	Yorkshire
1992	Surrey
1993	Middlesex
1994	Somerset
1995	Hampshire
1996	Warwickshire

SUNDAY LEAGUE CHAMPIONS

1969	Lancashire
1970	Lancashire
1971	Worcestershire
1972	Kent
1973	Kent
1974	Leicestershire
1975	Hampshire
1976	Kent
1977	Leicestershire
1978	Hampshire
1979	Somerset
1980	Warwickshire
1981	Essex
1982	Sussex
1983	Yorkshire
1984	Essex
1985	Essex
1986	Hampshire
1987	Worcestershire
1988	Worcestershire
1989	Lancashire
1990	Derbyshire
1991	Nottinghamshire
1992	Middlesex
1993	Glamorgan
1994	Warwickshire
1995	Kent
1996	Surrey

SECONDXI ONE DAY COMPETITION

1986	Northamptonshire
1987	Derbyshire
1988	Yorkshire
1989	Middlesex
1990	Lancashire
1991	Nottinghamshire
1992	Surrey
1993	Leicestershire
1994	Yorkshire
1995	Leicestershire
1996	Leicestershire

AUSTRALIA

The colonies of New South Wales and Victoria opposed each other in a first-class cricket match for the first time in 1855–56. Prior to that, the only major inter-colonial games had been between Tasmania and Victoria; the former, however, became progressively weaker in relation to the latter and thus were not considered as serious rivals for what could be described as the championship of Australia.

In the period 1855–56 to 1871–72, Victoria generally got the better of their arch-enemy. The wickets were dreadful and in the first 10 years it was unusual for an innings total to exceed 100. In 1862–63, when New South Wales won the annual match after losing five in succession, an umpiring dispute caused the game to be cancelled for the next two seasons.

The first individual hundred in the series, and indeed the first first-class hundred ever scored in Australia, came in 1867–68, when Dick Wardill hit 110 for Victoria – he also made 45 not out in the second innings, as his team won by seven wickets. Wardill, a Liverpudlian, captained Victoria and was one of the main promoters behind the English team, led by W.G. Grace, which came out to Australia in 1873–74. Wardill, however, did not play against Grace's side. In the winter of 1873, it was discovered that he had embezzled his employers out of some £7,000. He eluded the police, but committed suicide.

Whilst Wardill was the outstanding batsman of the period, Sam Cosstick was Victoria's greatest bowler – fast round-arm and, of course, a slogging bat. Cosstick was employed by the Melbourne Club as groundsman and professional.

Of the two established English players who were tempted to stay in Australia, after touring with the English team, Charles Lawrence was employed by the Albert Club in Sydney, whilst William Caffyn was initially in Melbourne, but after one season switched to Sydney.

With Victoria apparently too good for New South Wales, it was decided in 1872–73 that Victoria should not only play a combined New South Wales, Tasmania and South Australia team, but that the latter should be allowed 13 men! The odds were too great, Victoria losing by five wickets.

Two months later Victoria opposed New South Wales in an XI-a-side game and, with Sam Cosstick taking eleven for 51, the former proved victorious.

From 1874–75 it was the turn of New South Wales to dominate Australian cricket. The two rivals now played home and away each season. New South Wales won seven successive games – Charles Bannerman, who was to score the first Test hundred, was the batting star, whilst F.R. Spofforth developed into a unique bowler. He began as a tearaway but, by studying the skills of such slow merchants as Shaw and Southerton, he mixed his deliveries and was therefore quite lethal whatever the wicket.

In the 1880s the two sides were evenly matched; frequently one victory in the first fixture was reversed in the second. Billy Murdoch, who captained three Australian sides to England, scored the first triple hundred for New South Wales in 1881–82. Charles Turner (The Terror) bowled fast-medium with his fast yorker being dreaded by the opposition; he also belonged to New South Wales.

South Australia opposed Victoria in a first-class match for the first time in 1880–81 (the former had previously played Tasmania). The Adelaide side found an outstanding all-rounder, George Giffen. His figures were quite formidable: in one game against Victoria he hit 271 and took 16 wickets; other combinations were 237 and 12, 135 and 13, 166 and 14. He was considered Australia's answer to W.G. Grace.

BRADMAN *greatest of all batsmen. His Test batting average of 99.94 says it all.*

THE SHEFFIELD SHIELD

Lord Sheffield, the leading patron of Sussex cricket, agreed to finance an English team to Australia for the 1891–92 season. Soon after his arrival in Australia, in November 1891, Lord Sheffield offered to pay for a trophy which could be competed for by the three main cricketing colonies. By the end of this tour, the cricketing authorities in Australia had set up the Australasian Cricket Council, one of whose tasks was to purchase a suitable trophy, with money which Lord Sheffield donated. The three colonies each played home and away matches with the other two in 1892–93. All matches were played out and Victoria won all their four contests, thus being the first winners of the Sheffield Shield.

This three-way contest was to continue as such until 1925–26. Of the 30 seasons played (no matches were played 1915–16 to 1918–19), New South Wales won 17 times, Victoria 10 and South Australia three.

The best sequence of wins came between 1901–02 and 1906–07 when New South Wales recorded six successive titles. Victor Trumper, the outstanding batsman of his generation, was New South Wales's great run-getter in this period. Albert Cotter, the fastest bowler of the day, also represented New South Wales.

A major change came for the 1926–27 season. Queensland were admitted to the Sheffield Shield and simultaneously timeless matches for the Shield were abandoned, with four-and-a-half day matches introduced. Queensland had been created as a colony in 1859, had first played (being allowed odds) against another

HISTORIC SHEFFIELD SHIELD *Australia's principal cricket trophy: Queensland's success in 1991–95.*

colony in 1863–64, and had taken part in first-class matches since 1892–93. (The new entrants were not destined to win the Shield until 1994–95.) This season was also unusual as South Australia claimed the title for the first time since 1912–13. South Australia relied on the brilliant leg breaks of Clarrie Grimmett.

Don Bradman arrived and dominated Australian domestic cricket, just as he did Test cricket. Initially he played for New South Wales, but the season he switched to South Australia, the latter immediately won the title again. Queensland remained the minnows, winning only 12 times in their first 83 matches up to the Second World War.

Unlike Queensland, Western Australia took their first title during their first Shield season of 1947–48. The result was not quite as impressive as it might seem, for the new competitor only played four matches, whilst the rest played seven. This system remained in place until 1956–57 – with the exception of 1954–55 when a bizarre arrangement was tried whereby Western Australia played only two games and the rest only four. It ceased after one season.

New South Wales had a run of nine consecutive Shield titles between 1953–54 and 1961–62. The state had two great all-rounders, Richie Benaud and Alan Davidson, as well as the batting of Norman O'Neill. Ray Lindwall, the fearsome fast bowler, switched from New South Wales to Queensland for the 1954–55 season.

In 1961–62, three West Indian Test players, Gary Sobers, Rohan Kanhai and Wesley Hall, were imported for the Sheffield Shield. Hall took 43 wickets for Queensland, Kanhai made 533 runs for Western Australia and Sobers topped both batting and bowling for South Australia. What was perhaps more important, the crowds flocked to see the overseas stars – South Australia's gate receipts rose by two and a half times.

The 1970s saw Western Australia out in front – six titles in nine seasons to 1980–81. The period also saw seasons when the Australian Packer players were banned from the Shield and the increase of international games meant that the top players missed many matches. The attendances at Shield games dropped to a new low. Even in the Western Australian ground at Perth, spectator numbers for 1977–78, when the state were the reigning champions and then retained the title, dropped by a third.

The season of 1977–78 saw the raising of Tasmania to Shield status. In their first five seasons, they played one match against each opponent, while the rest played home and away. To avoid a percentage system, the points gained by Tasmania were multiplied by nine and divided by five.

The Australian states introduced a one-day knockout competition in 1969–70. Tasmania were part of the competition from the start and New Zealand were also included – the Kiwis in fact won the first title. The innings were limited to 40 eight-ball overs until 1978–79 and since then 50 six-ball overs. In 1978–79 Tasmania won the competition. In the same year, the island state won its first Shield match. Much of the team's success was due to the skills of Jack Simmons, the Lancashire all-rounder. After many years of endeavour, Queensland finally won the Shield in the 1994–95 season.

SHEFFIELD SHIELD

1892–93	Victoria
1893–94	South Australia
1894–95	Victoria
1895–96	New South Wales
1896–97	New South Wales
1897–98	Victoria
1898–99	Victoria
1899–00	New South Wales
1900–01	Victoria
1901–02	New South Wales
1902–03	New South Wales
1903–04	New South Wales
1904–05	New South Wales
1905–06	New South Wales
1906–07	New South Wales
1907–08	Victoria
1908–09	New South Wales
1909–10	South Australia
1910–11	New South Wales
1911–12	New South Wales
1912–13	South Australia
1913–14	New South Wales
1914–15	Victoria
1919–20	New South Wales
1921–22	Victoria
1922–23	New South Wales
1923–24	Victoria
1924–25	Victoria
1925–26	New South Wales
1926–27	South Australia
1927–28	Victoria
1928–29	New South Wales
1929–30	Victoria
1930–31	Victoria
1931–32	New South Wales
1932–33	New South Wales
1933–34	Victoria
1934–35	Victoria
1935–36	South Australia
1936–37	Victoria
1937–38	New South Wales
1938–39	South Australia
1939–40	New South Wales
1946–47	Victoria
1947–48	Western Australia
1948–49	New South Wales
1949–50	New South Wales
1950–51	Victoria
1951–52	New South Wales
1952–53	South Australia
1953–54	New South Wales
1954–55	New South Wales
1955–56	New South Wales
1956–57	New South Wales
1957–58	New South Wales
1958–59	New South Wales
1959–60	New South Wales
1960–61	New South Wales
1961–62	New South Wales
1962–63	Victoria
1963–64	South Australia
1964–65	New South Wales
1965–66	New South Wales
1966–67	Victoria
1967–68	Western Australia
1968–69	South Australia
1969–70	Victoria
1970–71	South Australia
1971–72	Western Australia
1972–73	Western Australia
1973–74	Victoria
1974–75	Western Australian
1975–76	South Australia
1976–77	Western Australia
1977–78	Western Australia
1978–79	Victoria
1979–80	Victoria
1980–81	Western Australia
1981–82	South Australia
1982–83	New South Wales
1983–84	Western Australia
1984–85	New South Wales
1986–87	Western Australia
1987–88	Western Australia
1988–89	Western Australia
1989–90	New South Wales
1990–91	Victoria
1991–92	Western Australia
1992–93	New South Wales
1993–94	New South Wales
1994–95	Queensland
1995–96	South Australia
1996–97	Queensland

LIMITED-OVERS COMPETITIONS

V & G AUSTRALASIAN COLA-COLA COMPETITION

1969–70 New Zealand 140–4 (31.4 overs) beat Victoria 129 (34.6 overs) by 6 wkts

1972–73 Western Australia 170 (38.2 overs) beat Queensland 79 (23.5 overs) by 91 runs

AUSTRALASIAN COCA-COLA COMPETITION

1969–70 Victoria 192–2 (33.4 overs) beat South Australia 190 (38.7 overs) by 8 wkts

1972–73 New Zealand 170–9 (35 overs) beat Queensland 132 (31.3 overs) by 38 runs

GILLETTE CUP

1973–74 Western Australia 151–3 (26.6 overs) beat New Zealand 150 (36.3 overs) by 7 wkts

1974–75 New Zealand 77–2 (17 overs) beat Western Australia 76 (26.1 overs) by 8 wkts

1975–76 Queensland 236–7 (40 overs) beat Western Australia 232 (39 overs) by 4 runs

1976–77 Western Australia 165–9 (39.3 overs) beat Victoria 164 (37.3 overs) by 1 wkt

1977–78 Western Australia 185–3 (37.1 overs) beat Tasmania 184-9 (40 overs) by 7 wkts

1978–79 Tasmania 180–6 (40 overs) beat Western Australia 133 (50 overs) by 47 runs

MCDONALD'S CUP

1979–80 Victoria 199–6 (47.4 overs) beat New South Wales 198–8 (50 overs) 4 wkts

1980–81 Queensland 188–9 (48 overs) beat Western Australia 116 (32.5 overs) by 72 runs

1981–82 Queensland 224–8 (47 overs) beat New South Wales 197 (44.4 overs) by 27 runs

1982–83 Western Australia 198–6 (49.1 overs) beat New South Wales 195–6 (50 overs) by 4 wkts

1983–84 South Australia 256–6 (49 overs) beat Western Australia 248–9 (49 overs) by 8 runs

1984–85 New South Wales278–7 (50 overs) beat South Australia 190 (45.5 overs) by 88 runs

1985–86 Western Australia 167 (38 overs) beat Victoria 148 (36.5 overs) by 19 runs

1986–87 South Australia 325–6 (50 overs) beat Tasmania 239–9 (50 overs) by 86 runs

1987–88 New South Wales 219–7 (50 overs) beat South Australia 196–6 (50 overs) by 23 runs

FEDERATED AUTOMOBILE INSURANCE

1988–89 Queensland 253–4 (50 overs)beat Victoria 90 (32.4 overs) by 163 runs

1989–90 Western Australia 88–3 (19.1 overs) beat South Australia 87 (34.5 overs) by 7 wkts

1990–91 Western Australia 236–3 (44.5 overs) beat New South Wales 235–7 (50 overs) by 7 wkts

1991–92 New South Wales 199–9 (50 overs) beat Western Australia 130 (40.1 overs) by 69 runs

MERCANTILE MUTUAL CUP

1992–93 New South Wales 187–6 (49.4 overs)beat Victoria 186 (50 overs) by 4 wkts

1993–94 New South Wales 264–4 (50 overs) beat Western Australia 218–9 (49 overs) on faster scoring rate

1994–95 Victoria 170–6 (44.5 overs) beat South Australia 169 (46.4 overs) by 4 wkts

1995–96 Queensland 167–6 (44.5 overs) beat Western Australia 166 (49.1 overs) by 4 wkts

SOUTH AFRICA

The first competition organized for major teams in South Africa was instituted in 1876. The silver inscription on the competition trophy – a cricket bat – reads: "Presented to the cricketers of the Colony of Good Hope by the municipality of Port Elizabeth". Named the Champion Bat Competition, the trophy was won twice by King William's Town, and once each by Kimberley, Port Elizabeth and Western Province. The final competition took place in 1890.

SIR DONALD CURRIE *the ship-owner who presented South Africa's major trophy.*

The Champion Bat Competition, which was considered of first-class status only in 1890, was put in abeyance when the Currie Cup was established. Sir Donald Currie, the founder of the Castle Shipping Line, which carried passengers and goods between the United Kingdom and South Africa, donated a cup which was to be presented to the South African team which performed best against the 1888–89 England touring team.

Kimberley were awarded the cup and from 1889–90 onwards the Currie Cup was competed for by the major sides in the country. In the first year, the single Currie Cup game took place when Transvaal challenged Kimberley and won. The second season was a repeat of the first, except that Kimberley won the cup back. There was no competition in 1891–92 because of the tour of an England side – this was indeed to be the pattern for many years to come. If a first-class touring side visited South Africa, the Currie Cup was abandoned for the season.

Frank Hearne, the Kent all-rounder, emigrated to South Africa and was engaged as coach to Western Province at Newlands from 1889. He also played for Western Province, making a material difference to the strength of that side. They won the Currie Cup in 1892–93 and took the title in three out of the next four competitions.

The Boer War caused a gap between 1898–99 and 1901–02, then Transvaal won the title, all the matches being staged in Port Elizabeth.

It is amusing now to note the career of P.H. de Villiers. He had played for Western Province, but moved to Transvaal and fought on the Boer side. According to legend, he was wearing his cricketing gear when captured by the British, shipped out as a P.O.W. to Ceylon, where he organized what he called the Curry Cup, amongst fellow prisoners, then a P.O.W. team against Ceylon match, which the Governor of Ceylon attended.

The Edwardian era saw the emergence of some quite brilliant googly bowlers: Aubrey Faulkner of Transvaal, who emigrated to England in 1913; A.E.E. Vogler, who played for three different provinces and in 1906 decided to move to England to qualify for Middlesex, but changed his mind after a year; and Gordon White of Transvaal. A fourth notable spin bowler was Reggie Schwarz. When he came to England with the 1907 South Africans, he was so successful that he topped the first-class bowling table with 137 wickets at 11.79 each. Curiously, whilst at Cambridge University, Schwarz not only failed to gain a blue, but never played in a first-class game for the University. He played for Transvaal from 1902–03 to 1909–10. Both White and Schwarz died whilst serving in the Forces during the First World War.

The great batsman of South African cricket was Dave Nourse, whose career began with Natal in 1896–97 and ended 40 years later with Western Province in 1935–36. Long before his final game, he was known as the Grand Old Man of South African cricket.

Virtually all cricket in South Africa had been played on matting wickets, but this slowly changed. By the time Wally Hammond's England side toured in 1938–39, all the principal grounds had turf wickets and the only matting wickets encountered by the tourists were in Rhodesia.

A major change in the Currie Cup Competition occurred in 1951–52 when the provincial sides were divided into two sections. Section A then comprised Eastern Province, Natal, Transvaal and Western Province; Section B comprised the Orange Free State, Rhodesia, Border, North-Eastern Transvaal and Griqualand West. The authorities reverted to a single division in 1960–61, but in 1962–63 went back to two divisions.

Natal were, by and large, the strongest team from the 1930s right through to the late 1960s and had three notable players in the 1950s and early 60s: Roy McLean, Jackie McGlew and Trevor Goddard.

Transvaal wrested the cup from Natal in 1968–69. They were to dominate the competition for the next 20 years during which, because of the political situation, South Africa was excluded from the Test arena. Apart from "rebel" tours, the Currie Cup was the most important feature of cricket in South Africa at this time.

In 1982–83, for example, Transvaal played in all the competition's 22 matches and lost just one. The team was led by Clive Rice; the leading scorer was Jimmy Cook; the bowling was opened by Vincent van der Bijl; and Alan Kourie, slow left arm, was the principal wicket-keeper. In the season under discussion, Graeme Pollock achieved little but he had been a mainstay of Transvaal from 1978–79, when he left Eastern Province.

The major domestic limited-overs competition commenced in 1969–70 on an unofficial basis sponsored by Gillette, but in the second year it was recognized by the authorities and ran on a knock-out basis until 1979–80, after which the semi-finals were played over two legs (home and away). From 1986–87, the teams were divided into two pools with the top two sides going into the semi-finals. Over limits were originally 60 per side, but were reduced to 55, though for the season 1986–87 only 50 overs were used. Datsun, Nissan and Total Power successively replaced Gillette as sponsors.

In 1981–82 a new competition, played under lights and sponsored by Benson & Hedges, was introduced. This, using coloured clothing and other novelties, took the public interest away from the original competition, so much so that 1992–93 saw the end of the day-time limited-overs competition.

TREVOR GODDARD AND JACKIE MCGLEW *two of South Africa's greatest batsman through the 1950s and 1960s.*

CURRIE BECOMES CASTLE

The beginning of the 1990s saw the political situation in South Africa change. The two governing bodies of cricket in the country, the South African Cricket Union and the South African Cricket Board, joined together to form the United Cricket Board of South Africa. One of the consequences of the amalgamation was a restructuring of the Currie Cup. The name was changed to the Castle Cup and two new regions were granted first-class status: Western Transvaal and Eastern Transvaal. The Springbok emblem, which had been the symbol of South African cricket for many decades, was discontinued.

Eastern Province wrested the top place in domestic cricket from Rice's Transvaal during this period – in 1991–92 Eastern won the Castle Cup for the third time in four years. They were led by Kepler Wessels. Another side to flourish was the Orange Free State, managed by Eddie Barlow, whose stars were the West Indian Franklyn Stephenson and the fast bowler Allan Donald. Below the top level, further changes took place in that the lower division of the first-class scene was divided into two sections, the UCB Bowl and the President's Competition. The latter was for B sides or Second XIs. However, in 1992–93 first-class status was revoked for the B sides. This lasted just one season, the B sides being reinstated as first-class for 1993–94. The efforts made by Eddie Barlow in the Free State paid off as the side won the Castle Cup for the first time in 1992–93, then the following year performed the double by retaining the title and taking the Benson & Hedges Night Competition as well.

Cricket in South Africa is proving ever more popular and its base is growing as the talents of the black and coloured cricketers are being discovered and utilized, notably in Soweto.

CASTLE CUP

1889–90	Transvaal
1890–91	Kimberley
1892–93	Western Province
1893–94	Western Province
1894–95	Transvaal
1896–97	Western Province
1897–98	Western Province
1902–03	Transvaal
1903–04	Transvaal
1904–05	Transvaal
1906–07	Transvaal
1908–09	Western Province
1910–11	Natal
1912–13	Natal
1920–21	Western Province
1921–22	Natal, Transvaal, Western Province
1923–24	Transvaal
1925–26	Transvaal
1926–27	Transvaal
1929–30	Transvaal
1931–32	Western Province
1933–34	Natal
1934–35	Transvaal
1936–37	Natal
1937–38	Natal, Transvaal
1946–47	Natal
1947–48	Natal
1950–51	Transvaal
1951–52	Natal
1952–53	Western Province
1954–55	Natal
1955–56	Western Province
1958–59	Transvaal
1959–60	Natal
1960–61	Natal
1962–63	Natal
1963–64	Natal
1965–66	Natal, Transvaal
1966–67	Natal
1967–68	Natal
1968–69	Transvaal
1969–70	Transvaal Western Province
1970–71	Transvaal
1971–72	Transvaal
1972–73	Transvaal
1973–74	Natal
1974–75	Western Province
1975–76	Natal
1976–77	Natal
1977–78	Western Province
1978–79	Transvaal
1979–80	Transvaal
1980–81	Natal
1981–82	Western Province
1982–83	Transvaal
1983–84	Transvaal
1984–85	Transvaal
1985–86	Western Province
1986–87	Transvaal
1987–88	Transvaal
1988–89	Eastern Province
1989–90	Eastern Province, Western Province
1990–91	Western Province
1991–92	Eastern Province
1992–93	Orange Free State
1993–94	Orange Free State
1994–95	Natal
1995–96	Western Province

BENSON & HEDGES NIGHT SERIES

1981–82	Transvaal 265–7 (47.3 overs) beat Natal 263 (49.3 overs) by 3 wkts
1982–83	Transvaal 277–4 (42.0 overs) beat Western Province 275–9 (45 overs) by 6 wkts
1983–84	Natal 125–3 (29.2 overs) beat Eastern Province 124 (37.3 overs) by 7 wkts
1984–85	Transvaal 179–3 (36.2 overs) beat Northern Transvaal 176 (43.1 overs) by 7 wkts
1985–86	Western Province 265–4 (45 overs) beat Northern Transvaal 253–9 (45 overs) by 12 runs
1986–87	Western Province 205–6 (45 overs) beat Transvaal 164 (41.4 overs) by 41 runs
1987–88	Western Province 190–5 (44 overs) beat Transvaal 189 (44.3 overs) by 5 wkts
1988–89	Orange Free State 213 (45 overs) beat Western Province 152 (39.4 overs) by 61 runs
1989–90	Eastern Province 205–9 (45 overs) beat Natal 202 (44.5 overs) by 1 wkt
1990–91	Western Province 168–4 (39.3 overs) beat Natal 164–8 (45 overs) by 6 wkts
1991–92	Eastern Province 246–4 (44.1 overs) beat Western Province 244–2 (45 overs) by 6 wkts
1992–93	Transvaal 193–7 (45 overs) beat Natal 192–8 (45 overs) by 1 run
1993–94	Orange Free State 108–3 (28.1 overs) beat Natal 103 (36.2 overs) by 7 wkts
1994–95	Orange Free State 291–8 (50 overs) beat Eastern Province 177–8 (50 overs) by 113 runs
1995–96	Orange Free State 290–6 (45 overs) beat Transvaal 148 (37.4 overs) by 142 runs

PAUL ADAMS *(South Africa) bowls against the West Indies in Karachi at the quarter finals of the 1996 Cricket World Cup.*

UCB BOWL

1977–78	Northern Transvaal
1978–79	Northern Transvaal
1979–80	Natal B
1980–81	Western Province B
1981–82	Boland
1982–83	Western Province B
1983–84	Western Province B
1984–85	Transvaal B
1985–86	Boland
1986–87	Transvaal B
1987–88	Boland
1988–89	Border
1989–90	Border, Western Province B
1990–91	Border, Western Province B
1991–92	Eastern Transvaal
1992–93	Boland
1993–94	Transvaal B, Western Province B
1994–95	Natal B
1995–96	Griqualand West

NEW ZEALAND

SIR RICHARD HADLEE *whose 431 Test wickets created a new record.*

The first three-day game between two New Zealand Provinces – Otago v Canterbury – at Dunedin in January 1864 is considered as the starting point of first-class cricket in the country. These two sides met annually in the single New Zealand first-class game until 1873–74, when Auckland, Nelson and Wellington joined the sides designated first-class. Taranki acquired first-class status in 1882–83 and Hawkes Bay in 1883–84.

The provinces were presented with a trophy by Lord Plunket, the Governor-General, in 1906–07. This was awarded by the New Zealand Cricket Council to Canterbury on the grounds that the province had given the best performance against the MCC side which toured New Zealand the same season.

The trophy – a shield – was to be competed for on a challenge basis. Auckland in December 1907 were the first successful challengers and they managed to retain the shield for over three years. Surprisingly, no other side held the trophy for more than a single year, except when it was put in abeyance during the First World War.

In 1921 the New Zealand Cricket Council decided to scrap the challenge system in favour of a league. Despite the fact that various New Zealand sides had imported professionals from England to improve the standard of cricket, it cannot be said that the quality prior to the First World War was particularly high. There was no question of the New Zealand side warranting Test-match status and touring sides to the country were not up to Sheffield Shield rank.

The four major associations which comprised the initial Plunket league were Auckland, Canterbury, Otago and Wellington. Hawkes Bay was designated a minor association. The Hawke Cup was the trophy for the minor associations and continued to be run on a challenge basis, even when the Plunket Shield switched to a league.

After the Second World War, two more sides were promoted to first-class status and joined the Plunket Shield, Central Districts with its headquarters at Palmerston North in 1950–51, and Northern Districts in 1956–57. In general, the sides were fairly evenly matched and, apart from a four-season period in the 1930s when Auckland won successive titles, no side has been champion for more than two consecutive summers. The notable Auckland players of that purple patch were Mervyn Wallace, Graham Vivian, Bill Carson and Jack Cowie – the first three were batsmen, whilst Cowie was New Zealand's outstanding fast bowler.

Directly after the Second World War, New Zealand produced a record-breaking batsman, Bert Sutcliffe. Initially, he played for Auckland, but then switched to Otago, for whom he hit two triple-centuries, the highest being 385 against Canterbury in 1952–53. This remains the Plunket Shield record.

After the appearance of Bert Sutcliffe, came the debut of John Reid, who played for Wellington from 1947–48 to 1964–65, apart from two seasons with Otago. The Hadlee family were the major force for Canterbury. Walter Hadlee's career as a batsman commenced in the 1930s and continued until 1951–52. His three sons all represented the province. Richard Hadlee was the greatest cricketer New Zealand has yet produced. Though initially he was a tearaway fast bowler, he developed into not only the most accurate bowler of his generation, but also a very aggressive left-hand middle-order batsman. The brothers Martin and Jeff Crowe, first with Auckland until Martin moved to Central Districts, were major batsmen of the 1980s.

In 1975–76 the Shell Oil Company took over sponsorship of the Plunket Shield. At first there was a Shell Cup for the league winners and a Shell Trophy for a knockout competition, but in the 1979–80 season the trophy was given to the league winners and the cup to the winners of a limited-overs competition. This limited-overs competition had commenced in 1971–72 under the sponsorship of the NZ Motor Corporation. Gillette sponsored it for two seasons.

SLOW LEFT-ARM *Daniel Vettori is New Zealand's latest spin discovery.*

LIMITED-OVERS COMPETITIONS

NZ MOTOR CORPORATION TOURNAMENT

1971–72	Canterbury 129–3 (33.3 overs) beat Wellington 127 (36.5 overs) by 7 wkts
1972–73	Auckland 209–6 (40 overs) beat Otago 144 (34 overs) by 65 runs
1973–74	Wellington 212–9 (34 overs) beat Auckland 209–7 (35 overs) by 1 wkt
1974–75	Wellington 181–7 (35 overs) beat Northern Districts 165–8 (35 overs) by 16 runs
1975–76	Canterbury 233–6 (35 overs) beat Wellington 153–7 (35 overs) by 80 runs
1976–77	Canterbury 178–7 (34.1 overs) beat Northern Districts 176–7 (35 overs) by 3 wkts

GILLETTE CUP

1977–78	Canterbury 211–9 (30 overs) beat Northern Districts 154–9 (30 overs) by 57 runs
1978–79	Auckland 156 (34.6 overs) beat Canterbury 143–9 (35 overs) by 13 runs

NATIONAL KNOCKOUT TOURNAMENT

1979–89	Northern Districts 183–8 (50 overs) beat Otago 182–8 (50 overs) by 2 wkts

SHELL CUP KNOCKOUT TOURNAMENT

1980–81	Auckland 188–7 (49.1 overs) beat Canterbury 186 (49.3 overs) by 3 wkts
1981–82	Wellington 205–2 (47.5 overs) beat Canterbury 204–7 (50 overs) by 8 wkts
1982–83	Auckland 212–5 (49.1 overs) beat Northern Districts 210 (49.2 overs) by 5 wkts
1983–84	Auckland 130–5 (33.3 overs) beat Wellington 129–6 (35 overs) by 5 wkts
1984–85	Central Districts 156–2 (43.2 overs) beat Wellington 153 (48.2 overs) by 8 wkts
1985–86	Canterbury [details??] [details??]
1986–87	Auckland[details??] [details??]
1987–88	Otago [details??] [details??]
1988–89	Wellington [details??] [details??]
1989–90	Auckland 198–8 (50 overs) beat Central Districts 176–9 (50 overs) by 22 runs
1990–91	Wellington 214–8 (50 overs) beat Central Districts 140 (42.4 overs) by 74 runs
1991–92	Canterbury 252 (49.4 overs) bet Wellington 249 (49.4 overs) by 3 runs
1992–93	Canterbury 183–8 (50 overs) bet Otago 169–9 (50 overs) by 14 runs
1993–94	Canterbury 240–7 (50 overs) beat Central Districts 215 (49 overs) by 25 runs
1994–95	Northern Districts 256–8 (50 overs) beat Wellington 108(29.3 overs) by 148 runs
1995–96	Canterbury 329–5 (50 overs) beat Northern Districts 213 (44.4 overs) by 116 runs

PLUNKET/SHELL

PLUNKET SHIELD

Canterbury to Dec 17, 1907
Auckland Dec 17, 1907 to Feb 1, 1911
Canterbury Feb 1, 1911 to Feb 12, 1912
Auckland Feb 12, 1912 to Jan 31, 1913
Canterbury Jan 31, 1913 to Dec 27, 1918
Wellington Dec 27, 1918 to Jan 24, 1919
Canterbury Jan 24, 1919 to Jan 4, 1920
Auckland Jan 4, 1920 to Jan 10, 1921
Wellington from Jan 10, 1921

1921–22	Auckland
1922–23	Canterbury
1923–24	Wellington
1924–25	Otago
1925–26	Wellington
1926–27	Auckland
1927–28	Wellington
1928–29	Auckland
1929–30	Wellington
1930–31	Canterbury
1931–32	Wellington
1932–33	Otago
1933–34	Auckland
1934–35	Canterbury
1935–36	Wellington
1936–37	Auckland
1937–38	Auckland
1938–39	Auckland
1939–40	Auckland
1940–45	No competition
1945–46	Canterbury
1946–47	Auckland
1947–48	Otago
1948–49	Canterbury
1949–50	Wellington
1950–51	Otago
1951–52	Canterbury
1952–53	Otago
1953–54	Central Districts
1954–55	Wellington
1955–56	Canterbury
1956–57	Wellington
1957–58	Otago
1958–59	Auckland
1959–60	Canterbury
1960–61	Wellington
1961–62	Wellington
1962–63	Northern Districts
1963–64	Auckland
1964–65	Canterbury
1965–66	Wellington
1966–67	Central Districts
1967–68	Central Districts
1968–69	Auckland
1969–70	Otago
1970–71	Central Districts
1971–72	Otago
1972–73	Wellington
1973–74	Wellington
1974–75	Otago

SHELL TROPHY

1975–76	Canterbury (Cup), Canterbury (Trophy)
1976–77	Northern Districts (Cup), Otago (Trophy)
1977–78	Canterbury (Cup), Auckland (Trophy)
1978–79	Otago (Cup), Otago (Trophy)
1979–80	Northern Districts
1980–81	Auckland
1981–82	Wellington
1982–83	Wellington
1983–84	Canterbury
1984–85	Wellington
1985–86	Otago
1986–87	Central Districts
1987–88	Otago
1988–89	Auckland
1989–90	Wellington
1990–91	Auckland
1991–92	Central Districts, Northern Districts
1992–93	Northern Districts
1993–94	Canterbury
1994–95	Auckland
1995–96	Auckland
1996–97	Canterbury

PAKISTAN

The Dominion of Pakistan was created on July 18, 1947. It was formed from two separate parts of the former Indian Empire: in the West, Pakistan comprised Baluchistan, Sind, North West Frontier Province and West Punjab; Eastern Pakistan was made up of East Bengal and the Sylhot district of Assam. In March 1971, Eastern Pakistan broke away to form the new independent country of Bangladesh. The three main cricketing centres in the new 1947 Pakistan were all in the western section – at Lahore, Karachi and Peshawar.

The only first-class matches involving a Pakistan side staged in 1947–48 were Sind v Bombay, played in Bombay and Punjab University v Punjab Governor's XI.

In 1948–49, the West Indian side touring India played two first-class matches in Pakistan and a few months later a Pakistan team toured Ceylon.

Pakistan was admitted as a member of the ICC in July 1952 and played its first Test, against India, in the 1952–53 season. The first domestic first-class competition in Pakistan was arranged for the following season. The competition was called the Qaid-i-Azam ("The Great Leader") Trophy, a reference to Mohammad Ali Jinnah, who founded the Pakistan State.

Seven teams competed in the first competition: Punjab, Karachi, Sind, North West Frontier Province, Bahawalpur, Services and Railways. Two other sides were entered, East Pakistan and Baluchistan, but both withdrew. These two did, however, compete in the second season, 1954–55.

It was soon clear that the sides were ill-matched and it was agreed that in 1956–57 Karachi and Punjab should enter three teams each. There have been numerous changes both in the teams taking part and in the way the competition has been run – in some years the contest has been spread over two seasons, for example.

In 1960–61, when the leading Pakistani cricketers were touring overseas, the Board of Control instituted the President Ayub Trophy, donated by Field-Marshal Ayub Khan. In 1970–71, this was replaced by the BCCP Trophy, which lasted two seasons, to be replaced by the Patron's Trophy.

At present, both the Patron's Trophy and the Qaid-i-Azam Trophy are considered first-class competitions. The following other competitions have been ranked as first-class in the seasons given:

Inter-University Championship 1958–59, 1959–60
Quadrangular Trophy 1968–69
Punjab Governor's Gold Cup 1971–72
S.A. Bhutto Cup 1972–73, 1973–74, 1975–76, 1976–77
Pentangular League 1973–74, 1974–75, 1975–76, 1976–77
Punjab Championship 1973–74, 1974–75, 1975–76
Kardar Shield 1973–74, 1974–75
A.S. Pirzada Memorial Trophy 1974–75, 1975–76
Invitation Tournament 1977–78, 1978–79, 1979–80
PACO Cup 1980–81, 1981–82 1982–83, 1984–85, 1985–86, 1986–87
President's Cup 1986–87

The principal limited-overs competition is for the Wills Cup. This commenced in 1980–81 as a 45-overs-a-side contest, the teams being divided into two leagues with the top two teams in each league meeting in a knockout semi-final round. In 1986–87, the matches were raised to 50 overs per side, but have since been cut back again to 45.

JAVED MIANDAD *Pakistan's longest-serving Test batsman.*

QAID-I-AZAM TROPHY

1953–54	Bahawalpur
1954–55	Karachi
1956–57	Punjab
1957–58	Bahawalpur
1958–59	Karachi
1959–60	Karachi
1961–62	Karachi Blues
1962–63	Karachi A
1963–64	Karachi Blues
1964–65	Karachi Blues
1966–67	Karachi
1968–69	Lahore
1969–70	PIA
1970–71	Karachi Blues
1972–73	Railways
1973–74	Railways
1974–75	Punjab A
1975–76	National Bank
1976–77	United Bank
1977–78	Habib Bank
1978–79	National Bank
1979–80	PIA
1980–81	United Bank
1981–82	National Bank
1982–83	United Bank
1983–84	National Bank
1984–85	United Bank
1985–86	Karachi
1986–87	National Bank
1987–88	PIA
1988–89	ADBP
1989–90	PIA
1990–91	Karachi Whites
1991–92	Karachi Whites
1992–93	Karachi
1993–94	Lahore
1994–95	Karachi Blues
1995–96	Karachi Blues

PATRON'S TROPHY

1970–71	PIA
1971–72	PIA
1972–73	Karachi Blues
1973–74	Railways
1974–75	National Bank
1975–76	National Bank
1976–77	Habib Bank
1977–78	Habib Bank
1978–79	National Bank
1979–80	IDBP
1980–81	Rawalpindi
1981–82	Allied Bank
1982–83	PACO
1983–84	Karachi Blues
1984–85	Karachi Whites
1985–86	Karachi Whites
1986–87	National Bank
1987–88	Habib Bank
1988–89	Karachi
1989–90	Karachi Whites
1990–91	ADBP
1991–92	Habib Bank
1992–93	Habib Bank
1993–94	ADBP
1994–95	Allied Bank
1995–96	ADBP

WILLS CUP

1980–81	PIA 230 (45 overs) beat United Bank 225 (44.1 overs) 5 runs
1981–82	PIA 132–3 (32.5 overs) beat Lahore 131 (42.3 overs) by 7 wkts
1982–83	PIA 206–9 (45 overs) beat Habib Bank 173 (43.2 overs) by 33 runs
1983–84	Habib Bank 182–3 (41 overs) beat PIA 181 (39.4 overs) by 7 wkts
1984–85	No competition
1985–86	PIA 257–3 (45 overs) beat United Bank 254–9 (45 overs) by 3 runs
1986–87	Habib Bank 155–7 (49.2 overs) beat United Bank 154 (48.1 overs) by 3 wkts
1987–88	PIA 212–8 (47.4 overs) beat United Bank 206–8 (49 overs) by 2 wkts
1988–89	United Bank 228–6 (45 overs) beat PIA 228 (45 overs) by losing fewer wkts
1989–90	Habib Bank 178–2 (42.4 overs) beat PIA 177 (46.3 overs) by 8 wkts
1990–91	Habib Bank 241–4 (45 overs) beat United Bank 185–9 (45 overs) by 6 wkts
1991–92	Habib Bank 254–5 (39 overs) beat PIA 234–4 (43 overs) by 5 wkts
1992–93	National Bank 272–5 (48 overs) beat Habib Bank 269–6 (50 overs) by 5 wkts
1993–94	Habib Bank 249–5 (50 overs) beat Rawalpindi 203–8 (50 overs) by 46 runs
1994–95	National Bank 215–2 (43.2 overs) beat PIA 211 (44.4 overs) by 8 wkts
1995–96	PIA 125–3 (30.5 overs) beat Rawalpindi 124 (42.4 overs) by 7 wkts
1996–97	Allied Bank 252–4 (42.1 overs) beat Nat. Bank 251–9 (50 overs) by 6 wkts

WASIM AKRAM *who, with Waqar Younis, provides Pakistan's opening attack.*

WEST INDIES

LEARIE CONSTANTINE *the star all-rounder for West Indies in the 1930s.*

The match between Barbados and Demerara played in Bridgetown on February 15 and 16 1865 is considered as the start of first–class cricket in the West Indies. In 1868–69, Trinidad played Demerara in two matches, both in Port of Spain, and are considered "first-class" from those matches. Matches between the three colonies continued intermittently for 20 years or more, but attempts to organize some sort of proper competition between the colonies came to nothing – despite the fact that in 1886 G.N. Wyatt of British Guiana had managed to pick a fairly representative West Indian side to tour the United States.

At last in September 1891, Trinidad agreed to take part in a triangular inter-colonial tournament in Bridgetown. Barbados won the competition and were declared champions. Their success was due in the main to the brothers Clifford and Percy Goodman, the former being a fast medium bowler and the latter a batsman.

This initial tournament generated great enthusiasm. A trophy was purchased and the basic rules established, that the two losing colonies played each other, then the winner challenged the reigning champion.

Jamaica was too far away to compete in this tournament and the island had to wait for overseas touring sides before it could field a representative XI. Jamaica's first first-class game was therefore against R.S. Lucas's English touring team in 1894–95.

Between 1911–12 and 1921–22 the Intercolonial Tournament was not staged. In the early days of 1920, Trinidad went to Barbados on a "Goodwill Tour". Barbados won both first-class games and Tim Tarilton hit a record 304 not out, when Barbados made 623 for five in the second game – at which point Harold Austin declared. Austin was the leading figure at this time in West Indian cricket. He captained two West Indian tours to England and was one of five brothers who played first-class cricket.

The 1921–22 contest for the Intercolonial Trophy proved to have a disappointing end. Rain caused delays and the Trinidad team were forced to leave to catch their boat before the final was played out.

The next competition, in Georgetown, saw Barbados win by an innings in the final. In 1924–25, Jamaica opposed Barbados for the first time in Bridgetown, having played another island in first-class matches only once before, when Trinidad visited Kingston in 1905–06. In the 1924–25 games – three were played – all ended as draws, the pitches being perfect for batting.

In the 1920s, Trinidad gradually overtook Barbados as the major force in the Caribbean. British Guiana were also building up their strength and in 1929–30 won the Intercolonial Trophy for the first time since 1895–96 – throughout the 1930s, the trophy was in the hands of either Guiana or Trinidad and the once all-powerful Barbados team was out in the cold.

Trinidad's outstanding cricketer from the First World War was Learie Constantine, an all-rounder whose fast bowling, hurricane hitting and brilliant fielding could change the course of any match. In the mid-1930s, however, he more or less emigrated to England. George Headley was the second great international West Indian star; his career batting record gave an average just a shade under 70. Unfortunately, he lived in Jamaica and thus took no part in the Intercolonial Trophy matches.

THE SHELL SHIELD

The 1938–39 season saw the end of the old trophy, but there were several one-off tournaments in the seasons which followed. Even during the Second World War, Barbados and Trinidad played regular first-class matches, but a proper competition did not re-emerge until 1965–66 when the Shell Oil Company sponsored a trophy. At first the competition involved Barbados, British Guiana, Jamaica, Trinidad and "Combined Islands" (i.e. Leewards and Windwards). In the second season, the Leewards and Windwards played as separate sides, but from 1969 to 1981 the two groups combined again. From 1981–82, the Leewards and Windwards have participated as individual competitors. In 1987–88, the Shell Shield was replaced by the Red Stripe Cup.

Barbados were the major force in the days of the Shell Shield, winning the trophy 12 times out of the 21 occasions on which it was held. In the 1960s, Barbados had Gary Sobers, the most talented cricketer of his time, as captain. Conrad Hunte and Seymour Nurse were the main batsmen and the much-feared Charlie Griffith led the bowling attack. In the second half of the 1970s, when Barbados won five titles in a row, their fast attack comprised Wayne Daniel, Joel Garner and Vanburn Holder, whilst Gordon Greenidge and Desmond Haynes opened the batting.

The Combined Islands, or to be specific, the Leeward Islands, found two quite outstanding cricketers, Viv Richards and Andy Roberts, both born on the small island of Antigua. The Combined Islands took the title in 1980–81.

The principal limited-overs competition for the West Indies began as the Gillette Cup in 1975–76. The competition has been fairly even; no side has won fewer than 50 games, whilst the best record, by Barbados, is under 70.

Two countries in the West Indies have also had their own internal first-class competition. The Jones Cup was originally established in 1954 for competition between the three counties of British Guiana (Guyana since 1966): Demerara, Berbice and Essequibo. The final of this competition was ruled first-class by the West Indies Board from 1971–72. In 1985–86, the title was changed from the Jones Cup to the Guystac Trophy, then to the Sookram Trophy in 1989–90. It ceased to be first-class in 1991.

The Beaumont Cup, donated by the former South African Test cricketer Rolland Beaumont, began as a competition between North and South Trinidad in 1926. It was ruled first-class in April 1959 and in 1970–71 was expanded to include East and Central Trinidad. The following year, the trophy was replaced by the Texaco Cup. In 1978–79, Tobago was added to the competition, but the next season the West Indies Board withdrew first-class status.

GILLETTE CUP

GILLETTE CUP

1975–76 Barbados 191 (49.3 overs) beat Trinidad 148 (39.5 overs) by 43 runs
1976–77 Barbados 97–2 (27 overs) beat Trinidad 95 (33.3 overs) by 8 wkts

GEDDES GRANT-HARRISON LINE TROPHY

1977–78 Jamaica and Leeward Islands shared the trophy as the final was abandoned
1978–79 Trinidad 214–9 (50 overs) beat Barbados 158 (47.1 overs) by 56 runs
1979–80 Guyana 327–7 (50 overs) beat Leeward Islands 224 (41.1 overs) by 103 runs
1980–81 Trinidad 128–6 (42 overs) beat Barbados 127 (49 overs) by 4 wkts
1981–82 Leeward Islands 95–5 (29.3 overs) beat Barbados 94 (37.5 overs) by 5 wkts
1982–83 Guyana 211–8 (41 overs) beat Jamaica 83 (25 overs) by 128 runs
1983–84 Jamaica 213–7 (41 overs) beat Leeward Islands 212–9 (42 overs) by 2 wkts
1984–85 Guyana 140–5 (41 overs) beat Jamaica 139 (46.1 overs) by 5 wkts
1985–86 Jamaica 173–4 (34.3 overs) beat Leeward Islands 169–8 (39 overs) by 6 wkts
1986–87 Jamaica 252–6 (46 overs) beat Barbados 249–3 (49 overs) by 4 wkts
1987–88 Barbados 219–9 (46 overs) beat Jamaica 218–8 (46 overs) by 1 wkt

GEDDES GRANT SHIELD

1988–89 Windward Islands 155–9 (49.3 overs) beat Guyana 154–9 (50 overs) by 1 wkt
1989–90 Trinidad 180–5 (44.2 overs) beat Barbados 178–9 (47 overs) by 5 wkts
1990–91 Jamaica 232–6 (49.5 overs) beat Leeward Islands 228–8 (50 overs) by 4 wkts
1991–92 Trinidad 167–2(37.3 overs) beat Barbados 163 (49.3 overs) by 8 wkts
1992–93 Guyana and Leeward Islands shared the shield as the final was abandoned
1993–94 Leeward Islands 289–6 (50 overs) beat Barbados 255 (46.1 overs) by 34 runs

SHELL-SANDALS TROPHY

1994–95 Leeward Islands188 (49 overs) beat Barbados 110 (31 overs) by 78 runs
1995–96 Trinidad and Guyana joint winners after rain prevented the final being completed

CHAMPION TEAMS

1891–92 Barbados
1893–94 Barbados
1895–96 Demerara
1897–98 Barbados
1890–00 Barbados
1901–02 Trinidad
1903–04 Trinidad
1905–06 Barbados
1907–08 Trinidad
1908–09 Barbados
1909–10 Trinidad
1910–11 Barbados
1911–12 Barbados
1921–22 No result
1922–23 Barbados
1923–24 Barbados
1924–25 Trinidad
1925–26 Trinidad
1926–27 Barbados
1928–29 Trinidad
1929–30 British Guiana
1931–32 Trinidad
1933–34 Trinidad
1934–35 British Guiana
1935–36 British Guiana
1936–37 Trinidad
1937–38 British Guiana
1938–39 Trinidad

SHELL SHIELD / RED STRIPE CUP

SHELL SHIELD

1965–66 Barbados
1966–67 Barbados
1967–68 No competition
1968–69 Jamaica
1969–70 Trinidad
1970–71 Trinidad
1971–72 Barbados
1972–73 Guyana
1973–74 Barbados
1974–75 Guyana
1975–76 Barbados, Trinidad
1976–77 Barbados
1977–78 Barbados
1978–79 Barbados
1979–80 Barbados
1980–81 Combined Islands
1981–82 Barbados
1982–83 Guyana
1983–84 Barbados
1984–85 Trinidad
1985–86 Barbados
1986–87 Guyana

RED STRIPE CUP

1987–88 Jamaica
1988–89 Jamaica
1989–90 Leeward Islands
1990–91 Barbados
1991–92 Jamaica
1992–93 Guyana
1993–94 Leeward Islands
1994–95 Barbados
1995–96 Leeward Islands

DESMOND HAYNES *of the West Indies, Barbados and Middlesex.*

INDIA

At first it appears odd that the first major cricket club in India should be established in Calcutta and through the nineteenth and much of the twentieth century be regarded as the premier club in India, when the most important competition in the sub-continent until the 1930s was centred a thousand miles away in Bombay.

The origins of the Calcutta Cricket Club are obscure. What is known is that in 1792 the club was established at Eden Gardens and that in 1804 Robert Vansittart, an Old Etonian, hit the first recorded century on the Eden Gardens ground. The Calcutta Club, however, was exclusively European and as such gave no encouragement to the Indians to learn or participate in cricket. It was aloof and remained so well into the twentieth century.

In contrast, the Parsees of Bombay took readily to cricket. Their first organized club was set up in 1848 and in 1877 the Parsees opposed the Europeans for the first time – the Indians were not successful. Undeterred by their defeat, the number of Parsees playing cricket multiplied as did their clubs and in 1886 they were in a position to finance a team to tour England. A programme of 28 matches was arranged against modest opposition – as the organizers pointed out, this was a tour on which to learn. Socially the matches were a great success and, at the behest of Queen Victoria, the Parsees played at Windsor against Prince Christian Victor's Team. A second such tour took place in 1888. On this visit was M.E. Pavri, who was to become the greatest Parsee cricketer of his day. He played for Middlesex in 1895, while he was in England qualifying as a doctor.

First-class cricket in India commenced in 1892–93 when the Parsees opposed the Europeans of Bombay Presidency, in two matches arranged for three days each. This fixture then became the major annual contest in India. In that first season, an English team toured the sub-continent, playing four first-class games.

In 1905–06, the Hindus joined in the European-Parsee contest, which therefore became a triangular series. In 1912–13, with the advent of a Muslim side, the contest became quadrangular, but it remained confined to Bombay and Poona. Similar communal tournaments were later arranged in Nagpur (Central Provinces Quadrangular), Lahore (Northern India Tournament) and Karachi (Sind Tournament). Apart from the Bombay Tournament, the status of the matches in these communal contests is very complicated and readers interested in the subject are advised to consult the *Guide to First Class Cricket Matches Played in India* published in 1986.

It was not until the MCC toured India in 1926–27 that any substantial moves were made to create an Indian Cricket Board of Control. A board was duly formed and encouraged the formation of cricket associations based on the various Indian provinces.

VIJAY MERCHANT *India's premier batsman in the 1930s and 1940s.*

THE RANJI TROPHY

In a meeting held in Simla in July 1934, the Board arranged a Cricket Championship of India which became known as the Ranji Trophy, when H.H. Sir Bhupindra Singh Mahinder Bahadur, Maharaja of Patiala, presented a trophy for the new competition in memory of K.S. Ranjitsinhji who had recently died.

India was divided into four zones, North, South, East and West, and each zone ran a knockout competition. The four winners then went into a national semi-final and then a final to decide the ultimate winners. In the first season, the competing sides were as follows:

North: Northern India, Army, United Provinces, Delhi, South Punjab
South: Madras, Mysore, Hyderabad
East: Central Provinces and Berar, Central India
West: Sind, Western India, Gujarat, Bombay, Maharashtra.

The Ranji Trophy continues today as India's equivalent of the English County Championship. An extra zone, Central, was created in 1952–53 and in 1957–58 the zonal knockouts were replaced by zonal leagues. The teams competing in 1995–96 were:

North: Delhi, Punjab, Haryana, Services, Himachal Pradesh, Jammua and Kashmir
South: Karnataka, Tamil Nadu, Hyderabad, Andhra, Kerala, Goa
East: Orissa, Bengal, Assam, Bihar, Tripura
West: Bombay, Baroda, Maharashtra, Gujarat, Saurashtra
Central: Railways, Madhya Pradesh, Uttar Pradesh, Vidarbha, Rajasthan

Bombay have been the dominant team throughout the 60 or so years of the contest which continued to be held during the Second World War, unlike all other first–class competitions worldwide. Bombay have been winners 32 times; no other side has claimed the title more than six times.

RANJITSINHJI *the Indian Prince who played Test cricket for England.*

The outstanding feature of the Ranji Trophy has been the high scores achieved – records in the *Indian Cricket* annual show more than 60 batsmen with a seasonal average over 100. Three exceeded 200, with Rusi Modi in 1944 hitting 1,008 at an average of 201.60. He played for Bombay as did such noted batsmen as Sunil Gavaskar, Vijay Merchant, Ajit Wadekar and Polly Umrigar. Among the bowlers, the left-arm spinner Rajinder Goel, playing for Haryana, has taken 640 Ranji Trophy wickets – a hundred more than the second on the list. Yet Goel has never appeared in Test cricket. Second and third in the list of most effective bowlers come two more spinners, Venkataraghavan of Tamil Nadu and Chandrasekhar of Karnataka, both of course well-known Test cricketers.

Apart from the Ranji Trophy and the various communal tournaments between the wars, the most notable competition was the Moin-ud-Dowlah Gold Cup. This was originally staged at Secunderabad in 1927–28. Run by the Nawab Behram-ud-Dowlah, it was strictly for invited teams and the various Indian rulers gathered together notable players in order to build a strong XI and win the trophy. The tournament lapsed when the founder Nawab died. After a gap of 11 seasons, the cup was revived in 1948–49 and finally ended in 1978–79. By no means all the annual contests are considered first-class.

In 1961–62 the Board of Control established a new competition which was aimed to give a higher standard of cricket than the Ranji Trophy. It was named the "Zonal Tournament" for the Duleepsinhji Trophy – but was more usually known as the "Duleep Trophy". Duleepsinhji was a nephew of Ranjitsinhji and both played Test cricket for England.

Indian independence in 1947 saw the end of the communal tournaments, though the Cricket Club of India staged a zonal tournament in Bombay for three seasons, the last being 1948–49.

No look at Indian first-class cricket would be complete without mentioning the Maharajkumar of Vizianagram. He was one of the major patrons of Indian cricket between the wars and vied with the Maharajah of Patiala for having the last word on cricketing affairs. In 1930–31, the MCC cancelled their proposed tour of India owing to the civil unrest created by Gandhi's independence movement. Vizianagram chose a picked team of Indian players and engaged the leading England batsmen, Hobbs and Sutcliffe. He then tried to fulfil the fixtures left vacant by the MCC. Vizianagram stated: "The cancellation of the MCC tour gave the greatest disappointment to Indian cricketers, and I was fired with a passion to devise ways and means to compensate India." A fixture list of 16 matches was arranged plus entry into the Nawab's Gold Cup.

The two major limited-overs competitions of the present day are the Deodhar Trophy and the Wills Trophy. The former, established in 1973–74, involves teams on the same basis as the Duleep Trophy.

The Wills Trophy is competed for by the five zonal winners of the Ranji Trophy, plus two representative sides which draw their players from the Ranji Trophy teams not involved. This competition began in 1977–78.

KAPIL DEV *who took 434 wickets for India.*

DULEEP TROPHY

This competition is run between the five zones into which India is divided for the Ranji Trophy. Originally a knockout competition, it was changed to a league from 1993–94. In 1988–89, the trophy was shared as rain prevented a first-innings decision.

1961–62	West Zone
1962–63	West Zone
1963–64	West Zone
1964–65	West Zone
1965–66	South Zone
1966–67	South Zone
1967–68	South Zone
1968–69	West Zone
1969–70	West Zone
1970–71	South Zone
1971–72	Central Zone
1972–73	West Zone
1973–74	North Zone
1974–75	South Zone
1975–76	South Zone
1976–77	West Zone
1977–78	West Zone
1978–79	North Zone
1979–80	North Zone
1980–81	West Zone
1981–82	West Zone
1982–83	North Zone
1983–84	North Zone
1984–85	South Zone
1985–86	West Zone
1986–87	South Zone
1987–88	North Zone
1988–89	North Zone, West Zone
1989–90	South Zone
1990–91	North Zone
1991–92	North Zone
1992–93	North Zone
1993–94	North Zone
1994–95	North Zone
1995–96	South Zone

RANJI TROPHY

1934–35	Bombay
1935–36	Bombay
1936–37	Nawangar
1937–38	Hyderabad
1938–39	Bengal
1939–40	Maharashtra
1940–41	Maharashtra
1941–42	Bombay
1942–43	Baroda
1943–44	Western India
1944–45	Bombay
1945–46	Holkar
1946–47	Baroda
1947–48	Holkar
1948–49	Bombay
1949–50	Baroda
1950–51	Holkar
1951–52	Bombay
1952–53	Holkar
1953–54	Bombay
1954–55	Madras
1955–56	Bombay
1956–57	Bombay
1957–58	Baroda
1958–59	Bombay
1959–60	Bombay
1960–61	Bombay
1961–62	Bombay
1962–63	Bombay
1963–64	Bombay
1964–65	Bombay
1965–66	Bombay
1966–67	Bombay
1967–68	Bombay
1968–69	Bombay
1969–70	Bombay
1970–71	Bombay
1971–72	Bombay
1972–73	Bombay
1973–74	Karnataka
1974–75	Bombay
1975–76	Bombay
1976–77	Bombay
1977–78	Karnataka
1978–79	Delhi
1979–80	Delhi
1980–81	Bombay
1981–82	Delhi
1982–83	Karnataka
1983–84	Bombay
1984–85	Bombay
1985–86	Delhi
1986–87	Hyderabad
1987–88	Tamil Nadu
1988–89	Delhi
1989–90	Bengal
1990–91	Haryana
1991–92	Delhi
1992–93	Punjab
1993–94	Bombay
1994–95	Bombay
1995–96	Karnataka
1996–97	Bombay

DEODHAR TROPHY

This competition is played between the five zonal teams. Originally played on a knockout basis, it was changed to a league from 1993–94. Since 1979–80, the competition has been held in a single zone during one week. The overs limit was 60 between 1973–74 and 1979–80 and thereafter has been reduced to 50.

1973–74 South Zone 185 (52.1 overs) beat West Zone 101 (38 overs) by 84 runs
1974–75 South Zone 263–5 (60 overs) beat West Zone 255–9 (60 overs) by 8 runs
1975–76 West Zone 185 (55.2 overs) beat South Zone 161 (49 overs) by 24 runs
1976–77 Central Zone 207–7 (56 overs) beat South Zone 206–9 (60 overs) by 3 wkts
1977–78 North Zone 177–0 (38.5 overs) beat West Zone 174 (53 overs) by 10 wkts
1978–79 South Zone 247 (59.4 overs) beat North Zone 218 (56.1 overs) by 29 runs
1979–80 West Zone 246–6 (48 overs) beat North Zone 245–9 (50 overs) by 4 wkts
1980–81 South Zone 275–5 (50 overs) beat West Zone 189–7 (50 overs) by 86 runs
1981–82 South Zone 260–5 (50 overs) beat Central Zone 147 (50 overs) by 113 runs
1982–83 West Zone 198–9 (46 overs) beat North Zone 185–9 (46 overs) by 13 runs
1983–84 West Zone 309 (48.4 overs) beat North Zone 266 (47.2 overs) by 43 runs
1984–85 West Zone 218–4 (37.5 overs) beat North Zone 214–8 (45 overs) by 6 wkts
1985–86 West Zone 227–9 (47 overs) beat North Zone 196 (44.5 overs) by 31 runs
1986–87 North Zone 207–1 (39.5 overs) beat West Zone 206–9 (48 overs) by 9 wkts
1987–88 North Zone 223–3 (45.2 overs) beat West Zone 221–7 (50 overs) by 7 wkts
1988–89 North Zone 243–6 (45 overs) beat South Zone 239–8 (46 overs) by 4 wkts
1989–90 North Zone 319–6 (50 overs) beat South Zone 263–8 (50 overs) by 56 runs
1990–91 West Zone 304–3 (44 overs) beat East Zone 260 (41.4 overs) by 44 runs
1991–92 South Zone 158–7 (35 overs) beat Central Zone 122 (33.2 overs) by 36 runs
1992–93 East Zone 257–9 (50 overs) beat North Zone 254–4 (50 overs) 1 wkt
1993–94 East Zone
1994–95 Central Zone

WILLS TROPHY

This competition is played on a knockout basis between the five zonal winners of the previous seasons's Ranji Trophy plus two representative sides, who choose their players from the other Ranji Trophy teams. The overs limit is 50 per side, although in the first two seasons 60 overs per side were played. In 1993–94, Ranji Trophy one-day matches were introduced as qualification for the following season's Wills Trophy.

1977–78 Wills XI 214–3 (52.3 overs) beat President's XI 213–4 (60 overs) by 7 wkts
1978–79 Delhi 253–7 (60 overs) beat Bombay 253 (56.1 overs) by losing fewer wickets
1979–80 No competition
1980–81 Wills XI 218–7 (49.3 overs) beat President's XI 216–8 (50 overs) by 3 wkts
1981–82 Bombay 225–7 (50 overs) beat President's XI 210–8 (50 overs) by 15 runs
1982–83 Bombay 158 (47.1 overs) beat Delhi 99 (42.1 overs) by 59 runs
1983–84 President's XI 269–6 (42 overs) beat Karnataka 242–9 (42 overs) by 27 runs
1984–85 Wills XI 252–4 (46.1 overs) beat President's XI 249 (49.4) by 6 wkts
1985–86 Bombay 228–9 (46.2 overs) beat Delhi 226–5 (47overs) by 1 wkt
1986–87 Delhi 258–8 (50 overs) beat Maharashtra 159 (37.4 overs) by 99 runs
1987–88 President's XI 244–5 (47 overs) beat Karnataka 184 (45.5 overs) by 60 runs
1988–89 Delhi 205–2 (44.1 overs) beat Railways 200 (48.2 overs) by 8 wkts
1989–90 Wills XI 265–4 (47.3 overs) beat Delhi 261–9 (49 overs) by 6 wkts
1990–91 Bombay 257–3 (46.5 overs) beat Wills XI 254–9 (49 overs) by 7 wkts
1991–92 President's XI 234–8 (50 overs) beat Wills XI 206–8 (50 overs) by 28 runs
1992–93 President's XI 128 (43.2 overs) beat Delhi 128 (44.4 overs) on scoring rate
1993–94 No competition
1994–95 Bombay 265–1 (36.4 overs) beat Haryana 263–7 (50 overs) by 9 wkts
1995–96 Wills XI 299–5 beat Bengal 224–6 by 75 runs
1996–97 Bombay

TABLE OF RESULTS 1977-78 TO 1994-95

	P	W	L	NR	Winner	R-up
President's XI	33	20	12	1	4	4
Wills XI	35	22	12	1	5	2
Bombay	24	18	5	1	5	1
Delhi	24	16	8	0	3	4
Karnataka	11	5	5	1	0	2
Railways	5	3	2	0	0	1
Maharashtra	7	3	4	0	0	1
Haryana	8	3	5	0	0	1
Bengal	18	5	12	1	0	1
Madhya Pradesh	4	2	2	0	0	0
Tamil Nadu	6	1	5	0	0	0
Uttar Pradesh	12	1	11	0	0	0
Andhra	1	0	1	0	0	0
Baroda	2	0	2	0	0	0
Bihar	3	0	3	0	0	0
Gujarat	1	0	1	0	0	0
Hyderabad	5	0	4	1	0	0
Orissa	2	0	2	0	0	0
Rajasthan	2	0	2	0	0	0
Punjab	1	0	1	0	0	0

Matches decided on the toss of a coin are included as No Result.

SRI LANKA

The major match on the island from the early years of the twentieth century was Europeans v Ceylonese, which had its tentative beginnings as far back as 1887. This contest, however, has not been seriously considered as of "first-class" status and, in fact, ended in 1933 because the European side could no longer match that of the Ceylonese.

A representative Ceylon Cricket Association was formed in 1922 and from 1924 organized a club championship with the principal clubs on the island taking part.

The *Ceylon Cricketer's Companion* for 1925 actually heads its main section: "First-class Cricket in 1924". It lists 15 first-class clubs, but most matches were of one-day duration and were only played two-innings-a-side if time allowed. In 1937, the championship developed into the Daily News Trophy. A second change of title came in 1950 when it became the P. Saravanamuttu Trophy. The best-known of the cricketers from Ceylon in the 1920s was Dr C.H. Gunasekara, who had played for Middlesex whilst studying medicine in England immediately after the First World War. Gunasekara captained Ceylon in the 1930s. F.C. de Saram, who obtained a blue at Oxford, represented Ceylon from 1930–1 to 1953–54.

So far as recognized first-class matches are concerned, Ceylon was confined to matches played by representative Ceylon teams overseas or games against visiting touring sides. Until air travel superseded voyages by boat, most England and Australia Test teams sailing between the two countries made fleeting stops at Colombo whilst their ships took on fuel. When at all possible a match was arranged between the tourists and a team from the island.

The first game against the tourists took place in October 1882, when the England side, which was to go on to win the 'Ashes' for the first time, opposed eighteen of Colombo. It was not until eight years later that the Australians stopped long enough to play in Colombo. Between these two visits England sent its first touring side to India. The England team commenced their matches in Colombo and played two games, the first a three-day fixture against All-Ceylon, the second a two-day match against Colombo CC. Both provided the visiting side with innings victories.

The greatest jolt to English pride came in October 1924 when the

WORLD CUP WINNERS *Arjuna Ranatunga and Asanka Gurusinha are seen with the 1997 trophy.*

DULEEP MENDIS *captained Sri Lanka in its first Test at Lord's.*

powerful England side en route to Australia were bowled out for 73, W.T. Greswell taking eight for 38. Greswell, who worked for the family business in Ceylon, played with success for Somerset when on leave in England.

After the Second World War, the major game for many years was Ceylon v Madras. This was instituted in 1952–53 as the Gopalan Trophy – named after M.J. Gopalan who performed a brilliant bowling feat in a game between the two sides in 1932–33. The match was played in each home venue alternately.

In 1972, Ceylon changed its name to Sri Lanka. Sri Lanka was raised to full membership of the ICC in 1981 and thus attained Test-match status. It was not, however, until 1988–89 that the Sri Lankan Board of Control designated the Lakspray Trophy competition as first-class – Lakspray had taken over sponsorship of the P. Saravanamuttu Trophy in 1982–83.

The teams taking part in the initial first-class competition were Air Force, Burgher RC, Colombo CC, Colts CC, Galle CC, Moratuwa SC, Moors SC, Nomads SC, Nondescripts CC, Panadura SC, Sinhalese SC and Tamil Union. Nondescripts and Sinhalese shared the first first-class title.

The Sinhalese club possessed the two leading batsmen of that season, L.R.D. Mendis and A.P. Gurushinha, as well as the best bowler, N. Ranatunga.

In 1990–91, the Lakspray Trophy was renamed the Sara Trophy after the new sponsors. In addition to the Sara Trophy, an inter-Provincial tournament was ranked as first-class from 1989–90, the sides competing for the Singer Trophy.

A list of current first-class domestic sides is difficult to compile because clubs compete in a non-first-class section before being entered into the first-class part of the Sara Trophy.

SINGER TROPHY

1989–90	Western Province City
1990–91	Western Province City
1991–92	Western Province North
1992–93	No competition
1993–94	Western Province City
1994–95	Western Province City
1995–96	No competition

SARA TROPHY

1988–89	Nondescripts, Sinhalese SC
1889–90	Sinhalese SC
1990–91	Sinhalese SC
1991–92	Colts
1992–93	Sinhalese SC
1993–94	Nondescripts
1994–95	Bloomfield, Sinhalese SC
1995–96	Colombo

ZIMBABWE

The territory now known as Zimbabwe was occupied – and from 1890 administered – by the British South Africa Company and it is believed that the first cricket match there took place as early as August 1890 near Fort Victoria. The new country was named Southern Rhodesia and in 1923 obtained self-government as a British colony. The first English cricket side to visit Southern Rhodesia was Lord Hawke's Team of 1898–99.

J.D. Logan, a well-known South African cricket patron, asked Lord Hawke to purchase a cup which could be used as a trophy competed for by the principal clubs in Rhodesia. It was not, however, until 1903–04 that a suitable competition was organized, with Matabeleland as the first winners. After the Second World War, with many of the best players gathered around Salisbury (now Harare) and this being in Mashonaland, this district dominated the competition to the extent that it was hardly worth playing.

Rhodesia (now Zimbabwe) were granted Test-match status in July 1992 and for the 1993–94 season organized a first-class programme of domestic matches, the Logan Cup being the trophy. The teams competing in that first year were: Mashonaland, Mashonaland Under 24, Mashonaland Country Districts and Matabeleland.

In 1995–96 the competition became rather hollow as a result of many of the leading Zimbabwean players being unavailable for matches. The Zimbabwe Board therefore decided to reduce the number of first-class domestic sides to two, Mashonaland and Matabeleland, and these two played three matches to decide the title.

Before the independent state of Zimbabwe was created in 1981, Rhodesia had played as a first-class team in the South African Currie Cup. The first such match was against Transvaal on March 15 and 16, 1905 in Johannesburg. But it was not until 1929–30 that a second game was played – in that season five Currie Cup matches were arranged and all five were lost. The next Currie Cup contest came in 1931–32; again Rhodesia played five games, but this time with quite contrasting results – four of the five ended in victory. Denis Tomlinson was the all-round star of the side and went on to be selected for South Africa. Despite this success, Rhodesia did not again enter the Currie Cup until 1946–47. From then on they were regular competitors and latterly entered a Rhodesian B team in the Castle Bowl competition.

A number of Rhodesian cricketers have made their name in English County cricket, notably Paddy Clift and Brian Davison, then more recently Graeme Hick. Those who have had success for Zimbabwe in Test cricket during the 1990s include David Houghton, Eddon Brandes, brothers Andrew and Grant Flower, and Heath Streak – not forgetting John Traicos who is the only cricketer to represent both South Africa and Zimbabwe at Test level.

HEATH STREAK *opened the bowling for Zimbabwe in the 1996–97 Test v England.*

ANDY FLOWER *Test batsman for Zimbabwe.*

ARGENTINA

FERGUSON *of Argentina nearly run out in the 1979 ICC Trophy match v Papua New Guinea.*

Although cricket was played by some British troops who were interned in the country in 1806, the first cricket club was not established in the Argentine until 1831. The continuing influx of Britons who were assisting in building the railways in the 1860s led to more clubs and more cricket, and in 1868 an Argentine side went to Montevideo in Uruguay.

The major match of the Argentine season, North v South, was founded in 1891, the principal cricketers of the day being the Leach family, several of whom had played for Lancashire. The Argentine Cricket Association was formed in 1913, by which time the MCC had already toured the country, bringing with them a team up to first-class standard. The first first-class matches played in the country were in fact the three games between the 1911–12 MCC side and a representative Argentine XI.

Between the two World Wars three sides from England – MCC in 1926–27, Sir Julien Cahn's in 1929–30 and Sir Theodore Brinckman's in 1937–38 – toured the country playing first-class matches. Argentina also opposed both Brazil and Chile during the same period. In 1932, a South American side, comprising mainly players from Argentina, toured the British Isles and played a number of first-class matches. After the Second World War, the MCC sent a side to Argentina in 1958–59, but the standard of cricket had dropped considerably and the major games were not considered first-class.

As an associate member of ICC, Argentina have taken part in the ICC Trophy, but with little success.

BANGLADESH

After the partition of India, the country now known as Bangladesh formed the eastern section of Pakistan. Four first-class teams from East Pakistan took part in competitions, namely Dacca, Dacca University, East Pakistan and Rajshahi. Bangladesh became an independent nation in 1973, by which time cricket there was in a poor state. However, the MCC were persuaded to visit the country in 1976–77. Four matches were played including one three-day fixture against Bangladesh. A second tour took place in 1980–81, with three "Test" matches all of which were drawn.

Bangladesh have taken part in all six ICC Trophy tournaments. In 1982 and 1990, they reached the semi-finals. In the latter year, they were unfortunate to meet Zimbabwe and were beaten. However, 1997 proved to be Bangladesh's great year and the country celebrated winning the ICC Trophy in style.

In the 1988–89 season, Bangladesh hosted their first official one-day international tournament, the teams taking part being Bangladesh, India, Pakistan and Sri Lanka. Bangladesh were outplayed by their visitors. Since then Bangladesh have taken part in the Sharjah tournament.

BERMUDA

Since a British garrison was stationed in Bermuda continuously from 1701 until the 1950s, it seems likely that cricket must have been played on the islands in the eighteenth century. It is not, however, until 1844 that records of a match exist. The following year Bermuda Cricket Club was formed. With the colony's close proximity to the United States, it is hardly surprising that the first team to tour Bermuda came from the States – Philadephia Zingari opposed the Garrison in three matches in 1891. The early years of the twentieth century saw regular tours between Bermuda and Philadelphia. The principal Bermudan cricketers of the period were the brothers J.R. and G.C. Conyers. The former was a fine batsman, whilst the latter bowled slow right arm. The 1912 Australian tourists to England played a game against Bermuda on their way home and had difficulty in beating the home side.

In the inter-war period, the most

important event was the 1933 tour by Sir Julien Cahn's English team. Five matches were played and a general holiday was proclaimed for the major fixture against Somerset CC, the leading club of the day.

After the Second World War, various West Indian sides visited Bermuda. The first tour by Bermuda to England took place in 1960, at which time W.F. Hayward was the driving force behind the team. Further tours took place, both to England and to Canada.

The major domestic match in Bermuda is the Cup Match between the two clubs, Somerset and St Georges. Alma Hunt is considered the best cricketer Bermuda has produced and he came close to being selected for the West Indies. Bermuda joined the ICC in 1966 and competed in the first ICC Trophy in 1979. The West Indies are continuing to encourage cricket in Bermuda and the country was invited to take part in the Shell–Sandals Limited-Overs competition, which involves the first-class West Indian sides, in October 1996. Though they failed to win a match, Bermuda impressed the West Indies Board and it is hoped that Bermuda will at some date in the near future compete in the first-class Red Stripe competition.

BURMA

Some kind of cricket was played in Burma in 1824 when British troops took Rangoon. Through the nineteenth century cricket was regularly played among the various regiments stationed in the country. King Thebaw seemed quite keen on the game in the 1870s, but refused to field and "was in the habit of using very injurious language to anyone who bowled him".

In the 1920s, the two principal sides were the Burma Athletic Association and the Rangoon Gymkhana. Burma opposed the MCC in a first-class match in 1926–27, at a time when Hubert Ashton, the Essex cricketer, was working for the Burmah Oil Company.

After the Japanese occupation during the Second World War, there was limited cricket among the British residents, but in recent years it has all but died out as little or no cricket has been played there.

CANADA

Although there are stray references to cricket in Canada in the eighteenth century, it was during the 1820s that the game really became established. Toronto Cricket Club was founded in 1827 by George A. Barber, a master at Upper Canada College, who also encouraged cricket there. In 1859, George Parr's England side, sponsored by the Montreal Club, toured Canada and United States. By 1864 a club was formed in Winnipeg and in the next decade cricket reached the West Coast. In 1844, came the first Canada v USA match, attended by 5,000 spectators and at which it is reported $100,000 changed hands among the betting fraternity.

The Marquis of Lansdowne, Governor-General in the 1880s, was a very keen cricketer and gave much encouragement to the sport, helping to sponsor the 1887 Canadian tour to England: there had been an earlier one in 1880, but this had collapsed when it was discovered that the Canadian captain was in fact a deserter from the British Army.

England teams made a number of visits to Canada through the late nineteenth century and the first half of the twentieth century, but Canadian cricket was relatively weak – baseball thrived whilst cricket was very much in second place.

The most famous inter-war event in Canadian cricket was the 1932 tour by the Australians – the visitors included Bradman in their side and he duly created a new Canadian record by scoring 260 not out against Western Ontario.

Although Canada toured England in 1954 and played some first-class matches, the game was not making great strides in Canada itself, as many of the players were British exiles. In the 1960s, though, due to the influx of immigrants from the West Indies and the Indian subcontinent, the number of active cricketers increased. In 1968, the Canadian Cricket Association was incorporated. The country entered the ICC Trophy in 1979 and has competed in all the subsequent contests. In 1996, a series of one-day internationals between India and Pakistan were staged at the Toronto Cricket Club – the first matches of such standing to be played in Canada. Two difficulties face cricketers in Canada today: one is that most grounds are also public parks and the second is that government funding has been substantially reduced. It is estimated that there are at present about 10,000 adult players.

CHINA

In the nineteenth century the main centre of cricket in China was Shanghai. The annual match between Shanghai and Hong Kong commenced in 1866 and Shanghai sent a team to Japan in 1893.

In 1929 there was a Shanghai Cricket League comprising six teams. Another centre of cricket at this time was Wei-Hai-Wei, most of the players there being from the Royal Navy.

The development of the game in Peking was spasmodic – when Peking Civilians opposed British Legation Guard in 1931, it was noted that this was the first game in the city for several years. The Mission Boys' School in Chungking also had an established cricket ground in the 1930s.

So far as the Chinese themselves were concerned, very few attempted to play the game, though B. Oeitiongham, from China, came close to obtaining a place in the Eton XI in 1926 and appeared for Eton 2nd XI. Later, the post-war period saw cricket disappear from China, but in the 1990s the Beijing International Sixes Tournament was founded and in the third such tournament in 1996 an all-Chinese team competed for the first time. It is to be hoped that cricket will grow in popularity.

CORFU

The single ground for cricket is in fact the main square in Corfu Town, part of the playing area being the tarmac of the car parking area round the square.

The Ionian Islands were a British Protectorate from 1815 to 1863 and inter-regimental games were played by the troops stationed there. The Greeks continued to play cricket after the islands reverted to Greece and two Greek clubs were established, playing either against each other or against visiting British sides. Sir Percy Kahn kept cricket going there between the wars, but the Second World War saw the end of matches. A revival took place following an appeal in the *Cricketer* magazine in 1952. Since that date the popularity of Corfu with British tourists has meant that cricket is played on a regular basis.

DENMARK

Cricket was introduced to Denmark in the 1860s by the British engineers involved in laying out the country's railway system. It was not until after the First World War that teams from England began to make fairly regular visits to Denmark and not until the 1950s that Denmark began to play the Netherlands in "Test" matches.

Denmark has taken part in four of the five ICC Trophy competitions, missing only 1982 owing to financial difficulties. In both 1979 and 1986, they came third, losing in 1979 to Sri Lanka in the semi-finals and to the Netherlands in 1986. In 1997, Denmark reached the last eight but, with Scotland and Kenya in their group, failed to reach the semis.

The best-known Danish cricketer to date is Ole Mortensen, who had a successful career with Derbyshire, bowling right arm fast medium.

The European Championship was inaugurated in 1996 and the initial tournament was staged in Denmark. The home side finished in third place, beating the England side in a play-off.

OLE MORTENSEN *the Danish bowler who had a successful career with Derbyshire.*

FIJI

The first cricket in Fiji took place in about 1874. The founding father of cricket's rapid development was the Attorney-General, J.S. Udal. The islanders took to the game, so much so that in 1894–95 a Fijian team toured New Zealand and played the major provinces. The team comprised six Europeans and six Fijians. These games were recognized as first-class. In 1908, one of the smallest islands in the Fijian group actually sent a touring team to Australia.

The major problem in the colony was the lack of touring sides visiting the islands for any but the briefest of stays. In the late 1930s, Philip Snow came to Fiji. He made every effort to promote the game and two further tours were organized to New Zealand, in 1947–48 and 1953–54.

Fiji was elected an associate member of the ICC in 1965; in the 1970s, various Indian teams toured. The country has taken part in the ICC Trophy competitions, but the game is battling for popularity against rugby and is certainly not as strong as it was in the 1940s.

FRANCE

Considering the proximity of France to the Kentish heartland of cricket, it is surprising that the game has never really established itself among the French. A visit by English cricketers to Paris was arranged for 1789, but cancelled just before the team crossed the Channel, because of the Revolution.

In the 1820s and onward, cricket was played extensively in the Pas de Calais among the Nottingham lace workers who had emigrated there, but few French names are found in the extant scores. In the 1860s, fashionable Paris toyed with cricket and again one or two English touring sides were organized – this time they actually arrived! However, most of the "French" players were English residents in the capital.

This enthusiasm for cricket among English residents continued through to the twentieth century. In 1930, there was a French Cricket Federation and two leagues, one in Paris and the other in the north. The Standard Athletic Club of Paris sent a team to England annually, but no French players were among the sides. The only time cricket was part of the Olympic Games was in 1900 when the Devon County Wanderers, representing England, opposed "France". The former won by 158 runs.

After the Second World War various British army sides played cricket in France and made up so-called French teams to oppose Belgium and the Netherlands.

In the last 10 years or so, the number of French-born cricketers has grown and in 1995 the MCC toured France, playing seven matches. The country takes part in the European Nations Cup. Nottinghamshire also sent a team to play France in 1995. An application to join the ICC as an associate member was made but was turned down, though it is hoped that a fresh application in 1998 might be successful.

GERMANY

There are many reports of cricket matches in Germany in the nineteenth century. A club was formed in Berlin in 1858 and Hamburg played Frankfurt in 1863. A cricket festival in Hamburg in 1865 included a match billed as France v Germany, but virtually all the players were English. A book of cricket instructions was published in Stuttgart in 1893; although the written part is fairly accurate, the illustrations were clearly by someone with no cricket knowledge. The bowlers wear pads and gloves, the bats resemble Indian clubs and the wicket is the same width as its height!

The Berlin Cricket League was founded in 1898 and even continued in the First World War. In 1927, a correspondent from Berlin wrote to *The Cricketer* suggesting that a German side tour England. The tour eventually took place in 1930 and the German team, which significantly comprised German-born players, played four games. In 1937, the Gentlemen of Worcestershire paid a visit to Germany.

With many British troops stationed in Germany after the Second World War, there were frequent tours to Germany by English club sides, but their matches were against British regimental sides rather than German-born cricketers. The resumption of cricket by German players is a fairly recent development.

In 1992, the German team was undefeated in the European Cricketer Cup held in England and went on to play the MCC at Lord's for the first time. It has to be admitted that not one of the XI at Lord's was German-born. Nevertheless, Germany's cricket association became an affiliated member of the ICC in 1991 and in the last few seasons German cricket has begun to make progress beyond the British expatriate community. New leagues are springing up and matches being played against other European nations.

GIBRALTAR

The first recorded match in the colony took place in 1822. Most of the cricket on the Rock has involved the military stationed there.

Gibraltar Cricket Club was founded in 1883. The Gibraltar Cricket Association was formed in 1960 and nine years later joined the ICC as an associate member.

The Cryptics visited Gibraltar in 1927 and the Yorkshire Gents toured in 1935. Teams from Gibraltar have made some trips to Portugal. The principal team is Gibraltar Cricket Club – a reduction of British Forces in recent years has meant that this club dominates the domestic scene.

Gibraltar had to withdraw from the 1979 ICC Competition, but have taken part, with not much success, in the four subsequent tournaments.

HONG KONG

Britain acquired Hong Kong as a result of the Opium Wars of the 1840s and cricket is reported to have been played there as early as 1840. The Hong Kong Cricket Club was formed in 1851 and its series of matches against Shanghai commenced in 1866. In 1882, the Hong Kong side under Captain J. Dunn was travelling homeward from Shanghai when their ship was sunk in a typhoon, with all lives lost. In all, 37 matches were played between the two sides, the final game taking place in 1948.

In 1890, Hong Kong began its series against Singapore, and the colony has also played matches in more recent times against Malaysia. The Hong Kong teams have been predominantly British with the Chinese taking little interest, but in recent years there has been a growing number of Chinese playing at junior level. The Hong Kong Sixes competition has brought world-class players to the colony and the competition has drawn the cricket world's attention to the territory for the first time.

Hong Kong took part in the ICC Trophy for the first time in 1982 and have played in the four subsequent competitions. In 1994 and 1997, they did well enough to reach the second round, but both times, were outplayed by the top ICC Trophy sides.

IRELAND

Although there is a reference to cricket supposedly being banned in Ireland by Cromwell's Commissioners in 1656, it is very probable that hurling rather than cricket was the subject. Hurling goes back to 1200 BC according to the standard works of reference; cricket in Ireland, in terms of an actual match, does not appear until AD 1792. The match in question, played in Phoenix Park, Dublin, was arranged by Colonel Lennox, later the Duke of Richmond, and involved the Dublin Garrison against "All-Ireland". The Phoenix Club in Dublin was founded in about 1830 and at about the same time cricket was introduced into Dublin University.

The original Irish Cricket Union was formed in 1884–85, though the present governing body did not come into being until 1923. The most important matches by representative Irish teams in the nineteenth century were against the MCC, I Zingari and Scotland, and the first recognized first-class games by Ireland came in May 1902 when an Irish side came to England and played successively against London County, the MCC, and Oxford and Cambridge Universities. Prior to this, the Dublin University team had played four first-class matches in 1895.

IRISH EYES ARE SMILING *Ireland celebrate their victory over Middlesex in the 1997 Benson & Hedges cup.*

The status of matches by Ireland up to 1947 is very complex and readers are advised to study the *Guide to First-Class Matches in the British Isles*, published by the Association of Cricket Statisticians, if they wish to know the full details.

At present, only Ireland's match against Scotland is given first-class status. In 1980, Ireland was admitted into the English Gillette competition and has been a regular competitor since, but the side has yet to win a game. They have also taken part in the Benson & Hedges Cup since 1991.

In 1994, Ireland competed in the ICC Trophy for the first time, winning four games out of seven. In 1997, they had a successful run and reached the quarter-finals.

ISRAEL

Part of the Ottoman Empire until 1917, the country became a British Mandate in 1920. Within a few years cricket was being played on a regular basis by the British Forces and civil administration in what was then Palestine. In 1935, Lord Melchett took a team to Palestine and five matches were played, the main one being a two-day game against Jerusalem Sports Club.

Israel became an independent state in 1948. Its national side took part in the first ICC Trophy Tournament in 1979 and has continued to play in the subsequent competitions. Its results, however, have been disappointing – after the first three tournaments, Israel had won only one out of 19 matches. Israel took part in the European Championships (replacing Wales, who withdrew) in 1996, but failed to win a game.

The structure of cricket in the country is being revamped, and proper coaching schemes and cricket at youth level are now operating. These should improve the standard of the game, especially as Steve Herzberg, the Kent cricketer, has been appointed National Coach.

ITALY

Although there had been occasional cricket matches in Italy from the late eighteenth century, cricket on an organized basis and involving Italians did not really take off until the 1980s.

Italy became an associate member of the ICC in 1995 and played in the ICC Trophy, for the first time in 1997, but with little success. At club level, however, more has been achieved. The Cesena Club won the European Club Championship in 1996, and brought the title to Italy for the second year running.

JAPAN

Probably the first game in Japan took place in 1863 when British residents in Yokohama opposed visitors from the Royal Navy. According to reports, due to unrest in the city, the players were armed!

The one regular fixture before and after the First World War was Yokohama v Kobe. It commenced in 1884 and in the 1930s was a three-day match. In 1919, a team from Shanghai visited Japan and played in both Kobe and Yokohama, but such visits seem to have been rare.

In more recent years, cricket has had a slightly higher profile and a cup competition has been established since 1993. Some native Japanese are taking up the game, which in the past was exclusively played by expatriates. A hopeful sign is the emergence of five University sides, but there is a scarcity of suitable grounds.

KENYA

The British East Africa Company secured what was to become Kenya Colony in 1888; the first cricket match of note took place in 1899 and in 1910 the annual fixture Officials v Settlers was established. Kenya invited the MCC to tour in 1930; this invitation was refused, but the Incogniti accepted a similar invitation. However, the Incogs were unable to raise a full side and the plan was abandoned.

In 1933 the Asian community had developed their cricket to the extent that a match against Europeans was arranged. This fixture vied with Officials v Settlers as the major game of the season, and both continued after the Second World War. The first "international" took place in 1951 when Kenya opposed Tanganyika. The following year a team from Natal toured Kenya and in 1953 came the formation of the Kenya Cricket Association.

The MCC finally toured East Africa, including Kenya, in 1957–58 under the leadership of the former England Test captain Freddie Brown. Basil D'Oliveira captained a South African non-European side to Kenya in 1958.

In the first ICC Trophy contest of 1979, Kenya played as part of East Africa, but in 1982 they broke away, playing as a separate country. The standard of cricket has improved over the years and in the 1997 ICC Trophy, Kenya reached the final.

The most important series of matches played in Kenya took place in Nairobi in September and October 1996, when Kenya, Pakistan, South Africa and Sri Lanka met. The competition, sponsored by the Sameer Group, was won by South Africa. Kenya had taken part in the World Cup of 1996 and caused a major upset by beating the West Indies, but it proved to be their only victory in the five matches they played.

SONG AND DANCE *Kenyan players celebrate their victory over Australia at the 1996 World Cup.*

MALAYSIA

The present Malaysia Cricket Association was formed in 1963 and includes Sarawak and Sabah (formerly North Borneo). Cricket began there in the second half of the nineteenth century, when the Malay States came under the protection of the British Government. There are good grounds at Kuala Lumpur, Ipoh and Penang.

The major match between the wars was Federated Malay States (i.e. Perak, Selangor and Negri Sembilan) against Straits Settlements (Singapore, Penang and Malacca). This was usually a three-day game played over the August Bank Holiday. At this time, the Singapore Cricket Club acted as the unofficial controlling body.

In 1927, a strong Australian touring side was defeated in Kuala Lumpur and the All Malaya team of this period was about first-class standard, though their matches are not generally recognized as first-class.

In the first two ICC Trophy competitions, Malaysia failed to win a match, but in 1986 they gained three victories. The country only had moderate success in 1990 and 1994. The highly successful 1997 ICC competition was staged in Malaysia and, although the home side did not reach the final eight, cricket in the country as a whole is on the increase and the main domestic tournaments are flourishing.

NAMIBIA

This sparsely populated country was a German colony from 1890 until 1915. From 1920 the League of Nations gave a mandate to South Africa to administer the country. Namibia became an independent nation in 1990.

Namibia took part in the ICC Trophy competitions of 1994 and 1997, but with little success. From 1996 South Africa allowed Namibia to compete in the UCB Bowl. In April 1996, a South African Country Districts side visited Windhoek and played three one-day matches against local sides. With the encouragement of South Africa, cricket standards in Namibia should improve. Namibian teams now play regularly in South Africa.

THE NETHERLANDS

An early comment on Dutch cricket went:

> "In matters of cricket the fault of the Dutch
> Is hitting too little and missing too much."

Even in the 1920s, this was considered libellous. Cricket in the Netherlands goes back to 1855, when some South African students at Utrecht University introduced the game, but it failed to take root and the first proper Dutch club was formed in 1875.

In the 1880s, it is believed, there were some hundred or so clubs. In 1883, the Nederlandse Cricket-Bond was founded and in 1892 the first Dutch side visited Britain. Prior to the First World War, the best known Dutch cricketer was C.J. Posthuma, who appeared in some first-class matches in England.

Between the wars the major British club to go on tour in the Netherlands was the Free Foresters. In fact, they scarcely missed a single season without going across the North Sea. Despite the obvious difficulties, cricket continued to be played every season between 1940 and 1945, though owing to travel restrictions matches were played on a regional basis.

The Free Foresters resumed their annual tour in 1946. In 1964 the Australians, who went to the Netherlands briefly whilst on tour to England, were beaten in a one-day game. In the first two ICC Trophy contests, the Netherlands did not shine, but in 1986 they reached the final and were narrowly defeated by Zimbabwe. The 1990 final was again Netherlands v Zimbabwe, but the latter won by a larger margin. 1994 saw the Netherlands finish in third place, beating Bermuda in the play-off. In the 1997 ICC Trophy, the Dutch team were unfortunate to come up against Bangladesh after having achieved a place in the last eight.

Due to their success in the 1994 ICC Trophy, the Netherlands qualified for the 1996 World Cup on the Indian sub-continent. However, they failed to win any of their five matches, their best performance being at Peshawar against England when they lost by 49 runs.

ZUIDERENT *batting against England in the 1996 World Cup.*

NIGERIA

The British presence in Nigeria commenced with the annexation of Lagos island in 1861, but it was not until 1914 that the colony of Nigeria, as such, was established. The neighbouring Gold Coast had, however, played for the first time in 1904. It was in 1926 that matches between Gold Coast and Nigeria were commenced and these continued through to recent times. In the mid-1930s, two Cricket Associations were formed, one for Europeans and one for Africans. The two organizations merged in 1956.

Political instability has affected the development of cricket and many other such activities – the civil war in the late 1960s is estimated to have cost a million lives. Nigeria is part of West Africa insofar as the ICC Trophy competition is concerned. West Africa first participated in 1982, when they failed to win a match. The side did not take part in the 1986 and 1990 tournaments, but returned in 1994 when, after again failing to win a match in the main competition, West Africa played in the Wooden Spoon Deluxe Group and won all three games. 1997 saw the side improving very little.

Nigeria won the 1988 triangular tournament against Ghana and Gambia, beating Gambia by 10 wickets and Ghana by an innings and 15 runs.

PAPUA NEW GUINEA

Until 1918, the country was divided into two halves, the northern half being a German colony and the southern a British colony. Cricket was taught at the various missionary stations of the British colony before the First World War, but the northern half did not see cricket until about 1921, when it became a League of Nations Mandate.

In the 1930s, two mission stations, at Samarai and Kwato, played cricket against each other every Saturday – there was no time limit, but as soon as one match was complete the next commenced. In Port Moresby a competition was established in 1937 for sides in the capital.

A Board of Control was founded in 1972 and the country, which was to become independent in 1975, joined the ICC in 1973. In the 1982 ICC Trophy, Papua finished in third place, beating Bangladesh in the play-off. The country also reached the second round in 1990, but has not been so successful in the last two contests.

THE MATCH AT BANBURY *Papua New Guinea play Argentina in the 1979 ICC Trophy.*

PORTUGAL

The British played some cricket in Portugal in the eighteenth century and there are references to informal games during the Peninsular Wars. A club was established in Oporto in 1855 and, when a second club came into being in Lisbon, an annual fixture began between the two sides, both being entirely composed of British residents. Cricket teams from England, notably the Cryptics, have made regular trips to Portugal since the 1920s.

In the nineteenth century, Tom Westray took a side out to Portugal once or twice. Pelham Warner gives an interesting account of his visit with Westray's side, when matches were played against Oporto and All-Portugal.

For many years Portugal and its cricketers remained aloof from competitive matches, but in 1995 it joined the European Nations Cup and, to the surprise of most rivals, took the title, but the majority of players are of English descent.

SCOTLAND

There are odd references to cricket in Scotland in the eighteenth century, but only involving the military or the landed gentry. The game did not become established in the country generally until the middle of the nineteenth century and the first match by a so-called Scotland team took place in 1865. The Scottish Cricket Union was formed in 1879, dissolved in 1883 and re-established in 1908. Much confusion has been caused to cricket statisticians by the fact that Scotland apparently played two matches simultaneously in 1878, one against Yorkshire, the other against England. However, on closer inspection the Yorkshire game involved "Gents of Edinburgh".

The first first-class match involving Scotland took place in 1905, when the opponents were the touring Australians. The West Indies were played in 1906 and South Africa in 1907.

The first recorded inter-county game was in 1851, East Lothian playing Stirling. The Scottish County Championship was established in 1902 and continued, with gaps for the two World Wars, until 1995. Aberdeen, Forfar, Perthshire and Stirlingshire played every year. Apart from those counties, others which at one time were champions were Clackmannan, Ayrshire and West Lothian.

In 1996, there was a drastic reorganization of major club cricket in Scotland. A new National Scottish League has been created, of two divisions, with 10 clubs in each and with promotion and relegation. Division 1 comprises Aberdeenshire, Arbroath Utd, Carlton, Freuchie, Grange, Heriots FP, Prestwick, Strathmore, Watsonians and West Lothian. The authorities have, however, established a knockout competition for the old Scottish counties.

Scotland were admitted to the English Benson & Hedges competition in 1980 and the NatWest Trophy in 1981. Their success has been very limited, with only two wins in the former contest and none in the latter.

Scotland entered the ICC Trophy competition for the first time in 1997 and finished in third place.

Mike Denness of Ayrshire moved to Kent and captained England in the 1970s.

SINGAPORE

Singapore was founded in 1819 and from 1826 formed part of the Straits Settlements. The first reported cricket took place in 1852 and Singapore was from then considered the centre of cricket in the Settlements. In 1890–91, a triangular tournament was staged in Singapore between Hong Kong, Ceylon and the Settlements, the home side being victorious. Three years afterwards, a team was sent to Ceylon. Matches between the Federated Malay States and the Straits Settlements were played on a regular basis between the wars. In May 1927, a strong Australian side, including Bill Woodfull and Charles Macartney, played two games against Singapore, both of which the tourists won by an innings.

After the Japanese occupation, the Singapore Cricket Club was flourishing again in 1947; Hong Kong made several visits to both Singapore and Malaya. Singapore became an independent state in 1965 and its team has taken part in the ICC Trophy since 1979. At present, there is a flourishing league with 19 teams and two divisions. In April 1996, Singapore staged the Singer Tournament – limited-over matches between India, Pakistan and Sri Lanka.

SPAIN

Occasional cricket matches were played in Spain from the second half of the nineteenth century, but it cannot be said that any serious matches were staged until the British began to take up residence there after the Second World War. Spain joined the ICC in 1992 as an affiliated member and in 1995 opposed both Italy and Portugal for the first time in matches arranged for two days. Barcelona and Javea are two of the main cricketing centres.

In June 1989, the first Spanish cricket tournament took place in Madrid, involving four teams: Madrid, Malaga, Balearic XI and Barcelona. The home team were the winners.

TANZANIA

Until the First World War Tanganyika was a German colony, whilst the second element of Tanzania was the British Protectorate of Zanzibar, ruled by the Sultan. There was some cricket in Zanzibar in the nineteenth century, but cricket in Tanganyika did not become established until the 1920s, and it was not until after the Second World War that, with the formation of the Twigas CC in 1951, international games commenced. The Twigas opposed the Kenya Kongonis and also toured England. The MCC visited Dar-es-Salaam for the first time in 1957–58 and the South African Non-European side also visited the country in the same season.

Under the captaincy of J.M. Brearley, the MCC toured Tanzania (created 1964) and in the game against Tanzania at Dar-es-Salaam the home country had the best of a high-scoring draw in January 1974, the home side gaining a lead on first innings.

Tanzania participates in the ICC Trophy as part of East & Central Africa, a combination of countries which had been admitted to the ICC in 1966.

UGANDA

The first cricket in Uganda was played in Entebbe, which was the original government headquarters in 1893. The cricket ground there was considered the equal of any in central Africa and the country's first international game took place there in 1914 when Uganda opposed the British East African Protectorate (Kenya).

Between the two World Wars, the major domestic fixture was Armed Forces v Uganda Kobs, a two-day game staged to coincide with the King's birthday. The Uganda Kobs is an organization involved in all sports, not only cricket, and has been responsible for tours to England. There was also a triangular communal competition between European, Goan and Indian teams. Later on it was expanded to include an African side.

When Idi Amin became head of state in 1971 and began his policy of expelling Asians, cricket was very seriously affected. Of the dozen or so clubs in existence prior to his taking over, only the African Club remained and even this struggled to exist. The game is slowly recovering from the devastating blows of the Amin period, and it is estimated that there are now at least 200 adult cricketers playing. In 1995, a team toured England, playing 12 matches. Uganda participates in the ICC Trophy as part of the East & Central Africa side. It had little success, however, in the 1997 competition.

UNITED ARAB EMIRATES

Some four years after starting his project to build an international cricket stadium in Sharjah, Abdul Rehman Bukhatir saw his ambitions realized when the Asian Cup, involving India, Pakistan and Sri Lanka, was staged at his ground. Some 15,000 spectators watched India beat Pakistan in the final on April 13, 1984.

Since that momentous day, more one-day internationals have been played in Sharjah than at any other venue and in the 1995–96 season the total reached 100. Domestic cricket in the seven Emirates has flourished on the back of the international stadium and both leagues and knockout competitions are operating.

In 1994, the United Arab Emirates entered the ICC Trophy for the first time. They outplayed all their rivals, winning all nine matches, and beating Kenya in the final by two wickets. This success qualified the team for the 1996 World Cup. However, they failed to make much impression on the Test-playing opponents and the Emirates' only victory was at the expense of the Netherlands.

THE 1996 WORLD CUP *Mazhar Hussain hit the highest score for his side against England.*

UNITED STATES OF AMERICA

The first report of a match in New York – between New Yorkers and Londoners – was published in 1751. Between then and 1780, cricket flourished but the War of Independence seems to have brought cricket, and certainly reports of cricket in the press, to a standstill. The game revived, though, and the creation of the St George's Club in 1839 had a great influence on cricket's popularity. The club sent a team to Toronto in 1840 to oppose the local side there and from this stemmed the first United States v Canada match of 1844.

By this time cricket was well-established in Philadelphia, and in the 1850s there were regular matches between various clubs from the two great cities. The first English touring side of 1859 played in both New York and Philadelphia.

The American Civil War had a disastrous effect on American cricket – not only were the international matches against Canada stopped for the duration, but financial problems prevented any English teams from touring. In addition, the war did much to encourage cricket's rival, baseball. The latter was so much easier to organize and play, and thus the troops involved in the war spent their spare moments with baseball rather than cricket.

By the 1870s Philadelphia, rather than New York, had become the cricketing centre of the States. When an international tournament was arranged in Halifax, Nova Scotia in 1874, the United States were represented by the Philadelphians who duly won the tournament and the Halifax Cup. This cup was taken back to Philadelphia and used as the trophy for what was probably the first cricket league competition in the world. This "Halifax Cup Tournament" was destined to run until 1926.

WALTER BEVELL *bowling for the USA v Sri Lanka in the 1979 ICC Trophy.*

Although the Philadelphians toured England, playing county teams, from 1883 to 1908 and were granted first-class status for three of their five tours, first-class domestic cricket in the United States was a very occasional affair: such contests as Gentlemen v Players, American-born v English Residents and Philadelphia v Rest of United States. No first-class competition was ever staged, the only other first-class games being between Philadelphia and English or Australian touring sides.

After the First World War cricket of any serious nature almost died out, though a league kept going in the Chicago area, and English residents in Hollywood, under the leadership of the film star and former England Test cricketer C. Aubrey Smith, played friendly games.

The most outstanding American cricketer of the Edwardian era was the in-swing bowler J. Barton King, whilst the best batsman was George Patterson.

The post-war revival of cricket was engineered by John Marder, who established the United States Cricket Association in 1961 and in 1968 organized a team to tour Great Britain, playing a series of 21 matches.

The country joined the ICC in 1965 and has been a regular competitor in the ICC Trophy Competition since it started in 1979. It has to be admitted, however, that the rise of American cricket in the last 20 years has been largely due to players from the West Indies or the Indian sub-continent rather than any great development among American-born players. In 1996, a United States Cricket Federation was created as a rival to the 1961-vintage Cricket Association. Clearly this duality needs solving.

VANUATU

Until 1980 this independent country was the Anglo-French condominium of the New Hebrides, situated between the Solomon Islands and Fiji. At present, it is reported that there are some 400 active cricketers and 12 teams.

South of Vanuatu are the Loyalty Islands of Mare, Lifou and Ouvea, and in the 1960s cricket was played there, having first come to the islands through the London Mission Society in the nineteenth century.

It seems that little cricket is played in the Solomon Islands at the moment, though at one time the game was popular on some of the islands, notably Gavatu and Makambo.

The man responsible for the introduction of cricket to many South Pacific islands was the Oxford blue, the Rev. J.C. Patteson. He was appointed Bishop of Melanesia in 1861, but 10 years later was murdered by natives on Nukapu.

TEST CRICKET

The first plans for international cricket were made in 1789, when the Duke of Dorset, a patron of Kent cricket and at the time the British Ambassador in Paris, arranged for a side captained by William Yalden, the Surrey wicket-keeper, to play matches in France. However, when the side reached Dover to board the ferry, they were met by the Duke coming the other way. He was fleeing from the French Revolution, and that was the end of that idea.

The world had to wait until 1844 before the first international cricket match took place, and this match nowadays sounds as unlikely as that abortive tour of France. It was a match between the United States and Canada, played in New York. In those days, North America was considered the strongest cricketing area outside England, and this was reflected in the calibre of the English side sent on the first cricketing tour. It went to Canada and the USA in 1859 under the captaincy of George Parr, captain of Nottinghamshire. It included the leading batsmen of the day in Parr and the Cambridgeshire pair Tom Hayward and R. Carpenter, and the best bowlers in John Jackson of Nottinghamshire and John Wisden (he of the *Cricketers' Almanack*) of Sussex. Other famous names included Julius Caesar of Surrey and John Lillywhite of Sussex. The team won all five matches played (against 22 on the opposition side) and staged three exhibition matches.

EARLY TOUR *Stephenson and Caffyn.*

Two years later, in 1861–62, a team toured Australia. Many of the 1859 tourists couldn't agree terms, but two went: H.H. Stephenson, the captain, and William Caffyn, both of Surrey, who had five Surrey colleagues with them. Again, most of the 12 matches were against 22 players, and two were lost. There were also two exhibitions, in one of which the World beat Surrey by six wickets.

There followed two more tours to Australia, during the second of which in 1873–74 W.G. Grace led the side, and two more to America, one by an amateur team in which W.G. was merely the leading batsman, before the first important tour of Australia in 1876–77. The team for this tour was led by James Lillywhite (Jr) of Sussex, the nephew of Fred and cousin of James (Sr) and John, all of Sussex. They mostly played against sides of 15, 18 or 22 players but on this tour, for the first time, three matches were played which are considered now to be "first-class". The first was against New South Wales, who followed on but held on for a draw when an innings defeat was the likeliest outcome. The other two first-class games were against Australia and have come to be regarded as the first two Test matches.

Not that they were known as Test matches then, although the term "Test match" in relation to cricket had been used as early as the first English tour to Australia in 1861–62. This sentence regarding the tourists appeared in Hammersley's *Victorian Cricketer's Guide*, published in Melbourne in 1862: "Of the thirteen matches played, five only can be termed 'test matches'; the three played at Melbourne and the two at Sydney". It wasn't until the 1880s that the term "Test match" to describe the England-Australia matches gradually became more widespread. Even then, which matches qualified for the description was disputed until the beginning of the twentieth century. It was then that the list in *Australian Cricket and Cricketers* by C.P. Moody, published in Melbourne in 1894, came to be regarded as the official list.

ASHES 1997 *Australia all out for 118 in the first Test at Edgbaston.*

CORNHILL Insurance
Nº11 TOTAL Nº8
1 118 47
WICKETS 9
LAST MAN BOWLERS
17 11 10
31 OVERS FLD 2
LAST WKT FELL 110
1 2 3 4 5 6 7 8 9 10 11 S
OVERS REMAINING 59
1ST INNS 2ND INNS
ENGLAND
AUSTRALIA
FRIENDS
CLEANAWAY
TETLEY'S

ENGLAND v AUSTRALIA

The side captained by James Lillywhite in that first Test match at Melbourne on March 15, 16, 17 and 19, 1877 was not quite representative of England's best, as the leading batsmen Grace, Daft and Shrewsbury did not tour, but the bowling was up to scratch. England were also lacking their wicket-keeper, Ted Pooley of Surrey, who was under arrest in New Zealand. This came about because of a well-known betting ploy which Pooley had used to his advantage against the locals. He bet a spectator at one of the matches England played against 22 opponents that he could forecast the score of all 22 batsmen. The spectator gave him odds of 20–1 for each, which Pooley took at £1 to a shilling. He then wrote down 0 for each man, it being usual to have quite a few ducks in these games. In fact there were 11, so Pooley won £11 and lost 11s, i.e. he required £10.9s to settle. The spectator refused to pay, there was a fight causing damage to property, and Pooley was arrested. He was awaiting trial when the first-ever Test began. As the party consisted of only 12 players, opening batsman Selby was forced to keep wicket.

The first ball in the first of more than 1,400 Tests was bowled by Alfred Shaw of Nottinghamshire and received by Charles Bannerman of New South Wales. Five of the Australian team were born in the British Isles including the two who scored most runs, Bannerman and Tom Horan, and the two who got most wickets, Tom Kendall and W.E. Midwinter. Midwinter also played for England, and is the only player to have played for England in Australia and for Australia in England. He became insane and was to die in an asylum aged 49.

ALFRED SHAW *First Test bowler.*

The star of the first Test was Charles Bannerman, who scored twice as many runs as any player on either side. Bannerman scored the first Test century, 165, before retiring hurt with a split finger at 240 for 7. The English fielding was appalling, with half the team suffering from stomach upsets after the boat journey from New Zealand. Australia, 245 and 104, beat England, 196 and 108, by 45 runs. The Australian captain was D.W. Gregory.

UNBROKEN RECORDS

This first Test established three records of interest which still stand, and one will be impossible to break. This belongs to James Southerton, the England bowler from Petworth, Sussex who played most of his cricket for Surrey, as he lived at Mitcham. Born on November 16, 1827, he was 49 at the time of the Test, and not surprisingly remains the "first-born" of all Test players. He also remains the oldest player to make his Test debut (although not the oldest Test player, a record held by Wilfred Rhodes). As it happens he was also the first Test player to die, in June 1880, three months before G.F. Grace. The other record is held by Charles Bannerman, whose first innings 165 was 67.3 per cent of his side's all-out total, the highest proportion still. It is strange to think that a record set in the first innings of the first Test still stands.

A second Test was arranged two weeks later for the benefit of the touring professionals, which led to cries of "fix" by gamblers who'd lost by betting on England in the first, and who claimed that England deliberately lost to ensure a big return gate. If it were true it worked, for 15,000 saw England win by four wickets to square the rubber. An odd statistic of this match is that the five Yorkshiremen in the side (Andrew Greenwood, George Ullyett, Tom Emmett, Allen Hill and Tom Armitage) scored 329 of the 356 runs from the bat, or 92.5 per cent of the runs.

To emphasize the unrepresentative nature of early Tests, the next touring side was an amateur outfit led by Lord Harris, reinforced by two of the Yorkshire professionals named above. The match which became the only Test of the series was billed as Gentlemen of England (with Ullyett and Emmett) versus An Australian XI. The England team's one-Test collection included the improbable Test players The MacKinnon of MacKinnon and the Reverend Vernon Peter Fanshawe Archer Royle. Australia's new discovery, the "Demon Bowler" F.R. Spofforth, was far too good for them, taking 13 wickets including the first Test hat-trick, as Australia won by 10 wickets.

In 1880 an Australian team toured England under W.L. Murdoch (who later was to play one Test for England). No Tests had been arranged, because the English thought the Aussies incapable yet of facing the full might of England. However, Charles Alcock, secretary of Surrey (who years earlier had played in the first FA Cup Final and arranged the first soccer international match), arranged a Test at the Oval. The first Test match in England took place on September 6, 7 and 8. W.G. Grace played and scored 152, England forced the follow-on and won by five wickets. Spofforth couldn't play through injury, but there were three Graces in the England side, the brothers W.G., E.M. and G.F. G.F. Grace made a pair but took a brilliant catch.

BANNERMAN *first Test century.*

Sadly, he caught a chill and died at Basingstoke a fortnight later, the second Test player to die.

Australia really established their credentials in the 1881–82 season, when they beat a strong English touring side 2–0 with two draws. In a match against Victoria, the state side needed only 94 in the fourth innings to win and the odds against England were 30–1. Most England players put £1 on themselves to win and, with Ted Peate getting six for 30, they dismissed Victoria for 75 and collected £30 winnings. But it then transpired that two England players, who had played noticeably badly, had been bribed with £100 to throw the match. They invited Midwinter to join them, but he reported the matter to the captain, Alfred Shaw. For his honesty, Midwinter was beaten up by the two conspirators.

HORNBY AND BARLOW

One of the big shocks in cricket came in 1882. There was one Test at the Oval, played on August 28 and 29. Unusually, both teams were at something like full strength,

SHAW'S TEAM *toured America, Australia and New Zealand in 1881–82.*

Murdoch captaining Australia and A.N. Hornby England (Hornby's Lancashire team-mate R.G. Barlow was also playing – the two are immortalized in Francis Thompson's famous poem *At Lord's*, which contains the refrain "O my Hornby and my Barlow long ago").

Australia won the toss and batted, and were rushed out for 63. When England batted, Spofforth bowled W.G. Grace for 4, but England battled on to 101, a lead of 38. In Australia's second innings, Hugh Massie launched an attack on the England bowling and scored 55 in an opening stand of 66, but the batting collapsed again and Australia were all out for 122. England needed a mere 85 to win. Openers Hornby and Barlow were both bowled by Spofforth at 15, but Grace and Ullyett took the score past 50 and all seemed over. Yet both were out by 53, and Spofforth and his steady ally Henry Boyle gradually ate through the remaining England wickets until the last one fell at 77 – Australia won by seven runs. Spofforth took seven wickets in each innings. W.G. Grace described the Australian wicket-keeper J.M. Blackham as "perfection". Blackham was an outstanding keeper who played Test cricket for 18 years and was on the first eight tours to England. Nearly 40,000 watched the two days' play and in the excitement at least one spectator died of a heart attack.

English cricket followers could hardly believe this result – the masters, at full strength, had been beaten. The *Sporting Times* published its famous obituary notice, framed in a black border, which read: "In affectionate remembrance of English cricket which died at the Oval on 29th August 1882, deeply lamented by a large circle of sorrowing friends and acquaintances. R.I.P. N.B. – The body will be cremated, and the ashes taken to Australia."

THE ASHES

In the English winter after this defeat, the Honourable Ivo Bligh took a party to Australia at the invitation of the Melbourne Cricket Club. It consisted of eight amateurs and four professionals. Fast bowler Fred Morley was injured when the ship taking them to Australia collided with a sailing ship, and was not much use. Three matches were arranged against the Australian team which had won at the Oval, but these were still not recognized as part of a Test match series – indeed the matches were billed as "Mr Murdoch's XI against the Hon. Ivo F.W. Bligh's Team". The Honourable Ivo Bligh, before departure for Australia, said at a dinner that he would be bringing "the Ashes of English cricket" back to England.

Bligh appeared to have little chance when Australia won the first Test, which included New Year's Day as the middle of its three days, by nine wickets. Morley got out of his bed for the second Test, but the star was Willie Bates of Yorkshire. He took seven wickets in each innings, including a hat-trick, England's first in Tests. He also scored 55 with the bat, becoming the first to score 50 and take 10 wickets in a Test. England won by an innings.

England won a well-fought decider by 69 runs, with Dick Barlow the hero, taking seven for 40 as Australia, needing 153, were dismissed for 83.

At this juncture, according to legend, some Melbourne ladies burned a bail, placed the ashes in a small urn and presented them to Bligh as the "ashes of England cricket" which he had won back. The urn was labelled "The Ashes" and carried a short type-written poem. It was given to Bligh in an embroidered velvet bag, and urn and bag are now kept in the Memorial Gallery at Lord's.

However, after this a fourth Test was arranged for Sydney and finished in a four-wicket win for Australia despite A.G. Steel's 135 for England. Blackham made two 50s for Australia, the only wicket-keeper to achieve this in the first 50 years of Test cricket. In this match Midwinter, after his beating by the two English players, returned to the Australian side for his last six Tests.

In 1884 England staged the first home Test series against Australia, as opposed to the single matches of 1880 and 1882. Although Australia had the better of two drawn matches, England won the only match to be decided, at Lord's, by an innings and five runs. A.G. Steel excelled again with 148 out of 379. In the final match at the Oval, the Australian captain, W.L. Murdoch, scored 211, the first double-century in Tests. That England saved the match was largely due to Surrey all-rounder Walter Read scoring 117 batting at number 10 and putting on 151 with William Scotton, the Nottinghamshire opener, who was ninth out for 90, scored in 340 minutes. The ninth-wicket stand remains the biggest for England against Australia.

END OF THE CENTURY

As the nineteenth century approached its end, big names and outstanding performances established the appeal of the Test match, in which England and Australia were now seen to compete on level terms. England won in 1884–85 by 3–2, with William Barnes of Nottinghamshire staking his claim as the leading all-rounder of the day. There were more disputes over money (all tours were privately run) and Blackham's continuous spell of playing in all the first 17 Tests ended when the Australian team asked for 50 per cent of the takings from the second Test and were dropped wholesale. This tour, as were many around this time, was organized by the trio of Arthur Shrewsbury and Alfred Shaw, of Nottinghamshire, and James Lillywhite, of the famous Sussex cricketing family, who was now an umpire. Shrewsbury, in the last Test, became the first Test captain to make a century.

In 1887–88 two rival teams went to Australia: that of Shrewsbury, Shaw and Lillywhite and G.F. Vernon's team captained by Lord Hawke. The two teams combined to play one Test at Sydney, with England winning after dismissing Australia for 42 and 82, George Lohmann and Bobby Peel taking 10 and nine wickets respectively.

The double tour was, not surprisingly, a financial disaster. This, plus the fact that in 1888–89 a third Test-playing country entered the lists with England taking a party to South Africa, meant the frequency of the meetings between England and Australia decreased a little. Australia exacted revenge for their dismal two-innings total of 124 at Sydney by dismissing England for 53 and 62 in the first Test of 1888. This caused W.G. Grace to assume the England captaincy for five years during which time England had the better of things.

The first Test of 1894–95 at Sydney was sensational. Australia made 586, with Syd Gregory scoring 201, the first Test double-century in Australia, George Giffen 161, and captain J.M. Blackham 74 at number 10, his ninth-wicket partnership with Gregory realizing 154, and remaining to this day a record for the series. England, out for 325, followed on and, thanks to 117 from opener Albert Ward and solid all-down-the-order contributions, made 437, setting Australia 177 to win. Bobby Peel (6 for 67) and Johnny Briggs then took advantage of a sticky sixth-day wicket to dismiss Australia for 166 and a 10-run victory. The aggregate runs scored, 1,514, was at the time a record for all first-class cricket. It was to be 87 years, when England again came from behind to beat Australia at Headingley in 1981, before the second instance of a side winning a Test after following on. England had to win the fifth Test to take the series 3–2.

DAWN OF THE GOLDEN AGE

The "Golden Age" of cricket was dawning, with great players and great deeds abounding. In the second Test of 1896, K.S. Ranjitsinhji of Sussex, who personified the Golden Age with his wristy leg glances, became the first Indian to play Test cricket and made a century (154 not out) on his debut, the second English batsman to do this after Grace. In the same match Australia's George Giffen, in his 30th Test, became the first player to complete 1,000 runs and 100 wickets in Tests. Bobby Peel ended his Test career with 6 for 23 in the final Test, having taken 102 Australian wickets – the following year Lord Hawke sacked him from Yorkshire for being drunk.

Under the captaincy of G.H.S. Trott, Australia had the ascendancy in the last two series of the nineteenth century, with the batting of Joe Darling and Clem Hill outstanding.

In the first Test of 1899 at Trent Bridge, which was drawn, W.G. Grace played his last Test, captaining England at the age of nearly 51. By coincidence, the player who was to break his record as the oldest Test player, Wilfred Rhodes, made his debut in the same match. Also making his debut (with a duck) was Victor Trumper, a batsman whom many Australians compared with the later Bradman. Trumper was another who exemplified the Golden Age, batting with a style, grace and modesty that came from genius. In the second Test, he made 135 not out to help win the only match of the series to be decided.

In 1901–02 A.C. MacLaren picked Syd Barnes, whose bowling had been mostly for Rishton and Burnley in the Lancashire League. The Yorkshire committee refused to allow the leading bowlers of the summer, Rhodes and George Hirst, to tour. Barnes, who came to be acknowledged as one of the greatest-ever bowlers in the game, took six wickets in the first Test, which England won by an innings and 124, and 13 wickets in the second Test, which Australia won (Monty Noble also took 13 wickets). Then Barnes injured his knee, and Australia won the series 4–1. With Trumper, Hill, Syd Gregory and Reggie Duff among the batsmen, and Hugh Trumble to bowl, Australia had one of its greatest sides.

When the party came to England in 1902, England too had one of its best sides, with MacLaren, Ranjitsinhji, C.B. Fry, J.T. Tyldesley, F.S. Jackson and Gilbert Jessop among the batsmen and Rhodes, Hurst, Len Braund and W.H. Lockwood among the bowlers (or all-rounders, as number 11, Rhodes, finished his career with 2,325 Test runs, average over 30). Wicket-keeper A.F.A. Lilley was also outstanding. This series marked perhaps the apogee of the Golden Age.

In the first Test at Edgbaston, England made 376 for 9 declared (Tyldesley 138) and dismissed Australia for 36, still their lowest score in Tests (Rhodes 7 for 17). Australia were 46 for 2 in the follow-on when rain intervened. The Lord's Test was washed out with England 102 for 2 (Albert Hopkins had dismissed both Fry and Ranjitsinhji without a run on the board). Clem Hill made 119 in the only Test ever to be played at Sheffield (Bramall Lane) and Australia won by 143.

Australia won the series at Old Trafford. Trumper and Duff had 100 up in 57 minutes, and by lunch, at 173 for 1, Trumper had completed his century. But Jackson scored a century for England, Australia were shot out for 86 and England needed only 124 to win. At 92 for 3 and 107 for 5, it seemed a doddle. Alas, Fred Tate, father of the more famous Maurice, was making his Test debut. He had already expensively dropped Joe Darling, Australia's top scorer in the second innings, and now, coming in last with 8 to get, and instructions to leave it to Rhodes, he was bowled, giving Australia victory by three runs.

'GOLDEN AGE' GIANTS *Brilliant sportsmen C.B. Fry and Prince Ranjitsinhji.*

The last Test at the Oval, although "dead", was even closer, and one of the most exciting on record. Australia made 324 and 121, leaving England, with a first-innings 183, a target of 263, which looked hopeless when Jessop went in at 48 for 5. Jessop then played one of the most famous of all innings, 104 in 75 minutes (then the fastest, and still the second-fastest ever Test century), Hirst stuck for 58 not out and, when Rhodes came in as last man, 15 were still required. According to legend, the two Yorkshiremen agreed to get them in singles. They didn't, in fact, restrict themselves to singles, but got the runs for a famous one-wicket victory.

ENTER THE MCC

England regained the Ashes in 1903–04, when R.E. Foster, of the famous Worcestershire family of cricketers, made 287 on his debut in the first Test, which remained the highest Test score for 26 years. He put on 130 for the last wicket with Rhodes (40 not out), the highest last-wicket stand for England in Tests. In the fifth Test Rhodes opened the innings. This was the first tour sponsored by the MCC rather than private sponsors. Such teams were always known as MCC until 1977–78 when the TCCB suggested that henceforth they should be called England.

The 1907–08 series was notable for the debut of C.G. Macartney of New South Wales in the first Test at Sydney, and the fact that Jack Hobbs of Surrey was only 12th man, even though the side was not the strongest. Australia, needing 274, were 124 for 6, but won by two wickets. Hobbs made his debut in the second Test at Melbourne and made 83 and 28, and England won by one wicket, thanks to a last-wicket stand of 39, ending with a snatched run which, with a better throw, would have caused a run-out and a tie. A partnership which was then a record for Test cricket and remains Australia's highest for the eighth wicket turned the series Australia's way finally in the third, setting up a 4–1 win. Roger Hartigan of Queensland, batting at number 8 in his Test debut, scored 116 at Adelaide, helping Clem Hill (160), who came in at 9, add 243 in the second innings. Hartigan was to play in only one more Test.

England picked 25 players in the Test series of 1909, and lost 2–1. Australia's main debutant was Warren Bardsley, who in the fifth Test at the Oval made 136 and 130 to become the first to score centuries in each innings of a match. For England, Frank Woolley made his debut in this match.

The 1911–12 series in Australia was the last for Clem Hill, who led Australia, and Victor Trumper, who were the only batsmen at the time to have passed 3,000 Test runs. Trumper made 113 as Australia won the first Test, but England won the rest, with Jack Hobbs in the form that made him the best batsman of his day. He made 662 runs, average 82.75, including 178 at Melbourne out of 323 for the first wicket with Wildred Rhodes (179). This remains the highest opening stand for England against Australia, so Rhodes, the erstwhile number 11, still figures in the record Ashes stands for both England's first and last wickets.

TRIANGULAR TEST SERIES

There was a triangular Test series in England in 1912, the only one in Test history, in which Australia and South Africa were the visitors. England won it by beating Australia in a "timeless" Test in the 12th match, but rain spoiled the whole experiment, which wasn't repeated.

The First World War interrupted Test cricket, and Australia dominated on resumption in 1920–21. There were 14 centuries in the series, 10 for Australia, skipper Warwick Armstrong making three of them. Arthur Mailey of New South Wales took 9 for 121 in the fourth Test, the only time an Australian has taken nine wickets in an Ashes Test. Australia won the series 5–0.

Less than two months after the last Test they were beginning the first in England, and Australia continued their run by winning the first three Tests. The final two were drawn. The fast bowlers J.M. Gregory and E.A. McDonald did most of the damage.

Before the next series, in 1924–25, Herbert Sutcliffe and Maurice Tate had made their Test debuts against South Africa. Sutcliffe was to form the best-known of all opening partnerships with Hobbs. Their first three opening stands against Australia were 157, 110 and 283. It was another series in which 14 centuries were scored, and half of them were scored by Hobbs (3) and Sutcliffe (4). Maurice Tate of Sussex took 38 wickets at 23.18 in the series, easily the best bowler on either side. But Australia still managed to win the series 4–1. Newcomers Bill Ponsford of Victoria and Vic Richardson of South Australia (grandfather of future Australian captains Ian and Greg Chappell) both made centuries and Jack Ryder of Victoria made 201 not out.

England at last regained the Ashes in 1926. After four draws in a rain-affected season, England began their second innings at the Oval 22 in arrears. On a sticky wicket on the third day Hobbs (100) and Sutcliffe (161) opened with a legendary stand of 172. England won the match by 289 runs. In the second Test, Harold Larwood of Nottinghamshire made his Test debut.

The majestic Walter Hammond of Gloucestershire, who made his Test debut against South Africa in the previous winter, was the star of the 1928–29 series, even though Don Bradman made his debut in the first Test. Patsy Hendren scored 169 and Larwood took eight wickets in the match as England won the first Test by 675 runs. They won the second at Sydney by eight wickets as England scored 636, the highest Test innings so far, with Hammond getting 251. Hammond made 200 in the next Test and 119 not out and 177 in the fourth, establishing a third-wicket partnership of 262 with Douglas Jardine which remains England's highest for the wicket against Australia. He ended the series with what is still an Ashes record for England of 905 runs (average 113.12). Bradman made two hundreds and averaged 66.85 but, even in competition with Bradman and Hammond, the 19-year-old New South Wales batsman Archie Jackson, making his debut in the fourth Test, played one of the great innings of the series in his first knock, 164. Sadly ill-health cut short his career.

BRADMAN AND BODYLINE

The 1930 series was the last for Hobbs, and the one in which Don Bradman established his reputation as the greatest batsman the world has seen. England won the first Test, despite Bradman's 131 in the second innings. The series was levelled at Lord's with Bradman getting 254 in a brilliant innings, until 1990 the highest Test score made at Lord's. With skipper W.M. Woodfull getting 155, Australia totalled 729 for 6 declared, the highest ever made at Lord's. The third and fourth Tests were drawn, but Bradman established a new Test record with an innings of 334 at Headingley, including 309 on the first day, still a Test record. Despite 161 and 54

RUN-GETTER SUPREME *Don Bradman (right) with Stan McCabe in 1934.*

from Sutcliffe, Australia won the match by an innings and the series at the Oval, with Bradman getting 232 and W.H. Ponsford 110. Bradman's 974 runs in the series (average 139.14) is still a record for all Test cricket.

In order to combat the new superbatsman, Douglas Jardine, the England captain for the 1932–33 tour to Australia, employed a tactic which he called leg-theory and which the Australians called bodyline. It produced the most bitter tour of all, with the Australian Board calling the English unsporting, questions being raised in parliament and much diplomatic activity aimed at preventing a secession of Australia from the Empire. The method involved packing the leg-side with fielders and bowling short, with Harold Larwood of Nottinghamshsire, as the world's fastest and most accurate bowler, being the main weapon.

The controversy itself is explained in another chapter, but the tactic worked. In Bradman's absence through illness, England won the first Test at Sydney overwhelmingly despite Stan McCabe's magnificently defiant 187 not out. Sutcliffe, Hammond and the Nawab of Pataudi each scored centuries. The Nawab followed Ranjitsinhji and his nephew Duleepsinhji in being the third Indian prince to play for England and the third to score a century on his debut against Australia. Australia levelled at Melbourne when Bradman scored his only century of the series, but England won all three remaining matches, with Lancashire's Eddie Paynter famously being brought from a nursing home at Brisbane to bat for four hours and turn the match with 83.

The bodyline argument came to its head in the third Test at Adelaide when Aussie captain Woodfull and wicket-keeper Bill Oldfield were both badly injured. Larwood did most to win the series with 33 wickets at 19.51, but such was the bitterness that he became a scapegoat and did not play for England again.

The 1934 series belonged to

LARWOOD *Controversial fast bowler.*

Bradman again, as Australia won 2–1. Australia won the first Test, which was notable for A.G. Chipperfield of New South Wales being the first man to be out for 99 on his debut. He had sat through lunch on the second day with his score on 99, and was caught behind third ball afterwards. England won by an innings at Lord's when, on a sticky wicket, Yorkshire's Hedley Verity took 14 wickets for 80 on one day – the most taken in a day in an Ashes Test. Verity's 15 for 104 remains the third-best analysis in Ashes matches after J.C. Laker's 19 wickets in 1956 and R.A.L. Massie's 16 in 1972. Bradman made 304 in the drawn fourth Test at Headingley and with Bill Ponsford (181) added 388 for the fourth wicket, then the highest stand in Ashes matches, and still the record for the fourth wicket. Australia won the series at the Oval, where Bradman (244) and Ponsford (266) did even better, adding 451 for the second wicket. This remains the second-highest partnership in all Test cricket, being passed only by the New Zealand third-wicket pair A.H. Jones and M.D. Crowe (467) in 1990–91.

When England returned to Australia for the first series after the bodyline controversy, in 1936–37, Bill Voce, Larwood's main ally on bodyline, returned to the side, having been left out for the 1934 series. Voce proved the most successful bowler of the series with 17 wickets in the first two Tests, both won overwhelmingly by England. In the second, Voce took three wickets in four balls (O'Brien, Bradman and McCabe, all for ducks) to have Australia 1 for 3, after Hammond had made 251 not out for England. However, Bradman turned the tide in the third Test with clever captaincy. On a Melbourne sticky wicket, after England declared at 76 for 9, 124 behind, Bradman sent in his tailenders while the wicket eased. He came in at number 7 with the score 97 for 5. He scored 270, and shared a stand of 346 with Jack Fingleton (136). This remains the highest sixth-wicket partnership in Test cricket. A second-innings 212 at Adelaide after England led on first innings and 169 in the last Test at Melbourne were Bradman's further contributions as Australia came back from two down to win 3–2.

Opening bat Charlie Barnett of Gloucestershire got the 1938 series off to a good start by reaching 98 not out at lunch in the first Test at Trent Bridge, completing his century to the first ball afterwards. Len Hutton and Denis Compton, in their fourth and second Tests respectively, each got a century in their first Ashes innings, and Lancashire left-hander Eddie Paynter topped them all with 216 not out. Compton and Paynter's stand of 206 is still the best sixth-wicket stand for England against Australia. Stan McCabe made 232 in reply, in an innings Bradman thought was the best he'd seen. He scored 72 of the 77 added for the last wicket with Fleetwood-Smith. Australia followed on, but centuries from W.A. Brown and Bradman saved the match. Hammond scored 240 and Brown 206 not out (carrying his bat) in a drawn second Test.

The third Test, at Old Trafford, was abandoned with no play at all. Australia finally forced a result in the fourth at Headingley, thanks to the bowling of Bill O'Reilly, who took five wickets in each innings. With the series undecided, the fifth Test at the Oval was played to a finish and records tumbled. Len Hutton scored 364 in 13 hours 17 minutes, then the highest score in Tests and still the highest in Ashes matches. His partnership of 382 with fellow-Yorkshireman Maurice Leyland remains England's highest second-wicket partnership, and his partnership of 215 for the sixth wicket with Joe Hardstaff Jr is the highest for England in Ashes matches. England's total of 903 for 7 declared is the highest total in Tests. L.O.B. Fleetwood-Smith conceded the most runs in a Test innings – 298 (he got one wicket). With Bradman and Fingleton absent hurt, England won by an innings and 579 runs, still the biggest margin of victory in a Test match.

After the war, the two batting giants of the 1930s, Hammond and Bradman, led the two sides in the 1946–47 series but, as after the First World War, England took a long time to regain form, and Australia won 3–0. Bradman's fitness and participation were doubtful, but in the first Test he received a "not-out" decision to a strong appeal for a catch by Jack Ikin at second slip and went on to score 187, adding 276 with Lindsay Hassett (128) for the third wicket – still an Ashes record. Australia won by an innings and 322 runs after storms and floods twice interrupted the England batting. More records fell in the second Test at Sydney when Bradman and Sidney Barnes each scored 234 and made a fifth-wicket partnership of 405 which remains a record for all first-class cricket. The drawn Adelaide Test was remarkable for the first of only two instances (1990–91 was the second) of two batsmen getting centuries in each innings of a Test – Denis Compton and Arthur Morris.

The Australian side which toured England in 1948 was possibly the strongest ever. It went through the season unbeaten, for the first time ever, and won the Tests 4–0. The first Test was won after Bradman and vice-captain Hassett had made 138 and 137, but the match was most noticeable for Denis Compton's highest innings against Australia of 184. He played an even better innings in the drawn Test at Old Trafford: hit on the head at 4, he retired at 33 for 2, resumed stitched up at 119 for 5 and was not out 145 when the innings ended. Australia won at Headingley after N.W.D. Yardley's declaration at 365 for 8 set Australia 404 to win in 344 minutes on the last day. Arthur Morris (182) and Don Bradman (173 not out) put on 301 for the second wicket in 217 minutes and Australia won at 404 for 3. In the first innings, Neil Harvey scored a century in his first Test against England.

Bradman made his last appearance in Tests at the Oval. England were dismissed for 52 (Ray Lindwall 6 for 20) with Hutton batting throughout the innings for 30. Bradman was cheered all the way to the wicket, given three cheers by the players, and then bowled second ball by Eric Hollies for 0 – a mere four runs would have given him a Test match career average of 100. Morris made 196 and Australia won by an innings.

HUTTON HITS BACK

Freddie Brown and Lindsay Hassett were the new captains for the tour of Australia in 1950–51, in which the Aussies won the first four Tests and England at last won the final match. After the war, England suffered 11 defeats and three draws before they finally beat Australia. The luck tended to go Australia's way, particularly in the first Test at Melbourne. Trevor Bailey and Alec Bedser did well to bowl Australia out for 228 on a good pitch. On an unplayable sticky pitch 20 wickets then fell on the third day. England declared at 68 for 7, Australia declared at 32 for 7, and England were reduced to 30 for 6. On the last morning Hutton, who was held back to number 8, scored 62 not out of the last 92 runs, but England were 70 short. There were remarkable innings at Adelaide: Morris 206 for Australia out of 371, Hutton 156 not out, carrying his bat through the innings, out of 272. At Melbourne Bedser took five wickets in each innings and Reg Simpson of Nottinghamshire made his highest Test score of 156 not out, as England won by eight wickets. Hutton was easily the outstanding batsman, his average of 88.83 being more than twice that of anybody else on either side.

The Ashes returned to England in 1953, by virtue of an eight-wicket win at the Oval after four closely fought draws. Since the previous series, Len Hutton had become the first professional to be chosen to lead England on a permanent basis. Perhaps the best match was at Lord's, where Hutton played one of his best innings, 145, to give England a narrow first-innings lead. But at the close on the fourth day, England had been reduced to 20 for 3, needing 343. Willie Watson, in his first Ashes match, and not out overnight, then played a masterly defensive innings of 109 in 346 minutes and, with the help of Trevor Bailey (71 in 257 minutes), saved the day, England being 282 for 7 at the close.

By 1954–55 England had some fast bowlers in Frank Tyson and Brian Statham to challenge the dominance that Lindwall and Miller had established over England. In the first Test, however, Hutton put Australia in, and Morris (153) and Harvey (162) allowed them to declare at 601 for 8, and to win by an innings. But in the Tests in Sydney and Melbourne, Tyson in particular bowled brilliantly in the fourth innings to win matches after Australia had led on first innings, and England got on top to record a 3–1 series victory.

England, now captained by Peter May, again came from behind in 1956 to win the series 2–1. The Surrey spinners, Jim Laker and Tony Lock, helped win the Headingley Test by an innings with 18 wickets between them, then at Old Trafford Laker produced the Test bowling performance of all time in another innings win, with 9 for 37 in the first innings and 10 for 53 in the second. His 19 wickets in the match is a record for all first-class cricket, let alone Tests, the next highest being 17. Laker's 46 wickets (at 9.60) in the series is also an England-Australia record, beaten only by the 49 that S.F. Barnes took against South Africa in 1913–14.

BOWLED OVER BY BENAUD

Australia, led by Richie Benaud, regained the Ashes in 1958–59 emphatically, 4–0, but the tour was marred by bitterness over the bowling styles of the Australian bowlers Ian Meckiff, Keith Slater, Gordon Rorke and Jim Burke. Only Burke, who was principally a batsman, came to England. Meckiff, Slater and Burke were eventually called for "throwing", while Rorke's drag helped get the Laws changed. One of the statistical highlights of the tour was Trevor Bailey's 68 in 458 minutes at Brisbane. His 357-minute 50 is the slowest in all first-class cricket. Burke replied in kind for Australia with 28 in 250 minutes.

BENAUD *Successful Aussie skipper.*

Australia's retention of the Ashes in 1961 was more satisfactory. After Australia had won at Lord's and England at Headingley, the series was won by Benaud's inspired bowling at Old Trafford. England were set 256 to win, after Alan Davidson (77 not out) and Graham McKenzie (32) had added 98 for Australia's last wicket. At 150 for 1, with Ted Dexter a dazzling 76 in 84 minutes, England were coasting, but Benaud had Dexter caught behind, May bowled round his legs for a duck, and England subsided to a 54-run defeat, with Benaud completing a spell of 5 for 12 in 25 minutes.

In a series mostly dominated by batsmen, of whom Ken Barrington, with an average of 73.75 was much the best, the 1962–63 series was drawn 1–1. It was the last series for the Australian stalwarts Neil Harvey and Alan Davidson, who topped the bowling with 24 wickets at 20.00.

Australia won the only match to be decided in 1964. The first two Tests were spoiled by rain, Geoff Boycott making his Test debut in the first. The series was won at Headingley, largely as a result of an innings by Peter Burge of Queensland, who scored 160, the last 122 coming out of 211 as he nursed Australia from 178 for 7 to 389, a lead of 121. At Old Trafford Australia's 656 for 8 declared (new captain Bobby Simpson 311, Bill Lawrey 106) was replied to with 611 (Ken Barrington 256, skipper Ted Dexter 174). The main interest at the Oval was Fred Trueman becoming the first bowler to claim 300 wickets in Tests by getting Neil Hawke caught.

M.J.K. Smith was England's new captain in 1965–66, when batsmen generally held the advantage as the sides drew 1–1. Doug Walters of New South Wales made his Test debut at Brisbane with 155. England won at Sydney when Bob Barber made 185 out of 303 in less than five hours on the first day. Australia won at Adelaide with Simpson (225) and Lawry (119) opening with a stand of 244. Ken Barrington played his last match at

BOYCOTT *batting at Headingley, 1977, where he scored his hundredth hundred.*

Adelaide by scoring 60 and 102, thus completing 10 consecutive innings there of over 50. In the fifth Test at Melbourne, Bob Cowper made 307 for Australia, still the only Test triple-century made in Australia.

There was another 1–1 in 1968. Australia won the first Test with a good all-round performance, but rain saved them in the second after they were out for 78. England squared the series at the Oval with five minutes left. With Australia needing 352 to win and being 86 for 5 at lunch, a freak storm flooded the ground. Spectators helped in mopping up and play started at 4.45. England grabbed the last five wickets for 15 runs, mainly through Derek Underwood (7 for 50). Basil D'Oliveira, who had been dropped after the first Test when England's top scorer, was reinstated for the last, made 158 and took a vital wicket, only to be dropped again when the touring party to South Africa was announced. His subsequent reinstatement led to the cessation of Test cricket with South Africa.

Six Tests were arranged for 1970–71, when the English tourists were led by Ray Illingworth. The third Test, due to be played at Melbourne, was abandoned without a ball bowled, and was rearranged. Greg Chappell made his debut at Perth and made 108 in a draw. England won at Sydney by 299 runs with John Snow of Sussex taking 7 for 20 as Australia were out for 116, Lawry carrying his bat for 60 not out. At the rearranged Melbourne Test, the crowd invaded the pitch at Ian Chappell's century and took the caps of Chappell and Colin Cowdrey plus a stump. England were set to score 271 in four hours to win but, with two batsmen injured, did not attempt the task, Boycott and John Edrich batting out time at 161 for no wicket, much to the disgust of the crowd. Dennis Lillee made his Test debut at Adelaide and took five wickets in his first innings. England won again at Sydney in the last Test, when Lawry was dropped and Ian Chappell became captain. In Australia's first innings a bouncer from Snow hit Terry Jenner on the head and he was taken to hospital. When Snow went to field on the boundary a drunk grabbed his shirt, and beer cans were thrown. Illingworth led the players off the field. Australia led by 80 after the resumption but, set 223 to win, were bowled out for 160. England took the series 2–0.

The 1972 series was closely fought. Tony Greig made his debut in the first Test and top-scored in each innings with 57 and 62. England won by 89. At Lord's, Bob Massie, of Western Australia, made an astonishing debut, taking eight wickets in each innings (8 for 84 and 8 for 53), and Australia levelled the series. England won the fourth Test at Headingley when freak weather conditions caused the outbreak of a fungus called *Fusarium oxysporum* on the wicket, and Underwood took 10 wickets in the match. This made the Aussies suspicious, but they had batted first. An eighth-wicket stand of 104 between Illingworth and Snow to put England ahead was crucial. However, Australia drew the series by winning the last Test at the Oval by five wickets. Ian Chappell (118) and Greg Chappell (113) provided the first instance of brothers each scoring centuries in the same innings of a Test.

"LILIAN THOMSON"

Australia won decisively in 1974–75 by 4–1, thanks mainly to "Lilian Thomson", otherwise Jeff Thomson and Dennis Lillee, the opening fast bowlers. They took 57 wickets between them in the first five Tests, England winning the last when Thomson was unfit and Lillee bowled only six overs.

The first World Cup competition, held in England in 1975, meant only a four-match rubber that year. A win in the first Test was enough to give Australia the series. Lillee, Thomson and Max Walker each got five wickets in an innings at Edgbaston, where Graham Gooch made his debut with a pair. At Headingley England, now with Tony Greig as captain, set Australia 445 to win in the fourth innings They reached 220 for 3 at the close of the fourth day, but then the match was abandoned as vandals, protesting against the conviction of a man they claimed was innocent, wrecked the pitch with oil and knives. England, following on in the last Test, were saved by a slow 149 by Bob Woolmer, which took 499 minutes.

A one-off Centenary Test was played in March 1977 at Melbourne and coincidentally was won by Australia by the same margin as the first-ever Test – 45 runs. The heroes were Dennis Lillee, with 11 wickets, and Derek Randall, who in his first England-Australia Test scored 174 as England reached 417, the highest fourth-innings score between the countries.

THE PACKER SERIES

The Centenary Test was used to finalize plans for Kerry Packer's World Series Cricket (referred to elsewhere in this book) in which Packer bought up Test players for his own series of matches. The 1977 Ashes series was therefore deprived of the England captain, a ringleader in the project. Mike Brearley took over; England won 3–0. In the third Test, Ian Botham made his debut, taking five first-innings wickets. Geoff Boycott also returned to Test cricket after a 30-match disagreement with the selectors and made 107, adding with Alan Knott (135) 215 for the sixth wicket, equalling England's record for Ashes matches. At Headingley Boycott scored 191, becoming the first player to complete his hundredth hundred in a Test match.

By the time England toured Australia in 1978–79, the whole group of Packer players had been named and were not considered for the Tests. England easily won the series by 5–1. Allan Border made his debut in the third Test at Melbourne, but the discovery of the tour was fast bowler Rodney Hogg of South Australia, who topped the averages and took 41 wickets, a record for an Ashes series in Australia.

England also toured the following season, when WSC had been disbanded. It was a three-match tour as the West Indies also toured Australia (the whole thing was part of a deal with WSC). Australia took back all the WSC players, but England recalled only Underwood. Australia won all three matches in a series dominated by bowlers, Allan Border making the only century of the series.

A second Centenary Test was played at Lord's in 1980, on the anniversary of the first Test played in England (though that was at the Oval). It was completely spoiled by rain and drawn.

The 1981 series was one of the most remarkable of all. Australia (with Kim Hughes as captain and Terry Alderman making his debut by taking nine wickets) won a low-scoring first Test by four wickets. At Lord's, where the match was drawn, England captain Ian Botham made a pair and was received back into the pavilion in complete silence. His 12 matches as captain had produced four draws and eight defeats. He was replaced at Headingley by Brearley, but remained in the team.

BOTHAM BOUNCES BACK

The third Test at Headingley saw a change in the fortunes of both England and Botham that came straight out of schoolboy fiction. Australia made 401 (Botham 6 for 49) and dismissed England for 174 (Botham 50). England followed on, and when Botham arrived at the wicket were 105 for 5. Soon they were 135 for 7 – still 92 behind. Bookmakers quoted the odds against them winning as 500–1. Dennis Lillee and Rodney Marsh of Australia took a little interest in England at these attractive odds. Botham then proceeded to add 117 with Graham Dilley (56), 67 with Chris Old (29) and 37 with Bob Willis (2). He finished 149 not out. Botham's century came in 87 balls, 62 of the last 64 runs coming in boundaries. He scored 106 in the final session of the fourth day. It looked a magnificent but probably futile gesture, as Australia still needed a mere 130 runs to win. But Botham quickly got a wicket in Australia's second innings and so inspired Bob Willis that Willis grabbed eight wickets for 43 and at 111 all out Australia had been beaten by 18 runs. It was only the second time in 905 Tests that a team had won after following on. Rodney Marsh had the consolations of his winning bet and of passing Alan Knott's record of wicket-keeping dismissals in Tests, a record he still holds, while his fellow-gambler Dennis Lillee had the further consolation of becoming the leading wicket-taker in England-Australia Tests, a status he too retains.

Botham played a quiet role at Edgbaston until Australia, needing 151 to win, reached 105 for 4. He then took five wickets for one run in 28 balls and England had won by 29 runs. At Old Trafford he began his second innings at 104 for 5 and scored 118, reaching his century in 86 balls. England totalled 404, won by 103 and retained the Ashes. The sixth Test was drawn. Amid all this, Terry Alderman took 42 wickets, still the most in an Ashes series by an Australian.

Australia got back the Ashes 2–1 in 1982–83. England were weakened by the absence of players who had gone on a "rebel" tour to South Africa and been given a three-year ban. In a drawn match at Perth, some hooligans invaded the pitch and, in making a rugby tackle on one of them, Alderman dislocated his shoulder and took no further part in the series. Kepler Wessels, the first South African to play for Australia, scored 162 in the second Test to help Australia win by seven wickets (Geoff Lawson took 11 wickets). Australia won the third Test and England the fourth. This was very close, all four innings being between 284 and 294. Australia required 292, and were 218 when last man Jeff Thomson joined Allan Border. In a partnership of over two hours they refused 29 singles in order to manipulate the strike, but Thomson was out at 288 for 21, leaving Border 62 not out. The last wicket belonged to Botham who completed 1,000 runs and 100 wickets against Australia. Kim Hughes and Geoff Lawson were the series' most successful batsman and bowler respectively.

Allan Border and David Gower were the new captains for the 1985 series which, by winning the last

ALLAN BORDER *In a long Test career he scored a record number of runs.*

two Tests by an innings, England took 3–1. England won the first Test, in which Tim Robinson made 175, and Australia the second, with Border getting 196. The next two Tests were high-scoring, rain-affected draws. Rain at Edgbaston kept Australia, at 335 for 8 at the end of the second day, apparently safe from defeat, but England were inspired on the third day, grabbing the last two wickets and scoring 355 for 1 at the close. Gower (215) and Robinson (148) added 315 for the second wicket and, with Gatting, a returned "South African rebel", getting 100, England declared at 595 for 5. A controversial dismissal of Wayne Phillips on the last day sealed Australia's fate. He slashed, Allan Lamb jumped to avoid injury, the ball struck his foot in mid-air and was caught by Gower. He was given out by the square leg umpire. It was difficult to see, even on slow-motion television, exactly what happened. England's loss of only five wickets in winning was at the time the least in any Ashes victory. Richard Ellison of Kent took 10 wickets in the match. England won as clearly at the Oval, with Gooch getting 196 and Gower 157. With 732 runs (average 81.33) Gower was the most successful batsman, but Gatting with 527 (average 87.83) topped the averages. Allan Border also made more than 500 runs. Ellison, with 17 wickets at

10.88, topped the bowling but Botham had most wickets: 31.

England kept the Ashes in 1986–87 when Gatting had taken over the captaincy. They won the first and fourth Tests comfortably and Australia's victory in the last was academic. Chris Broad made centuries in three successive Tests and topped the batting averages at 69.57, but his 487 runs was topped by Australia's Dean Jones, who scored 511. Gladstone Small topped the bowling averages with 12 wickets at 15.00 each, but again an Australian, Bruce Reid, had most wickets: 20.

BROAD STUMPS UP

Australia celebrated the Bicentenary of British colonization in 1988 with a one-off Test match at Sydney. Chris Broad, out for 133, his fourth century in six Tests in Australia, smashed a stump out of the ground and was fined £500 by his manager. England forced Australia to follow on, but 184 not out by David Boon saved the game and won the Man-of-the-Match award.

An under-rated Australian party in 1989 soon changed their opponents' estimation of them. At Headingley they made 601 for 7 declared (Mark Taylor 136, Steve Waugh 177 not out). England made 430 but, set 402 to win in the fourth innings, lost by 210 runs. Australia then made it 2–0, winning by six wickets at Lord's (Waugh got 152 and 21, both not out). The next Test was spoiled by rain, but Steve Waugh, by scoring 43, took his total runs for the series to 393 before being out, a record in Ashes matches. A fourth Test win by nine wickets, Australia's 100th victory over England in 267 contests, sealed the Ashes for Australia, who however heaped further humiliation on England at Trent Bridge. Mark Taylor and Geoff Marsh batted throughout the first day, scoring 301 runs. Next day they took their stand to 329, the highest opening stand in Ashes Tests, beating the Hobbs and Rhodes stand of 323 in 1911–12. Taylor made 219, Marsh 138, Australia 602 for 6 declared, and Australia won by an innings and 180. The sixth Test was drawn. For the first time in an Ashes series, three batsmen from one side topped 500 runs: Taylor, Dean Jones and Steve Waugh. Waugh topped the averages at 126.50, but Taylor's aggregate of 839 remains the third-highest in a Test series, beaten only by Bradman and Hammond. By taking 41 wickets at 17.37, Terry Alderman became the first bowler to take 40 or more wickets in a Test series twice.

Graham Gooch was England captain in 1990–91. In a low-scoring game at Brisbane, which lasted only three days, England got a first-innings lead of 42 but set Australia only 157 to win – which Taylor and Marsh scored without loss. The story was repeated at Melbourne: an England first-innings lead of 46, a target of 197, an eight-wicket win for Australia. Bruce Reid took 13 wickets. The next two Tests were drawn, the most notable occurrence being the debut of Mark Waugh at Adelaide, making him and Steve the first twins to play Test cricket. Mark Waugh began his Test career with 138. Australia wrapped up the series 3–0 at Perth. David Boon and Bruce Reid were best batsman and bowler of the series, in both aggregate and average.

Allan Border captained Australia for the last time in Ashes matches on the tour of 1993. Shane Warne made an explosive entry into Ashes Tests by bowling Mike Gatting with a fizzing leg break on his first ball – the fifth bowler to take a wicket with his first ball in Ashes matches, but the first to do it by hitting the stumps. Warne took eight wickets in the match and Australia won by 179 runs. Gooch, the England captain, was out "handled the ball" in the second innings for 133, having punched it away as it bounced up after a defensive shot.

At Lord's Australia declared at 632 for 4 and won by an innings and 62. By losing only four wickets in winning, Australia set a new record for the series. Boon made 164 not out, Michael Slater 152 and Mark Taylor 111. Warne again took eight wickets.

One of four England Test debutants at Trent Bridge, Graham Thorpe, made 120 not out in the second innings, allowing England to declare and set Australia 371 to win – they were 202 for 6 at the close. But Australia repeated the old slaughter at Headingley, declaring at 653 for 4 (Border 200 not out, Steve Waugh 157 not out in an unbroken fifth-wicket stand of 332). Australia won by an innings and 148 runs, and Graham Gooch resigned the England captaincy. Mike Atherton took over for the last two Tests. Australia won by eight wickets at Edgbaston, but England at last managed a win at the Oval by 161 runs, their first against Australia in 19 Tests. Graham Gooch scored most runs in the series, 673, but Steve Waugh topped the averages with 83.20. Angus Frazer topped the bowling averages, having played in only one match, with eight wickets at 16.38, but Shane Warne had most wickets, 34.

Mike Atherton took his first side to Australia in 1994–95, when Mark Taylor had assumed the Australian captaincy. After Michael Slater (176) and Mark Waugh (140) had helped Australia to 426 at Brisbane, Taylor declined to enforce the follow-on when England made only 167 (Craig McDermott 6 for 53), but eventually won by 184 runs, Warne getting 8 for 71 in the second innings. At Melbourne, England were set 388 to win and were dismissed for 92, Warne getting the first hat-trick in Ashes Tests for 91 years. England had much the best of the third Test but couldn't snatch the last three Australian wickets. Greg Blewett made a century on debut and added another in the fourth Test, but England won it comfortably by 106 runs. Looking to level the series in the last Test at Perth, they collapsed badly in the fourth innings to 27 for 6, were all out for 123 and lost by 329 runs. Blewett topped the series batting averages by virtue of his two centuries in the last two Tests, but Slater's 623 runs was easily the highest. McDermott, with 32 wickets, and Warne, with 27, were the best bowlers.

WAUGH'S SCORE *at Lord's in 1989 during his run of 393 runs before being out.*

TEST RESULTS

ENGLAND v AUSTRALIA

	Matches	Eng	Aus	Draw	Series	Eng	Aus	Draw
In Australia	150	52	73	25	35	12	18	5
In England	135	38	38	59	32	15	13	4
Totals	285	90	111	84	67	27	31	9

ENGLAND v SOUTH AFRICA

The third country to play Test matches was South Africa. Major R. Gardner Warton retired early in 1888 after five years' service in South Africa on the General Staff and decided to take a party of cricketers back the following winter. Seven of the party had played first-class cricket, and the other five were club standard. After playing sides of 15, 18 and 22 players, they played two matches against 11 South Africans. These two matches have become recognized as the first two Tests in South African cricket. England were overwhelmingly superior and remained so for some years, resulting in some English cricketers acquiring flattering Test records. The English side was led by C.A. Smith of Sussex, who later found fame in Hollywood as C. Aubrey Smith, usually playing a typical Englishman. For three of the party, the two Tests represent their entire careers in first-class cricket. England won the matches, at Port Elizabeth and Cape Town, by eight wickets and an innings and 202 runs. Johnny Briggs of Lancashire took 7 for 17 and 8 for 11 in the second match. In this match J.E.P. McMaster, an Irishman, played his only first-class game. He was out for a duck and did not bowl or take a catch.

A strong touring side played one Test in South Africa in 1891–92 and won by an innings and 189. It included Australian Test players J.J. Ferris and W.L. Murdoch, who made their debuts for England. Similarly Frank Hearne of Kent, who had played twice for England against South Africa in 1888–89, made his debut for South Africa, having settled there. His brothers, Alec and George Gibbons, were in the England side, the second occasion on which three brothers had appeared in the same Test. Another Hearne, J.T., was also in the England side but, although often referred to as a cousin of the other three, his relationship was slightly more distant. Harry Wood, the Surrey wicket-keeper, scored 134 not out, batting number 8, the first instance of a wicket-keeper making a Test century.

Lord Hawke, the power behind Yorkshire for many years, took sides to South Africa in 1895–96 and 1898–99 which won all their Tests. In the first tour, when three Tests were played, George Lohmann, the Surrey bowler, produced analyses of 7 for 38 and 8 for 76, 9 for 28 and 3 for 45, and 7 for 42 and 1 for 45. In the second innings of the first Test, South Africa were dismissed for a record low score of 30. In the second tour, when England introduced nine new Test players, South Africa actually took a first-innings lead of 106 at Johannesburg but lost by 32 after Pelham Warner carried his bat for 132 not out, the first player to carry his bat on his Test debut. James Sinclair of Transvaal was run out for 86 in this match, South Africa's first 50, and in the second scored his country's first century. He also took 6 for 26 in England's first-innings 92, almost single-handedly giving South Africa a lead of 85, but South Africa were out for 35 in their second knock. Albert Trott became another Australian Test player to play also for England.

It was not till 1905–06 that the next party went to South Africa, led by Pelham Warner. It was not a bad side, but South Africa had improved considerably. In the first Test, at Johannesburg, South Africa were 93 behind on first innings and set 284 to win. They got to 239 for 9, when captain Percy Sherwell joined A.W. "Dave" Nourse, and the two put on a winning 48. Nourse, batting number 8, scored 18 and 93, both times not out. They then won the second Test by nine wickets and the third by 243 runs. C.M.H. Hathorn and G.C. White made centuries, and in South Africa's first innings, 385, every player made double figures. S.J. "Tip" Snooke took 8 for 70 in England's second innings and 12 wickets in the match. England won the fourth Test, but South Africa took the last by an innings. South Africa in this series employed four leg-break bowlers, R.D. Schwarz, G.A. Faulkner, G.C. White and A.E.E. Vogler, who perfected the new invention of googly bowling, which seemed well-suited to the South African matting wickets.

FIRST OVERSEAS TESTS

South Africa played their first Tests overseas in 1907, when the team that had beaten England in the winter played three Tests in England. The weather interrupted all three, the only result coming in a low-scoring match at Headingley, where England won by 53 runs. C.B. Fry was the only batsman to average over 40 for the series and Colin Blythe of Kent was easily the most successful bowler with 26 wickets at only 10.38 each.

Jack Hobbs went to South Africa in 1909–10 and topped the batting averages with 67.37, but South Africa won an exciting series 3–2. While Colin Blythe topped the bowling averages, it was Bert Vogler and Aubrey Faulkner who won the series, with 36 and 29 wickets respectively. In this series, England played George Simpson-Hayward of Worcestershire, the last of the great under-arm bowlers. He got a wicket with his fifth ball in Tests and returned 6 for 43. In the series he took 23 wickets at 18.26 each.

South Africa played in the rain-sodden triangular series in England in 1912, but lost all three games to England – largely because of Sydney Barnes, who took 34 wickets – and could manage only a draw in their three with Australia.

Barnes was their tormenter in 1913–14, as well. England sent their strongest tourists so far, with Hobbs, Wilfred Rhodes, C.P. Mead and Frank Woolley also in the party. England won 4–0. Barnes set a record for all Tests, which still stands, by taking 49 wickets in the series, and he played in only the first four Tests. His best haul was 9 for 103 in the second innings of the second Test at Johannesburg. He took 17 for 159 in this Test, a record which has been passed only once since, by Jim Laker in 1956. Amongst the carnage, the new South Africa captain, Herbie Taylor, batted bravely for 508 runs, average 50.80.

SHARP BOWLER *Bert Vogler.*

It was not until after the First World War that another side went to South Africa, and Taylor made 176 in the first Test of 1922–23 to give South Africa a win. England won the second Test by one wicket, recovering from 86 for 6 to 173 for 9. England won the rubber in the final Test at Durban, when C.A.G. "Jack" Russell of Essex made 140 and 111, the second player and first Englishman to make a century in each innings of a Test. He suffered from ill-health and this was the last of his 10 Tests, in which he averaged 56.87. Herbie Taylor topped the batting aggregates and averages, however, with 582 runs at 64.66.

The South African tourists in 1924 faced Hobbs and Herbert Sutcliffe, who made his Test debut in the first Test at Edgbaston. They put on 136 in their first opening stand, the first of their 15 Test century stands, but it was England's

LEN HUTTON *hits high to leg against South Africa at the Oval in 1947.*

bowlers who caused the sensations. Maurice Tate, another debutant, took a wicket with his first ball in Tests and finished with 4 for 12, but partner A.E.R. Gilligan, the captain, had 6 for 7. Eleven extras helped South Africa to 30, equalling their record lowest score. It remains the second-lowest score in all Tests. Hobbs (211) and Sutcliffe (122) opened with a stand of 268 in the second Test at Lord's. England at 531 for 2 declared, lost only two wickets in winning by an innings, a Test record. England won the series 3–0, an oddity being the England appearance in a rain-ruined Old Trafford Test of J.C.W. MacBryan of Somerset. In this his only Test, he did not bat, bowl, or dismiss anybody in the field. England's Patsy Hendren topped the batting averages with 398 runs at 132.66, but South Africa's Bob Catterall made most runs, 471.

Walter Hammond made his Test debut in South Africa in 1927–28, an exciting series in which England won the first two matches, the third was drawn and South Africa won the last two. George Bisset, whose only four Tests were in this series, took 7 for 29 in England's second innings of the last Test to ensure the tied series. His 25 wickets were the most of the series. The South African press were very critical of his omission from the party to tour England in 1929. Bruce Mitchell made his debut for South Africa in this series, in which England won the only two Tests to be decided. It was a series in which English batsmen made 10 centuries, four to Herbert Sutcliffe. Even so, Frank Woolley topped the averages with 126.00.

The 1930s were better for South Africa. They won 1–0 in 1930–31 by winning the first Test by 28 runs (E.P. Nupen took 11 wickets) and drew the rest. The fourth Test was the last played in South Africa on matting wickets. Then in 1935, under Herbie Wade, they won their first Test in England and with it the series. In the Lord's Test Bruce Mitchell made 164 and X.C. Balaskas, in his only match of the rubber because of injury, took nine wickets. South Africa drew the other games. In the first Test, Dudley Nourse (son of "Dave") and Eric Rowan made their debuts. Mitchell was the most successful batsman of the series.

"TIMELESS TEST"

The 1938–39 series in South Africa featured the famous "timeless Test" at Durban. England had established a 1–0 lead in a series dominated by batsmen, so the last Test, as it could decide the rubber, was played to a finish. Alan Melville, making his Test debut, captained South Africa in this series, while Wally Hammond captained England.

At Durban, South Africa made 530, with centuries from P.G.V. van der Bijl and Dudley Nourse, and England 316. Then, with Melville getting 103, South Africa made 481, setting England 696 to win. Paul Gibb (120) and Bill Edrich (219) put on 280 for the second wicket, Hammond (140) and Edrich 89 for the third, and Hammond and Paynter (75) 164 for the fourth. Finally, at tea on the 10th day, with England still 42 short at 654 for 5, rain caused the match to be abandoned, as England had to leave on a two-day rail journey to catch their ship at Cape Town. It is the longest first-class match, and the 1,981 runs scored was a record, since beaten twice in India. During the series, Eddie Paynter scored a century in each innings at Johannesburg and his highest Test score, 243, at Durban. He topped the series aggregates with 653 runs, but Hammond, who made 609, topped the averages at 87.00. Edrich, who made 219 to help save the final match, had previously made only 48 runs in his nine Test innings before this, and was on the point of being dropped.

COMPTON RUNS AND RUNS

In the first series after the war, there was a run-feast for Compton, Edrich, Nourse, Melville and Mitchell. It was Compton's record-breaking season, when he scored more runs and centuries than anybody before or since. Compton made 753 in the Tests, average 94.12, but Edrich had a higher average, 110.40, with 552 runs. Nourse, Mitchell and Melville scored 621, 597 and 569 respectively, with averages in the 60s. Edrich proved his worth by topping the bowling averages, too, with 16 wickets at 23.12. Melville (189 and 104 not out) made a century in each innings in the first Test, and Mitchell (120 and 189 not out) did it in the fifth. Compton (208) and Edrich (189) added 370 for the third wicket at Lord's, then a third-wicket record for all Tests, still a record for any wicket in England v South Africa matches. Melville's 117 at Lord's was his fourth century in successive Test innings, dating back to before the war, all against England. South Africa drew the first and last Tests, but England won 3–0.

England continued to have the better of the exchanges. They won 2–0 in 1948–49, although they were narrow victories, the first by two wickets with a leg bye off the last ball of the match. On the first day of Test cricket at Ellis Park, Johannesburg, Hutton (158) and Cyril Washbrook (195) put on 359 for the first wicket, then a record for all Tests, and still England's highest opening partnership. England won 3–1 in 1951, when captain Dudley Nourse made 208 at Trent Bridge, batting in great pain from a fractured thumb. Eric Rowan made 236 at Headingley, which helped him top the batting averages. Peter May made a century here on his Test debut. Alec Bedser's 30 wickets really decided the series. The most remarkable incident occurred at the Oval, when Len Hutton, having played a ball from Athol Rowan into the air, played it again as it was about to land on the stumps. However, Russell Endean was moving to catch it, and Hutton became the only batsman in Test cricket to be given out "obstructing the field". In 1955 all five Tests produced a result, the first time

BEDSER *Last wicket v South Africa.*

this had happened in England. England won the first two Tests and South Africa the third and fourth. Alec Bedser's Test career ended at Old Trafford with a then world-record 236 wickets. An exciting series was decided at the Oval when England won by 92 runs. Peter May, the captain and top run-scorer in the series, made 89 not out in England's second innings, while Hugh Tayfield, who took most wickets in the series, bowled 52 overs unchanged over five hours in a spell which brought four wickets for 54 runs.

In 1956–57 South Africa tied the rubber by winning the last two Tests after England had won the first two with the third a draw. South Africa collapsed in their second innings in the first two Tests, being out for 72 each time. In the second, at Cape Town, Russell Endean prevented a ball rebounding on to his stumps with his hand, and became the first player to be given out "handled the ball" in Tests. In the drawn match, Tayfield bowled a record 137 deliveries without conceding a run in the first innings, and took 8 for 69 in the second. In the fourth Test, which South Africa won by 17 runs, he took 9 for 113 in the second innings, a record for South Africa, and 13 wickets in the match, remaining the only South African to achieve this, and having done it twice. Tayfield was naturally the best bowler of the series with 37 wickets, the most by a South African in a Test series, although Trevor Bailey topped the averages. England won easily in 1960, where the most noteworthy incidents concerned Geoff Griffin at Lord's, in his second Test. After becoming the first South African to get a Test hat-trick, he was no-balled 11 times for throwing. It was the end of his Test career.

APARTHEID AND AFTER

England won the series 1–0 in 1964–65 by winning the first Test by an innings and then securing four draws. Ken Barrington averaged 101.60. In a three-match series in 1965, however, South Africa won 1 0 by taking the second Test at Trent Bridge, thanks to 125 from Graeme Pollock and five wickets in each innings from brother Peter. Series planned for South Africa in 1968–69 and England in 1970 were cancelled because of apartheid and the D'Oliveira affair, which is dealt with elsewhere in this book. Unfortunately for South Africa, they were building at that time their strongest-ever side.

Cricket relations resumed in 1994 when South Africa toured England and played a three-match series. Kepler Wessels captained South Africa, having previously played for Australia. After making a century on his debut for Australia against England in 1982–83, he made another on his debut for South Africa at Lord's. South Africa won convincingly by 356 runs. Following a high-scoring draw at Headingley, South Africa appeared in command at the Oval until England's last man, Devon Malcolm, was hit on the helmet by a bouncer on the morning of the third day. Vowing vengeance, he then took 9 for 57 in four hours to shoot out South Africa for 172, leaving England to get 205 for 2 and an eight-wicket win. Malcolm's analysis is the sixth-best in Tests in all time.

England returned to South Africa in 1996–97 after 32 years. After a rain-spoiled first Test, England saved the second, at Johannesburg, when captain Mike Atherton (185 not out) and wicket-keeper Jack Russell (29 not out) batted out time for over $4^1/_2$ hours. Atherton's innings lasted 643 minutes. Russell took 11 catches in the match, a record number of dismissals for all Test cricket. Russell took his dismissals to 27, second only to Marsh of Australia in all Tests. After two more draws, South Africa won the last Test and the series at Cape Town by 10 wickets.

TEST RESULTS

ENGLAND v SOUTH AFRICA

	Matches	Eng	SA	Draw	Series	Eng	SA	Draw
In South Africa	63	25	14	24	15	9	4	2
In England	47	22	6	19	11	8	2	1
Totals	110	47	20	43	26	17	6	3

LEAP AT LORD'S *South African captain Kepler Wessels makes Mike Atherton jump in 1994 .*

AUSTRALIA v SOUTH AFRICA

In 1902 the Australian party which won the Ashes in England played three Tests in South Africa on their way home. In the first they managed to save the game after following on, but they won the last two, despite Test South Africa's J.H. Sinclair scoring 100 in 80 minutes in the last Test, the fourth-fastest in Tests and still the fastest for South Africa.

The South Africans visited Australia in 1910–11 and lost 4–1. Although Trumper topped the batting averages, Aubrey Faulkner scored most runs – 732, a South African record for a series. South Africa failed to beat Australia in a Test after this until 1952–53, 25 Tests later. At Johannesburg in 1921–22, Jack Gregory scored a century in 70 minutes for Australia, still the fastest in Tests. In the two series in the 1930s, Australia won nine Tests and one was drawn. Bradman dominated the batting in Australia in 1931–32, making 806 runs and averaging 201.50. At Adelaide he made 299 not out, running out the number 11 batsman when going for a quick single at the end of an over. Clarrie Grimmett took 33 wickets in this series, and in South Africa in 1935–36 took 44, the third-highest of all time and best for Australia.

It was 4–0 again for the Australians after the war when matches resumed in South Africa in 1949–50. There was an outstanding performance at Durban by Neil Harvey. Dudley Nourse, having dismissed Australia for 75, 236 behind, decided not to enforce the follow-on on a wearing pitch. South Africa were dismissed for 99, leaving Australia to get 336. Harvey came in at 59 for 3, and in a patient innings of 151 not out in 5½ hours steered Australia to a five-wicket win.

With the retirements of Nourse and the Rowan brothers, Eric and Athol, South Africa sent a young side under Jack Cheetham to Australia in 1952–53 with low expectations. After Harvey had made his fifth century in successive matches to help win the first Test, South Africa won their second match ever against Australia at Melbourne, thanks largely to 162 not out from Endean and 13 for 165 by Tayfield, still the best analysis by a South African in Tests. South Africa then drew the series with an extraordinary performance in the last Test at Melbourne. Australia, with Harvey making 205, totalled 520. South Africa made 435 and needed 295 in the fourth innings, and won by six wickets. Harvey made 834 runs in the series to average 92.66, the fourth-highest aggregate ever. Tayfield took 30 wickets.

Australia won 3–0 in South Africa in 1957–58, under Ian Craig, who in the fifth Test in 1952–53 had become Australia's youngest Test player at 17 years 239 days (a record he still holds), and now became the youngest Test captain of all (since superseded) in 1957–58 when he took a side to South Africa. Australia easily won 3–0, with Benaud and Davidson doing particularly well as bowlers. South Africa then narrowly failed to win the series in Australia in 1963–64, under Trevor Goddard. Graeme Pollock and Denis Lindsay made debuts in the first Test, which Australia won. Pollock made 122 at Sydney and, while still not 20 years old, 175 at Adelaide. He and Eddie Barlow (201) added 341 for South Africa's third wicket, a record for any wicket for South Africa and for the Australia-South Africa series. This levelled the series and South Africa might have won it in the last Test had there been time – they needed less than 100 with all wickets standing at the close.

CHRISTMAS PRESENT

There were to be no more close shaves. In 1966–67 in South Africa the home team won 3–1 for their first series win over Australia. Nobody would have guessed this outcome on the second day of the series, Christmas Eve, when Australia passed South Africa's total of 199 with only one wicket down. But South Africa made 620 in the second innings (Lindsay 182) and won by 233 runs, their first victory over Australia at home. Lindsay's six catches in Australia's first innings was at the time a Test record. After Australia won the second Test, Mike Procter made his debut for South Africa in the third, and South Africa won this and the fifth for their historic win. Lindsay topped the run aggregates with 606, and took 24 catches in the series, third in the all-time list.

Even this performance was nothing to 1969–70 when South Africa's team for the third Test was possibly their best ever. They won all four of the Tests played. Barry Richards made his debut in the first Test, and scored 140 in the second at Durban, where Graeme Pollock made 274, the highest score for South Africa in Tests. South Africa's 622 for 9 declared remains their highest. South Africa won by an innings and 129, and won the last two Tests by over 300 runs. Lindsay conceded no byes in any Test. Pollock and Richards topped the batting, Procter the bowling. It was Richards' only Test series before South Africa were ejected from the Test arena. His average for Tests is therefore 72.57. Pollock ended his Test career with 2,256 runs, average 60.97.

At the time of their expulsion from Tests, South Africa had won eight Tests, drawn three and lost only one in their last three series against Australia and England. Led by Ali Backer, the team included some outstanding players. The contests between the countries were revived in 1993–94, with Allan Border and Kepler Wessels as captains, and three matches played in each country, the results being 1–1 with one draw each time. Australia came from behind in both series, which were generally disappointing, with umpiring disputes and unimaginative tactics. In the last, Allan Border made his final Test appearance with a record number of appearances (156) and runs (11,174).

Australia won a three-match series in South Africa in 1996–97 by 2-1, winning the first two Tests, .he second by two wickets in an exciting finish. South Africa won the third. Steve Waugh was the leading batsman of the series for Australia with 313 runs, average 78.25, and the most successful bowlers were Australians Jason Gillespie and Glenn McGrath, with 14 and 13 wickets respectively.

GREAT BATSMAN *Graeme Pollock.*

TEST RESULTS

AUSTRALIA v SOUTH AFRICA

	Matches	Aus	SA	Draw	Series	Aus	SA	Draw
In South Africa	36	18	9	9	9	6	2	1
In Australia	23	13	5	5	5	2	0	3
In England	3	2	0	1	1	1	0	0
Totals	62	33	14	15	15	9	2	4

ENGLAND v WEST INDIES

An all-amateur English side toured the West Indies in 1894–95, and tours were made regularly after this, being organized by the MCC from 1910. The first West Indian party toured England in 1900. It was during the fourth tour to England in 1928 that three Tests were played in the 41-match programme. England won all three by an innings and Hobbs averaged 106.00. In 1929–30, however, the series was shared 1–1 with two draws. The England team, under the Honourable F.S.G. Calthorpe on his debut, was not the best, as England were also touring New Zealand. George Gunn, aged 50, was recalled after a record gap of 17 years, 316 days. The West Indians' J.E.D. Sealy, still their youngest Test player at 17 years, 122 days, had not been born when Gunn had played his previous Test. Gunn is the fourth-oldest Test player. The oldest, Wilfred Rhodes, ended his career in the same series, aged 52 years, 165 days. Clifford Roach made the West Indies' first Test century in the first Test, and George Headley, on his debut, made 176 in the second innings, aged 20. After England won the second Test (Hendren 205 not out), the West Indies achieved their first Test victory in the third with Roach getting 209 and Headley a century in each innings. The fourth Test, at Kingston, Jamaica, was a timeless Test intended to settle the series but, after rain had washed out the eighth and ninth days, it was left drawn. Several Test records, since beaten, were set: the longest Test (now second), the highest total (England's 849, now second), the highest score (Andy Sandham's 325, now eighth) and the highest aggregate runs (1,815, now second). Calthorpe, leading by 563, did not enforce the follow-on. The West Indies, needing 836 to win in the fourth innings, were 408 for 5 at the close (Headley 223). Headley, with 703 runs, had the highest aggregate, but Hendren topped the averages at 115.50.

In 1933 in England, the West Indian fast bowlers Learie Constantine and Manny Martindale bowled bodyline at Old Trafford, but Jardine scored a century. England won 2–0.

GEORGE HEADLEY *the first outstanding West Indian batsman.*

There was an extraordinary match at Bridgetown in the first Test of 1934–35. the West Indies made 102 on a sticky wicket which grew more spiteful. R.E.S. Wyatt, the England captain, declared at 81 for 7. The West Indian captain, George Grant, reversed his batting order hoping the pitch might improve. But when Headley came in and was dismissed for a duck at 51 for 6, he declared, giving England a day and a bit to get 73 to win! They were 29 for 4 and 48 for 6, but got home by four wickets. Nevertheless the West Indies won the second and fourth Tests to win 2–1. Headley, who scored 270 in the fourth Test, averaged 97.00.

In the last Test series played before the war in 1939, England won at Lord's and drew the remaining two Tests. Headley scored a century in each innings at Lord's. Hutton averaged 96.00, with 480 runs. Learie Constantine was among those who played their last Test.

On resumption in 1947–48, debutants in the first Test in Barbados were Everton Weekes and Clyde Walcott for the West Indies and Jim Laker for England. Frank Worrell made his debut in the second Test. A second Test curiosity was the debut of Andy Ganteaume of Trinidad. He made 112 in his only Test innings, but was not picked again, so strong did the West Indies' batting become. Worrell was only twice out for a series average of 147. After two draws, the West Indies won the last two Tests.

GREAT CAPTAIN *Frank Worrell.*

CALYPSO CLASSIC

West Indian cricket really came of age in 1950, under the captaincy of John Goddard, and based on the batting of Worrell, Weekes and Walcott and two debutant slow bowlers, Alf Valentine and Sonny Ramadhin. Valentine must have wondered what it was all about as he took the first eight wickets to fall in his first Test at Old Trafford. He had taken only two wickets in first-class cricket before coming to England. Nevertheless, England won. It all turned round at Lord's in the second Test when Ramadhin took 11 wickets to add to Valentine's seven and the West Indies won by 322. Walcott got 168 not out, but the West Indian steel bands were telling everybody that it was "at Lord's where they done it ... with those little pals of mine, Ramadhin and Valentine". The calypso was famous. The West Indies slaughtered England at Trent Bridge (Worrell 261) and the Oval, where a defiant Hutton carried his bat for 202 not out. The West Indies won 3–1.

Strangely, the West Indies did not win another series against England for 13 years. In 1953–54 the MCC sent a strong team led by Len Hutton to the West Indies, but the West Indies won the first two Tests. England won at Georgetown, and there was a high-scoring draw at Trinidad where, in the first innings, the West Indies made 681 for 8 declared, then their highest Test score. Weekes made 206, Worrell 167 and Walcott 204. Weekes and Worrell put on 338, still a West Indies' record for the third wicket. England squared the series by winning in Jamaica, where Trevor Bailey took 7 for 34 in the first innings and Len Hutton scored 205. Gary Sobers made his debut, batting number 9. Hutton scored 677 runs in the series, average 96.71, and Walcott 689, average 87.25. Ramadhin was the top bowler.

English batsmen finally found a way to play Ramadhin in the first Test of 1957 at Edgbaston. After being shot out for 186 (Ramadhin 7 for 49), and facing a deficit of 288, they had reached 113 for 3 (two more for Ramadhin). Peter May (285) and Colin Cowdrey (154) then added 411, still a record for the fourth wicket in all Test cricket. England won the series 3–0, with Peter Loader getting a hat-trick at Headingley. At Trent Bridge, Tom Graveney made 258 and Frank Worrell carried his bat for 191.

England also won 1–0 in 1959–60, by virtue of winning the second Test in Trinidad, where the crowd rioted and threw bottles after a run-out decision. Sobers made 709 runs in the series at 101.28.

TONY GREIG *in 1973–74. wickets and a controversial run-out attempt.*

WISDEN TROPHY

The Wisden Trophy was a new prize on offer in 1963. The West Indies won it 3–1 and have relinquished it for only two series since. Frank Worrell captained the West Indies; the drawn match at Lord's was the most exciting, with all results possible until the last ball, England needing six to win with the last pair in. In fact they defended in the last over, because Cowdrey had been forced to return to the wicket with his fractured left arm in plaster to ensure the draw. Sobers was the captain defending the Trophy in 1966, and he did much to make sure the West Indies kept it 3–1 by scoring 722 runs, average 103.14, and taking 20 wickets and 10 catches. At Lord's he added 274 with his cousin David Holford, still theWest Indies' sixth-wicket record in all Tests.

England, under Cowdrey, won the Wisden Trophy 1–0 in 1967–68, thanks to a generous declaration by Sobers in the fourth Test which enabled them to win with three minutes to spare. In the last Test, England, chasing 308 to win, scraped a draw at 206 for 9. Sobers was again the best batsman, averaging 90.83, and John Snow took 27 wickets in four Tests. In 1969, England easily won a three-match series 2–0, but lost the Wisden Trophy in 1973 when the West Indies won 2–0 and have never been able to get it back. In this series, there was a bomb alert at Lord's which cost 89 minutes but allowed many of the public to tread the sacred turf.

A five-Test series in 1973–74 saw the West Indies win the first and England the last. Outstanding individual performances came in the second Test from Dennis Amiss, who saved the game with 262 not out in a total of 432 for 9, in the third from Lawrence Rowe, who made 302, and in the fifth from Tony Greig, who took 13 wickets in England's 26-run win. On the second day of the first Test, Greig ran out Kallicharran as the batsman was leaving the ground at close of play. Umpire Sang Hue was forced to give him out, but an off-the-field conference by administrators, umpire and captains led to his reinstatement.

The West Indies, under Clive Lloyd, were beginning their long mastery of all countries in 1976, when they won the series 3–0. Vivian Richards scored 232 in his first innings against England. Gordon Greenidge made a century in each innings at Old Trafford and Viv Richards made 291 at the Oval, bringing his total of runs in the calendar year to 1,710, still the world's record. Dennis Amiss's 203 was unable to affect the result. Richards made 829 runs in the series, the fifth-highest on record. He averaged 118.42.

Richards topped the averages in 1980 and 1980–81 as well. The West Indies beat England, led by Ian Botham for the first time, 1–0 in 1980, by virtue of winning the first Test by two wickets. Rain cut short the remaining games. The West Indies won 2–0 in 1980–81, when pitch vandals caused a delay in the first Test at Trinidad in protest against the omission of local wicket-keeper Deryck Murray. The second Test at Georgetown was cancelled when the Guyanan Government withdrew Robin Jackman's visitor's permit because he had played in South Africa, which was banned from international cricket at the time for political reasons. England's manager, Ken Barrington, died of a heart attack during the third Test. It was a sad tour all round.

BLACKWASHED

In 1984 and 1985–86 the West Indies won all 10 Tests in what were called "blackwashes". All the margins were big. In both series it was the West Indian fast bowlers Malcolm Marshall and Joel Garner who did most damage to England. In 1984, in the second Test at Lord's, England got a first-innings lead, and David Gower was able to declare on the last morning and set the West Indies 342 to win. Greenidge made 214 not out and the West Indies won by nine

'BIG BIRD' *Joel Garner, the tall and dangerous West Indies fast bowler.*

wickets. Greenidge made another double-century at Old Trafford. In the 1985–86 series, 94 of the 98 England wickets to fall were taken by fast bowlers. Viv Richards made 110 not out in the fifth Test, his century coming in 56 balls, still the fastest hundred in terms of balls received in Test cricket.

England's run of defeats ended in the first rain-interrupted Test of 1988, but normal service was soon resumed and the West Indies won the next four in a rainy summer, in which only three centuries were made. For one reason or another, England had four captains in this series: Mike Gatting, John Emburey (2), Chris Cowdrey and Graham Gooch. Marshall, with 35 wickets, was the star.

England under Gooch unluckily lost 2–1 in 1989–90. England won the first Test by nine wickets, the second was washed out with no play at all, and in the third, chasing only 150, they were forced to come off at 120 for 5 because of bad light after Gooch's hand had been broken, amid suggestions of a West Indies' "go-slow" until it was too dark to continue. The West Indies levelled at Barbados, with Curtley Ambrose getting 8 for 45 in the second innings, and won the series at Antigua, where Greenidge and Haynes set a first-wicket partnership record for the West Indies with 298.

The 1991 series was drawn 2–2. England won at Headingley, where Graeme Hick made his long-awaited debut. But it was Graham Gooch, who carried his bat in the second innings for 154 out of England's 253, who was the hero. Rain spoiled an even Test at Lord's and the West Indies took a 2–1 lead by winning at Trent Bridge and Edgbaston. England tied the rubber at the Oval after the West Indies followed on.

The 1993–94 series, when Mike Atherton and Richie Richardson were captains, was the series of Brian Lara. The West Indies won the first three Tests, coming from behind in the third at Trinidad, bowling England out for 46 in the second innings, their lowest total against the West Indies and only one more than their lowest ever. Ambrose took 6 for 24. England then won in Barbados with Alec Stewart making a century in each innings. However, everything became secondary to Brian Lara's performance in the last Test in Antigua, where he scored 375 runs, the highest-ever Test innings. It took 766 minutes, and he faced 538 balls and hit 45 boundaries. His aggregate for the series was 798, average 99.75.

In 1995 Dominic Cork made an impressive debut for England at Lord's, with 7 for 43 in the second innings to get England level after the West Indies won at Headingley, but the West Indies went ahead again on a dangerous pitch at Edgbaston, exploited by the fast bowlers. A hat-trick by Cork helped level it again at Old Trafford, and the fifth and sixth Tests were drawn, with the West Indies making 692 for 8 declared at the Oval, their highest total against England.

GOOCH *An inspiring batsman, in 1991.*

TEST RESULTS

ENGLAND v WEST INDIES

	Matches	Eng	WI	Draw	Series	Eng	WI	Draw
In England	65	18	28	19	15	5	8	2
In West Indies	50	9	20	21	11	2	3	6
Totals	115	27	48	40	26	7	11	8

ENGLAND v NEW ZEALAND

New Zealand entered the Test fold in 1929–30 when A.E.R. Gilligan's touring side to Australia played three Tests against New Zealand, captained by T.C. Lowry. The first was at Christchurch, and England won by eight wickets. C.S. Dempster proved the best New Zealand batsman, scoring his country's first century (136) at Wellington, and incidentally putting on 276 with John Mills (117) for the first wicket, which remains the highest stand for New Zealand against England for any wicket.

For the first 40 years or so of their meetings, England had much the better of the matches between the countries. In the second of the two-match 1932–33 series, Walter Hammond made 336 not out, the highest Test score at the time. Since he was only once out, his average of 563.00 for the series remains, unsurprisingly, a record for all Tests.

In 1949 at Lord's Martin Donnelly scored 206, which remains the only double-century by a New Zealander against England. In 1954–55 at Auckland, New Zealand were dismissed for 26, the lowest score by any country in Tests. New Zealand were nevertheless given their only five-Test tour to date in 1958, managing only one draw, in a rain-ruined match at the Oval. In 1965 John Edrich scored 310 not out for England at Headingley. In another defeat for New Zealand in 1969, Glenn Turner carried his bat at Lord's for 43 not out in a total of 131, and at 22 years 63 days remains the youngest ever to perform the feat in Tests. Dick Motz, at the Oval, became the first New Zealander to take 100 Test wickets.

Although New Zealand lost 2–0 in a three-match series in 1973, there was evidence that better things were coming. Set 479 to win at Trent Bridge, they passed 400 with only five out, but were all out for 440. At Lord's New Zealand made 551 for 9 declared. Captain Bev Congdon made 176 and 175 in these innings. Vic Pollard also made two centuries and averaged 100.06.

The 1974–75 series was overshadowed by the accident to New Zealand debutant Ewen Chatfield, who suffered a hair-line fracture of the skull when struck by a ball from Peter Lever. He swallowed his tongue and his heart stopped. Fortunately MCC physio Bernard Thomas resuscitated him and he made a full recovery.

ARISE, SIR RICHARD

England toured New Zealand after a tour of Pakistan in 1977–78, in which Geoffrey Boycott, because Mike Brearley had broken his arm, took over the England captaincy. New Zealand won at Wellington, where Richard Hadlee took 6 for 26 (10 in the match) to dismiss England for 64 in the second innings. It was New Zealand's first win over England in their 48th Test. The series was drawn, with Geoff Howarth making a century in each innings at Auckland.

England made a clean sweep, 3–0, in 1978, but in 1983 New Zealand won their first Test in England, by five wickets at Headingley, although losing the series 3–1. The 1983–84 series saw New Zealand's big breakthrough. Dismissing England for 82 and 93 at Christchurch, they won by an innings and 132. Richard Hadlee was the star, taking eight wickets and top-scoring with 99 in 81 balls. Two draws gave New Zealand their first series win against England.

On their next trip to England in 1986, New Zealand repeated the formula, winning the middle one of three Tests for another 1–0 win.

A dull series in 1987–88 did not produce a win, the main excitement being the century made by Mark Greatbatch on his debut. England won the final Test to win 1–0 in 1990, where the chief interest was the farewell to Test cricket of the already knighted Sir Richard Hadlee at Edgbaston. His eight wickets in the match took his total of Test victims to 431, then the world record. England's successes continued in the 1990s, with a 2–0 win in 1991–92, notable for an unusual ending to the first Test.

IAN BOTHAM'S *356th Test wicket; Jeff Crowe lbw breaks the record, Oval 1986.*

With New Zealand's last pair together, 4 needed to avoid an innings defeat, and three overs remaining, captain Martin Crowe decided a boundary would save the game, as England would not have time to bat. Trying to hit a 4, he miscued and was caught at cover. In this match four players, two from each side, were out in the 90s, a Test record. New Zealand's Dipak Patel and John Wright were run out and stumped respectively for 99.

Thanks to an innings win at Trent Bridge, England won the 1994 series 1–0, and then won the 1996–97 series 2–0, after New Zealand had saved the first Test at Auckland with a last-wicket stand of 166 minutes between Nathan Astle (102 not out) and Danny Morrison (14 not out). They had come together with New Zealand only 11 ahead and England to bat again.

TEST RESULTS

ENGLAND v NEW ZEALAND

	Matches	Eng	NZ	Draw	Series	Eng	NZ	Draw
In New Zealand	38	15	2	21	15	9	1	5
In England	40	21	2	17	12	10	1	1
Totals	78	36	4	38	27	19	2	6

AUSTRALIA v WEST INDIES

The West Indies played their first Tests against Australia when touring in 1930–31. They lost the first four Tests, but won the last. Bradman and Ponsford each topped 400 runs for Australia, and Grimmett took 33 wickets, while George Headley made two centuries for the visitors. The same 4–1 result was recorded in the West Indies' next tour in 1951–52, but the matches were more closely fought, particularly at Melbourne, where Australia needed a last-wicket stand of 38 to win.

Ian Johnson led the first Australian Test tour to the West Indies in 1954–55 and won 3–0 in a series remarkable for heavy scoring, 21 centuries being scored. At Bridgetown, the West Indies' captain Denis Atkinson (219) and wicket-keeper Clairmonte Depeiza (122) came together at 147 for 6, facing a total of 668, and put on 347, which remains the highest seventh-wicket partnership in Test cricket. At Kingston, in the fifth Test, five Australian batsmen scored centuries and five West Indian bowlers conceded over 100 runs, as Australia made 758 for 8 declared, the fourth-highest total in Tests (three of the four at Kingston!). But in this match Clyde Walcott made a century in each innings to become the only batsman to perform this feat twice in one Test series. In fact, he made five centuries in all, and his aggregate of 827 is sixth in the all-time list. Neil Harvey, however, topped the averages at 108.33.

FRANK WORRELL TROPHY

The series in Australia in 1960–61 is one of the great series, and led to the presentation of the Frank Worrell Trophy, named after the West Indian captain, to the winners. It got off to a superb start at Brisbane with the first of only two tied Tests. Australia required 233 to win and recovered from 92 for 6 to require 6 with three wickets left when the last over began, bowled by Wes Hall. A leg-bye was followed by Benaud caught behind for 52. A bye to the keeper came from the fourth ball and a single from a dropped skier from the fifth. Grant was run out with a throw from the boundary when going for a third and winning run off the sixth – 232 for 9, level. On the seventh ball another winning run was tried but, when Solomon threw down the wicket from sideways on for another run out, the match was tied. Alan Davidson became the first player to complete 100 runs and 10 wickets in a Test. Australia won the second Test, the West Indies the third, and the fourth was drawn after Ken Mackay and Lindsay Kline survived 100 minutes for Australia's last wicket at Adelaide. Rohan Kanhai made a century in each innings. Australia won the deciding Test by two wickets. Conrad Hunte topped the batting for the West Indies and Neil Hawke the bowling for Australia.

Australia beat an ageing West Indian touring side 3–1 in 1968–69 with Doug Walters making four centuries in four matches, including 242 and 103 in the fifth Test at Sydney. He averaged 116.50. Two wins kept Australia on top in the West Indies in 1972–73.

After the West Indies, with a new resurgent team led by Clive Lloyd, had won the first World Cup, the series in Australia in 1975–76 was billed as for the "world championship". After Australia won the first Test and the West Indies the second, the West Indies disappointed, and Australia won the last four Tests. The destroyers were Dennis Lillee and Jeff Thomson, ably assisted by Gary Gilmour, in the bowling, and skipper Greg Chappell in the batting, his average of 117.00 being twice anybody else's.

World Series Cricket meant the teams in the West Indies in 1977–78 weren't representative. However, the West Indies' 3–1 win gave them the Frank Worrell Trophy which they were to hold for 17 years. Back with full-strength sides in Australia in 1979–80, the West Indies confirmed their new superiority. Their fast-bowling battery of Andy Roberts, Michael Holding, Joel Garner and Colin Croft were the masters. While the 1981–82 series was drawn 1–1, the West Indies won 3–0 at home in 1983–84 in a series remarkable for the fact that they did not lose a second-innings wicket all series. With the West Indies superior all round, Allan Border nevertheless

GREG CHAPPELL *had a superb series in 1975–76, averaging 117 and leading Australia to a 5–1 series victory.*

made most runs in the series, and at Trinidad he scored 98 not out and 100 not out, batting for over 10½ hours. The West Indies won a very bad-tempered series in 1984–85. Australian captain Kim Hughes resigned in tears after the second Test, and Allan Border took over. The West Indies won the first three Tests but Lloyd declared too late in the fourth and Australia held out for a draw, ending a run of 11 successive wins by West Indies. Australia then won the fifth Test at Sydney.

TOP TEST BOWLER *Malcolm Marshall, the Windies' most successful bowler, in 1990–91.*

Under Viv Richards, the West Indies won 3–1 in Australia in 1988–89 when the short-pitched bowling of their four fast bowlers caused a lot more ill-tempered comment. The West Indies won the first three Tests to ensure retention of the Frank Worrell Trophy. Courtney Walsh surprised himself with a hat-trick in the first Test, spread over both innings – the last wicket in the first and the third and fourth to fall in the second innings. In a brave 13-wicket performance at Perth, Merv Hughes bettered this with a unique Test hat-trick with wickets in three separate overs. In the West Indies' first innings he took the ninth wicket with the last ball of one over and the tenth with the first ball of the next. He completed the hat-trick with his first ball of the West Indies' second innings. In the third Test at Melbourne, Malcolm Marshall took his 300th Test wicket. Australia won the fourth Test and drew the last, with Dean Jones getting 216.

The West Indies maintained their superiority 2–1 in 1990–91, but it was another bad-tempered series, remarkable for the dismissal of Dean Jones in the second Test at Georgetown. Thinking he was bowled (not hearing a no-ball call), he was returning to the pavilion when Carl Hooper, who fielded the ball, pulled a stump from the ground. Jones was given run out, which turned out to be an umpiring mistake.

The same 2–1 score for the West Indies was repeated in 1992–93 in Australia, but they had to win the last two Tests. Brian Lara announced his arrival in the top flight with an innings of 277 in the drawn third Test. The West Indies won the fourth Test by one run. Australia were set 186 to win, and seemed out of it at 74 for 7, but the last-wicket pair put on 40 and just failed to clinch the series. Having escaped, the West Indies won the last Test in three days by an innings. Curtley Ambrose, with 19 wickets in the two Test wins and 33 in all, was the man of the series.

Australia, under Mark Taylor, at last beat the West Indies in 1994–95, West Indies' first series defeat in 15 years and the first on their own soil for 22 years. In fact, they had won 20 and drawn 9 of their 29 previous series. After three Tests, in which Australia won the first, rain the second and the West Indies the third, the final decisive Test was fought at Kingston, Jamaica. Australia won decisively by an innings and 53 runs, with outstanding contributions from the Waugh twins, Steve (200) and Mark (126), who put on 271 together, more than half Australia's total and more than either of the West Indies' innings.

The West Indies went to Australia in 1996–97 to try to reassert their mastery but lost the first two Tests by 123 and 124 runs. They came back to win the third Test by six wickets, but Australia clinched the Frank Worrell Trophy in the fourth by an emphatic margin of an innings and 83 runs. An easy 10-wicket win for the West Indies in the final Test only narrowed the defeat to 3–2. Wicket-keeper Ian Healey topped the series' batting averages for Australia with 356 runs at 59.33 while Glenn McGrath topped the bowling with 26 wickets at 17.42. Rick Ponting achieved the curious bowling figures for the series of one wicket for no runs, having come on to complete an over when Steve Waugh was injured. So Australia emphasized that, for the time being, they were the world's leading power.

TEST RESULTS

AUSTRALIA v WEST INDIES

	Matches	Aus	WI	Draw	Series	Aus	WI	Draw
In Australia	52	25	18	9*	11	6	4	1
In West Indies	34	10	11	13	7	3	4	0
Totals	86	35	29	22*	18	9	8	1

* includes one tie

SOUTH AFRICA v NEW ZEALAND

The first Test series not to involve either England or Australia began in 1931–32 when the South African tourists, who had lost 5–0 in Australia, played two Tests in New Zealand, winning both easily. Twenty-one years later South Africa won a repeat two-match tour 1–0, notable for a stand between Jackie McGlew (255 not out) and Anton Murray (109) of 246, still South Africa's biggest in Tests for the seventh wicket.

SUTCLIFFE SOLDIERS ON

In 1953–54 New Zealand toured South Africa for a five-match series. Although South Africa won 4–0, the series is remembered for the magnificent innings of 80 not out by Bert Sutcliffe in Johannesburg in a match which spanned Christmas. On Christmas Day, the New Zealand party was devastated as news came through of a train smash at home which killed 151 people, including the fiancée of tourist Bob Blair, who was playing. New Zealand had to go in to bat. The pitch was very fiery and South African fast bowler Neil Adcock, in his second Test, bowled Chapple and Poore off their chests and sent Sutcliffe and Miller to hospital. Sutcliffe, going in at 9 for 2, was immediately hit on the head (no helmets then) and sank to the turf. After five minutes, he was helped from the field and rushed to hospital, where he fainted under treatment. However, at 81 for 6, with New Zealand still needing 41 to avoid the follow-on, he returned to the wicket, face pale and head swathed in bandage, to a great welcome from the crowd. Inspired, Sutcliffe pulled his third ball for six, and when Adcock was brought on, cut him for four. He went on to play an innings of controlled, graceful violence. He was 55 not out when New Zealand reached 154 for 9, having had his bandages readjusted after they had been disturbed by his onslaught. And then the crowd stood in silence as 22-year-old Blair, who had been left in the hotel, came out to bat, to be met by Sutcliffe. They added 33 for the last wicket in 10 minutes, during which time Sutcliffe hit Tayfield for three sixes in an over and took a single to keep the strike, only to see Blair himself hit a six. It was Blair's only scoring stroke – he was soon stumped and walked off with Sutcliffe's arm around him.

In 1961–62 New Zealand, led by John Reid, who scored 546 runs, won their first Tests overseas and drew the series 2–2. In 1963–64 in New Zealand, with anti- apartheid demonstrators in evidence, all three Tests were drawn, though South Africa might have won them all.

The countries resumed their matches with a three-match series in South Africa in 1994–95. New Zealand won the first Test but South Africa took the last two to become the first side to come from behind this century to win a three-Test series. South Africa were then guests at Auckland for New Zealand's centenary match – the centenary of organized cricket – and spoiled the party by overturning a first-innings deficit to win by 93 runs.

TEST RESULTS

SOUTH AFRICA v NEW ZEALAND

	Matches	SA	NZ	Draw	Series	SA	NZ	Draw
In New Zealand	8	4	0	4	4	3	0	1
In South Africa	13	8	3	2	3	2	0	1
Totals	21	12	3	6	7	5	0	2

ENGLAND v INDIA

Indian cricket has a long tradition, and an English side toured India in 1888, but outstanding Indian players such as Ranjitsinjhi, Duleepsinjhi and the Nawab of Pataudi played their Test cricket for England until 1932, when India's inaugural Test took place at Lord's. England beat a side led by C.K. Nayudu by 158 runs. In 1933–34 England, led by recent "bodyline" captain Douglas Jardine, toured India, who played their first three home Tests. England won 2–0. "Lala" Amarnath made his country's first Test century. However, on the 1936 tour of England, Amarnath, India's best player, was sent home before the first Test after dissension in the Indian camp. The Maharajkumar of Vizianagram led the tourists. England won 2–0. In the drawn Test at Old Trafford, 588 runs were scored on the second day (398 for the loss of six wickets by England, who declared at 571 for 8, and 190 for no wicket by India). This remains the most runs scored in one day in a Test match.

There were distinguished debuts in the first series in England after the Second World War – Alec Bedser and Godfrey Evans for England, Gul Mahomed, A.H. Kardar, Vijay Hazare and Vinoo Mankad for India. England were too strong and won the only match decided. India won their first Test in 1951–52, however. It was at Madras, the last of five, and it allowed India to tie the rubber 1–1. Mankad took 12 wickets, 34 in the series.

The four-match series in 1952, which England won 3–0, was notable for the debut of Fred Trueman at Headingley. India were 0 for 4 in their second innings, Trueman having taken three wickets in eight balls. Things were even worse for India in 1959 when England, under P.B.H. May, recorded the first 5–0 success in any rubber in England. But it all changed when England sent a not-quite-representative side to India in 1961–62. After three draws, India won the last two Tests for their first series win over England. Nari Contractor was India's captain, Vijay Manjrekar and Salim Hurani their best batsman and bowler. Ken Barrington averaged 99 for England. The Nawab of Pataudi Jr made his debut in this series, and captained India in their next two against England, but without registering a win in eight Tests. This was despite a brave captain's innings at Headingley in 1967, when he made 148 out of 510 when India followed on – Geoffrey Boycott made 246 not out for England.

Under Ajit Wadekar, however, India won the next two series. In 1971, John Snow knocked over Sunny Gavaskar as they collided when the opener was going for a quick single, and Snow was disciplined by being dropped for the second Test. After two draws, India came from behind to win the third and last Test at the Oval, when Chandrasekhar's 6 for 38 shot England out in the second innings for 101. It was England's first defeat in 27 Tests. In 1972–73, in a five-match series, India recovered from losing the first Test to win 2–1. Chandrasekhar's 35 wickets in the series remains a record for India. England won all three Tests in 1974, the last for the loss of only two wickets. David Lloyd made 214 not out and, by virtue of playing only one other innings, averaged 260 in his first Test series.

Captain Tony Greig led England to a 3–1 win in India in 1976–77, their first there for 43 years, contributing immensely himself with an innings of 103 at Calcutta, batting for 414 minutes, including the whole of one day. England won

GREAT ALL-ROUNDER *India's leading Test wicket-taker, Kapil Dev.*

SUNNY DAY *Gavaskar during his double century at the Oval in 1973.*

again, 1–0, in 1974, but the series will be remembered for Gavaskar's magnificent innings at the Oval, when India were set 438 to win. He batted for 490 minutes and made 221, by which time India were 389 for 4. They finished just short at 429 for 8.

England beat India by 10 wickets in India's Golden Jubilee Test at Bombay in 1979 (celebrating the formation of the Board of Control for Cricket). Two outstanding English performances came from Ian Botham (the first to score a century and take 10 wickets in a match – in fact 114 and 13 for 106) and Bob Taylor (the first wicket-keeper to make 10 dismissals in a Test).

There were six Tests in India in 1981–82. India won the first; there then followed five long draws. Captain Gavaskar made 172 in 708 minutes in the second Test, and was on the field for all but four balls of the five days. In Madras, Gundappa Viswanath, Gavaskar's brother-in-law, made 222 in 638 minutes, the highest score by an Indian against England. In 1982 England won the first Test and drew the remaining two.

TRAGIC TOUR

The series in 1984–85 was marked by tragedy. The Indian Prime Minister, Mrs Indira Gandhi, was assassinated three days after the touring party arrived, and before the first Test the British Deputy High Commissioner to Western India was murdered, having entertained the tourists the day before. England won the series 2–1, despite losing the first Test when 18-year-old spinner Laxman Sivaramakrishnan took six wickets in each innings, and despite Mohammad Azharuddin becoming the first Test cricketer to make centuries in each of his first three Tests. He averaged 109.75 in his first series. At Madras, Mike Gatting and Graeme Fowler each made double centuries in England's 652 for 7 declared.

India, led by Kapil Dev, had their revenge in 1986 in England, winning 2–0 with one drawn. Dilip Vengsarkar set a record by becoming the first overseas player to make three Test centuries at Lord's.

England's 1–0 win in three Tests in 1990 was notable for the match at Lord's when Graham Gooch made 333 and 123, the first being the highest innings in England-India Tests and his total of 456 being the highest aggregate in a Test. He is the only batsman in first-class cricket to score 300 and 100 in the same match. England's total of 653 for 4 declared is the highest in England-India Tests. For India, Azharuddin made a century in 87 balls; Kapil Dev, partnering the number 11, hit a Test-record four successive sixes in an over, the last saving the follow-on; and the 17-year-old Sachin Tendulkar took a breathtaking catch in the deep. At Old Trafford, Tendulkar, at 17 years 122 days, became the second-youngest Test century-maker, and at the Oval, India made their highest score against England: 606 for 9 declared. Gooch's aggregate of 752 runs (average 125.33) is a record for a three-match series. Azharuddin did his best for India with 426 runs.

India's revenge in 1992–93 was complete, as they won all three matches, two by an innings and the other by eight wickets. Newcomer Vinod Kambli made 224 in his third Test match. Both he and his former school-fellow Tendulkar averaged 100 for the series. In 1996 in England, the home side won a well-fought series 1–0. Saurav Ganguly became only the third batsman to score a century in his first two Test innings. He averaged 105.00 for the series.

TEST RESULTS

ENGLAND v INDIA

	Matches	Eng	India	Draw	Series	Eng	India	Draw
In England	41	22	3	16	13	11	2	0
In India	43	10	11	22	10	4	4	2
Totals	84	32	14	38	13	15	6	2

AUSTRALIA v NEW ZEALAND

ALLAN BORDER *at Christchurch on his way to a record career Test aggregate.*

Surprisingly, Australia and New Zealand did not meet each other in Test cricket until after the Second World War, when a match played at Wellington on March 29 and 30 1946 was retrospectively granted Test status by the ICC and thus became the first Test played after the war. W.A. Hadlee, father of Richard and his brothers, captained New Zealand and W.A. Brown captained Australia. New Zealand were dismissed for 42 and 54 and Australia won by an innings and 103. Bill O'Reilly took eight wickets in his last Test. The most notable Australian debutants were Ray Lindwall and Keith Miller.

Although each country toured the other in the 1960s, Tests were not resumed until 1973–74 in Australia with a three-Test tour in each country. Australia won 2–0 at home and drew 1–1 away, when New Zealand recorded the first victory over their neighbours at Christchurch, with Glenn Turner (101 and 110 not out) becoming the first New Zealander to get a 100 in each innings of a Test. At Wellington, both Chappell brothers performed the feat for Australia: Ian 145 and 121 and Greg 247 not out and 133, Greg's total of 380 runs being a new record for one Test. Australia won the series in 1976–77 and 1980–81 before New Zealand again won a match to tie the series in 1981–82.

In 1985–86, New Zealand, under J.V. Coney, went to Australia and won the series 2–1, thanks largely to the brilliant bowling of Richard Hadlee, who took 33 wickets at 12.50. His 9 for 52 in the first innings of the first Test at Brisbane is still the fourth-best innings analysis in Tests. Martin Crowe backed Hadlee up by being the top batsman. New Zealand proved it was no fluke by beating Australia 1–0 in the same season in New Zealand. In the third Test at Auckland, they came from a deficit of 56 to win by eight wickets.

Australia won 1–0 in Australia in 1987–88 but only after their last pair held out for four overs to draw the last Test. Hadlee in this match equalled Botham's world record number of Test wickets, 373. In 1989–90, there was one Test in each country, New Zealand recording the only win at Wellington.

The first Test in New Zealand in 1992–93 at Christchurch was notable for Allan Border passing Sunil Gavaskar's Test aggregate of 10,122 – Border's 88 took him to 10,161. Australia won, but New Zealand won the third Test to square the series. In 1993–94, the sides met in Australia. With Martin Crowe forced to go home after the drawn first Test, Australia won the second by an innings and 222 and the third by an innings and 96. Craig McDermott took his 200th Test wicket, and at Brisbane Allan Border played his 150th Test and held his 150th catch, as well as scoring a century.

TEST RESULTS

AUSTRALIA v NEW ZEALAND

	Matches	Aus	NZ	Draw	Series	Aus	NZ	Draw
In New Zealand	41	22	3	16	13	11	2	0
In Australia	43	10	11	22	10	4	4	2
Totals	84	32	14	38	23	15	6	2

AUSTRALIA v INDIA

India's first Test series against Australia was played in 1947–48, and was Don Bradman's last home season. It was a weakened Indian side under Lala Amarnath and Australia won 4–0, with one Test ruined by rain after India, ironically, had gained a first-innings lead. Bradman made a century in the first Test, two in the third and another in the fourth, and finished with an average of 178.75.

Australia comfortably won a shortened tour of India in 1956–57, and on the first full tour of India in 1959–60 won 2–1. India's win by 119 runs in the second Test at Kanpur was due to Jasu Patel, who took 9 for 69 and 5 for 55. The first are the best innings figures by an Indian bowler in Tests. Captain Richie Benaud and Alan Davidson each took 29 wickets in Australia's series win.

In 1964–65 India managed to draw the next series 1–1, a crowd of 42,000 watching them scrape home on the last day at Bombay with two wickets to spare.

Australia maintained their superiority through the rest of the 1960s and 1970s, winning 10 Tests to India's three, but the 1977–78 series in Australia, with World Series Cricket weakening the Aussies, was very exciting.

Australia won the first Test by 16 runs and the second by two wickets (after an Indian declaration), before India comfortably won the next two Tests. In the last Test, Australia made 505 and (not enforcing the follow-on) 256 and India, after a first-innings 269, needed 493 to win. With 10 players reaching double figures, they got to 415 for 6, but eventually lost by 47.

In 1979–80, in India, the Indians won their first series against Australia by 2–0. Aussie skipper Kim Hughes made most runs, 594, but the Indian bowling, led by Kapil Dev with 28 wickets, was decisive. In three three-match series in the 1980s, each side won one Test only, in 1980–81 when they tied 1–1. With Dennis Lillee bowling well in the high-scoring series, Australia needed only 143 in the last innings of the series to take the series 2–0 but, with two bowlers (Kapil Dev and Doshi) bowling with leg injuries, India skittled Australia for 83 to tie the series. In this Test, at Melbourne, Indian skipper Sunil Gavaskar was so incensed at an lbw decision against him that he persuaded his opening parnter, C.P.S. Chauhan, to leave the field with him. India's manager, S.K. Durrani, met them at the gate and persuaded Chauhan to return, with what turned out to be an excellent result for them.

Australia completely outplayed India in Australia in 1991–92, winning 4–0. Australia's Allan Border won his 126th cap in the first Test, passing Sunil Gavaskar's previous record of 125. Craig McDermott, with 31 wickets, was the player of the series. In the last Test, Kapil Dev became the second bowler in Test history, after Richard Hadlee, to claim 400 Test wickets.

In 1996–97 Australia, in India for a one-day tournament, played a one-off Test at Delhi. Sachin Tendulkar captained India for the first time. With keeper N.R. Mongia getting 152 and Anil Kumble nine wickets, India won easily by seven wickets.

NAYAN MONGIA *cover-drives on his way to a century at Delhi, October 1996.*

TEST RESULTS

AUSTRALIA v INDIA

	Matches	Aus	Ind	Draw	Series	Aus	Ind	Draw
In Australia	25	16	3	6	6	4	0	2
In India	26	8	6	12*	7	3	2	2
Totals	51	24	9	18*	13	7	2	4

* Includes one tie

WEST INDIES v INDIA

Tests between the West Indies and India started with J.D.C. Goddard's team visiting India for a five-Test series in 1948-49. The strong West Indian side, which had recently beaten England, included Everton Weekes and Clyde Walcott. Everton Weekes, having made a century in his last Test innings against England, scored centuries in his first four in India, including two in the third Test. Weekes was then run out for 90 when attempting a sixth successive century. The West Indies won the only match decided, the fourth Test. In the last, India, chasing 361 to win, were 355 for 8 at the close, with their last player, P. Sen, absent hurt. Weekes made 779 runs, average 111.28.

The West Indies maintained their supremacy in four series in the 1950s and 1960s, winning 11 matches to none. In India in 1958–59, there were complaints about the use of bouncers by the West Indians Wes Hall and Roy Gilchrist and Gilchrist was sent home for bowling beamers. In 1961–62, the West Indies achieved a 5–0 whitewash. At Bridgetown the Indian captain, N.J. Contractor, suffered a fractured skull when hit by a ball from C.C. Griffith, which ended his Test career.

However. India scored their first victory against the West Indies in 1970–71, in the West Indies, and it was enough to win the series. India won the second Test at Port-of-Spain, the Test in which Sunil Gavaskar made his Test debut. He scored 65 and 67 not out. Dilip Sardesai made 112 as India won by seven wickets. In India's first innings, 34-year-old Jack Noriega, whose four Tests all came in this series, took 9 for 95 in his second Test, the best analysis recorded by a West Indian. In the fifth Test (his fourth), Gavaskar became only the second batsman (after K.D. Walters) to score a century and a double-century in the same Test. He scored 774 runs in the series, average 154.80. Ajit Wadekar was the successful skipper.

With Clive Lloyd as captain, the West Indies won excitingly in 1974–75 in India by 3–2. Gordon Greenidge (with 93 run out and 107) and Viv Richards (4 and 3) made their debuts in the first Test. The West Indies won the final deciding Test, by 201 runs, Lloyd making 242 not out, and topping the batting, while Andy Roberts' 32 wickets was then a series record for the West Indies.

The 1975–76 series in the West Indies was a sour affair. After the West Indies won the first Test, India levelled in the third with a magnificent win. They were set 403 to win in the fourth innings and, with Gavaskar getting 102 and Viswanath 112, won by six wickets. Their score of 406 for 4 remains the highest fourth-innings total made to win a Test match. The West Indies won the fourth and final Test with what the Indians regarded as intimidatory bowling on a variable pitch. In protest, Bedi declared India's first innings total at 306 for 6, with two players injured. India were all out 97 in the second innings with five players absent hurt, although at first it was assumed Bedi had declared with five wickets down to reinforce his protests about the dangerous bowling. The West Indies needed only 13 to win. Patel, one of the injured batsmen, was only once out and averaged 207 for the series.

India took their revenge in 1978–79 with their first series win over the West Indies in India. Alvin Kallicharran and Gavaskar were captains. It was a high-scoring, six-Test series, with the only result coming in the fourth Test in Madras. India won by three wickets in a match which became a bouncer war. Gavaskar led the series batting with 732 runs, average 91.50, while Karsan Ghavri took 27 wickets.

The West Indies have dominated since, with India's only successes being twice to tie series 1–1 in India. In 1982–83, the West Indies won a Test remarkably by taking four Indian wickets and scoring 173 for 6 in the final session of play, with four balls of their allotted 26 overs left. In 1983–84 at Ahmedabad, Gavaskar scored the runs that took his Test aggregate past the record of 8,114 set by Geoffrey Boycott.

In the tied series in India in 1987–88 there was a remarkable Test debut by Narendra Hirwani, a little-known bespectacled leg-spinner from Gorakhpur who took 8 for 61 and 8 for 75 in India's victory at Madras. His 16 for 136 remain the best match figures by a debutant in a Test match, narrowly beating Bob Massie's 16 for 137 for Australia against England in 1972.

In 1994–95, the West Indies tied the series in the last Test to maintain their 15-year unbeaten record. Jimmy Adams, who made 174 and 78, both times not out, ended the series with an average of 173.33.

With the batting geniuses Brian Lara and Sachin Tendulkar captaining the sides, the West Indies won the series of 1996–97 by virtue of a single win at Bridgetown. On an increasingly difficult wicket they were bowled out for 140 in the third innings but dismissed India, needing only 120 in the fourth, for 81.

161 NOT OUT *Clive Lloyd on his way to 161 at Calcutta in 1983–84, when he led West Indies to a 3–0 series win.*

TEST RESULTS

WEST INDIES v INDIA

	Matches	WI	Ind	Draw	Series	WI	Ind	Draw
In India	37	14	5	18	8	5	1	2
In West Indies	33	14	2	17	7	6	1	0
Totals	70	28	7	35	15	11	2	2

WEST INDIES v NEW ZEALAND

J.D.C. Goddard's strong West Indian side which toured Australia in 1951–52 played two Tests in New Zealand, the first between the countries. They won the first by five wickets and drew the second.

New Zealand won a match in the West Indies' next visit in 1955–56, but lost the series 3–1, thanks to the batting of Everton Weekes. New Zealand's win came in the last Test when the West Indies were dismissed for 77, their lowest Test score at the time. The third series in New Zealand, 1968–69, was drawn. Seymour Nurse played innings for the West Indies of 168 and 258, averaging 111.60 for the series. All five Tests were drawn in New Zealand's first tour to the West Indies in 1971–72, but in 1979–80 back in New Zealand they won the three-Test series 1–0. The West Indians behaved badly after New Zealand's one-wicket win (from a leg-bye) in the first Test, and only Desmond Haynes attended the presentation. In the second Test, the West Indies refused to take the field after tea on the third day as a protest against an umpire, but did so eventually and saved the match.

The West Indies got their revenge 2–0 in the Caribbean in 1984–85 amid a flurry of bouncers from Marshall and Garner. After a draw in 1986–87, the West Indies won both two-Test series in the 1990s by 1–0.

TEST RESULTS

WEST INDIES v NEW ZEALAND

	Matches	WI	NZ	Draw	Series	WI	NZ	Draw
In New Zealand	17	7	4	6	6	3	1	2
In West Indies	11	3	0	8	3	2	0	1
Totals	28	10	4	14	9	5	1	3

INDIA v PAKISTAN

The bitter rivalry between India and Pakistan began in 1952–53, when India hosted Pakistan's first Test series after the partition of India. A.H. Kardar, Pakistan's first captain, had previously played for India (as Abdul Hafeez), as had Amid Elahi. India won the first match, Pakistan the second. In this match, Nazar Mohammad of Pakistan carried his bat for 124 not out in a score of 331 and became the first player to be on the field for an entire Test match. India took the series 2–1. It was a low-scoring series with the bowling of Vinoo Mankad for India and Fazal Mahmood for Pakistan having the upper hand.

FIRST AMONG RIVALS *Javed Miandad of Pakistan leg-glides against India. His 280 not out is the highest between the countries.*

From then on, draws dominated the series, there being a run of 13 consecutively. The 1954–55 series in Pakistan was the first-ever five-Test series not to produce a result. The 1960–61 series in India also produced five draws. Fear of defeat was stifling adventure.

War between the countries in 1965 kept them apart for 17 years, Tests resuming in 1978–79, when Pakistan won 2–0 despite the debut of Kapil Dev in the first Test. Fast bowlers Imran Khan and Sarfraz Nawaz were decisive on the fast pitches. India, under Gavaskar, reversed the result in India the following season by winning 2–0, Kapil Dev's 32 wickets at 17.68 being the vital difference between the sides. India's win at Bombay was their first over Pakistan for 27 years.

In 1982–83, it was Pakistan's turn again in a record-breaking series. They won 3–0, captain Imran Khan's 40 wickets remaining the best series haul for any Pakistani in Tests. At Hyderabad, Mudassar Nazar (231) and Javed Miandad (280 not out) put on 451 for the third wicket, equalling the then highest stand in Test cricket. And at Lahore, Mudassar became the second Pakistani to carry his bat in a Test innings, the first having been his father, Nazar Mohammad, 30 years earlier, also against India, $3\frac{1}{2}$ years before Mudassar was born.

The only series of four succeeding ones to produce a result was in 1986–87 in India when, after four dull draws, Pakistan won an exciting final Test. It seemed unlikely when their first-innings total of 116 was passed by India with four wickets down, but they then took the last six wickets for 19. By setting India 221 to win, Pakistan were confident, but Gavaskar played a great innings of 96 in 323 minutes, being eighth out at 180. India were dismissed for 204 and Pakistan won by 16 runs.

A series in 1989–90 in Pakistan resulted in four draws, making a total of 33 out of 44 Tests played. India have not yet won in 20 Tests in Pakistan.

TEST RESULTS

INDIA v PAKISTAN

	Matches	Ind	Pak	Draw	Series	Ind	Pak	Draw
In India	24	4	2	18	5	2	1	2
In Pakistan	20	0	5	15	5	0	2	3
Totals	44	4	7	33	10	2	3	5

ENGLAND v PAKISTAN

Pakistan toured England under A.H. Kardar in 1954 to play four Tests against Len Hutton's Ashes-winning side. England won the second Test, at Trent Bridge, by an innings, and in the draws at Lord's and Old Trafford dismissed Pakistan for 87 and 90 respectively. So it was a big shock when Pakistan tied the series at the Oval with a 24-run win. Pakistan's tail-enders did wonders, changing 51 for 7 to 133 in the first innings and doubling 82 for 8 to 164 in the second. But Fazal Mahmood, with six wickets in each innings, was the hero. His 20 wickets in the series was equalled by John Wardle for England, whose wickets cost only 8.80 each.

Pakistan did not win another match for nine series, five of which England won. In 1968–69 in Pakistan, the matches were held amidst rioting – the third Test at Karachi being abandoned with England 502 for 7 in the first innings; Alan Knott, seeking his first Test century, was 96 not out. Days later, England left for home. Pakistan had successes without winning. At Edgbaston in 1971 they scored 608 for 7 declared, with Zaheer Abbas making 274, and at the Oval in 1974 they got 600 for 7 declared, with Zaheer contributing 240.

Pakistan won their second match against England at Lord's in 1982, when Mohsin Khan scored the first Test double-century there for 33 years, and Pakistan won by 10 wickets. Despite the all-round efforts of skipper Imran Khan, England won the series 2–1. But in Pakistan in 1983–84, Pakistan, under Zaheer Abbas, won their first series against England 1–0, by virtue of winning the first Test at

Karachi. When set to score 65 in the fourth innings, they lost seven wickets getting them.

Pakistan have won all four series against England since. An innings win at Headingley was enough in 1987 when, in the Oval Test, Pakistan scored 708, their highest total in Tests, with Javed Miandad getting 260.

The 1987–88 tour of Pakistan was notable for the argument in Faisalabad between England captain Mike Gatting and umpire Shakoor Rana, who refused to continue without an apology from Gatting for his behaviour. A whole day's play was lost until Gatting apologized under instruction from the TCCB. The only result went to Pakistan by an innings in the first Test, Abdul Qadir getting 9 for 56 in the first innings, the best Test analysis by a Pakistani, and the fifth-best in all Test cricket.

Pakistan won 2–1 in 1992. At Lord's, needing 138, they were 95 for 8, but got home when fast bowlers Wasim Akram (45 not out) and Waqar Younis (20 not out) added 46 to win. There were reprimands for bad behaviour for Pakistani players at Old Trafford, as well as 205 from Aamir Sohail. England won at Headingley, but Pakistan took the series with a 10-wicket win at the Oval. The wickets of the fast bowlers Wasim (21) and Waqar (22) made the vital difference.

In 1996, Pakistan won a three-match series 2–0, with better all-round cricket and five batsmen averaging over 60: Moin Khan (best with 79.00), Ijaz Ahmed, Salim Malik, Inzaman-ul-Haqand Saaed Anwar, while leg-breaker Mushtaq Ahmed took most wickets.

TEST RESULTS

ENGLAND v PAKISTAN

	Matches	Eng	Pak	Draw	Series	Eng	Pak	Draw
In England	37	13	7	17	10	5	3	2
In Pakistan	18	1	2	15	6	1	5	2
Totals	55	14	9	32	16	6	10	3

NEW ZEALAND v PAKISTAN

New Zealand first toured Pakistan in 1955–56, playing their first Test on matting at Karachi. Pakistan won the first two of a three-Test series. Of the 15 series between the countries, Pakistan have won 10 to New Zealand's two.

New Zealand's first series win came in 1969–70 in Pakistan when they won by five wickets in Lahore. It was New Zealand's first series win against any opposition and came 40 years after their first Test. In Karachi, Pakistan fielded the third instance of three brothers playing in one Test when Hanif, Mushtaq and Sadiq Mohammad all played, Hanif in his last Test. New Zealand's second series win was by 2–0 in New Zealand in 1984–85, revenge for a 2–0 defeat in Pakistan earlier in the season. Richard Hadlee's 16 wickets had much to do with it, although New Zealand only won the last Test by two wickets, their 278 for 8 (captain Jeremy Coney 111 not out) being the highest innings of the match.

Richard Hadlee made his Test debut against Pakistan in 1972–73 but Pakistan won the only Test decided by an innings. In a drawn Test at Auckland, New Zealand's Brian Hastings (110) and Richard Collinge (68 not out) added 151 for the last wicket, still the highest last-wicket stand in Tests.

Javed Miandad has been the outstanding batsman in Pakistan v New Zealand Tests, with the highest score (206 at Karachi in 1976–77) and the only instance of a century in each innings (at Hyderabad in 1984–85). The best partnership is 350 by Mushtaq Mohammad and Asif Igbal (Dunedin, 1972–73) and the best bowling 12 for 130 by Waqar Younis (Faisalabad 1990–91).

In 1996–97, a two-match series in Pakistan ended 1–1, with Pakistan's debutant Mohammad Zahid taking 11 for 130 in the second Test at Rawalpindi, the best by a Pakistani on Test debut and seventh-best by a debutant in all Tests.

TEST RESULTS

NEW ZEALAND v PAKISTAN

	Matches	NZ	Pak	Draw	Series	NZ	Pak	Draw
In Pakistan	20	2	12	6	7	1	5	1
In New Zealand	19	3	6	10	8	1	6	1
Totals	39	5	18	16	15	2	11	2

NEW ZEALAND v INDIA

Less than a week after finishing their first series in Pakistan in 1955–56, New Zealand began their first Test series against India. India won two of a five-match series, both by an innings, and had the better of the draws. "Fergie" Gupte's 34 wickets was the main difference between the sides, New Zealand's Bert Sutcliffe getting most runs, 611, and Vinoo Mankad, with 526 runs and 12 wickets, being a valuable all-rounder.

India won the two series in the 1960s, in 1967–68 winning their first Test away from home, and taking the series 3–1 thanks to excellent spin bowling. New Zealand were deprived of their first series win over India in 1969–70 when in the third and deciding Test rain interrupted once too often. Dismissing India for 89 on a damaged pitch in their first innings, New Zealand set India to get 268 to win and India were 76 for 7 when rain ended it.

New Zealand had to wait until 1980–81 for their first series success. In a rainy series in New Zealand, they won the only match decided by 62 runs at Wellington, captain Geoff Howarth being the match-winner with 137 in the first innings. Each side won at home in series in the late 1980s. A one-off Test in Hamilton in 1993–94 was drawn, and India retained their superiority with a 1–0 win in 1995–96, a victory at Bangalore being sufficient, with monsoon rains at Madras and Cuttack. The highest innings in the matches is 239 by New Zealand's Graham Dowling at Christchurch in 1967–68.

TEST RESULTS

NEW ZEALAND v INDIA

	Matches	NZ	Ind	Draw	Series	NZ	Ind	Draw
In India	21	2	9	10	6	0	5	1
In New Zealand	14	4	4	6	5	2	2	1
Totals	35	6	13	16	11	2	7	2

AUSTRALIA v PAKISTAN

On the way home from England in 1956, Ian Johnson's Australia played a Test in Pakistan, the first between the countries. Gul Mahomed played for Pakistan after eight appearances for India. The first day at Karachi, on a matting wicket, produced 95 runs, still the lowest for a full day's play in Tests: Australia 80, Pakistan 15 for 2. Pakistan eventually won by nine wickets, Fazal Mahmood taking 13 wickets for 114 runs.

Australia gained revenge 2–0 during a second visit in 1959–60, which preceded a tour of India. Captain Richie Benaud took 18 wickets in the three Tests. Single Tests in each country were played in 1964–65, both drawn. Aussie skipper Bobby Simpson got a century in each innings at Karachi and Ian Chappell made his debut at Melbourne.

Chappell was captain of Australia when Pakistan made their first three-match tour in 1972–73, and Australia won 3–0. Mushtaq Mohammad led Pakistan on tours in 1976–77 and 1978–79 and both tours ended 1–1. In the first, Imran Khan's hauls of six wickets in each innings at Sydney sealed Pakistan's first victory in Australia.

Pakistan's first rubber victory followed in 1979–80 in Pakistan, with Javed Miandad as captain. A seven-wicket win in Karachi was followed by two draws. At Lahore, Allan Border scored 150 and 153, the first player to reach 150 in each innings of a Test. Under Imran Khan, Pakistan won 3–0 in 1982–83, all easy wins. Leg-breaker Abdul Qadir's 22 wickets in the series were crucial.

The first five-Test series between the countries was won 2–0 by Australia at home in 1983–84. Graham Yallop was the most successful batsman, Geoff Lawson the best bowler. At the end of the series, three great Australians announced their retirements: Greg Chappell, who during the match had set an Australian record for runs scored at 7,110, beating Bradman's 6,996, and a world record for catches held (122, since beaten); Dennis Lillee, whose 355 wickets was then a world record; and Rodney Marsh, whose 355 wicket-keeping dismissals remains a world record.

Pakistan won 1–0 in Pakistan in 1988–89, thanks partly to captain Javed Miandad's batting, but the Australians objected officially to the umpiring at Karachi (this was the season after England captain Mike Gatting's dispute with an umpire in Pakistan). Australia won 1–0 in 1989–90, Pakistan 1–0 in 1994–95 and Australia 2–1 in 1995–96, all in their own countries. The home side has thus won the last eight series. This last series began in a bitter atmosphere after Australian players had made allegations of attempted bribery by at least one Pakistan player to lose in Pakistan the previous season. A Pakistani judge had rejected the charges and the Australian Board were unable to persuade the ICC to launch a full enquiry. However, the bad feeling passed and the series proved to be well-fought.

TEST RESULTS — AUSTRALIA v PAKISTAN

	Matches	Aus	Pak	Draw	Series	Aus	Pak	Draw
In Pakistan	17	2	7	8	7	1	5	1
In Australia	23	12	4	7	8	5	0	3
Totals	40	14	11	15	15	6	5	4

WEST INDIES v PAKISTAN

In 1957–58, A.H. Kardar took a Pakistan team on a five-match tour of the West Indies. It proved to be record-breaking. In the first Test at Bridgetown, Nasim-ul-Ghani of Pakistan became the youngest Test player till then at 16 years 248 days, Conrad Hunte made 142 in his first Test innings and, when Pakistan followed on 473 behind, Hanif Mohammad scored 337, the second-highest Test score till then, in 16 hours 10 minutes, then the longest innings in first-class cricket.

In the third Test at Kingston, Gary Sobers, aged 21, scored 365 not out, the highest score in Tests until 1993–94. With Hunte (260), he put on 446 for the second wicket, currently the fourth-highest Test stand. The West Indies made 790 for 3 declared, the third-highest Test score. In the fourth Test, Sobers made a century in each innings. Pakistan won the last Test, the West Indies taking the series 3–1. In the series, Sobers made 824 runs, average 137.33, while Hanif and Hunte also topped 600.

The following season, Pakistan won 2–1 in Pakistan, captain Fazal Mahmood getting 21 wickets in the three Tests. There was a gap of 15 years before the countries met again, and in the seven series since the West Indies have won three and drawn four.

In 1974–75 at Karachi both sides made their highest scores in Pakistan. Pakistan made 406 for 8 declared, with Wasim Raja and Majid Khan making centuries, and West Indies replied with 493, Alvin Kallicharran and Bernard Julien getting hundreds. Both matches in the series were drawn.

The final Test of 1976–77 in the West Indies was reached with the sides 1–1, West Indies winning the decider. In 1980–1981 in the Tests in Pakistan, West Indies won the only match decided, at Faisalabad, allowing Clive Lloyd to complete three series as captain against Pakistan by winning two series and drawing one.

Two series in the 1990s when Viv Richards and Imran Khan were captains were both drawn 1-1, as was the series in 1990–91.

There was a particularly fine performance by Abdul Qadir at Faisalabad in 1986–87 when he took 6 for 16 in helping rout the West Indies for 53, their lowest-ever total in Tests. At Bridgetown in 1987–88, Pakistan had a great opportunity to win their first series in the West Indies when in the last Test the West Indies, set 266 to win, and so draw the series, were 207 for 8. Jeffrey Dujon (29) and Winston Benjamin (40) provided the runs. In this match, a spectator was struck by Abdul Qadir after abusing him and the Pakistan manager paid the spectator not to press charges.

There was more trouble on Pakistan's next tour of the West Indies in 1992–93. Four Pakistan players were arrested on a beach in Grenada for "constructive possession" of marijuana. The Pakistanis, who protested their innocence, threatened to call off the tour, which was locally billed as for the "world championship". The charges were dropped, but the first Test was delayed by one day. The West Indies' eventual 2–0 win was the biggest since the first series in 1957–58. Richie Richardson was the winning captain.

TEST RESULTS — WEST INDIES v PAKISTAN

	Matches	WI	Pak	Draw	Series	WI	Pak	Draw
In West Indies	16	8	3	5	4	3	0	1
In Pakistan	15	4	4	7	5	1	1	3
Totals	31	12	7	12	9	4	1	4

ENGLAND v SRI LANKA

Sri Lanka was the eighth country to achieve Test status when in 1981–82 England played a Test in Colombo after touring India. Bandula Warnapura was Sri Lanka's first Test captain. England won by seven wickets. The first 50 for Sri Lanka was scored by Arjuna Ranatunga, who was 18 years 78 days old. Sri Lanka had the better of a draw at Lord's in 1984, when Sidath Wettimuny batted for 636 minutes, the longest Test innings at Lord's, to score 190, the highest score by a foreign batsman playing his first Test in England. So far, the teams have not played a series, only single Tests. England won in 1988 and 1991 but in 1992–93 Sri Lanka recorded their first victory at Colombo when, captained by Arjuna Ranatunga, they won by five wickets.

So far Sri Lanka have shown a definite liking for Lord's. The only three centuries made by their batsmen were made there, as was their best bowling performance, 5 for 69 by Rumesh Ratnayake in 1991.

TEST RESULTS

ENGLAND v SRI LANKA

	Matches	Eng	SL	Draw	Series	Eng	SL	Draw
In Sri Lanka	2	1	1	0	2	1	1	0
In England	3	3	0	1	3	2	0	1
Totals	5	3	1	1	5	3	1	1

FIRST TEST CAPTAIN *Bandula Warnapura at Colombo, February 1982.*

PAKISTAN v SRI LANKA

Sri Lanka visited Pakistan for a three-Test series in 1981–82. Pakistan, weakened in the first two Tests because of disputes over the captaincy, won 2–0. Imran Khan, returning in the third Test for Pakistan, took 14 wickets. In 1985–86, the result was repeated in Pakistan, but in a series which followed in Sri Lanka, Sri Lanka won at Colombo and drew the series. Pakistan won the series in 1991–92 and 1993–94, when the third Test was cancelled owing to civil disturbances following an election in Sri Lanka. In 1995–96, however, Sri Lanka won the series in Pakistan 2–1. After losing the first Test by an innings, Sri Lanka came from 110 behind on first innings to win the second by 42 runs and then took the third by 144.

TEST RESULTS

PAKISTAN v SRI LANKA

	Matches	Pak	SL	Draw	Series	Pak	SL	Draw
In Pakistan	12	6	2	4	4	3	1	0
In Sri Lanka	5	3	1	1	2	1	0	1
Totals	17	9	3	5	6	4	1	1

INDIA v SRI LANKA

Sri Lanka played a Test in Madras in 1982–83 which ended evenly poised with India needing 40 to win with three wickets left. In their first three-Test series, in Sri Lanka in 1985–86, Sri Lanka won 1–0, winning the second Test at Colombo, their first Test win in their 14th Test in five years. Sri Lanka battled hard to force the draw in the final Test at Kandy to win their first series.

In India in 1986–87 the Indian batting was far too strong, Dilip Vengsarkar and Kapil Dev each averaging over 100, and India won 2–0. Sri Lanka have not beaten India in a Test since. At Chandigarh in 1990–91, India's 21-year-old slow left-armer Venkatapathy Raju took 6 for 12 in the first innings and ended the match with the astonishing analysis of 53.5 overs, 38 maidens, 37 runs and 8 wickets.

After winning in Sri Lanka 1–0 in 1993–94, India won all three Tests in India later in the season by an innings. In the third Test, Kapil Dev took his 432nd Test wicket to pass the total of Richard Hadlee and become the highest wicket-taker in Test history.

In August 1997 Sri Lanka broke the 39-year-old record for the highest Test score by making 952 for 6 against India at Colombo. Sashan Jayasuriya and Roshan Mahanama made a record Test stand by adding 576 for the second wicket.

TEST RESULTS

INDIA v SRI LANKA

	Matches	Ind	SL	Draw	Series	Ind	SL	Draw
In India	8	6	0	2	4	3	0	1
In Sri Lanka	6	1	1	4	2	1	1	0
Totals	14	7	1	6	6	4	1	1

NEW ZEALAND v SRI LANKA

Sri Lanka visited New Zealand and Australia in 1982–83 with a weak side because 14 players had been banned for 25 years for touring South Africa, and three other key players had injuries. New Zealand won both Tests comfortably.

New Zealand won 2–0 in Sri Lanka in 1983–84, the drawn Test being the most noteworthy. Set 266 to win in 350 minutes, New Zealand, because of illness and injury, made no attempt and ended at 123 for 4. Only 117 were scored on the fifth day, a record for a last full day in Test cricket. In 1986–87 in Sri Lanka, only one drawn Test was played, the other two being cancelled because of public disturbance, after a bomb killed 150 near the tourists' hotel. There was another series without a result in 1990–91, but there were records in the first Test at Wellington. Sri Lanka made their then highest score, 497 for 9 declared, with Aravinda de Silva getting 267, still his country's highest. Facing a deficit of 323, New Zealand then made 671 for 4, still their highest score, with Martin Crowe getting 299, also still his country's best. Crowe and Andrew Jones (186) put on 467 for the third wicket, still the highest stand for any wicket in Test cricket. Sri Lanka won 1–0 in 1992–93 at home, but again there was a bomb before the Tests started, and six New Zealanders voted to return home. The first Test was drawn, but Sri Lanka won the second of a two-match series. The win was repeated in New Zealand in 1994–95, denting the celebrations for the centenary of organized cricket in New Zealand. At least New Zealand had the consolation of their wicket-keeper Adam Parore setting a new Test record of not conceding a bye while 2,323 runs were scored. The previous record, 1,484, was set by Alan Knott. New Zealand comfortably won a home series 2–0 in 1996–97.

TEST RESULTS — NEW ZEALAND v SRI LANKA

	Matches	NZ	SL	Draw	Series	NZ	SL	Draw
In New Zealand	9	4	1	4	4	2	1	1
In Sri Lanka	6	2	1	3	3	1	1	1
Totals	15	6	2	7	7	3	2	2

AUSTRALIA v SRI LANKA

Right at the end of the 1982–83 season, in April, Australia played a Test against Sri Lanka in Kandy, and lost only four wickets in winning by an innings and 38. In 1987–88 Sri Lanka played one match in Australia and lost by an innings and 108, with only 10,607 attending the four days. Since then there have been three series of two or three Tests each, with three draws being the sum of Sri Lanka's achievement. Sri Lanka's best chance of a win so far was at Colombo in 1992–93 when they made their highest Test score to date of 547 for 8 declared and led on first innings by 291. Wicket-keeper Romesh Kaluwitharana, on his Test debut, scored 132 not out from 158 deliveries. Set to get only 181 to win, Sri Lanka reached 127 for 2, but a dazzling catch by Allan Border to dismiss Aravinda de Silva turned the match, and Sri Lanka, having been on top for all but the last session, lost eight wickets for 37 runs to lose by 16. They drew the remaining two Tests, which were evenly fought. However, in the next series in Australia in 1995–96 Sri Lanka lost 3–0.

TEST RESULTS — AUSTRALIA v SRI LANKA

	Matches	Aus	SL	Draw	Series	Aus	SL	Draw
In Sri Lanka	4	2	0	2	2	2	0	0
In Australia	6	5	0	1	3	3	0	0
Totals	10	7	0	3	5	5	0	0

STARTLING DEBUT *Romesh Kaluwitharana for Sri Lanka in 1992–93.*

SOUTH AFRICA v WEST INDIES

South Africa's re-admittance to Test cricket after the apartheid ban which lasted 22 years was marked by the first meeting between them and the West Indies in a one-off Test at Bridgetown, Barbados, in the 1991–92 season. Unfortunately, the overall attendance was only 6,500 because of a spectator boycott over the omission from the West Indies team of fast bowler Anderson Cummins, which Bajans saw as just the last of a series of rebuffs to local players over recent years. As a placard said: "No Cummins, no goings". They missed a great match which South Africa might have won. All South Africa's players except skipper Kepler Wessels, who had made 24 appearances for Australia, were debutants, and one, Andrew Hudson, immediately became the first South African to make a century on Test debut by scoring 163, which helped give South Africa a first-innings lead of 83. When the West Indies were then dismissed in their second innings for 283, South Africa needed only 201 to win. When the last day began, they were 122 for 2, needing only another 79 runs. On a variable pitch, they managed to get only 26 of them, losing eight wickets in 20 overs, mostly to Curtley Ambrose, who finished with figures of 6 for 34.

TEST RESULTS

SOUTH AFRICA v WEST INDIES

	Matches	WI	SA	Draw	Series	WI	SA	Draw
In West Indies	1	0	1	0	1	0	1	0
Totals	1	0	1	0	1	0	1	0

INDIA v ZIMBABWE

Zimbabwe became the ninth Test-playing country in 1992–93 when they entertained India in Harare. Their captain, David Houghton, scored 121, becoming the first player to make a century in his country's inaugural Test since Charles Bannerman in the very first Test of all 116 years earlier. However, they took so long in scoring 456 (214.2 overs) that India replied in kind (307 in 169.4 overs) and the game petered out. A curiosity in the Zimbabwe team was John Traicos, who had played three Tests for South Africa in 1969–70. He became the 14th player to appear for two countries in Tests, and the first to be born in neither country (he was born in Egypt). The 45-year-old Traicos broke another record – it was 22 years 222 days since his previous Test, the longest gap in a Test career (previously the 17 years 316 days of George Gunn).

India played Zimbabwe again in Delhi later the same season and won by an innings and 13, thanks to 227 from 21-year-old Vinod Kambli, who took his total runs to 544 in his first four Tests.

TEST RESULTS

INDIA v ZIMBABWE

	Matches	Ind	Zim	Draw	Series	Ind	Zim	Draw
In Zimbabwe	1	0	0	1	1	0	0	1
In India	1	1	0	0	1	1	0	0
Totals	2	1	0	1	2	1	0	1

RECORD EQUALLED *David Houghton, captain of Zimbabwe, in 1992–93.*

NEW ZEALAND v ZIMBABWE

Ten days after their first-ever Test against India, Zimbabwe played New Zealand at Bulawayo, a usually drought-ridden town, but rain cut 10 hours from play, preventing a result, which meant that Zimbabwe became the only Test country to avoid defeat in each of their first two Tests. In the second of a two-Test series, however, New Zealand won convincingly after captain Martin Crowe had made 140 in the first innings.

Two Tests in New Zealand in 1995–96 were drawn, the first through rain, the second because batsmen were on top throughout.

TEST RESULTS

NEW ZEALAND v ZIMBABWE

	Matches	NZ	Zim	Draw	Series	NZ	Zim	Draw
In Zimbabwe	2	1	0	1	1	1	0	0
In New Zealand	2	0	0	2	1	0	0	1
Totals	4	1	0	3	2	1	0	1

SOUTH AFRICA v INDIA

South Africa entertained India in 1992–93 in their first home series since being banned from Test cricket and it was the first time the two countries had met. Doves for peace were released before the first Test in Durban. South Africa's Jimmy Cook, who, at 39 years 105 days, was the twentieth-oldest Test debutant, immediately made less welcome history as the first debutant to be out first ball of a Test. The South African captain Kepler Wessels scored 118 and became the first player to score Test centuries for two different countries, having already made four centuries in 24 appearances for Australia. When India batted, Sachin Tendulkar became the first

HISTORIC *Wessels in the Durban Test.*

player to be given out (run out) by the third umpire watching the television slow-motion replay, this being the first series of "trial by television". The match was drawn, as was the second at Johannesburg which South African President Nelson Mandela attended. South Africa won their first Test since their re-admission at Cape Town and a draw in the final Test gave them their first series. Solid batting all through and 20 wickets from fast bowler Allan Donald made the difference between the sides.

A series in India in 1996–97 resulted in a 2–1 win for India. Gary Kirsten made a century in each innings for South Africa in Calcutta. Mohammed Azharuddin made certain of victory with a second-innings 163 not out in the final Test, and was easily the series' best batsman. Javagal Srinath and Anil Kumble were the best bowlers. A return series in South Africa the same season, however, ended 2–0 in favour of South Africa. The fast bowling of Allan Donald and Shaun Pollock and the all-round play of Bruce McMillan, who scored most runs at an average of 98.66, were decisive.

TEST RESULTS

SOUTH AFRICA v INDIA

	Matches	SA	Ind	Draw	Series	SA	Ind	Draw
In South Africa	7	3	0	4	2	2	0	0
In India	3	1	2	0	1	0	1	0
Totals	10	4	2	4	3	2	1	0

SOUTH AFRICA v SRI LANKA

In 1993–94, South Africa played a three-match series in Sri Lanka. A maiden Test century by Jonty Rhodes saved South Africa in the first Test, after Arjuna Ranatunga had made 131 for Sri Lanka, who passed 300 in each innings. However, South Africa won the second by an innings and 208 runs, with Brett Schultz claiming nine wickets and Hansie Cronje scoring 122. Rain in the third Test made sure that South Africa would take the series 1–0. Brett Schultz's 20 wickets was the series' best performance.

TEST RESULTS

SOUTH AFRICA v SRI LANKA

	Matches	SA	SL	Draw	Series	SA	SL	Draw
In Sri Lanka	3	1	0	2	1	1	0	0
Totals	3	1	0	2	1	1	0	0

PAKISTAN v ZIMBABWE

Zimbabwe visited Pakistan in 1993–94, where three Tests were played in a curious series in which the highest individual score was 81, and the highest aggregate for the series 205. Pakistan won the first two Tests by 131 and 52 runs and the third was drawn. The dominant figure was Pakistan's Waqar Younis, whose 27 wickets was more than twice any other bowler's. In 1994–95 in Zimbabwe, the home side won theirfirst Test match, beating Pakistan by an innings and 64 in the first Test. Grant Flower scored 201 not out for Zimbabwe, adding 269 for the fourth wicket with his brother Andy (156) and an unbeaten 233 for the fifth with Guy Whittall.Pakistan fought back to win the second and third Tests and the series 2–1. Zimbabwe's Heath Streak, with 22 wickets at 13.55, shared Player of the Series award with Pakistan's Inzaman-ul-Haq, who scored 367 runs, average 73.40.

A two-match series in Pakistan in 1996–97 saw Pakistan win 1–0. In the drawn first Test, captain Wasim Akram made 257 not out for Pakistan, the highest score by a number 8 batsman in Test history. his 12 sixes was a new record for a Test innings and his eighth-wicket stand of 313 with Saqlain Mushtaq (79) was a new Test record.

TEST RESULTS

PAKISTAN v ZIMBABWE

	Matches	Pak	Zim	Draw	Series	Pak	Zim	Draw
In Pakistan	5	3	0	2	2	2	0	0
In Zimbabwe	3	2	1	0	1	1	0	0
Totals	8	5	1	2	3	3	0	0

WEST INDIES V SRI LANKA

One Test was played in Moratuwa, in 1993–94, when, in the first meeting between the countries play was so curtailed that it was possible only for Sri Lanka to score 190 (P.A. de Silva 53, W.K.M. Benjamin 4-46, C.E.L. Ambrose 3–14), the West Indies 204 (C.L. Hooper 62, R.B. Richardson 51, M. Muralitharan 4–47, S.D. Anurasiri 3–77) and Sri Lanka to get 43 for 2 in their second knock. Sri Lanka visited in 1996–97 for a two-match series which West Indies won 1–0.

TEST RESULTS

WEST INDIES v SRI LANKA

	Matches	WI	SL	Draw	Series	WI	SL	Draw
In Sri Lanka	1	0	0	1	1	0	0	1
In West Indies	2	1	0	1	1	1	0	0
Totals	3	1	0	2	2	1	0	1

SOUTH AFRICA v PAKISTAN

Pakistan visited Johannesburg for a single Test against South Africa in 1994–95, South Africa winnng the inaugural Test by 324 runs, their largest win in terms of runs in their interrupted 106 years of Tests. Two all-rounders shared the honours: Man-of-the-Match Fanie de Villiers with a whirlwind 66 not out from 68 balls at number 10 and 10 wickets in the match for 108, and Bruce McMillan with a maiden Test century and four match wickets for 78. Fanie de Villiers was the South African to take 10 wickets and score 50 in the Test.

TEST RESULTS

SOUTH AFRICA v PAKISTAN

	Matches	SA	Pak	Draw	Series	SA	Pak	Draw
In South Africa	1	1	0	0	1	1	0	0
Totals	1	1	0	0	1	1	0	0

SRI LANKA v ZIMBABWE

Test cricket's two youngest countries met in Zimbabwe in 1994–95, in a high-scoring three-Test series in which all three Tests were drawn. David Houghton's 266 in Bulawayo remains the highest innings in Tests for Zimbabwe.

Sri Lanka won both Tests in the series in 1996–97 when no Zimbabwe player scored more than 92 runs in the series. For Sri Lanka Hasha Tillekeratne made the only century, and Muttiah Muralithan took most wickets, 14.

TEST RESULTS

SRI LANKA v ZIMBABWE

	Matches	SL	ZIM	Draw	Series	SL	ZIM	Draw
In Zimbabwe	3	0	0	3	1	0	0	1
In Sri Lanka	2	2	0	0	1	1	0	0
Totals	5	2	0	3	2	1	0	1

SOUTH AFRICA v ZIMBABWE

South Africa made the short journey to Harare to play a single Test match against Zimbabwe early in the 1995–96 season. The home batsmen couldn't cope with the fast bowling of Allan Donald, who took 8 for 71, his best figures in Tests, in Zimbabwe's second innings. Andrew Hudson, with 135, had already helped South Africa gain a first-innings lead of 176, and South Africa needed only 108 in the fourth innings to win. They registered a comfortable victory by seven wickets.

TEST RESULTS

SOUTH AFRICA v ZIMBABWE

	Matches	SA	Zim	Draw	Series	SA	Zim	Draw
In Zimbabwe	1	1	0	0	1	1	0	0
Totals	1	1	0	0	1	1	0	0

ENGLAND v ZIMBABWE

England played a two-match Test series in Zimbabwe in 1996–97. In the first Test at Bulawayo, England gained a first-innings lead of 30 and, when Zimbabwe were dismissed for 234 in their second knock, needed 205 to win in a minimum 37 overs. A second-wicket partnership of 137 between Nick Knight and Alec Stewart took the score to 154, but England failed to press home the advantage and finished on 204 for 6, managing only a draw with the scores level, the first such instance in Test cricket. The second Test was spoiled by rain, so the scores finished level.

TEST RESULTS

ENGLAND v ZIMBABWE

	Matches	Eng	Zim	Draw	Series	Eng	Zim	Draw
In Zimbabwe	2	0	0	2	1	0	0	1
Totals	2	0	0	2	1	0	0	1

TEST RESULTS

TOTAL TEST RESULTS 1876–77 TO 1996–97

	Played	Won	Lost	Draw	Tied	Wins/losses ratio
West Indies	334	129	80	124	1	1.61
Australia	566	237	160	167	2	1.48
Pakistan	234	66	54	114	0	1.22
England	734	249	207	278	0	1.20
South Africa	209	53	86	70	0	0.61

	Played	Won	Lost	Draw	Tied	Wins/losses ratio
India	310	57	102	150	1	0.55
New Zealand	252	36	104	112	0	0.34
Sri Lanka	72	9	34	29	0	0.26
Zimbabwe	21	1	10	10	0	0.10

THE CRICKET WORLD CUP

For many years the pinnacle of the soccer world has been the World Cup. Although cricket's rules and regulations pre-date soccer's by over one hundred years, it was not until 1975 that the cricket authorities managed to organize a similar event. Even then, instead of being Test cricket it was confined to one-day matches. The World Cup, held every four years, has proved a popular success and nothing was more appropriate than that the 1996 World Cup should be won by Sri Lanka, until then considered by many to be inferior to the senior Test playing sides.

The first attempt in England to organize an international comptetition which involved more than one other country was staged in 1912. England invited Australia and South Africa to come and play a Triangular Tournament of Test Matches. Unfortunately, to quote a contemporary source "we had one of the most appalling summers ever known, even in England." It rained and rained. The cricket press forecast that it was an idea which would probably not be repeated for a generation. And so it proved.

In 1975 for the first World Cup, the *Wisden Almanack* commenced its report with "The First World Cup cricket tournament proved an outstanding success. Blessed by perfect weather, ideal conditions prevailed." Unlike the 1912 Triangular tournament, the authorities did not have to wait a generation to repeat the experiment.

HAPPY DAY *Kapil Dev (India) receives the Prudential Cup Trophy, World Cup Final 1983.*

WORLD CUP 1975

Venue: England

FIRST BLOOD TO WEST INDIES

The first World Cup was staged in England in June 1975. The trophy at stake was the Prudential Cup, Prudential having sponsored the competition to the tune of £100,000. There were eight countries competing: the six current Test-playing nations plus East Africa and Sri Lanka. It was noted with regret that South Africa were omitted. The teams were divided into two groups of four and the top two in each group would then meet in a knockout semi-final round. Each match would consist of 60 overs per side – the number used in the English Gillette Cup competition.

The first four matches commenced on June 7 at Lord's, Headingley, Old Trafford and Edgbaston. The most popular game was Australia v Pakistan at Headingley, where the ground sold out. Australia, batting first, reached 278 for 7, with Ross Edwards making a hard-hit 80. Pakistan lost Sadiq, Zaheer and Mushtaq cheaply and the game seemed all over, but Majid Khan was joined by Asif Iqbal and the score rose to 181 for 4 off 41 overs. Dennis Lillee returned to demolish the tail and bring Australia an easy win.

At Lord's, England completely outplayed India, after Dennis Amiss hit 137 – India's style was utterly cramped as they could only score 132 for 3 off their 60 overs, England winning by 202 runs. The minnows, Sri Lanka and East Africa, fell to the West Indies and New Zealand, Glenn Turner making 171 not out for the latter.

The second batch of games saw England beat New Zealand, Keith Fletcher making 131; Australia beat Sri Lanka, though only by 52 runs, a margin which would have been less if Jeff Thomson had not forced Wettimuny and Mendis to retire hurt when both were well established. India walked over East Africa – winning by 10 wickets with 30.1 overs to spare. The most exciting game was at Edgbaston, where an incredible tenth-wicket stand of 64 by Deryck Murray and Andy Roberts produced a one-wicket victory for the West Indies over Pakistan. Sarfraz Nawaz had blown away the top West Indian batsmen.

The third batch of games saw England outplay East Africa, while Pakistan, put in to bat, dealt convincingly with Sri Lanka. The most exciting game was West Indies v Australia at the Oval. Clive Lloyd put Australia in and the fast attack led by Andy Roberts kept the Australia total below 200. For Australia everything depended on Lillee and Thomson, but the former was out of sorts and a brilliant batting display by Alvin Kallicharran, who hit 35 off 10 deliveries from Lillee, saw the West Indies win with 14 overs to spare.

In the other game, an unbeaten century by Glenn Turner saw New Zealand home against India at Old Trafford.

The first semi-final produced bitter criticism of the Headingley pitch, which was green and damp. Australia put England in and none of the home batsmen could master the conditions. England were bowled out for 93, with Gary Gilmour, the left-arm seamer, returning figures of six for 16. Australia's batsmen found the pitch difficult but Gilmour hit an unbeaten 28 and his team won by four wickets.

In the second semi-final, the winner of the toss, Clive Lloyd, also put the opposition in. New Zealand fared better on the Oval pitch than England had done at Headingley, but they could only make a modest 158 and Kallicharran again starred as the outstanding Caribbean batsman.

EASY VICTORY *for Alvin Kallicharran and the West Indies over Australia.*

The final was staged at Lord's between Australia and the West Indies before a capacity crowd of 26,000. The West Indies were put in and lost their first three wickets for 50. Clive Lloyd joined Rohan Kanhai in a partnership which changed the game. Lloyd was on his best form, as was demonstrated when he hooked Lillee for six. With the latter batsmen all making useful contributions, the West Indian total reached a very respectable 291 for eight.

Australia were not daunted by the target set. Ian Chappell batted very competently for 62, opener Alan Turner made 40, but some brilliant fielding allied to a casual approach to running meant that no fewer than four Australians were run out, including most importantly both Greg and Ian Chappell. Despite these errors, Australia lost only by the narrow margin of 17 runs, the game not ending until nearly quarter to nine. Prince Philip presented the trophy to Clive Lloyd amid great cheers from the large contingent of West Indian supporters in the crowd. Clive Lloyd was also given the Man-of-the-Match award.

RESULTS

FINAL QUALIFYING TABLE

GROUP A

	P	W	L	Pts
England	3	3	0	12
New Zealand	3	2	1	8
India	3	1	2	4
East Africa	3	0	3	0

GROUP B

	P	W	L	Pts
West Indies	3	3	0	12
Australia	2	2	1	8
Pakistan	3	1	2	4
Sri Lanka	3	0	3	0

SEMI-FINALS ***England*** 93 (36.2 overs);
Australia 94–6 (28.4 overs)
Australia won by four wickets
Man of the Match: G.J. Gilmour
New Zealand 158 (52.2 overs);
West Indies 159–5 (40.1 overs)
West Indies won by five wickets
Man of the Match: A.I. Kallicharran

FINAL ***West Indies*** 291–8 (60 overs);
Australia 274 (58.4 overs)
West Indies won by 17 runs
Man of the Match: C.H. Lloyd

WORLD CUP 1979

Venue: England

ENGLISH WEATHER CAN'T KEEP THE CARIBS DOWN

138 NOT OUT *for Viv Richards in the 1979 Final.*

In 1975, the World Cup had been played in a flaming English June; four years later June was not quite so kind, though only one match was totally washed out. However the Prudential Assurance Company upped their sponsorship to £250,000 and, because of increased prices, the receipts for matches were nearly double those of 1975 though the spectator numbers dropped by 28,000. The format was the same as for the first World Cup and there was only one team change, Canada replacing East Africa. Each side was allowed 60 overs, but the umpires were now instructed to deal more harshly with wides and bumpers.

The first batch of matches took place on June 9 at Edgbaston, Lord's, Headingley and Trent Bridge, the match of the round being that at headquarters between England and Australia. All tickets were sold prior to the day, and Mike Brearley, viewing a dull grey morning, put the opposition in. Runs came very slowly – only 14 off the first 10 overs – and by the time the first wicket fell the scoreboard read 56 off 21 overs. Brearley amazed everyone by putting Geoff Boycott on to bowl, but his tactic proved correct as Boycott removed both Andrew Hilditch and Kim Hughes. This was followed by a rash of run outs – four in all – and England were set just 160 to win. Graham Gooch made 53, Brearley 44 and England won by six wickets.

In the three other games, the West Indies crushed India. 75 from Viswanath enabled the Indians to make 190 all out before Gordon Greenidge and Desmond Haynes opened for the West Indies with a stand of 138. The former went on to a century and, in partnership with Viv Richards, brought a nine-wicket victory. The Pakistan v Canada match saw a very similar result, Pakistan cruising home by eight wickets, with Sadiq making a top score of 57 not out.

The same scenario occurred at Trent Bridge, where New Zealand won by nine wickets against Sri Lanka, Glenn Turner being the star batsman with 83 not out.

The weather affected the second batch of matches – all three days of the West Indies v Sri Lanka game saw the players sitting in the Leeds pavilion. At Old Trafford, the first day of England v Canada was washed out. The match began an hour late on day two in very poor conditions. Canada were bowled out for 45, Chris Old taking four for 8. It took England 13.5 overs to knock off the runs.

At Trent Bridge play was possible on the first day of Australia v Pakistan. Australia were without Rodney Hogg and Pakistan scored freely to reach 286 for seven on a rain-interrupted day. On the second day, the Australian batting never looked like scoring the runs required and Pakistan sailed home. New Zealand's batsmen found no difficulty in scoring the 183 required off India's attack – Bruce Edgar hit 84 and with John Wright added 100 before the first wicket fell.

In the third batch of games, Sri Lanka took centre stage, being the first non-Test-playing country to win a game in the World Cup. Playing India at Old Trafford, they were without their captain, Anura Tennekoon, but still hit 238 for five, with three players making fifties. The Indian innings did not begin until the second day. India seemed confident whilst Sunil Gavaskar and A.D. Gaekwad put on 60 for the first wicket, but the leg breaks of Somachandra de Silva caused the middle order problems and Sri Lanka dismissed their opponents for 191.

Brilliant sunshine greeted the semi-finals. There was a very exciting game at Old Trafford. New Zealand put England in and, though both Mike Brearley and Graham Gooch made fifties, Richard Hadlee caused all the early batsmen problems. Derek Randall came in at number 7 to make the tail wag and push the total over 200. With John Wright batting well, New Zealand kept in touch with the target and required 14 from the final over – they couldn't manage it, England winning by nine runs. In the other semi, the West Indies scored a rapid 293 for six, Gordon Greenidge being the top run-getter with 73.

For Pakistan, Majid Khan and Zaheer added 166 for the second wicket in 36 overs, before Colin Croft took three wickets in 12 balls and seized the initiative.

A full house at Lord's saw an outstanding batting display by Viv Richards, 138 not out and, though Mike Brearley and Geoff Boycott opened England's reply with a stand of 129, the scoring rate was too low. Viv Richards was Man of the Match as the West Indies won by 92 runs.

RESULTS

FINAL QUALIFYING TABLES

GROUP A

	P	W	L	Pts
England	3	3	0	12
Pakistan	3	1	2	8
Australia	3	1	2	4
Canada	3	0	3	0

GROUP B

	P	W	L	NR	Pts
West Indies	3	2	0	1	10
New Zealand	3	2	1	0	8
Sri Lanka	3	1	1	1	6
India	3	0	3	0	0

SEMI-FINALS ***England*** 221–8 (60 overs);
New Zealand 212–9 (60 overs)
England won by nine runs
Man of the Match: G.A. Gooch

West Indies 293–6 (60 overs);
Pakistan 250 (56.2 overs)
West Indies won by 43 runs
Man of the Match: C.G. Greenidge

FINAL ***West Indies*** 286–9 (60 overs);
England 194 (51 overs)
West Indies won by 92 runs
Man of the Match: I.V.A. Richards

WORLD CUP 1983

Venue: England

UNDERDOGS INDIA BEAT THE ODDS

The third World Cup, again sponsored by Prudential, saw the company put £500,000 into the kitty. The total attendance rose to 232,081, but the number of matches was substantially increased, each team in the group playing six games instead of three. Again the competition was staged in England, with one team change from the previous tournament: Zimbabwe replaced Canada. The weather was much kinder than in 1979, though England suffered a very wet May.

The sensation of the first batch of matches came at Trent Bridge where Zimbabwe beat Australia by 13 runs. The Zimbabwean captain Duncan Fletcher rescued his side from a poor start with an innings of 69 and the total was 239–6. Fletcher then took four for 42 as Australia struggled against some accurate bowling and good fielding.

India also caused an upset by beating the West Indies at Old Trafford. For once, the Caribbean batting was not up to the mark, Andy Roberts and last man Joel Garner being their highest scorers as India won by 34 runs.

In the second batch of games the West Indies recovered their poise with a 101-run win over Australia, Winston Davis returning figures of seven for 51. England always looked like beating Sri Lanka, David Gower scoring 130, and for New Zealand Richard Hadlee bowled brilliantly as Pakistan crashed to three down before a run was on the board. New Zealand won by 52 runs.

Australia won at last in the third batch of games, trouncing India by 162 runs; Trevor Chappell made 110 and Ken MacLeay took six for 39. Zimbabwe were brushed aside by the West Indies at Worcester, Gordon Greenidge making 105 not out.

Round four saw a nail-biting finish at Edgbaston, where New Zealand beat England with one delivery unbowled and two wickets in hand. David Gower was again in splendid form for the home country, making 92 not out, but few of his compatriots could master Richard Hadlee. John Bracewell hit the penultimate ball for four to seal England's fate.

Australia managed to put Zimbabwe in their place when they played the return fixture at Southampton, whilst all England's batsmen – Fowler, Tavare, Gower and Lamb – flourished at the expense of Pakistan. On the same day, however, at Derby, Sri Lanka gained their single victory of the tournament, beating New Zealand by three wickets; Ashantha de Mel took five for 32 as the Kiwis were dismissed for 181, then Roy Dias hit 64 not out to bring Sri Lanka victory by three wickets. Zimbabwe nearly pulled off a sensation against India at Tunbridge Wells: India were five down for 17 and seven for 78, but Kapil Dev, coming in at number 6 hit 175 and, with Kirmani, added 126 for the 9th wicket. Even so, Zimbabwe batted well in reply, losing by just 31 runs. India went on to beat Australia by 118 runs at Chelmsford, Madan Lal taking four for 20 as Australia collapsed in the final innings, being 129 all out. This gave India a place in the semi-finals, against all the bookmakers' odds.

In the first semi-final, India met England at Old Trafford. To everyone's surprise, the England batting failed to score with any authority against a modest Indian attack and India had no trouble in reaching their target of 214, Yashpal Sharma hitting 61. In the other semi-final, Pakistan had the more difficult task of scoring from the formidable West Indian attack. Mohsin Khan made 70, but no one stayed with him and the West Indies were left needing 185. Viv Richards was in top form, making 80 not out as the Caribs won with 11.2 overs and eight wickets in hand.

The underdogs India therefore came to Lord's to meet Clive Lloyd's West Indians. Lloyd duly won the toss and naturally put India in. Facing Roberts, Garner, Marshall and Holding, the Indian batsmen were dismissed for 183, only Srikkanth managing to top 30. For the crowd it seemed as if the West Indies merely had an afternoon's stroll in order to win the £20,000 prize. Gordon Greenidge, that most prolific of one-day batsmen, was out for a single – a minor disappointment. Desmond Haynes and Viv Richards took the total to 50 in an easy manner, then Madan Lal, bowling medium-pace seamers, struck. He dismissed Haynes, Richards and Gomes. Clive Lloyd fell to Binny and the score was suddenly 66 for five, then 76 for six. Malcolm Marshall came to partner wicket-keeper Dujon. Three figures were on the board. Gradually the two seemed to be turning the game the West Indies' way, but Mohinder Amarnath dismissed both and India won by 43 runs.

ALL ROUND CRICKET *from Mohinder Amarnath helped India to the final at Lord's.*

RESULTS

FINAL QUALIFYING TABLES

GROUP A

	P	W	L	Pts
England	6	5	1	20
Pakistan	6	3	3	12
New Zealand	6	3	3	12
Sri Lanka	6	1	5	4

GROUP B

	P	W	L	Pts
West Indies	6	5	1	20
India	6	4	2	16
Australia	6	2	4	8
Zimbabwe	6	1	5	4

SEMI-FINALS ***England*** 213 (60 overs);
India 217–4 (54.4 overs)
India won by six wickets
Man of the Match: M. Amarnath

Pakistan 184–8 (60 overs);
West Indies 188–2 (48.4 overs)
West Indies won by eight wickets
Man of the Match: I.V.A. Richards

FINAL ***India*** 183 (54.4 overs);
West Indies 140 (52 overs)
India won by 43 runs
Man of the Match: M. Amarnath

WORLD CUP 1987

Venue: India and Pakistan

AUSSIES BATTLE THROUGH

BORDER AND GATTING *the captains greet each other at the 1987 Final.*

The fourth World Cup, sponsored by Reliance, was staged in India and Pakistan. The same eight sides as played in 1983 were assembled and, as in the third cup, each team played six matches to settle positions in two group tables. The number of overs per side was reduced from 60 to 50. The Group A matches were played in India and Group B in Pakistan. Each country staged a semi-final, with the final held in Calcutta.

The competition got off to an exciting start in Madras. Geoff Marsh hit 110 as Australia began the game by making 270–7. India made a confident reply, Gavaskar, Srikkanth and Sidhu all in good form, so that the total rose to 207 for two. Craig McDermott, however, removed India's middle order and Australia won off the penultimate ball by one run. The next day in Hyderabad saw a match of almost equal excitement, when New Zealand beat Zimbabwe by three runs. The Kiwis made 242. Zimbabwe seemed a one-man band as David Houghton batted totally unsupported and the score slumped to 104 for seven. Then Butchart arrived at number 9, the total doubled before the next wicket went down and New Zealand only won by dint of two run-outs, when Zimbabwe required six from the final over.

Heavy rain at Indore meant that the first Australia v New Zealand game was put off to the second day, and reduced to 30 overs per side. Through David Boon and Dean Jones, Australia made 199 for four. New Zealand made good progress and were 133 for two. They needed seven from the final over, but lost three wickets and made only three runs.

For the rest of the matches in Group A, the advantage remained with Australia and India, who both won five of six matches. In the final four games, India beat Zimbabwe by seven wickets and New Zealand by nine wickets, Sunil Gavaskar hitting a marvellous unbeaten 103 in the second game. Australia beat New Zealand by 17 runs, with Geoff Marsh scoring 126 not out, and Zimbabwe by 70 runs, Boon making 93.

Over in Pakistan, the host country had a tight match against Sri Lanka, winning by 15 runs only, in spite of 103 by Javed Miandad. A well-fought battle in Gujranwala, gave England a two-wicket win over the West Indies, Allan Lamb scoring 67, but England then came unstuck against Abdul Qadir whose spin brought Pakistan victory by 18 runs at Rawalpindi.

Pakistan went on to victory by one wicket over the West Indies.

Pakistan also beat England, but by a much larger margin, when Qadir again proved the best bowler. On the same day in Karachi, Viv Richards broke the World Cup record with an innings of 181 off 125 balls; Desmond Haynes also hit a century in the same game as Sri Lanka conceded 360 runs and lost by 191 runs. In the return fixture, Sri Lanka did much better but, needing 37 off the final four overs, Sri Lanka couldn't score off Patterson and Benjamin, so the West Indies won by 25. England, though, did manage to beat the West Indies in Jaipur and thus qualify for the semi-finals. Graham Gooch made 92.

In the first semi in Lahore, Australia batted well to make 267 for eight – for once Qadir failed to take a wicket. Javed Miandad and Imran Khan added 112 for the fourth Pakistani wicket after the first three batsmen fell cheaply, but Craig McDermott bowled accurately, taking five for 44 as the later home batsmen contributed little.

India put England in in Bombay. Gooch mastered the slow pitch and scored 115, giving England a total of 254. India looked on target so long as Azharuddin was attacking but, once Eddie Hemmings had him leg before, the English bowler took command. About 70,000 spectators came to watch the final in Calcutta. Australia decided to bat first. David Boon and Geoff Marsh took full advantage of some erratic opening overs by De Freitas and Small and this, in the end, proved the vital concession of the match. Allan Border and Mike Veletta kept Australia's runs flowing, so that England required 254. Gooch and Bill Athey took the England score to 66 for one; Mike Gatting and Allan Lamb made useful contributions, but England were gradually slipping behind the run rate. They needed 46 runs off the last five overs, but it was only narrowed to 17 off the final McDermott over, a task beyond Foster and Small. Australia, therefore, took the fourth World Cup by seven runs.

The main difference between this cup on the Indian subcontinent and those held in England was that the spin bowlers had much more opportunity – Hemmings and Emburey, for example, bowled 20 overs in the final – which was bound to add to the interest and break the dreadful monotony of pace.

RESULTS

FINAL QUALIFYING TABLES

GROUP A

	P	W	L	Pts
India	6	5	1	20
Australia	6	5	1	20
New Zealand	6	2	4	8
Zimbabwe	6	0	6	0

GROUP B

	P	W	L	Pts
Pakistan	6	5	1	20
England	6	4	2	16
West Indies	6	3	3	12
Sri Lanka	6	0	6	0

SEMI-FINALS ***Australia*** 267–8 (50 overs); ***Pakistan*** 249 (49 overs)
Australia won by 18 runs
Man of the Match: C.J. McDermott

England 254–6 (50 overs); ***India*** 219 (45.3 overs)
England won by 35 runs
Man of the Match: G.A. Gooch

FINAL ***Australia*** 253–5; ***England*** 246–8 (50 overs)
Australia won by seven runs
Man of the Match: D.C. Boon

WORLD CUP 1992

Venue: Australia and New Zealand

IMRAN HAS THE LAST LAUGH

FINAL BAT *Imran Khan in the Final.*

There was a sensible format for the fifth World Cup in Australia and New Zealand in 1992. With South Africa recently returned to the fold of international cricket and Zimbabwe joining the Test match countries for the first time, there were nine entrants who played each other on a league basis, the top four qualifying for the semi-finals and final. So every country played at least eight matches. However, in the event, neither finalist could claim to have got there without luck or controversy – Pakistan by virtue of a point awarded for a "no-result" in a match they would almost certainly have lost, and England with the help of a "wet weather" rule which guaranteed them a semi-final win when the match was still in the balance.

The tournament was sold with the maximum amount of aggressive hype by Australian television, but the home country's expected easy ride to the knockout stages received a jolt in the first match, when joint hosts New Zealand beat them by 37 runs. The New Zealand captain Martin Crowe made 100 not out in a total of 248 for six, and then, despite 100 from David Boon, Australia were bowled out for 211.

It was the start of a spectacular run by the New Zealanders who won their first seven matches and lost only to Pakistan in their last, by which time they had long qualified for the semi-finals. Martin Crowe, with 456 runs, was the highest scorer of the tournament, his average of 114 being 45 higher than the next best.

Australia also lost their second match, comprehensively beaten by nine wickets by South Africa, who made 171 for one wicket in reply to 170 for nine. Kepler Wessels, the South African captain, who had played Tests for Australia, made 81 not out. "This is the greatest moment in South African cricket," said Ali Bacher.

Apart from New Zealand, the only other team to march impressively on and clinch an early place in the semi-finals were England. A thrilling opening match with India was won by nine runs, and after six matches they had won five and drawn unluckily with Pakistan. After bowling Pakistan out for 74 (Pringle three for eight) England were 24 for one when persistent rain ended it. England finally lost to New Zealand and Zimbabwe when it didn't matter, giving Zimbabwe their only points.

South Africa became the third team to book a semi-final place by beating India in their last match, but the fourth semi-final place rested on the matches on the last day of the league section. The West Indies could have it by beating Australia, Australia could have it by beating the West Indies, but only if Pakistan lost, and Pakistan, who had started disastrously, could have it by beating New Zealand, provided Australia beat the West Indies. This last was what happened, thanks to Wasim Akram taking four for 32 and an innings of 119 not out by opener Ramiz Raja.

As it happened, Pakistan had to play New Zealand again in the semi-final in Auckland. New Zealand made an excellent 262 for seven, with Martin Crowe run out for 91, but Pakistan achieved the runs thanks to a patient 57 not out by Javed Miandad, who anchored the innings, and a spectacular knock by Man-of-the-Match Inzamam-Ul-Haq, who came in at 140 for four and scored 60 in 37 balls.

In the other semi-final, South Africa put England in and bowled only 45 overs in their allotted time, from which England made 252 for six. With 10.10 p.m. fixed for the end of the day-night match, South Africa had reached 231 for six with 13 balls remaining when a downpour stopped play. When the players returned, the umpires decreed there was time for only seven balls but, as under the rules the lowest-scoring over of England's innings was discarded, the target was not reduced. However, before play could begin, there was another stoppage, reducing the time allowed to only one ball. This time the target was reduced by one run to 21, and that was that.

Pakistan started slowly in the final, but scraped 249 for six. England batted disappointingly and were all out in the last over for 227, with Wasim Akram, who not only took three wickets but scored a vital 33 in 18 balls at the end of the Pakistan innings, becoming Man of the Match.

Martin Crowe was "Champion Player" of the tournament, winning cash and a Nissan motor car. Javed Miandad and South Africa's Peter Kirsten were the other batsmen to top 400 runs, while David Boon of Australia and Ramiz Raja each made two centuries. Wasim Akram took most wickets, 18, at the best average, 18.78, while Chris Harris (New Zealand), Ian Botham (England) and Mushtaq Ahmed (Pakistan) all captured 16 wickets.

The Pakistan skipper Imran Khan accepted the biggest prize, however, and couldn't help beaming at the way fortune had smiled for his team at half-way – after winning only one of their first five matches, they won all five thereafter.

RESULTS

FINAL QUALIFYING TABLES

GROUP A

	P	W	L	NR	Pts	NRR
New Zealand	8	7	1	0	14	0.59
England	8	5	2	1	11	0.47
South Africa	8	5	3	0	10	0.14
Pakistan	8	4	3	1	9	0.16
Australia	8	4	4	0	8	0.2
West Indies	8	4	4	0	8	0.07
India	8	2	5	1	5	0.14
Sri Lanka	8	2	5	1	5	-0.68
Zimbabwe	8	1	7	0	2	-1.14

NRR = Net Run Rate, calculated by subtracting runs per over conceded from runs per over scored, to be used in the event of a tie on points.

SEMI-FINALS ***New Zealand*** 262–7 (50 overs) (M.D. Crowe 91)
Pakistan 264–6 (49 overs) (Inzamam-Ul-Haq 60, Javed Miandad 57 not out)
Pakistan won by four wickets
Man of the Match: Inzamam-Ul-Haq

England 252–6 (45 overs) (Hick 83)
South Africa (revised target 252 in 43 overs) 232–6 (43 overs)
England won by 19 runs
Man of the Match: G.A. Hick

FINAL ***Pakistan*** 249–6 (50 overs) (Imran Khan 72, Javed Miandad 58, Pringle 3–22) ***England*** 227 (49.2 overs) (Fairbrother 62, Wasim Akram 3-49, Mushtaq Ahmed 3–41)
Pakistan won by 22 runs
Man of the Match: Wasim Akram

WORLD CUP 1996

Venue: India, Pakistan and Sri Lanka

SRI LANKA CONQUER THE WORLD

There were 12 participants in the 1996 World Cup – the nine from 1992 (Zimbabwe was now a Test-playing country) plus Kenya, the Netherlands and the United Arab Emirates. The teams were split into two groups of six, each team to play the five others in their group, the top four in each group to play in the quarter-finals of the knockout stage. The whole tournament lasted 33 days in which 35 matches were played. The schedule consisted of 37 matches, but both Australia and the West Indies forfeited their matches against Sri Lanka, refusing to travel there after a terrorist bomb had killed 80 people in Colombo.

Sri Lanka, who were given the points for a win, were therefore more or less guaranteed a quarter-final place, but they nevertheless earned it by beating their other three opponents, Zimbabwe, India (in Delhi) and Kenya, against whom they made a world record for a one-day international of 398 for five.

The group produced one of cricket's biggest shocks when Kenya defeated the West Indies. With only one professional in the side, Kenya made 166 and dismissed the West Indies for 93. The result caused a crisis meeting of the West Indian Board, and Richie Richardson was lucky to retain the captaincy. However, 93 not out in the West Indies' final match, helping them beat Australia and qualify for the quarter-finals, proved his character.

In Group B, South Africa were impressive in winning all five matches, but there were no real surprises.

In the first quarter-final, Sri Lanka confirmed their form with an exciting victory over England. Sri Lanka were responsible in this tournament for a tactical innovation in limited-overs cricket by launching a batting assault from the first ball, the philosophy being to score fast while the fielding restrictions are in force, rather than build a foundation for a late assault. Coming together at 12, Jayasuriya and Gurusinha added 100 in 65 balls. Jayasuriya made 82 in 44 balls, including 22 in one over from De Freitas.

The sub-continent would have liked to see India play Pakistan in the final, but the two met at Bangalore in the quarters. With Pakistan's skipper, Wasim Akram unfit, India won by 39 runs, after Pakistan had forfeited an over of their innings for a slow bowling rate.

The new favourites, South Africa, were beaten by 19 runs by a rejuvenated West Indies, for whom Brian Lara made 111, while Australia beat New Zealand, despite a final New Zealand total of 286 for nine, of which Chris Harris made 130 and Lee Germon 89. Mark Waugh's 110 helped Australia to a comfortable win in the end by six wickets. Thus all four sides from Group A qualified for the semi-finals. Both of these were extraordinary matches, one in cricketing terms, the other because of crowd disturbances.

At Calcutta, India put in Sri Lanka. Both openers were out in the first over, caught at third man. In fact, the first three batsmen contributed two runs, but Aravinda de Silva continued attacking, reaching 53 in 32 balls, and Sri Lanka recovered to 251 for eight. India reached 98 for one, but Sanath Jayasuriya then dismissed both Tendulkar (65) and Manjrekar (25) and India collapsed in disarray. At 120 for eight after 34.1 overs, the 110,000 crowd began throwing bottles on the pitch, and referee Clive Lloyd took the teams off for a 20-minute cooling-off period. However, when the players returned, the bottle-throwing resumed, and Lloyd awarded the match to Sri Lanka by default.

In the other semi-final, Australia began disastrously, and were 15 for four before Stuart Law (72) and Michael Bevan (69) squeezed the total to 207 for eight. At 165 for two, with Chanderpaul (80) and Richie Richardson established, the West Indies needed 43 in seven overs to win, but Shane Warne (4–36) inspired a panic. The last eight wickets went for 37 in 50 balls, leaving Richardson stranded on 49 not out and the West Indies five runs short of Australia.

Australia started well in the final, had 82 up in the first 15 overs and reached 137 before the second wicket fell, but Sri Lanka's bowlers then bowled very well and kept the final total down to a manageable 241 for seven. When Sri Lanka batted, a brilliant innings of 107 by Aravinda de Silva took his country to a convincing victory with runs and wickets in hand. Among the individual performances, Sachin Tendulkar made most runs, 523, while Australia's Mark Waugh and Aravinda de Silva of Sri Lanka also topped 400. Arjuna Ranatunga, the winning captain, averaged 120 by virtue of four not-outs.

ARAVINDA DE SILVA *in the final.*

RESULTS

FINAL QUALIFYING TABLES

GROUP A

	P	W	L	Pts
Sri Lanka	5	5	0	10
Australia	5	3	2	6
India	5	3	2	6
West Indies	5	2	3	4
Zimbabwe	5	1	4	2
Kenya	5	1	4	2

GROUP B

	P	W	L	Pts
South Africa	5	5	0	10
Pakistan	5	4	1	8
New Zealand	5	3	2	6
England	5	2	3	4
United Arab Emirates	5	1	4	2
The Netherlands	5	0	5	0

QUARTER-FINALS ***England*** 235–8; ***Sri Lanka*** 236–5 (40.4 overs)
India 287–8; ***Pakistan*** 248–9
West Indies 264–8; ***South Africa*** 245
New Zealand 286–9; ***Australia*** 289–4 (47.5 overs)

SEMI-FINALS ***Sri Lanka*** 251–8; ***India*** 120–8 (34.1 overs)
(Play ended because of crowd encroachment – match awarded to Sri Lanka)
Man of the Match: P. A. de Silva
Australia 207–8; ***West Indies*** 202
Australia won by five runs
Man of the Match: S. K. Warne

FINAL **Australia** 241–7 (Taylor 75, de Silva 3–42);
Sri Lanka 245-3 (46.2 overs) (Gurusinha 65, de Silva 107 notout)
Sri Lanka won by seven wickets
Man of the Match: P. A. de Silva

LEGENDS OF CRICKET

Becoming a legend in cricket is not a question of outstripping everyone else in statistics. Character, style, approach and temperament make mere figures secondary. In any case conditions change so much from era to era and from country to country that comparisons of figures tell only half the story. A player becomes a legend when he dominates an era, or shapes the course of cricket, or so transcends the game that he appeals to a wider audience. In short, he is a player who leaves a mark on the game and on the lives of those who follow it. All twelve in this section – including four players knighted for their services to cricket – comfortably satisfy the criteria. They represent cricket and sportsmanship at their best.

Another dozen players at least could easily have been included. Slow bowlers Rhodes, Grimmett, O'Reilly or Laker would clearly not be out of place, nor wicket-keepers Knott and Marsh. Many will wonder about the omission of Hutton, Compton, Trueman, George Headley, Worrell, Weekes, Barry and Viv Richards, Hanif, Kapil Dev, Doug Walters, Border and other famous players going back to the turn of the century, such as the immortal batsman, Victor Trumper. Short biographies of all of these and many more are included in the 'The Great Cricketers'.

The twelve players featured here represent well over 100 years of cricket history, from the 1870s and W.G. Grace to the present day and Brian Lara. They include at least one player from all seven of the long-established Test countries and four men who have been knighted for their services to the game: Hobbs, Bradman, Sobers and Hadlee.

Five are all-rounders: Grace, Sobers, Botham, Hadlee and Imran Khan – the last three in the exclusive club (Kapil Dev the only other member) of players with 3,000 runs and 300 wickets in Tests. Five batsmen represent five countries: Hobbs, 'The Master' of England; Gavaskar, 'The Little Master' of India; Bradman of Australia, the greatest run-maker in history; Pollock of South Africa, whose Test potential was sadly unfulfilled through politics; and Lara, today's West Indian record-breaker. Two fast bowlers complete the line-up: Dennis 'The Menace' Lillee and Malcolm Marshall, best of the modern West Indian battery.

LEAVING A MARK *Brian Lara will fore er be a legend to the young fans who in 1994 witnessed – and celebrated – his world-record innings of 501 not out for Warwickshire against Durham.*

BREW XI

BOTHAM

Ian Botham was the typical schoolboy hero who could turn a match round in a couple of hours of extravagant strokeplay or bowling. He was a player who could make things happen.

BOTHAM *bowling in his last Test series, v Pakistan 1992.*

BEEFY TO THE RESCUE

Ian Terance Botham should really have been a Yorkshireman, like his father, but he was born prematurely in Cheshire, which at the time meant he was not qualified for Yorkshire. Their loss was Somerset's gain. Making his debut for the county in 1974, the 18-year-old Botham soon showed the swashbuckling characteristics which were to make him famous. In a Benson & Hedges Cup match at Taunton, a fast short ball from West Indian fast bowler Andy Roberts struck the helmetless Botham on the face, half felling him. The blow cost him four teeth but, with the last man in, Botham, in great pain, won the match with a boundary: 45 not out, and the 6,500 crowd had had the privilege of seeing the first significant signs of an outstanding batting career.

It wasn't long before Botham was England's best all-rounder – an aggressive batsman, fine swing bowler and brilliant and charismatic fielder. He made his Test debut against the Australians at Trent Bridge in 1977, and soon had his first wicket – Aussie skipper Greg Chappell. He took five wickets in the Australian first innings, and repeated the feat in the following Test match, England winning both.

In the winter, he scored his first Test century, against New Zealand (and also took eight wickets in the match). By the following summer, when he hit two centuries against Pakistan and achieved his best-ever bowling performance, 8–34, the 22-year-old was the hottest property in cricket.

Over a quarter of Botham's first-class matches were Tests, well over a quarter of his total runs were made in Tests, and practically a third of his total wickets were taken in Tests. The Test match arena became his natural habitat. In 1979, he passed 1,000 Test runs and 100 Test wickets in his 21st Test, two fewer than the previous quickest (Mankad), and in 1979–80 in India's Golden Jubilee Test in Bombay he became the first player to score a century and take 10 wickets in a Test (114 and 13 for 106).

Botham became captain of England in 1980, but this proved to be the only area in which he failed. His form suffered and, after the second Test against Australia in 1981, he resigned the captaincy. This followed a chilling demonstration at Lord's when, after being bowled first ball in the second innings for a pair, his return to the pavilion was marked by a frosty silence.

In answer, at Headingley in the next match, Botham produced one of the greatest and most amazing all-round performances ever. Having taken six for 95 and scored 50 in the first innings, he went out to bat with England, following on, 105 for 5 in the second innings. Later, at 135 for 7 England still required 92 to avoid an innings defeat, with bookmakers quoting a victory at 500–1. In a heroic display of hitting, Botham smashed 149 not out and, with Bob Willis inspired to his best-ever bowling, helped dismiss Australia for 111 and give England an 18-run victory. He was only the second (after J.M. Gregory in 1920–21) to score a century and take five wickets in an innings in an Ashes Test.

> **"Ian Botham had the mourners dancing in the aisles at Headingley last night with the greatest comeback since Lazarus."**
>
> *PAT GIBSON, reporting on the 1981 England v Australia Test*

And that was not all – at Edgbaston in the next Test, Botham claimed five wickets for one run to finish off the Aussies and give England a 29-run win, and then a magnificent, controlled 118 at Old Trafford gave England a third consecutive win. In his 12 matches as England captain, he had failed to register a win – in the next three matches, he performed wonders to inspire three victories.

BOTHAM AT BAT *for Queensland in 1987–88.*

If his subsequent career did not produce comparable fireworks, the figures were outstanding nevertheless. He became the third (after Benaud and Sobers) to 2,000 Test runs and 200 Test wickets, and the youngest of them all at just over 26. Then in 1984 he became the first-ever Test player to reach 3,000 runs and 300 wickets.

In 1986, Botham became the leading wicket-taker in Test history when he passed Dennis Lillee's total of 355 (his final total of 383 has since been passed by Hadlee and Kapil Dev).

Throughout his career, Botham made his own rules and was the centre of much controversy. There have been court appearances over drugs (a fine) and assault (dismissed), disparaging remarks about touring Pakistan (apologized for), dissent in a Test (reprimand), a well-publicized row with Somerset (he went to Worcestershire and helped win championships in 1988 and 1989), a row over ball-tampering with Imran Khan, accusations of being too domineering and getting too fat, and countless tabloid stories of reckless behaviour.

However, balancing all this have been the successful appearances as captain in the BBC's quiz 'A Question of Sport', and famous walks for charity. And so far as cricket is concerned, he did it all.

CAREER FACT FILE

Born: November 24, 1955, Oldfield, Heswell, Cheshire
Teams: Somerset (1974–86), Worcestershire (1987–91), Durham (1992–93), Queensland (1987–88)
Tours: Pakistan 1977–78; New Zealand 1977–78, 1983–84, 1991–92; Australia 1978–79, 1979–80, 1982–83, 1986–87; India 1979–80, 1981–82; Australia and New Zealand (World Cup) 1991–92; Worcestershire to Zimbabwe 1990–91.
First-class career: (1974–93, 402 matches)
Batting: runs 19,399; average 33.97; highest score 228; centuries 38
Bowling: wickets 1,172; runs 31,902; average 27.22; best 8–34
Catches: 354
Tests: (1977–92, 102 matches)
Batting: runs 5,200; average 33.54; highest score 208; centuries 14
Bowling: wickets 383; runs 10,878; average 28.40; best 8–34
Catches: 120

BRADMAN

Bradman dominated batting as no player before or since. His figures remain about 50 per cent better than those of anybody else in cricket history.

BRADMAN *going out to bat in his testimonial match, Melbourne, 1948. He scored 123.*

RELENTLESSLY FLOWS THE DON

HIP HIP HOORAY *Bradman (left) receiving three cheers from the England players before his last innings in Tests, Oval, 1948.*

There can be no other choice than Sir Donald George Bradman as the best batsman the world has ever seen. Arguments have been advanced for other players, usually on the grounds of Bradman having good firm Australian wickets to bat on, but it is clutching at straws because Bradman's record on his four tours of England is phenomenal: he scored 9,837 runs, averaging 96.44. Because of the increase nowadays in the number of matches, especially Test matches, many have surpassed him in aggregates, but his career average stands on its own 24 above the next player's, and his Test average is nearly 40 above anybody else's. A measure of his stature is that his worth as a Test run-getter practically equalled that of Allan Border and Viv Richards added together!

Bradman spent his boyhood in Bowral, 80 miles from Sydney, and developed his hand and eye co-ordination by hitting golf balls against a wall with a stump. In his first Sheffield Shield match aged 19 he scored 118, and throughout his career he continued to score a century for every three innings he played. And not only single centuries – 37 times he went past 200, six times past 300, both still records. His highest score is 452 not out. And he scored his runs quickly, only 12 times in his career batting for longer than six hours. His runs came all round the wicket, from a great variety of shots, with the pull shot, in which he took a ball sometimes from around or outside off-stump and smashed it through midwicket, being particularly associated with him.

He came to England in 1930 with a huge reputation, and scored 236 in the first match at Worcester (he repeated the double-century on his next two visits). In the Headingley Test, he came in at number 3 and was 309 not out at close, eventually going on to 334, an Ashes record at the time (he repeated the triple-century on his next Test at Headingley). Many consider his innings in the Lord's Test his finest. Coming to the wicket in mid-afternoon, he was not out 155 at the close, and went on to 254. He himself picked this innings as his greatest because "every ball went where I wanted it to go". Never, at Test level, had an innings been so dominating. In that series, Bradman scored 974 runs, still a record for a single series, and averaged 139.14.

Bradman's dominance was such that "bodyline" was used to counter him in 1932–33, and it worked, as his average was "only" 56.57 – still the best on either side. He was dominant again in 1934 and was captain on his tour of England in 1938. The Second World War took six years out of Bradman's career and his health

> **"Every ball's the first ball whether I've just come to the wicket or reached 200. And I never consider the possibility that anybody will get me out."**
>
> *Don Bradman, on his batting*

wasn't perfect when cricket resumed. Nevertheless, he carried on at only slightly below his peak and led an Australian side to England in 1948 that remained unbeaten and is generally considered the best side to tour England. When he went out to bat in his last Test at the Oval, he needed only four runs to make sure of a Test average of 100, but he was bowled for a duck, some said because he still had a tear in his eye from his reception. If so, it would have been untypical of Bradman, who had the self-sufficiency of a genius.

Apart from his batting, Bradman was a brilliant fielder at cover-point and a very shrewd and thoughtful captain. He was knighted in 1949 and on his retirement became an influential figure in Australian cricket as an administrator. He was awarded Australia's highest honour, the companion of the Order of Australia, in 1981.

CAREER FACT FILE

Born:	August 27, 1908, Cootamundra, New South Wales, Australia
Teams:	New South Wales (1927–28 to 1933–34), South Australia (1935–36 to 1948–49)
Tours:	England 1930, 1934, 1938, 1948
First-class career:	(1927–28 to 1948–49, 234 matches)
Batting:	runs 28,067; average 95.14; highest score 452 not out; centuries 117
Bowling:	wickets 36; runs 1,367; average 37.97; best 3–35
Catches:	131 (plus 1 stumped)
Tests:	(1928–29 to 1948, 52 matches)
Batting:	runs 6,996; average 99.94; highest score 334; centuries 29
Bowling:	wickets 2; runs 72; average 36.00; best 1–8
Catches:	32

GAVASKAR

Sunny Gavaskar was a model opening batsman with a perfect defensive technique yet the flair to put the world's greatest bowlers to the sword.

GAVASKAR *a pensive captain*

THE LITTLE MASTER

Sunil Manohar Gavaskar was not quite 5ft 5in tall, a distinct disadvantage when facing tall, fast, West Indian bowlers, but he had such a perfect batting technique that he was for many years the best opening batsman in the world. Thoroughly consistent, he triumphed over all types of bowling on all wickets. His countrymen called him "the little master" and by the end of his career he had more Test runs and centuries than anybody before him. His 34 Test centuries, five more than Bradman, remains a record.

Gavaskar shone at school and university and made his first-class debut for Vazir Sultan Colts in 1966–67 as a 17-year-old. Appearing for Bombay the following year, he made his debut for India on a tour of the West Indies in 1970–71 and was sensational. He played in the last four Tests, and scored four centuries, including 220 in the last Test when suffering from toothache. His aggregate of 774 is the highest by a batsman in his debut series, and the highest by an Indian in a series. India won a match against the West Indies for the first time and took the series.

"Cool and ruthless, he ground them into the dust."

RAVI SHASTRI on Gavaskar's 236 not out against the West Indies' fast bowling, Madras 1983–84

Gavaskar suffered a reaction from this explosive start and shone less brightly in his next two series against England (although India won). His most famous feat on the 1974 tour was to get knocked over at Lord's by John Snow when attempting a run, for which act Snow was dropped for a match in punishment. Gavaskar's Test career was in doubt until in 1974 he made a fighting 101 at Old Trafford, an innings he rates as his most important, because it confirmed to himself that he had a place at the highest level. From then he did not look back. In 1976, he became the first Indian to score 1,000 Test runs in a calendar year, and he did so again in 1978 and 1979, when he scored 1,555, second only to Viv Richards' 1,710 in 1976.

In 1978–79, he passed Polly Umrigar's record Test aggregate for an Indian while getting a century in each innings of a Test – the first Indian to perform this feat twice. He replaced Bedi as captain of India for the visit of the West Indians the same season, and again at Calcutta scored centuries in each innings against them, and he remains the only batsman to do this three times in Tests.

AT BAT *Gavaskar in 1984.*

He was not captain for the tour to England in 1979, when he played probably his best innings in England. At the Oval, India needed to win to tie the series but were set 438 to achieve this. Gavaskar batted brilliantly and patiently on the last day to score 221, and when he was out at 389 for 4, with 49 wanted, India were almost within grasp of a famous victory. But they finished nine runs short of England's total with two wickets left. As captain again for the tour of Australia in 1980–81, when he caused a storm by asking his partner Chauhan to leave the field with him when he was angered at being given out lbw. Luckily, wiser heads prevailed. In 1981–82, he made his highest score, 340, for Bombay against Bengal in Bombay.

In 1982–83, Gavaskar became the first Indian to carry his bat through a Test innings when scoring 127 not out in a total of 286 against Pakistan. However, he lost the captaincy to Kapil Dev. With the West Indies the visitors to India in 1983–84, he reached 100 from 94 balls, equalling Bradman's record of 29 Test centuries. In the next Test, he passed Geoff Boycott's total of 8,114 Test runs and became the new world record holder. In the sixth Test, batting at number 4 but going in with the score 0 for 2, he scored 236 not out, his highest Test score.

He became captain again for a couple of series, making 47 times he captained his country in Tests. He completed 106 consecutive Test appearances, a record until overtaken by Allan Border. In his final Test series, against Pakistan in 1986–87, "the little master" passed 10,000 runs, the first player to do so. He ended on 10,122, another record since surpassed by Border. He played for the Rest of the World in MCC's bicentenary match at Lord's in 1987, scoring 188, his first century there. He retired after the 1987–88 World Cup.

CAREER FACT FILE

Born: July 10, 1949, Bombay, India
Teams: Bombay (1967–68 to 1986–87), Somerset (1980)
Tours: West Indies 1970–71, 1975–76, 1982–83; England 1971, 1974, 1975 (World Cup), 1979, 1982, 1983 (World Cup), 1986; Ceylon 1973–74, 1985–86; New Zealand 1975–76, 1980–81; Australia 1977–78, 1980–81, 1985–86; Pakistan 1978–79, 1982–83, 1984–85; Sharjah (not first-class) 1983–84, 1984–85, 1985–86; Rest of World to Australia 1971–72, to England 1987
First-class career: (1966–67 to 1987, 348 matches)
Batting: runs 25,834; average 51.46; highest score 340; centuries 81
Bowling: wickets 22; runs 1,240; average 56.36; best 3–43
Catches: 293
Tests: (1970–71 to 1986–87, 125 matches)
Batting: runs 10,122; average 51.12; highest score 236 not out; centuries 34
Bowling: wickets 1; runs 206; average 206.00; best 1–34
Catches: 108

GRACE

"W.G." was the most famous cricketer of all, a law unto himself, who with his brothers made Gloucestershire a first-class county.

W.G. GRACE *on an 1896 calendar.*

THE DOCTOR

GRACE AND FRIENDS *W.G., captain of the Gentlemen v Players at Lord's, 1894.*

William Gilbert Grace was not only the most famous cricketer of all time, but in his day the best-known Englishman. With his big beard and burly frame, he was instantly recognizable. He came from a cricketing family, the second-youngest of five brothers, and was coached as a boy in the back garden by an uncle, with his mother giving strong support. His brothers E.M., G.F., and Henry all played first-class cricket for Gloucestershire, the first two also for England (all three played together in one Test). His son, W.G. Jr, played for Gloucestershire, and another, C.B., for London County. Two nephews also played first-class cricket, one for Gloucestershire.

Grace scored 32 against an All-England XI when 15, and made his first-class debut aged 16 for Gentlemen of South. When he was 18, he scored 224 not out for England against Surrey at the Oval. An athlete in his younger days, he slipped off during the match to win a 440-yard hurdles championship at Crystal Palace.

He dominated the Gentlemen (i.e. amateurs) v Players match, which was to remain one of the showpieces of the season for 156 years. The Gentlemen had won only seven times in 35 years before Grace played for them, but the Players would win only seven times in 50 years afterwards. He began playing for Gloucestershire in 1868 and, when Gloucestershire became first-class in 1870, he captained them till 1898, when there was a dispute. Grace then moved to London County in 1900 and captained them for four years, during which time they were regarded as first-class, too.

> **"No one has by prowess and personality alike so long and so indisputably dominated the field."**
>
> *Cricket historian H.S. ALTHAM*

When 23, Grace had one of his best seasons, establishing a record aggregate of runs, 2,739, and the highest average, 78.25. His average was more than double the second highest, the 37.66 of Notts batsman Richard Daft. In this season, 1871, Grace also became the first to score 10 centuries in a season. He was the first to perform the double of 1,000 runs and 100 wickets in 1874 – although some record books claim he did it in 1873. The fact is that, such was Grace's charisma, a certain amount of fiddling with scores took place that year to give him the honour – the Society of Cricket Statisticians and Historians have now corrected Grace's figures. This fiddling reflected Grace's stature in the game, which has led to stories of his grandeur, such as the famous placard for a match: "Entrance 6d; if W.G. Grace plays, one shilling" and the occasion when, given out early, he refused to go, telling the umpire that the crowd had come to see him bat, not the umpire giving him out. Of course, some of the extra entrance money mentioned above would have gone to Grace, who although a "Gentleman" was far from being an amateur.

As a batsman, Grace was a master, seeing the ball early and sound in judgement of length. He scored all round the wicket. Although he scored 344 for the MCC against Kent in 1876, his career batting average of just under 40 would not be remarkable today. But one has to consider the genuinely fast bowling he faced and mastered on pitches which by today's standards would be regarded as extremely dangerous. Grace was the first player to score 20,000 runs, and the first to each target up to 50,000. He was the first to score 100 centuries.

As a bowler, his style has been described as "high, home and easy", delivering slows with the round-arm action of his day, but no doubt using all the cunning and competitiveness that made him stand out. He established yet another first – the first player to take 2,000 wickets.

At his peak he was called "the champion". He had already reached his peak before Test match cricket began. He toured North America in 1872 and took a team to Australia in 1873–74, but there were no first-class matches on the itinerary. Although he played his first Test in 1880, and captained England from 1888 to 1899, including the tour to Australia in 1891–92, he played only 22 Tests. He hit the first England Test hundred in his first innings in Tests, 152 at the Oval, the first Test played in England. Although his powers began to wane in the 1890s, he had a magnificent season in 1895, when he became the first batsman to score 1,000 runs in May – in 22 days, in fact. That season he completed his hundredth hundred. No wonder a "shilling testimonial" for him realised £9,000. In his later years, he became a bowls enthusiast and helped form the English Bowling Association in 1903.

CAREER FACT FILE

Born:	August 18, 1848, Downend, Bristol
Died:	October 23, 1915, Mottingham, Kent
Teams:	Gloucestershire (1870–99); Kent (1877 – 1 match as "given man"); London County (1900–04)
Tours:	North America 1872 (not first-class); Australia 1873–74 (not first-class), 1891–92
First-class career:	(1865–1908, 869 matches)
Batting:	runs 54,211; average 39.45; highest score 344; centuries 124
Bowling:	wickets 2,809; runs 50,980; average 18.14; best 10–49
Catches:	875 (plus 5 stumped)
Tests:	(1880–99, 22 matches)
Batting:	runs 1,098; average 32.29; highest score 170; centuries 2
Bowling:	wickets 9; runs 236; average 26.22; best 2–12
Catches:	39

HADLEE

With mental as much as physical assets, Hadlee became his country's greatest cricketer and the first bowler in the world to take 400 Test wickets.

HADLEE *batting for Notts in 1986.*

SIR RICHARD THE LIONHEART

CAREER FACT FILE

Born: July 3, 1951, St Albans, Christchurch, New Zealand
Teams: Canterbury 1971–72 to 1988–89, Nottinghamshire 1978–87, Tasmania 1979–80
Tours: Australia 1972–73, 1973–74, 1980–81, 1982–83 (not first-class), 1984–85 (not first-class), 1985–86, 1987–88; England 1973, 1975 (World Cup), 1978, 1979 (World Cup), 1983, 1986, 1990; India 1976–77, 1988–89; Pakistan 1976–77; Sri Lanka 1983–84, 1986–87; West Indies 1984–85; Sharjah 1986–87 (not first-class)
First-class career: (1971–72 to 1990, 342 matches)
Batting: runs 12,052; average 31.71; highest score 210 not out; centuries 14
Bowling: wickets 1,490; runs 26,998; average 18.11; best 9–52
Catches: 198
Tests: (1972–73 to 1990, 86 matches)
Batting: runs 3,124; average 27.16; highest score 151 not out; centuries 2
Bowling: wickets 431; runs 9,611; average 22.29; best 9–52
Catches: 39

If *Wisden* had made Hadlee a cricketer of the year in 1990, rather than 1982, the quote on this page might have read slightly differently: the world-class fast bowler had established a class of his own by being the first ever to take 400 Test wickets. In the years since, only Kapil Dev has joined him on the heights.

Richard John Hadlee comes from a cricketing family. His father, W.A., captained New Zealand, and of his four cricketing brothers D.R. played for New Zealand, and B.G. for Canterbury. His wife, Karen, played for New Zealand Women.

Tall and wiry rather than muscular, he began playing for Canterbury in 1971–72 and a year later made his Test debut against Pakistan. He really came to the fore in 1975–76 against India when, in the third Test, he took 4 for 35 and 7 for 23 to help win the match by an innings and square the series. These were the best match figures produced by a New Zealander at the time. In 1977–78 at Wellington, he was instrumental in New Zealand beating England for the first time, in the 48th match between them. He took 10 wickets, his 6 for 26 in the second innings skittling England for 64 when they were chasing 137. In 1979–80, he scored his first Test hundred, and his 11 wickets in the first Test against the West Indies set up the one-wicket win which gave New Zealand their first Test rubber at home after 50 years trying.

Hadlee then began an astonishing revival in the fortunes of Nottinghamshire, for whom he signed in 1978. In 1981, he took 100 wickets, the only bowler to do so, and Nottinghamshire won the championship for the first time for 62 years. From 1980 to 1987 at Nottinghamshire, he achieved complete domination over county batsmen, finishing top of the bowling averages five times and second twice.

Meanwhile he revived New Zealand, and had a hand in everything they achieved in the 1980s and beyond. New Zealand's win at Headingley in 1983 caused such euphoria that back home the demands on Hadlee led him to suffer a kind of mental breakdown. But a quick course in motivation by a psychologist soon had him back on form, and in England in 1984 he performed the double of 1,000 runs and 100 wickets, a very rare event since the introduction of one-day cricket. He also hit his highest score, 210 not out against Middlesex.

Because of the strains of the English season, he modified his run-up to a shorter one more economical on energy, and reaped great rewards. In Australia in 1985–86, he achieved his best analysis, 9 for 52, and his 33 wickets in the three-match series gave New Zealand their first series victory over Australia.

Hadlee said farewell to Nottinghamshire in 1987 by helping them to win the championship again. His Test wicket-taking continued: in 1988–89 he passed Ian Botham's world record by capturing his 374th wicket in India; he passed 400 in 1989–90 on his home ground of Christchurch and finished in 1990 with 431. It had taken only 86 Tests, a remarkable strike rate of five wickets per match. In nine of those Tests he had taken 10 wickets; 36 times he took five wickets in an innings. He was awarded an MBE in 1980 and a knighthood in 1990 on his final tour to England. Now he runs a plant nursery in Christchurch with his wife.

> **"A world-class fast bowler whose aggressive left-handed batting entitles him to all-rounder status."**
>
> *Five Cricketers of the Year, Wisden 1982*

WICKET RECORD *Hadlee helped to win the Championship in 1987.*

HOBBS

Hobbs was more than the finest batsman of his generation; he was an attractive stroke-maker and gallant opponent who cared little for statistics.

JACK HOBBS *going out to bat.*

THE MASTER

AFTER THE ASHES *Jack Hobbs batting in 1926, the year he helped England regain the Ashes after 14 years.*

There are those who still regard John Berry Hobbs as the greatest batsman of all, although his figures were eclipsed by Bradman. They base their view on his style, grace and mastery in all conditions, including the sticky wickets which do not occur in cricket in these days of covering whenever it rains. Hobbs himself would not have been the least concerned about his place in the pantheon. To quote Robertson-Glasgow, who bowled to him when he broke Grace's record of centuries, "he had the gift of smiling quietly at failure and triumph alike". Not that he failed often. He scored more runs and more centuries than any cricketer in history.

Hobbs joined Surrey in 1905 after playing four seasons for Cambridge, following in the footsteps of Tom Hayward, who was to be his opening partner and mentor till the First World War. W.G. Grace was captain of the Gentlemen of England in the first match Hobbs played for Surrey, in which he scored 88. Hobbs was soon into his stride. In 1907, he and Hayward shared four opening stands of over a hundred in one week and in 1909 put on 352 against Warwickshire. In 1907–08, Hobbs went to Australia and averaged 43.14 in his four Tests: in four more tours there he never averaged fewer than 50 in the Tests. In 1911–12, he enjoyed an outstanding tour, scoring 662 Test runs, average 82.75, and sharing with Wilfred Rhodes an opening stand of 323 at Melbourne, which remained an Ashes record opening stand for 77 years.

The war took seven years from Hobbs' career in what would have been his prime. Afterwards he had a new partner for Surrey, Andy Sandham, with whom he shared 63 opening stands of 100 or more, including a Surrey record of 428 against Oxford University in 1926. But the opening partner with whom Hobbs is most closely associated is Yorkshire's Herbert Sutcliffe, who began his Test career in 1924. Seven times they put on 200-plus together, and passed 100 on 26 occasions, 15 in Tests. In Australia in 1924–25, they had consecutive stands in Tests of 157, 110 and 283. Their most famous partnership occurred at the Oval in 1926, when they were required to open the second innings on a difficult rain-affected pitch and put on 172 (Hobbs 100), establishing a base for England to regain the Ashes after 14 years. A similar stand of 105 (Hobbs 49) in 1928–29 on one of the most spiteful of Melbourne stickies paved the way for a three-wicket win and a 3–0 winning lead in the series.

> **"He was the most perfectly equipped by art and temperament for any style of innings on any sort of wicket against any quality of opposition."**
>
> *R.C. ROBERTSON-GLASGOW, cricketer and writer*

On the domestic front, Hobbs caused tremendous excitement in 1925 as he closed in on Grace's record of centuries (then held to be 126). He was in tremendous form, and each time he didn't quite make a century it was said he'd "failed again". On August 15 he went to Taunton to play against Somerset and equalled the record in the first innings and passed it in the second. That season he scored 16 centuries, a record until surpassed by Denis Compton in 1947, and 3,042 runs, average 70.32. In 1926, when he averaged 77.60, he made his highest score, 316 not out for Surrey against Middlesex at Lord's, the highest score made at Lord's until Graham Gooch beat it 64 years later.

Hobbs had overlapped Grace in his first match for Surrey, and in his last Test series in 1930, when he was 47, he overlapped Bradman, then on his first triumphant tour of England. So Hobbs passed on the mantle of the world's leading batsman, having been the first to score 5,000 runs in Test cricket.

In his first-class career, Hobbs was involved in no fewer than 166 opening stands of 100 or more. His total of runs, 61,760, remains a record more than 60 years after his retirement, as does his total of centuries, 199. These two records appear slightly different, 61,237 and 197, in *Wisden*, which has preferred to stick with tradition rather than correct them in the light of research by the Association of Cricket Statisticians and Historians. It is of little concern. It was the manner of the runs not the number that counted. It is said that Hobbs could have had many more had he not often surrendered his wicket on scoring a century.

Hobbs was an outstanding fielder at cover, and a pretty reasonable swing bowler, who opened the bowling in three Tests in South Africa. He was knighted in 1953, and every year on his birthday, until his death in 1963, "the master" was feted at a special dinner organized by admirers, of whom John Arlott was delighted to be at the fore.

CAREER FACT FILE

Born: December 16, 1882, Cambridge
Died: December 21, 1963, Hove, Sussex
Teams: Surrey (1905–34)
Tours: Australia 1907–08, 1911–12, 1920–21, 1924–25, 1928–29; South Africa 1909–10, 1913–14; India and Ceylon (Vizianagram's XI) 1930–31
First-class career: (1905–34, 834 matches)
Batting: runs 61,760; average 50.70; highest score 316 not out; centuries 199
Bowling: wickets 108; runs 2,704; average 25.04; best 7–56
Catches: 340
Tests: (1907–08 to 1931, 61 matches)
Batting: runs 5,410; average 56.94; highest score 211; centuries 15
Bowling: wickets 1; runs 165; average 165.00; best 1–19
Catches: 17

IMRAN

One of the game's greatest all-rounders, Imran moulded the differing factions of Pakistani cricket into a major world power.

IMRAN KHAN *his greatest triumph: holding the World Cup aloft in 1992.*

CAPTAIN MARVEL

Imran Khan Niazi had a strange cricket career. A fierce critic of the structure of the first-class game in Pakistan, he did not play domestic cricket in his own country after 1980–81. Although he played county cricket in England from 1971 to 1988, his appearances were limited, as they were in his season in Australia, when he played five times for New South Wales. At the end of his career he was playing international cricket only.

He has a remarkable cricketing pedigree. Eight first cousins played first-class cricket, two of them, Majid Khan and Javed Burki, captaining Pakistan, as he himself was to do. Two uncles, Baqa Jilani and Jahagir Khan, played for India. While still at school, he made his first-class debut, aged 16½, for Lahore as a medium-fast bowler and opening bat. The chairman of selectors was his uncle, the captain his cousin. He was picked for the tour of England in 1971, making his Test debut at Edgbaston, aged 18½. He failed to take a wicket, but had already agreed to play for Worcestershire while studying at Worcester Royal Grammar School. He went to Oxford University and won blues in 1973–75. In 1974, after coming down from Oxford, he played in three Tests for the Pakistani touring side, slightly disappointingly (five wickets). After leaving Oxford he played for Pakistan International Airways for six years, after which he left Pakistani cricket. At the same time he played in England, moving from Worcestershire to Sussex in 1977.

He was given a third chance to establish himself in the Pakistan Test side in 1976–77 and seized it. With a yard or two of pace added, he was a genuine and thoughtful fast bowler. In three series that season, against New Zealand, Australia and the West Indies, he took 57 wickets. Twelve in the third Test at Sydney against Australia helped Pakistan win in Australia for the first time.

ANOTHER WORLD CUP *Imran bowling against Australia in the World Cup 1975.*

By 1981–82 he had become his country's leading wicket-taker, overtaking Fazal Mahmood, but internal strife in Pakistan's cricket politics led to eight players, including Imran, being omitted from the first two Tests against Sri Lanka. Restored in the third Test, Imran achieved his best Test bowling, 8 for 58, at Lahore (and 6 for 58 in the second innings).

After the turmoil, Imran was chosen as captain for the tour of England in 1982. Captaincy inspired him and, although the three-match series was lost 2–1, he took 21 wickets and scored 212 runs. Back in Pakistan, his side won all three Tests against Australia and then beat India 3–0 in a six-Test series. He took 53 wickets in the two series at an average of 13.75.

A shin injury kept him out of cricket for a season, but in Australia in 1983–84 he played in the last two Tests as captain and batsman only – a tribute to his genuine all-round qualities. He averaged 56.66.

He was not fully fit until 1985–86, the following season taking 18 wickets at only 11.05 each against the West Indies. In 1987, he led Pakistan to their first series victory in England, topping the series bowling with 21 wickets at 21.67, and scoring an imperious 118 at the Oval. In the West Indies the following winter, he took 23 wickets at 18.31, but Pakistan narrowly lost the final Test when they could have made themselves cricket's unofficial world champions. However, Imran achieved this in another way when he led Pakistan to win the World Cup in Australia in 1991–92, beating England in the final. He retired from cricket after this. As well as his skill as captain and as inspiration, he is one of only four cricketers (Botham, Hadlee and Kapil Dev being the others) to achieve 3,000 runs and 300 wickets in Tests.

Imran became a public figure, raising funds for a cancer hospital after his mother's death in 1985, embracing more rigorously the Muslim faith, marrying a rich heiress and entering politics.

"The sense of responsibility (of being captain) turned a fine cavalier into a great cricketer."

Five Cricketers of the Year, Wisden 1983

CAREER FACT FILE

Born: November 25, 1952, Lahore, Pakistan
Teams: Lahore (1969–70 to 1970–71), Worcestershire (1971–76), Oxford University (1973–75), Dawood Club (1975–76), PIA (1975–76 to 1980–81), Sussex (1977–88), New South Wales (1984–85)
Tours: England 1971, 1974, 1975 (World Cup), 1979 (World Cup), 1982, 1983 (World Cup), 1987; Sri Lanka 1975–76, 1985–86; Australia 1976–77, 1978–79, 1981–82, 1983–84, 1984–85 (not first-class), 1986–87 (not first-class), 1988–89, 1989–90, 1991–92; West Indies 1976–77, 1987–88; New Zealand 1978–79, 1988–89; India 1979–80, 1986–87, 1989–90 (not first-class); Sharjah (not first-class) 1984–85, 1985–86, 1988–89, 1989–90, 1990–91, 1991–92; Australia and New Zealand 1991–92 (World Cup); Rest of World to England 1987, 1988
First-class career: (1969–70 to 1991–92,382 matches)
Batting: runs 17,771; average 36.79; highest score 170; centuries 30
Bowling: wickets 1,287; runs 28,726; average 22.32; best 8–34
Catches: 117
Tests: (1971 to 1991–92, 88 matches)
Batting: runs 3,807; average 37.69; highest score 136; centuries 6
Bowling: wickets 362; runs 8,258; average 22.81; best 8–58
Catches: 28

LARA

The record-breaker who leapt into immortality with 876 runs which broke two of the most treasured records in cricket.

LARA *on his way to 132 against Australia, Perth, 1996–97.*

THE SEVENTH SON

ON THE WAY *Lara on his way to a century v England, Trent Bridge, 1995.*

To break one of cricket's greatest records would ensure a batsman a place in the record books forever, and a position in any gallery of greats. To break another, seemingly even more impregnable, only seven weeks later, sounds like something out of fiction. Yet Brian Charles Lara did it, and his place among the all-time greats was already secure at the age of 25.

Lara is the seventh son of 11 children and was born in the village of Cantaro in Santa Cruz, four miles outside Port of Spain. He was taken to the Harvard Club by an older sister when seven for cricket coaching. Former West Indies opening bat Joey Carew took him in hand and at 14 he was scoring centuries at Fatima College. He toured India with a schools team and later captained the West Indies Youth team to the Youth World Cup in Australia, and took a B side to Zimbabwe. He made his debut for Trinidad in 1987–88 and soon showed his class with 92 against the Barbados fast bowlers, Garner and Marshall.

He was devastated when his father Bunty died in 1988, just as Lara was chosen for the West Indies squad for the third Test against India at his local Queen's Park Oval. Unfortunately he was made 12th man and did not play.

His Test debut came in the final Test at Lahore on the tour of India in 1990–91, and he made 44 (at a critical time) and 5. He was on the tour of England in 1991 but was injured just when it looked as if he might make the Test side. His second appearance was in the historic first Test with South Africa after their return to Test cricket in 1991–92. He scored 17 and 64.

The following season he went to Australia, and in the third Test at Sydney announced his class to the world. After Australia had declared at 503 for 9, Lara went in at 31 for 2 and made 277 in a masterly innings, the fourth-highest at the time by a West Indian. He treated the Australian bowlers, who included McDermott, Hughes and Warne, with disdain, and was disappointed to be run out at 277, not afraid to admit he had his sights on Sobers' world-record 365. Lara topped the West Indies' batting averages.

Later that season he helped the West Indies beat Pakistan in the three-match so-called "World Championship of Test Cricket" by 1–0, averaging 43.20.

The following season England visited the West Indies. England had just reduced their deficit to 2–1 when the fifth Test began at St John's, Antigua. Lara went out to bat at 11 for 1, which soon became 12 for 2. In a rain-interrupted innings he advanced with first Adams, then Arthurton, then Chanderpaul to pass 300. As he went on and on, the talk at the start of the third day was of whether he could beat Sobers' 365. At 347 he was stuck for 18 minutes and was nearly yorked. Were nerves to deprive him? No: at 361 he smashed Caddick through the covers to equal the record, and next over he pulled Lewis to square leg for another boundary to beat the record. He accepted six minutes of congratulations but was out through tiredness for 375 after 13 hours' batting. Sobers was one of the first to congratulate him.

Before this innings Lara had agreed to join Warwickshire for the 1994 season. Seven weeks after his great feat he went out to bat for Warwickshire against Durham at Edgbaston. Durham had declared at 556 for 8; Lara came in at 8 for 1. When 12, he was "bowled" from a no-ball, and he was dropped by the wicket-keeper at 18. But then he went on remorselessly and, with the match heading for a draw, went for another record. He was dropped at 238 and again at 413. When possibly the last over of the match began he was 497 not out – Hanif Mohammad's world-record score was 499. Surprisingly, he blocked three balls and was struck on the head by the fourth, but the next went for 4 and he ended 501 not out. It came from 427 balls.

"Lara is the only batsman today who plays the game the way it should be played ... It's a pride and joy to watch him."

SIR GARFIELD SOBERS

Since then Lara's form has suffered through commercialism, rows and jealousy. He admits he was losing his appetite for the game. His saviour could be Clive Lloyd, new manager of the West Indies, who has become a father figure to him. Lara has regained his enthusiasm and ambition, and Lloyd says he will lead the West Indies into the 21st century.

N.B. the table opposite includes the West Indies' tour of Australia and the home Tests v India, 1996–97, but not Tests v Sri Lanka or domestic cricket, 1996–97.

CAREER FACT FILE

Born: May 2, 1969, Santa Cruz, Trinidad
Teams: Trinidad (1987–88 to 1996–97)
Tours: Pakistan 1990–91, 1991–92 (not first-class); England 1991, 1995; Australia 1991–92, 1992–93, 1996–97; Sri Lanka 1993–94; New Zealand 1993–94; India 1994–95; Australia and New Zealand 1991–92 (World Cup); India and Pakistan 1995–96 (World Cup); Sharjah (not first-class) 1991–92
First-class career: (1987–88 to 1996–97, 108 matches)
Batting: runs 10,404; average 55.00; highest score 501 not out; centuries 29
Bowling: wickets 1; runs 284; average 284.00; best 1–22
Catches: 134
Tests: (1990–91 to 1996–97, 43 matches)
Batting: runs 3,884; average 55.48; highest score 375; centuries 7
Bowling: runs 18; wickets 0
Catches: 56

LILLEE

The greatest fast bowler of his day, Dennis Lillee got a special kick from taking English wickets, and enjoyed the pleasure 167 times.

LILLEE *A smooth but menacing run-up.*

THE MENACE

CAREER FACT FILE

Born:	July 18, 1949, Subiaco, Perth, Western Australia
Teams:	Western Australia (1969–70 to 1983–84), Tasmania (1987–88), Northamptonshire (1988)
Tours:	New Zealand 1969–70, 1976–77, 1981–82; England 1972, 1975, 1980, 1981, 1983 (World Cup); West Indies 1972–73; Pakistan 1979–80; Sri Lanka 1982–83; International Wanderers to South Africa 1975–76; Rest of World to England 1988
First-class career:	(1969–70 to 1988, 198 matches)
Batting:	runs 2,377; average 13.90; highest score 73 not out; centuries 0
Bowling:	wickets 882; runs 20,695; average 23.46; best 8–29
Catches:	67
Tests:	(1970–71 to 1983–84, 70 matches)
Batting:	runs 905; average 13.71; highest score 73 not out; centuries 0
Bowling:	wickets 355; runs 8,493; average 23.92; best 7–83
Catches:	23

Dennis Lillee, for a decade, was one of the most feared fast bowlers ever to play cricket. By the time he retired, he had taken more wickets than any Test bowler before him. He had done it with great technique and with courage, for he had to overcome severe back problems. He had also done it in the way of most fast bowlers: with a swagger, a belligerence and no fear whatever of offending the cricketing establishment.

With a fine physique and limitless stamina, he made his debut for Western Australia in 1969–70 and took 32 Sheffield Shield wickets. The following season he was in the Test team against England, taking eight wickets in the series dominated by England's John Snow. In 1971, he played for Haslingden in the Lancashire League, reaping the benefit when he toured England in 1972 and took 31 Test wickets at 17.87. It was the most wickets an Australian had taken in a series in England at the time.

However, his fine progress broke down in the West Indies in 1972–73 when he ended the first Test, in which he was wicketless, with stress fractures in the back, which kept him in plaster for six weeks. His return to Tests was in 1974–75 against England, when he was at his best. With new partner Jeff Thomson, he shattered the English batting, his and Thomson's names being joined as the fearsome "Lilian Thomson". Australia regained the Ashes 4–1, and retained them with a single win in England in 1975. Lillee took 46 English wickets in the two series.

The pair demolished the strong West Indians in 1975–76 when Australia were the strongest team in the world, largely thanks to Lillee and Thomson. Lillee took 11 wickets as Australia won the Centenary Test against England in 1976–77, but then joined Kerry Packer's World Series Cricket. With his black moustache, smooth 19-step run-up, perfect action and a delivery which threatened dismissal or injury to the batsman, he was not a man Packer could do without.

> **"After two Tests their names (Lillee and Thomson) had become synonymous with pain and terror or triumph and victory, depending on one's nationality."**
>
> *DAVID FRITH on the 1974–75 Test series*

SHOUT IT OUT *Lillee appeals vociferously during the Tests in England in 1981.*

He returned to Tests in 1979–80, when, although less fast, he took 23 English wickets in three Tests, and went out to bat with an aluminium bat, actually scoring three runs with it before Brearley objected and the umpires ordered him to change it. Lillee held up the game for 10 minutes while he threw a tantrum. Later Brearley became his 100th English victim in Tests. In 1981, he took 39 wickets in a losing series in England, but did at least win a bet when backing England at 500–1 to win the Headingley Test from an "impossible" position which, thanks to Botham, they did. His worst behaviour came in 1981–82 when, after impeding Javed Miandad, the Pakistani captain, a player he was pleased to dislike, he kicked him. This earned a suspension from two one-day matches.

That same season, against the West Indies, he returned his best innings analysis in Tests with 7 for 83. Australia won the match, but the series was drawn. When Lillee had Gomes caught, he passed Lance Gibbs' record of 309 Test wickets. By the end of the match, his 85 Test wickets in 1981 were a new record for a calendar year.

Lillee was by now battling against back problems once more, and played in only four more Test series, three of them disappointingly, but in his final series in 1983–84 he took 20 Pakistan wickets in a winning series. He, Greg Chappell and Rodney Marsh then retired from Tests together. If Thomson had been a great partner for Lillee, Marsh was more so, though less conspicuous. Both ended with a record 355 Test victims (Lillee's since passed) and their 95 shared dismissals (c Marsh b Lillee) was also a world record.

Lillee signed for Northamptonshire in 1988, but an ankle injury restricted his appearances to seven matches, and the popular warrior finally called it a day.

MARSHALL

As West Indian fast bowlers go, Marshall is small in stature, high in strike-rate, and most successful of all in getting wickets.

MARSHALL *bowling in England, 1988.*

MR WHIPPY

Malcolm Denzil Marshall stands only 5ft 10½in tall, and when he was a boy wanted to be a wicket-keeper, like the West Indian Test keeper David Murray, who came from the same district in Barbados. A year or two before his first Test match he regarded himself as a batsman and useful medium-pace change bowler. Yet Malcolm Marshall became the deadliest fast bowler in the world, who elbowed his way into a Test side which included Roberts, Holding, Croft and Garner as fast bowlers and outshone them all in taking a record number of Test wickets for a West Indian. His assets were dedication, skill, ambition and fitness. He pursued a regular regime of 50 or 60 sit-ups a day, even at his peak. He managed to make an advantage of his lack of inches, explaining that with his speed in his run-up, his whippy action, co-ordination and balance, he came off the wicket faster than the batsmen expected – that is, his deliveries tended to skid off the wicket.

He played cricket all the time as a boy, taking up bowling in order to get his turn to bat to come round more quickly. He joined a club, got into the Barbados side at 19 and was lucky enough to be called up to tour India in 1978–79, in a side weakened by the defection of some players to World Series Cricket. He played in three Tests, and took only three wickets at 88.33 each, clearly not yet the finished article.

"There is more to being a great fast bowler than the ability to bowl fast. It takes fitness, stamina, common sense, commitment and aggression and Marshall has got them all."

WES HALL, former fast bowler and West Indian Minister of Sport

CELEBRATION *Marshall at Hampshire's B & H Cup win, Lord's 1992.*

In 1979, he began playing for Hampshire as a replacement for Andy Roberts, their previous highly successful West Indian bowler. After leaving the sunshine of Barbados, he arrived to play his first match at Southampton, running in to bowl with snow in the air. He took nine wickets and began a 14-year career with Hampshire, in which he was one of the leading bowlers on the county circuit all through the 1980s. In 1982 he took 134 wickets – 44 more than the next bowler.

He established his West Indies place in 1980, getting 15 wickets in four Tests on the tour of England, but it wasn't until 1983–84 in India that he opened the bowling regularly, again replacing Andy Roberts. He took 33 wickets at 18.81 on that tour and from then on was perhaps the most feared West Indian bowler.

Marshall always liked doing well against England and the Headingley Test in 1984 typifies his dedication – and not only as bowler. After bowling six overs on the first morning, he suffered a double fracture of his left thumb when fielding close to the wicket, and left the field. With Gomes on 96, he came in as last man to bat one-handed. Gomes got his hundred. Marshall then took 7 for 53 in England's second innings, his best Test bowling till then, and he even took a "caught and bowled". The West Indies won all five Tests.

The next winter in Australia he took 28 wickets at 19.78 and was "man of the series". Back home he took 27 New Zealand wickets in four Tests at 18.00, and the following season 27 more English wickets at 17.85, as the West Indies won 5–0 again. In that season, a bouncer gave England captain Mike Gatting a squashed nose and two black eyes. His lethal bowling contrasted with his happy demeanour off the field where he likes reggae music and a good joke and is companionable and considerate to all.

He enjoyed his best tour of England in 1988 when he took 35 wickets at only 12.65 each, including his best innings analysis in Tests, 7 for 22 at Old Trafford. The following winter, in Australia, his total of Test wickets passed 300, and later, in India, he took his 310th wicket to pass Lance Gibbs' record as the leading West Indian wicket-taker in Tests. There seemed little diminution of his powers in England in 1991, when he took 20 wickets at 22.10, bringing his total to 376, but to his dismay, for he loves Test cricket, he was not selected for further Tests and did not get the chance to push his total to 400.

He went to play for Natal in South Africa, which he captained in 1993–94. Like many great bowlers, he loved batting and was pleased to make his then highest score of 116 not out in 1982 for Hampshire against Lancashire, captained by his Test skipper Clive Lloyd. In 1993–94, he averaged 60 for Natal and improved his best to 120 not out against Western Province. In 1996–97, he was made coach of the West Indies Test side.

CAREER FACT FILE

Born: April 18, 1958, Bridgetown, Barbados
Teams: Barbados (1977–78 to 1990–91), Hampshire (1979–93), Natal (1992–93 to 1995–96)
Tours: India 1978–79, 1983–84, 1989–90 (not first-class); Sri Lanka 1978–79; Australia 1979–80, 1981–82, 1983–84 (not first-class), 1984–85, 1986–87 (not first-class), 1988–89, 1991–92 (not first-class); New Zealand 1979–80, 1986–87; England 1980, 1983 (World Cup), 1984, 1988, 1991; Pakistan 1980–81, 1985–86 (not first-class), 1986–87, 1990–91, 1991–92 (not first-class); Sharjah (not first-class) 1985–86, 1986–87, 1989–90; Australia and New Zealand (World Cup) 1991–92; Young West Indians to Zimbabwe 1981–82
First-class career: (1977–78 to 1995–96, 408 matches)
Batting: runs 11,004; average 24.83; highest score 120 not out; centuries 7
Bowling: wickets 1,651; runs 31,548; average 19.10; best 8–71
Catches: 145
Tests: (1978–79 to 1991, 81 matches)
Batting: runs 1,810; average 18.85; highest score 92; centuries 0
Bowling: wickets 376; runs 7,876; average 20.94; best 7–22
Catches: 25

POLLOCK

Big and strong, Pollock wielded one of the heaviest bats in cricket, yet his touch was so magical it seemed more like a wand than a bludgeon.

POLLOCK *batting against the 'rebel' English touring side in Johannesburg, 1981–82.*

THE GOLDEN BOY

DEFENCE *Pollock defends against the 'rebel' English tourists, 1981–82.*

Of all the fine players deprived of a full Test career because they were born in South Africa and were at their peak when that country was banned from international cricket, the greatest was Robert Graeme Pollock. Because his first-class career was almost entirely confined to domestic cricket in South Africa, and he did not play for an English county or an Australian state, the world at large remembers him most for a few scintillating innings played on tours of one kind or another. But what precious jewels they are.

He came from a cricketing family whose roots were Scottish – one grandfather was a Presbyterian minister. His father kept wicket for Orange Free State, his brother Peter was an outstanding South African Test bowler, two sons play for Transvaal and nephew Shaun (Peter's son) played for South Africa on their re-instatement into Test cricket. Graeme was exceptional as a schoolboy, hitting a century and taking 10 wickets in the same match when only nine. Like his father, he was right-handed in everything except batting. On leaving school, he joined Eastern Province and, at the age of 16 years 335 days, became the youngest player to hit a century in the Currie Cup. He owed much to the coaching of the Sussex player George Cox, who between 1931 and 1960 scored nearly 23,000 first-class runs. When the 17-year-old visited England with his parents in 1961, he played six innings for Sussex second XI. Little more than a year later, he became the youngest South African to hit a double-century and, at just turned 20, he was captain of Eastern Province.

Pollock made his Test debut in 1963–64 when he was selected to tour Australia. In the second major match of the tour, he batted against a combined XI at Perth and scored a century in 85 minutes. When he was out for 127, Sir Donald Bradman congratulated the 19-year-old on one of the best innings he'd ever seen. Pollock failed in his first two Tests, making only 43 in three innings, but at Sydney he scored 122, adding to his list of "youngests" by becoming the youngest South African to score a Test century – he was 19 years 318 days. His 122 came out of 186 added, the second 50 of his century needing 17 scoring shots. South Africa levelled the series by winning the fourth Test at Adelaide, when they made 595, then their highest. Pollock joined Eddie Barlow (201) at 70 for 2 and left at 411 for 3, scoring 175 in 283 minutes. He was the third player to score two Test centuries before he was 20 (R.N. Harvey and Mushtaq Mohammad the others).

When England visited South Africa in 1964–65, Fred Titmus got him in his first three Test innings for only 17 runs, and it was not until the final Test that he showed his true majesty with 137 and 77 not out. He was the second player (after George Headley) to score three Test hundreds before he was 21. In England in 1965, he helped South Africa win the rubber by scoring a typical 125 at Trent Bridge. It was scored out of 160 from 145 balls with 21 boundaries, the last 91 coming while his partner scored 10. During his innings he became the youngest-ever Test player to reach 1,000 runs. Just before this, he hit 203 not out against Kent at Canterbury.

Australia visited South Africa in 1966–67, South Africa winning the series 3–1. Previously they'd never beaten Australia in a match at home in 21 attempts in 64 years. Pollock, suffering from a thigh strain, hit 209 in the Cape Town Test and 105 at Port Elizabeth, his sixth Test century being scored on his 23rd birthday. He averaged 76.51 for the series, with 537 runs.

Pollock's last Test series was also against Australia, in 1969–70. It was a massacre, South Africa winning all four Tests by huge margins. Pollock topped the averages with 73.85 and played at Durban what remains the highest-ever innings for South Africa, 274. While he and Barry Richards scored 103 runs for the third wicket, Aussie skipper Bill Lawry said he'd never seen the ball hit with such power by two players at the same time. South Africa made 622 for 9, their highest total.

After this series, Pollock did not play Test cricket again, although there were tours with the Rest of the World side. South Africa's apartheid policy, which would not allow Basil D'Oliveira to tour there in 1968–69, led to England's cancellation, and demonstrations against South Africa's tours of England in 1970 and Australia in 1971–72, on both of which Pollock was selected, led to South Africa's ban from all Test cricket. Pollock's Test average of 60.97 is second only to that of Bradman. When the style of his batting and his statistics are considered, it is clear that Test cricket lost a great deal by South Africa's ban.

> **"If you ever score a century like that again, I hope I am there to see it."**
>
> *SIR DONALD BRADMAN on Pollock's 127 at Perth 1963–64*

CAREER FACT FILE

Born: February 27, 1944, Durban, Natal, South Africa
Teams: Eastern Province (1960–61 to 1977–78), Transvaal (1978–79 to 1986–87)
Tours: England 1965; Australia and New Zealand 1963–64; Rest of World to England 1966, 1967, 1968, 1970, to Australia 1971–72; Isaacs to England 1969 ((not first-class); International Cavaliers to England 1969; International Wanderers to South Africa 1974–75
First-class career: (1960–61 to 1986–87, 262 matches)
Batting: runs 20,940; average 54.67; highest score 274; centuries 64
Bowling: wickets 43; runs 2,062; average 47.95; best 3–46
Catches: 248
Tests: (1963–64 to 1969–70, 23 matches)
Batting: runs 2,256; average 60.97; highest score 274; centuries 7
Bowling: wickets 4; runs 204; average 51.00; best 2–50
Catches: 17

SOBERS

Sobers was a one-man cricket team, not only the world's best batsman but a bowler in three styles and a great fielder – the all-time all-rounder.

BEST OF THREE *Sobers had three styles of bowling, all effective.*

ALL-ROUND GREAT

SOBERS *plays hard through the slips.*

Sobers began his first-class career when he was not yet 17. Less than a year later, he was in the Test team against England, batting number 9. He made 14 not out and 26 and took 4 wickets. The following year against the Aussies he scored 231 runs and took six wickets – a promising start, as he was still only 18. All the time he was learning the craft that made him a master left-hand batsman on all types of wicket. At that time, he was bowling orthodox left-arm spin. He was always like lightning in the field and an outstanding catcher.

> **"Sir Garfield St Aubrun Sobers was cricket's eighth knight and probably its greatest-ever player."**
>
> *Cricketer and latterly writer*
> *PETER ROEBUCK*

It was the visit to the West Indies of Pakistan in 1957–58 which really made Sobers' name. In the third Test at Kingston, he made his first Test century, and then went on and on until captain Gerry Alexander declared at 790 for 3, the West Indies' highest score. Sobers himself had made 365 not out, the highest score ever made in a Test. In the next Test, he got 125 and 109 not out. His aggregate for the series was 824, his average 137.33.

Instantly famous, he cashed in at first by signing as a professional for Radcliffe and it was there that he developed a new bowling skill, left-arm medium-fast, or even sometimes fast, swing bowling. However, on tour in India during the English winter, he found the pitches unresponsive to his new quick style and tried out his left-arm off-breaks and googlies. His batting did not suffer with this pre-occupation with bowling and, with centuries in the first three Tests, he took his record to six centuries in six successive Tests. As a batsman, he kept still as long as possible and then seemed to uncoil, launching himself into his shots and hitting the ball very hard. He was not merely an aggressive slinger of the bat, though – his shots were precise, occasionally delicate, and he could defend as well.

When England arrived in the West Indies in 1959–60, Sobers first hit them for 154 when playing for Barbados, then in the first Test in his native Bridgetown, he scored 226, adding 399 for the fourth wicket with Frank Worrell (197 not out). It remains the West Indies' best stand in Tests. He amassed 709 runs in the series, averaging 101.28.

In the winter, he played in the famous series in Australia which began with the tied Test. He took 15 wickets in this series and from then on his bowling began to pay more dividends – in the 1961–62 series against India he took 23 wickets, his best in a single series. That year, he signed for South Australia, for whom he played 26 matches in three seasons.

After a successful tour of England in 1963, he was captain of the West Indies for the visit of Australia in 1964–65, and won the series 2–1. He had a superb tour of England in 1966, scoring 722 runs, average 103.14, and taking 20 wickets. The West Indies won 3–1 and three times Sobers passed 160. In the Lord's Test, with the West Indies 95 for 5 in their second knock, only 9 ahead of England, Sobers (163 not out) was joined by his cousin David Holford (105 not out) and the two added 274 unbeaten to turn the series. He had another spell in League cricket with Norton in the North Staffordshire League and then agreed to play for Nottinghamshire in 1968, a spell which was to last seven years.

Meanwhile England won the 1967–68 series in the West Indies 1–0, after a generous Sobers' declaration at 92 for 2, leaving England to get 215. They did so, for which Sobers was much criticized.

Sobers announced his arrival in county cricket in typical fashion. At Swansea in August, against Glamorgan, he hit every ball of the six-ball over from Malcolm Nash for six, a new record for first-class cricket.

Sobers, who had played nearly non-stop for around 20 years, began to suffer injuries in 1972–73 and did not play in the home series against Australia, relinquishing the captaincy of the West Indies. He was back in the side for the tour of England in 1973, scoring 150 not out at Lord's. On England's visit in the winter, Sobers became the first batsman to pass 8,000 runs in Test matches during his innings in the second Test at Jamaica which was to be his last series. He was the second player (after Richie Benaud) to score 2,000 runs and take 200 wickets in Tests. He was knighted in 1975. He has suffered operations to knees and eyes in retirement, but retains his immense popularity.

CAREER FACT FILE

Born: July 28, 1936, Bay Land, Bridgetown, Barbados
Teams: Barbados (1952–53 to 1973–74), South Australia (1961–62 to 1963–64), Nottinghamshire (1968–74)
Tours: England 1957, 1963, 1966, 1969, 1973; Australia 1960–61, 1968–69; New Zealand 1955–56, 1968–69; Ceylon and India 1966–67; India and Pakistan 1958–59; West Indian XI to England 1964; Rest of World to England 1965, 1967, 1968, 1970, to Pakistan 1970–71, to Australia 1971–72; Swanton to India 1963–64; Cavaliers to India 1962–63
First-class career: (1952–53 to 1974, 383 matches)
Batting: runs 28,315; average 54.87; highest score 365 not out; centuries 86
Bowling: wickets 1,043; runs 28,941; average 27.74; best 9–49
Catches: 407
Tests: (1953–54 to 1973–74, 93 matches)
Batting: runs 8,032; average 57.78; highest score 365 not out; centuries 26
Bowling: wickets 235; runs 7,999; average 34.03; best 6–73
Catches: 109

THE GREAT CRICKETERS

Although cricket is a statistician's delight, the great players are those who rise above figures and impress by personality, style and the excitement they generate. Thus any choice of 200 of the greatest must be subjective. Those included here would be on many lists.

A

Abdul Qadir

Born: September 15, 1955, Lahore, Pakistan
Teams: Punjab (1975–76); Lahore (1975–76 to 1984–85); Habib Bank (1975–76 to 1995–96)
First-class: 208 matches; 3,740 runs, average 18.33; 960 wickets, average 23.22
Tests (1977–78 to 1990–91): 67 matches; 1,029 runs, average 15.59; 236 wickets, average 32.80

It was Abdul Qadir who announced the renaissance of the leg-break and googly bowlers in Test cricket when he played three Tests against England in Pakistan in 1977–78. He disappointed in England the following summer when he was troubled by injury, but by the time he returned in 1982 he was a potent force and his six wickets at Lord's played a significant part in Pakistan's victory.

In 1982–83, he took 22 wickets in three tests as Pakistan had a clean sweep against Australia, and he became the first bowler to take 100 wickets in a Pakistan season. The following season, he took 19 wickets in three Tests as Pakistan beat England in a rubber for the first time, and 10 wickets at the Oval in August 1987 ensured Pakistan's series victory in England. Three months later, Qadir produced an outstanding display of leg-spin and googly bowling when he took nine for 56 and four for 45 to bring Pakistan an innings victory over England at Lahore. His first-innings figures are a record for Pakistan in Test cricket, and he became only the second Pakistani bowler to take 200 Test wickets.

His bouncy run to the wicket, unquenchable enthusiasm and passionate appeals established his character with the crowd. Often in disagreement with authority, he was a spin bowler with a fast bowler's attitude and temperament.

Bobby Abel

Born: November 30, 1857, Rotherhithe, Surrey
Died: December 10, 1936, Stockwell, London
Teams: Surrey (1881–1904)
First-class: 627 matches; 33,124 runs, average 35.46; 236 wickets, average 24.00
Tests (1988–96): 13 matches; 744 runs, average 37.20

A diminutive opening batsman, Bobby Abel became one of the great favourites at the Oval where he was dubbed "The Guv'nor". Surrey adopted a policy of recruiting young professionals in the late 1870s and engaged Abel as an off-break bowler. He was 23 before he made his first-class debut, and it was some years before he established himself. He did not score a century until 1886, and it was an innings of 144 against the Australians that season which really set him on this way, when he scored 1,000 runs in a season for the first time. He was to repeat that feat on 13 other occasions.

He toured Australia and South Africa with England sides, and, in Sydney, January 1892, he became the first England player to carry his bat through a completed Test innings. He was unbeaten for 132 out of 307. Three years earlier, he had hit 120 against South Africa in Cape Town.

In 1893, his career was threatened by an eye infection, but he recovered to exceed 2,000 runs every season between 1895 and 1902. In 1899, he made 357 not out against Somerset at the Oval, which remains the highest score ever made for Surrey. In the same season, he and Tom Hayward scored 448 for Surrey's fourth wicket against Yorkshire at the Oval, and this remained a world record for 50 years.

In 1901, he created another record when he scored 3,309 runs in first-class cricket. His team-mate Tom Hayward was to better this five years later.

Abel's eye problem reasserted itself, and his career came to an abrupt end in 1904. He coached Surrey in 1907. He also coached at Dulwich College and ran a sports shop.

Jimmy Adams

Born: January 9, 1968, Port Maria, Jamaica
Teams: Jamaica (1984–85 to 1996–97); Nottinghamshire (1994)
First-class: 111 matches; 6,649 runs, average 44.32; 56 wickets, average 36.62
Tests (1991–92 to 1996–97): 24 matches; 1,851 runs, average 66.10; 14 wickets, average 42.50

Jimmy Adams is an all-round cricketer in every sense – a stylish left-handed batsman, a slow left-arm bowler and a most competent wicket-keeper who has been used by the West Indies in limited-over internationals in this capacity. A courteous and intelligent man, he hit 79 and took four for 43 on his Test debut, against South Africa, and made his first Test century against England at Bouda, 1993–94. This was the second game of the series; in the first he had scored 95 not out and taken six catches to equal the Test record.

He played for several seasons in the Durham League, but assisted Nottinghamshire in 1994, and the following winter he hit two Test centuries against India. He toured England in 1995 and, at one time, was ranked number one batsman in the world, but he suffered a severe blow on the head at Taunton, from which it took him some time to recover.

The injury set back his career and, for a period, he lost his place in the West Indies' side, but he is still seen as a future captain.

Neil Adcock

Born: March 8, 1931, Sea Point, Cape Town, South Africa
Teams: Transvaal (1952–53 to 1959–60); Natal (1960–61 to 1962–63)
First-class: 99 matches, 451 runs, average 5.50; 405 wickets, average 17.25
Tests (1953–54 to 1961–62): 26 matches, 146 runs, average 5.40; 104 wickets, average 21.10

A tall, slim fast bowler, Neil Adcock found his way into the South African side after only nine first-class matches. He was an immediate success, taking three wickets in the second innings as South Africa beat New Zealand in Durban, and following this with eight for 87 in the match as the Springboks triumphed in Johannesburg. He finished his first Test series with 24 wickets, an outstanding achievement. He was a hostile bowler, full of passion, but he was troubled by various injuries, and it was not until his second tour of England in 1960 that he showed himself at his best. In five Tests, he took 26 wickets at 22.57 runs each, and his total for the tour was a record 108. These achievements were all the more remarkable when one considers that his new ball partner was no-balled out of Test cricket on this tour for his illegal action. Adcock is one of only five South African bowlers to have taken 100 wickets in Test cricket.

Following his retirement, he became a radio commentator.

Terry Alderman

Born: June 12, 1956, Subiaco, Perth, Western Australia
Teams: Western Australia (1974–75 to 1991–92); Kent (1984–86); Gloucestershire (1988)
First-class: 238 matches; 1,276 runs, average 8.34; 936 wickets, average 23.47
Tests (1981 to 1990–91): 41 matches; 203 runs, average 6.54; 170 wickets, average 27.15

Terry Alderman was a right-arm fast medium-pace bowler whose control and late movement proved too much for most English batsmen. He had not played Test cricket until he came to England in 1981, and nine wickets in the first match at Trent Bridge when he bowled unchanged through the second innings gave early indication of his worth. He finished the series, in which Australia were beaten, with a record 42 wickets in six Tests.

In 1982–83, Alderman's career suffered a severe setback when he dislocated a shoulder while tackling a pitch-invader during the first Test. The injury ended his season. He was due to tour England in 1985, but was withdrawn from the party when he revealed that he had signed to go to South Africa. He had enjoyed a good season for Kent in 1984 and was to have an outstanding one in 1986. He later assisted Gloucestershire with great success. He complemented his bowling with excellent slip fielding.

A key member of the overwhelmingly successful Australian side in 1989, he took 41 wickets in the series, five times capturing a wicket in his opening over. A modest and courteous man, fiercely competitive, he coached Western Australia in 1992–93.

ALDERMAN *40 series wickets twice.*

Gubby Allen

Born: July 31, 1902, Bellevue Hill, Sydney, Australia
Died: November 29, 1989, St John's Wood, London
Teams: Middlesex (1921–1950); Cambridge University (1922–23)
First-class: 265 matches; 9,232 runs, average 28.67; 788 wickets, average 22.32
Tests (1930 to 1947–48): 25 matches; 750 runs, average 24.19; 81 wickets, average 29.37

"Gubby" Allen's career spanned 29 years, yet he was never able to play in more than a handful of games each season. He appeared in county cricket before he went up to Cambridge, and was probably the fastest bowler ever to play for Middlesex. He had the perfect action for a pace man, and became a stylish batsman.

In 1929, he became the only man to take all 10 wickets in an innings of a county match at Lord's, Lancashire being the opponents, and the following year he made his debut for England against Australia. His selection was opposed in some quarters as he had been born in Australia, and his uncle was an Australian Test cricketer.

He toured Australia with Jardine's side, 1932–33, and took 21 wickets in the "bodyline" series, although he himself refused to bowl leg-theory. He captained England against India in 1936 and was appointed to lead the side to Australia, 1936–37. Allen was not a county captain, and many believed his appointment was due to his Australian connections and had been made in an attempt to heal the wounds that existed following the "bodyline" tour. England won the first two Tests but went on to lose the next three.

Allen played no more Test cricket before the Second World War but, astonishingly, was recalled to lead England in the West Indies, 1947–48, at the age of 45. He pulled a calf muscle on the boat on the way out, could not play in the first Test and, for the first time in history, the MCC went through a tour without a win to their credit.

Very close to his mentor Sir Pelham Warner, Allen succeeded him as the most influential administrator in the game, holding all the high offices. He was knighted for services to cricket in 1986.

Lala Amarnath

Born: September 11, 1911, Lahore, India
Teams: Hindus (1929–30 to 1939–40); Southern Punjab (1933–34 to 1951–52); Patiala (1953–54 to 1957–58); Uttar Pradesh (1956–57); Railways (1958–59 to 1960–61)
First-class: 186 matches; 10,426 runs, average 41.38; 463 wickets, average 22.98
Tests (1933–34 to 1952–53): 24 matches; 878 runs, average 24.38; 45 wickets, average 32.91

Although his given name was Nanik, Amarnath, the father of two Test cricketers, was always known as

"Lala". By the time the MCC toured India, 1933–34, he was recognized as an accomplished batsman and was selected for the first Test match. He hit a century in the second innings, the first to be scored for India in a Test. It was during this season that his medium-pace bowling developed, for he had originally been a wicket-keeper, and he arrived in England in 1936 as an all-rounder of international standing, which was confirmed by 32 wickets and three centuries in the early part of the tour. His anger at the way in which the tour was being managed caused this instinctive and impetuous cricketer to erupt, and he was sent home for disciplinary proceedings. Later enquiries found him "not guilty".

He played in the Lancashire League, toured England in 1946 and took eight wickets at Old Trafford. He captained India in Australia, 1947–48 and, although confronted by Bradman's great side, he was the leading wicket-taker in the series. He retained the captaincy for the home series against West Indies, 1948–49, and kept wicket in the fifth Test when Sen was injured, holding five catches.

Demanding more money and better travelling conditions, he was suspended from domestic cricket at the end of that series and, inexplicably, was omitted from the side that toured England in 1952. The tour was a disaster, and he was

gural series against Pakistan, 1952–53, leading India to their first victory in a Test rubber. He enjoyed a fine series, but learned that he was to be replaced for the trip to the West Indies. He left the game an embittered man.

He has found consolation in the achievements of his sons. Mohinder scored more than 4,000 Test runs and was Man of the Match in the World Cup Final, 1983.

Curtly Ambrose

Born: September 21, 1963, Swetes Village, Antigua
Teams: Leeward Islands (1985–86 to 1996–97); Northamptonshire (1989–1996)
First-class: 186 matches; 2,681 runs, average 14.89; 752 wickets, average 20.46
Tests (1987–88 to 1996–97): 61 matches; 850 runs, average 12.50; 266 wickets, average 21.27

Standing 6ft 7in and with a high, classic action, Curtly Ambrose is a fast bowler who presents an awesome sight for any batsman. He had to choose between cricket and basketball as a career, and, once he had made his choice, his advance was rapid. Successes in domestic cricket won him a place in the Test side against Pakistan. To their credit, Northamptonshire had recognized this potential and signed him, but the West Indies picked him for the tour of England, 1988, and his county debut was delayed. He played in all five Tests in England with considerable success, and that success has continued unabated.

In 1990, when England toured the Caribbean, he took eight for 45 in the second innings of the Barbados Test to bring off a sensational victory for the West Indies. Even more sensationally, he took six for 34 in the inaugural Test against South Africa, 1992, to bowl the West Indies to victory when the South Africans looked certain to win.

AMBROSE *Deadly when necessary.*

Leslie Ames

Born: December 3, 1905, Elham, Kent
Died: February 27, 1990, Canterbury, Kent
Teams: Kent (1926–51)
First-class: 593 matches; 37,248 runs, average 43.51; 24 wickets, average 33.37; caught 704, stumped 417
Tests (1929 to 1938–39): 47 matches; 2,434 runs, average 40.56; caught 74, stumped 23

AMES *Wicket-keeper with 100 100s.*

Les Ames was the outstanding wicket-keeper/batsman of the inter-war period, and he remains the only wicket-keeper to have scored a hundred hundreds in first-class cricket; eight of them came in Test matches. He joined Kent as a batsman in 1923, took up wicket-keeping and gained a regular place in the county side in 1927. This was the first of 17 seasons in which he scored 1,000 runs. In 1933, he made 3,058 runs.

In 1928, he created a new wicket-keeping record with 122 dismissals, but he beat this the following season with 128 dismissals. It is a record which is not likely to be beaten, nor is his record of 64 stumpings in 1932 when he claimed a hundred victims for the third time.

He holds another wicket-keeping record in that he made 417 stumpings in his career. Many of these came off "Tich" Freeman, the leg-spinner, with whom Ames had an almost supernatural understanding.

By 1938, he had begun to suffer from back trouble, and he did not keep wicket after the Second World War although he remained a prolific scorer. He was the first professional to become a selector, and he was both secretary and manager of Kent during a very successful period for the county.

Dennis Amiss

Born: April 7, 1943, Harborne, Birmingham
Teams: Warwickshire (1960–1987)
First-class: 658 matches; 43,423 runs, average 42.86; 18 wickets, average 39.88
Tests (1966–1977): 50 matches; 3,612 runs, average 46.30

Any young player who wanted to know what was meant by correct technique had only to watch Dennis Amiss to find the answer. To see this right-handed opening batsman at the crease was in itself an aesthetic pleasure. He was associated with Warwickshire from the age of 15, and since leaving the playing staff he has become chief executive of the club, piloting them through a period of outstanding success. He took some time to establish himself in the England side, having a torrid time against the West Indies at the Oval on his debut. It was not until 1972–73, at Lahore, when he hit 112 against Pakistan, that he claimed a permanent place in the England side, and he followed his first Test century with 158 and 0 at Hyderabad and 99 and 23 in Karachi. A century against New Zealand followed, but he reached his peak in the Caribbean, 1973–74, when he hit three centuries in the rubber including a match-saving unbeaten 262 in Jamaica, the highest score of his career.

He also scored 206 against West Indies at the Oval, 1976, and, in all, made 102 centuries of which 11 were in Tests. He joined Packer's World Series and was most unfortunate not to be restored to the England side after that flirtation.

Warwick Armstrong

Born: May 22, 1879, Kyneton, Victoria, Australia
Died: July 13, 1947, Darling Point, Sydney, New South Wales, Australia
Teams: Victoria (1898–99 to 1921–22)
First-class: 269 matches; 16,158 runs, average 46.83; 832 wickets, average 19.71
Tests (1901–02 to 1921): 50 matches; 2,863 runs, average 38.69; 87 wickets, average 33.59

Warwick Armstrong was totally professional in his approach to the game. He was born to be a winner, and he showed no mercy to his opponents. He was a giant of a man who became known as "The Big Ship". He was a fine right-handed batsman and a medium-pace bowler who had turned to leg-breaks by 1905. His standing as an all-rounder can be seen from the fact that in three of his four tours of England – 1905, 1909 and 1921 – he completed the "double". In 1905, he scored 1,902 runs and took 122 wickets. His first visit to England had been three years earlier.

He was a mighty force in the Australian side of the Edwardian period, a good stroke-player and a relentlessly accurate bowler, but his relationships with the Australian Board were always strained. He was one of six players to refuse to take part in the Triangular Tournament of 1912.

He became captain of Australia when cricket resumed after the First World War and scored three centuries in the 1920–21 series which Australia won 5-0. They followed England back to England and won the first three Tests of the 1921 series at the end of which Armstrong retired.

There were those in authority who had not wanted Armstrong to lead the great 1921 side, but his players never wavered in their loyalty to him. His captaincy was shrewd, forthright, calculating, persistent and even ruthless, and in many ways he bridged the gap between the Golden Age and the ultra-professional approach of today. Ten Tests as captain, eight wins and two draws is a record to be envied.

ASIF IQBAL *Gallant all-rounder who always gave his best.*

Asif Iqbal

Born: June 6, 1943, Hyderabad, India
Teams: Hyderabad (1959–60); Karachi (1961–62 to 1968–69); PIA (1964–65 to 1979–80); National Bank (1976–77); Kent (1968–82)
First-class: 440 matches; 23,329 runs, average 37.26; 291 wickets, average 30.15
Tests (1964–65 to 1979–80): 58 matches; 3,575 runs, average 38.85; 53 wickets, average 28.33

Asif Iqbal began his career in India but emigrated to Pakistan in 1961. He made his Test debut three years later, batting at number 10 and opening the bowling with his medium pace. An exciting batsman who could adapt his style according to the needs of the moment, he made his first Test century against England at the Oval, 1967, when he went in at number nine and scored 146 in 170 minutes, sharing a record stand of 190 with Intikhab Alam.

Asif was a dynamic cricketer with Kent whom he captained in 1968, and he played a major part in one of the most successful periods in that county's history. Between 1964 and 1977, he appeared in a record 45 consecutive Tests for Pakistan. He then announced his retirement from Test cricket, and a month later joined Kerry Packer's World Series. He had long pressed for better financial rewards for Pakistani players.

When the differences between Packer and the cricketing authorities were resolved, Asif returned to Test cricket and led Pakistan against India, 1979–80. It was the first time the two nations had met for almost 19 years, and this series marked the end of Asif's career. He has remained in the game mainly as an entrepreneur involved with Sharjah and as Pakistan's representative on the ICC for a time.

William Astill

Born: March 1, 1888, Ratby, Leicestershire
Died: February 10, 1948, Stoneygate, Leicestershire
Teams: Leicestershire (1906–39)
First-class: 733 matches; 22,731 runs, average 22.55; 2,431 wickets, average 23.76
Tests (1927–28 to 1929–30): 9 matches; 190 runs, average 12.66; 25 wickets, average 34.24

Ewart Astill was one of those great county professionals of the inter-war period whose achievements and abilities were never rewarded to the extent that they deserved. He made his debut in 1906, and he was ever-present in the next two seasons. As the First World War approached he lost form, but when he was demobilized after the war he was better than ever. A reliable middle-order batsman and a slow to medium-pace bowler who could turn the ball either way, he completed the all-rounder's "double" every season from 1921 until 1930 with the exception of 1927.

His consistency was finally rewarded when he was chosen to tour South Africa, 1927–28, and he made his Test debut at the age of 39. Two years later, he went to the West Indies and played in all four Test matches there.

He was a fine slip fielder and had a good cricket brain, and when he became the first professional to captain Leicestershire, 1935, the county enjoyed one of the most successful periods of their history.

Astill was a very good billiards player, an excellent pianist and vocalist, and a good ukulele player. He was an accomplished coach and did some fine work in this field.

Mike Atherton

Born: March 23, 1968, Manchester, Lancashire
Teams: Cambridge University (1987–89); Lancashire (1987–97)
First-class: 223 matches; 15,416 runs, average 43.92; 108 wickets, average 43.75
Tests (1989–97): 62 matches; 4,627 runs, average 41.68; 2 wickets, average 151.00

Seemingly destined to captain England from the time he made his debut for Lancashire, Michael Atherton is a solid, dependable if unspectacular opening batsman who has enjoyed the longest of reigns as England captain in a most difficult period. He made his Test debut in the Ashes series of 1989, catapulted into the England team because of several defections to a rebel tour of South Africa. He proved his worth a year later with Test centuries against India and New Zealand. A back operation which was virtually to end his spells of leg-break bowling and a loss of form against the West Indies and India brought one of the troughs of his career, but he returned in strength for the Ashes series of 1993. He had forged a good opening partnership with Gooch, and he made 80 and 99 run out in the Lord's Test and 55 and 63 at Headingley. Gooch stood down as captain when the Ashes were lost, and Atherton, 25 years old, succeeded him as captain. England won the last game in the series, their first success for 11 matches.

Although he did well in the Caribbean the following winter, England lost the series 3–1 and were bowled out for 46 in Trinidad. There was victory over New Zealand but problems against South Africa when television cameras spotted him ball-tampering, for which he was censured and fined. There was no success in Australia and his body-language did not inspire confidence or optimism, but he led England to victory over India, 1996, only to lose to Pakistan in the second half of the summer.

Attitude and performance in Zimbabwe brought heavy criticism of the England side, but redemption came in New Zealand where Atherton batted well, and he was reappointed England captain for the whole of the 1997 summer. He began by leading England to victory in the Texaco Trophy and scoring a century in the second match at the Oval.

Mohammad Azharuddin

Born: February 8, 1963, Hyderabad, India
Teams: Hyderabad (1981–82 to 1996–97); Derbyshire (1991 and 1994)
First-class: 184 matches; 12,857 runs average 52.47; 12 wickets, average 56.08
Tests (1984–85 to 1996–97): 71 matches; 4,362 runs, average 44.96; no wickets for 12 runs

One of the most exciting batsmen in world cricket, Mohammad Azharuddin created a record when he began his Test career with three centuries in successive matches against England, 1984–85. He proved that this was no temporary glory by being the leading run-scorer in England, 1986, and playing with confidence in all three Tests as India took the series. His form lapsed a little, but he reasserted himself with an innings of 199 against Sri Lanka at Kanpur, December 1986, and centuries against Pakistan followed.

He was named as captain of the side to tour New Zealand, 1989–90, and to England, 1990. He hit hundreds at Lord's and Old Trafford, both of them glorious to watch, for he is a wristy player with the full range of strokes and ever ready to use them.

Azharuddin became the most successful captain in Indian Test history, but a loss of form and poor results in South Africa, failure in the World Cup and eventually the loss of the series in England, 1996, when his form was below par, cost him the leadership. He continued to hold his place in the side and shine, but defeat in the Caribbean, where he was accused of indiscipline in his batting and events in his private life which caused public concern, led to his being dropped from the side.

B

Trevor Bailey

Born: December 3, 1923, Westcliff-on-Sea, Essex
Teams: Essex (1946-67); Cambridge University (1947–48); Prime Minister's XI, India (1963–64)
First-class: 682 matches; 28,641 runs, average 33.42; 2,082 wickets, average 23.13
Tests (1949 to 1958–59): 61 matches; 2,290 runs, average 29.74; 132 wickets, average 29.21

The best all-round cricketer to represent England in the 1950s and, indeed, the finest English all-rounder of the post-war period until the arrival of Ian Botham, Trevor Bailey played a mighty role in England's rise from the depths to the recapturing of the Ashes in 1953 and their subsequent eminence in world cricket.

Educated at Dulwich College, he became known to audiences at Lord's during the war before joining the Royal Marines as soon as he left school. He served in Europe, but he was demobilized in time to play for Essex in 1946. He went up to Cambridge the following year, and by 1949 he was recognized as a bowler of genuine pace, a most reliable and adaptable batsman and a brilliant close-to-the-wicket fielder. He was also a talented soccer player who got his blue and won an FA Amateur Cup medal with Walthamstow Avenue.

He had an excellent debut Test series against New Zealand, 1949, and when Hutton took over the captaincy of the England side Bailey was seen as an integral part of the plan to recapture the Ashes. At Lord's, 1953, he batted 257 minutes for 71 and added 163 with Willie Watson. This was one of the great rearguard actions of Test cricket. The partnership saved the match, and Bailey was a national hero. He bowled and batted well to help save the Headingley Test, and in the final victorious Test at the Oval, he hit 64 to complete a memorable series.

He went to the West Indies as Hutton's vice-captain, 1953–54, and had the remarkable bowling figures of seven for 34 in the first innings in Jamaica where Hutton made a double-century. Bailey's outstanding Test career continued until 1959, and even after that he continued to give fine service for Essex until 1967, captaining the county from 1955 until 1966. He performed the "double" eight times and is the only man to have scored 2,000 runs and taken 100 wickets in a post-war season, 1959.

Nicknamed "Barnacle" for his adhesive batting qualities in Test cricket, he could score quickly when needed. Since retirement, he has become a noted journalist, author and broadcaster. He is a man with a zest for life and a great generosity of spirit.

Warren Bardsley

Born: December 6, 1882, Nevertire, Warren, New South Wales, Australia
Died: January 20, 1954, Collaroy Plateau, Bondi, Sydney, New South Wales
Teams: New South Wales (1903–04 to 1925–26)
First-class: 250 matches; 17,025 runs, average 49.92; no wickets for 41 runs
Tests (1909–1926) 41 matches; 2,469 runs, average 40.47

Warren Bardsley was a stylish left-handed opening batsman of impeccable technique. He toured England four times and reached 2,000 runs on three of those trips.

He made his Test debut in 1909 and, in the fifth test, at the Oval, he scored 136 and 130, so becoming the first batsman to score a century in each innings of a Test match. He made three hundreds against South Africa, but he was to wait until 1926 for his third and final century against England. He made 193 not out at Lord's which, at the time, was the highest score that had been made in a Lord's Test.

He captained Australia in the next two Tests, at Headingley and Old Trafford, when Collins was ill.

Eddie Barlow

Born: August 12, 1940, Pretoria, South Africa
Teams: Transvaal (1959–60 to 1967–68); Eastern Province (1964–65 to 1965–66); Western Province (1968–69 to 1980–81); Derbyshire (1976–78); Boland (1981–82 to 1982–83)
First-class: 283 matches; 18,212 runs, average 39.16; 571 wickets, average 24.14
Tests (1961–62 to 1969–70): 30 matches; 2,516 runs. average 45.74; 40 wickets, average 34.05

Eddie Barlow was a tenacious all-rounder, a right-handed batsman and right-arm medium-pace bowler of strength and determination. He was an integral part of a powerful South African side in the 1960s, but his Test career was cut short by his country's expulsion from international cricket. He had six Test centuries to his credit, including 201 against Australia at Adelaide, 1963–64.

He spent three seasons with Derbyshire, taking over the captaincy mid-way through the first year. A modest and warm man, he proved a belligerent leader who drove the county to new levels of fitness and attainment.

Barlow became a fine ambassador for his country and for the game. He coached Gloucestershire in 1990 and 1991.

Syd Barnes

Born: April 19, 1873, Smethwick, Staffordshire
Died: December 26, 1967, Chadsmoor, Staffordshire
Teams: Warwickshire (1894–96); Lancashire (1899–1903); Wales (1927–30)
First-class: 133 matches; 1,573 runs, average 12.78; 719 wickets, average 17.09

Tests (1901–02 to 1913–14): 27 matches; 242 runs, average 8.06; 189 wickets, average 16.43
Sydney Barnes played four games for Warwickshire and 46 for Lancashire, but he preferred league cricket to the county game. In spite of this fact, those who saw him and those who played against him considered him the greatest bowler of his time and, in the opinion of many, he remains the greatest bowler the game has known. He bowled at medium pace, was a master of length and of variations in flight and could turn the ball either way. He was able to adapt his bowling to any conditions.

Barnes was not an easy man. Gaunt, dark and brooding, he did not suffer fools gladly, and he needed handling carefully. He was virtually unknown when A.C. MacLaren invited him to tour Australia, 1901–02. He took five for 65 and one for 74 in the first Test and had match figures of 13 for 163 in the second after which injury hampered his tour. He played one Test against Australia in 1902 and took seven wickets, and thereafter spent most of his time in the leagues, issuing forth only to tour with England when invited.

In Australia, 1911–12, he took 34 wickets, average 22.38, in five Tests. In the Triangular Tournament of 1912, he took 39 wickets, average 10.3, and in South Africa, 1913–14, he took 49 wickets, average 10.93, in four Tests, which remains a world record. That marked the end of his Test career. After the First World War he confined himself to the leagues and to the Minor Counties with Staffordshire, for whom he played until 1935 when he was 62 years old. He is said to have taken all 10 wickets in an innings seven times and to have taken 6,229 wickets, average 8.33, in competitive matches in his long career.

Ken Barrington

Born: November 24, 1930, Reading, Berkshire
Died: March 14, 1981, Needham's Point, Barbados
Teams: Surrey (1953–68)
First-class: 533 matches; 31,714 runs, average 45.63; 273 wickets, average 32.62

BARRINGTON *Popular and determined.*

Tests (1955–68): 82 matches; 6,806 runs, average 58.67; 29 wickets, average 44.82
Stocky, with a pronounced nose and chin which suggested defiance, Ken Barrington was a very sound middle order batsman, a rock on which England so often depended. He had to fight his way into a strong Surrey side, but in two years he was in the England side – 1955, the same year in which he was capped. He made 0 against South Africa on his debut, but he was to make amends for this with 20 Test centuries, the first nine of them abroad. His first in England was his highest, 256 against Australia at Old Trafford, 1964, when he and Dexter put on 246 for the third wicket.

Barrington was a very difficult batsman to dislodge, and he proved the banc of Pakistan in 1967 when he hit centuries in three successive Tests. He played his last Test against Australia at Headingly in 1968. The following winter, playing in a double-wicket tournament in Australia, he suffered a mild heart attack and was forced to retire. He became a selector and managed England touring sides. He was assistant manager and coach to the England side in the Caribbean, 1981, when he died suddenly of a heart attack in the middle of a Test match. A most popular man, he is much missed.

Bishen Bedi

Born: September 25, 1946, Amritsar, India
Teams: Northern Punjab (1961–62 to 1966–67); Delhi (1968–69 to 1980–81); Northamptonshire (1972–77)
First-class: 370 matches; 3,584 runs, average 11.37; 1,560 wickets, average 21.69
Tests (1966–67 to 1979): 67 matches; 656 runs, average 8.98; 266 wickets, average 28.71
A slow left-arm bowler whose action was an aesthetic delight, Bishen Bedi was a most popular cricketer whose brightly coloured patkas became a feature of Test cricket and of the English county scene for several years. He was only 15 when he first played in the Ranji Trophy, and his Test debut came against the West Indies in Calcutta, December 1966. His Test career ended with the last match in the 1979 series in England. Surprisingly, he was not very successful in Tests in England although he enjoyed triumphs with Northamptonshire, whom he captained with flair. He also led India in 22 Tests, but he was outspoken and never far from controversy, being banned once for giving an unauthorized television interview and leading a move for improved payments.

He twice took 25 wickets in a series against England in India and took 21 wickets in Australia, 1969–70. Since his retirement he has managed Indian sides.

Alec Bedser

Born: July 4, 1918, Reading, Berkshire
Teams: Surrey (1939–60)
First-class: 485 matches; 5,735 runs, average 14.51; 1,924 wickets, average 20.41
Tests (1946–55): 51 matches; 714 runs, average 12.75; 236 wickets, average 24.89

BISHEN BEDI *Bowler of gentle guile but outspoken off the field.*

ALEC BEDSER *soldier and cricketer.*

Alec Bedser played a handful of matches for Surrey in 1939, and then saw the early years of his career consumed by the war. He and his identical twin brother Eric were on the beaches at Dunkirk, but in the closing year of the war Alec Bedser came into prominence in matches at Lord's. He was a truly great right-arm medium fast bowler with a model action and an economic run to the wicket. A very strong man, he gave the impression that he could bowl all day and sometimes did. In the years immediately after the Second World War, he carried the England attack on his broad shoulders. He began his Test career with seven for 49 and four for 96 against India at Lord's, 1946, and followed with another 11 wickets at Old Trafford. In Australia, the following winter, he gained the respect of Bradman's men, but he was forced to plough a lonely furrow.

It was in 1953 that he finally gained the reward for his years of endeavour. When England regained the Ashes, Bedser was one of the heroes of the hour, claiming a record 39 wickets in five Tests. That outstanding achievement was almost the end of his Test career, for when he went to Australia with Hutton's side, 1954–55, he had an attack of shingles and lost his place in the side after the first Test. He played his last Test against South Africa at Old Trafford in 1955. He took four wickets which brought his total to 236, at the time a record for Test cricket.

He was a major force in Surrey's run of seven consecutive championships, and he led the side on occasions. He was an England selector for over 20 years and was first awarded the OBE and then knighted for his services to cricket.

Richie Benaud

Born: October 6, 1930, Penrith, New South Wales, Australia
Teams: New South Wales (1948–49 to 1963–64)
First-class: 259 matches, 11,719, average 36.50; 945 wickets, average 24.73
Tests (1951–52 to 1963–64): 63 matches, 2,201 runs, average 24.45; 248 wickets, average 27.03

Richie Benaud has argued that he would not have won a place in the Australian side had he not learned to bat. He was an exciting right-handed, forcing batsman, but he was an even greater leg-break and googly bowler, and he was a captain who must rank alongside Bradman and Armstrong as Australia's greatest. He, more than any other man, lifted Australian cricket from a period of tedium and gloom to a position of entertaining supremacy.

He made his Test debut against the West Indies, 1951–52, and played four Tests against South Africa the following season. He toured England in 1953 and made little impact, but he was an astute cricketer, and learned much. He was in the side that was shattered by Tyson and Statham, 1954–55, but he played a major part in Australia's revival weeks later when they won three Tests in the Caribbean. In the fifth match, at Sabina Park, he reached a maiden Test century in 78 minutes.

In 1956, he hit 97 at Lord's and when Australia went to India he took seven for 72 in Madras to set up his side's victory. He followed this with 11 wickets in the win in Calcutta. A year later, he dominated the series in South Africa with two centuries and 30 wickets.

He succeeded Craig as captain of Australia and immediately won back the Ashes, 1958–59, found success in India and was victorious in a thrilling series against Worrell's West Indians.

In 1961, he was troubled by an injured shoulder, yet his Australian side retained the Ashes when, at Old Trafford, Benaud himself put in a remarkable spell of bowling on the last afternoon to take six for 70 and win the match. When he departed from Test cricket, he could claim that he had led Australia in six Test series of which five were won and one drawn. His contribution as player and captain had been incalculable.

He worked to establish Kerry Packer's World Series and became a journalist and commentator. His wit, charm, lucidity and deep knowledge of the game have made him an outstanding personality.

Colin Blythe

Born: May 30, 1879, Deptford, Kent
Died: November 8, 1917, Passchendaele, Belgium
Teams: Kent (1899–1914)
First-class: 439 matches; 4,443 runs, average 9.87; 2,503 wickets, average 16.81
Tests (1901–02 to 1909–10): 19 matches; 183 runs, average 9.63; 100 wickets, average 18.63

"Charlie" Blythe was one of the two great left-arm spinners of the Edwardian period, the other being Wilfred Rhodes. Blythe was rhythmic and graceful, a master of flight with his long, sensitive fingers wrapped round the ball. He was a most intelligent bowler who made full use of his height. In 14 of his 15 full seasons in first-class cricket, he captured 100 wickets, and it is likely that he would have played more for England had he not been subject to epileptic fits.

Artistic (he played the violin) and highly strung, he had match figures of seven for 56 on his Test debut against Australia, 1901–02, and he was second only to Barnes among England bowlers for the series, and he enjoyed a fine tour of South Africa, 1905–06, taking 11 for 118 in Cape Town when England won their only match of the rubber. He had even greater success in 1907 when he took eight for 59 and seven for 40 against South Africa at Headingley, so becoming the only bowler to take 15 South African wickets in a Test in England.

He was at the height of his powers in 1914 and had played in four championship-winning sides. When war broke out he enlisted and was killed in action in 1917.

David Boon

Born: December 29, 1960, Launceston, Tasmania
Teams: Tasmania (1978–79 to 1996–97)
First-class: 267 matches; 18,811, average 46.10; 9 wickets, average 53.11
Tests (1984–85 to 1995–96): 107 matches; 7,422 runs, average 43,65; no wickets for 14 runs

Short, compact and strong, David Boon possesses a rock-like defence, but he also has a wide range of shots, specializing in a vicious square-cut. He played three Tests against the West Indies, 1984–85, and three on the tour of England a few months later, but it was not until he moved up to open the innings against India, 1985–86, that he recorded his first Test century. His partnership with Geoff Marsh became renowned, but when Mark Taylor came into the side Boon reverted to number three with equal success.

At first a slip fielder, he became a most capable short-leg, brave, reliable and most agile for a heavy man. He hit 200 against New Zealand at Perth, 1989–90, and runs flowed from him in every series. He was a foundation on which Australia built their success in the late 1980s and early 1990s. He announced his retirement from Test cricket before the World Cup, 1996, and scored a century against Sri Lanka in his penultimate appearance. It was his 21st Test hundred.

He has continued to captain Tasmania in the Sheffield Shield and took over the captaincy of Durham in 1997.

Allan Border

Born: July 27, 1955, Cremorne, Sydney, New South Wales
Teams: New South Wales (1976–77 to 1979–80); Gloucestershire (1977): Queensland (1980–81 to 1995–96); Essex (1986–88)

First-class: 385 matches; 27,131 runs, average 51.38; 106 wickets, average 39.25
Tests (1978–79 to 1993–94): 156 matches; 11,174 runs, average 50.56; 39 wickets, average 39.10

BORDER *Success became a habit.*

No cricketer has appeared in more Test matches than Allan Border, no batsman has scored more runs in Test cricket and nobody has approached his record of captaining his country in 93 Tests. He allied a straightforward, sound technique to a concentration and determination which were exemplary, and few left-handed batsmen have been so free of faults as he. He was a useful left-arm slow bowler and a very fine close-to-the-wicket fielder. He took over the captaincy of Australia in troubled times and led them to the summit, winning the World Cup along the way. He was very determined and tactically sound and was worshipped by his men.

He first came to light as a most accomplished left-hander when Australia had been ravaged by defections to Packer's organization. Stocky, with cheerful, gleaming blue eyes, he never allowed his concentration to take away his delight in the game, and he learned in a tough school. His maiden Test hundred came against Pakistan in 1979, and he was soon established as his country's number three. In 1979–80, he hit 150 not out and 153 against Pakistan in Lahore, the first batsman to hit 150 in each innings of a Test. In England, 1981, when Australia struggled, he batted 377 minutes with a broken finger to score an unbeaten 123 at Old Trafford.

He first became captain of Australia in 1984–85 and held the job until the end of the tour of South Africa, 1993–94. This marked the end of his Test career, but there was still one more world to conquer. He was a key member of the Queensland side that won the Sheffield Shield for the first time. He had also been part of an Essex side that won the county championship. His career was studded with 70 centuries of which 27 were in Tests, where his 156 catches were vital to Australia's success.

Bernard Bosanquet

Born: October 13, 1877, Bulls Cross, Enfield, Middlesex
Died: October 12, 1936, Wykehurst, Ewhurst, Surrey
Teams: Oxford University (1898–1900); Middlesex (1898–1919)
First-class: 235 matches; 11,696 runs, average 33.41; 629 wickets, average 23.80
Tests (1903–04 to 1905): 7 matches; 147 runs, average 13.36; 25 wickets, average 24.16

A tall, upstanding right-handed batsman who won his blue all three years at Oxford, Bosanquet was originally a medium-pace bowler. He played four Tests in Australia in 1903–04 and three against Australia in England in 1905. It was in the first of these Tests in England, at Trent Bridge, that Bosanquet took eight for 107 in the second innings and won the match. It is not as a player, however, that Bosanquet is best remembered, but as the perfecter of the googly, the off-break with the leg-break action – a delivery that is still known as the "Bosie" in Australia after its inventor.

Bosanquet developed the googly by playing billiards fives or "twisty grab". In the early part of the nineteenth century, it was feared that the googly would ruin the game, but it simply brought more mystery and vitality.

Bosanquet declined as a bowler after 1905, but advanced as a batsman and headed the national averages in 1908 when he hit 214 in 195 minutes for the Rest of England against the Champion County. He was an accomplished billiards player, ice hockey player and hammer thrower. He was father of the television news reader, the late Reginald Bosanquet.

Ian Botham

See Legends (pages 94–95)

Geoff Boycott

Born: October 21, 1940, Fitzwilliam, Yorkshire
Teams: Yorkshire (1962–86); Northern Transvaal (1971–72)
First-class: 609 matches; 48,426 runs, average 56.83; 45 wickets, average 32.42
Tests (1964 to 1981–82): 108 matches; 8,114 runs, average 47.72; 7 wickets, average 54.57

Geoffrey Boycott is one of the greatest opening batsmen that the game has known. He dedicated his life to the art of batting, practising assiduously and eschewing any shot that might even hint at threatening the loss of his wicket. When he walked out of Test cricket during the Tour of India, 1981–82, he had scored more runs than any other batsman in Test history and might well have scored more but for his own self-imposed exile from Test cricket for two years. His career was littered with controversy and he excited extremes of passion. A deeply sensitive man, he found that fame and success brought problems which were not always easy to cope with. His fans worshipped him; others saw his intense dedication as selfish.

His Test debut came against Australia at Trent Bridge, 1964, when he scored 48 and fractured a finger while fielding. In the last match of the series, he scored the first of his 22 Test centuries. The highest of these came at Headingley, 1967, when he made 246 not out against India, a record for the series, but the innings occupied 573 minutes and he faced 555 balls. He was disciplined for slow scoring and was omitted from the next Test.

Headingley was his spiritual home, and he stirred great emotions when he scored his 100th hundred on the ground in 1977 during the Test match against Australia. He went on to make 191. In all, he scored 151 centuries in first-class cricket, and in 1971 and 1979 he averaged over 100 for the season.

BOYCOTT *A favourite scoring shot.*

No other English batsman has achieved this feat once.

His relationship with his own county was often tempestuous although he captained the side from 1971 to 1978. He has become a well known television summarizer since leaving the game. His comments are both intelligent and perceptive.

Donald Bradman

See Legends (pages 96–97)

Johnny Briggs

Born: October 3, 1862, Sutton-in-Ashfield, Nottinghamshire
Died: January 11, 1902, Heald Green, Cheadle, Cheshire
Teams: Lancashire (1879–1900)
First-class: 535 matches; 14,092 runs, average 18.27; 2,221 wickets, average 15.95
Tests (1884–85 to 1899): 33 matches; 815 runs, average 18.11; 118 wickets, average 17.75

Short, cheerful and immensely popular, Johnny Briggs made his first-class debut at the age of 16. He was a right-handed batsman and a fine fielder, but he developed into a slow left-arm bowler, although it was not until 1886 that he was truly recognized in that capacity.

In 1888–89, in South Africa, he took 21 wickets in two Tests, and his 15 for 28 at Cape Town constituted a record for one day in Test cricket as did his eight for 11, all bowled, in the second innings.

He had both a century and a hat-trick for England against Australia and was wonderfully consistent. At Headingley, 1899, he took three for 53 on the first day against Australia. That evening he had a violent epileptic fit and played no more cricket until the next season when he seems to have been as good as ever. He suffered another violent attack, however, and was confined to Cheadle Asylum where he died at the age of 39.

Basil Butcher

Born: September 3, 1933, Port Mourant, Berbice, British Guiana
Teams: British Guiana (1954–55 to 1970–71)
First-class: 169 matches; 11,628 runs, average 49.90; 40 wickets, average 30.42
Tests (1958–59 to 1969): 44 matches; 3,104 runs, average 43.11; 5 wickets, average 18.00

In a West Indian side studded with stars, it was sometimes all too easy to overlook the worth of Basil Butcher, yet he was among the most consistent batsmen in the world as a number four or five and was particularly successful in England. He was also a useful leg-break bowler and a fine fielder. He made his Test debut in India, 1958–59, and reached his first Test century in the third mach of the series which he followed with an innings of 142 in the fourth.

In the dramatic Lord's Test of 1963 he scored a magnificent 133, and three years later, at Trent Bridge, he saved the West Indies with the highest score of his career, an unbeaten 209, and shared in century partnerships for three wickets. The West Indies had trailed by 90 in the first innings, and Butcher's knock not only saved them when defeat looked probable, but set up a remarkable victory.

Greatly respected by his opponents, he was a professional in the Lancashire League for many years.

C

Bhagwat Chandrasekhar

Born: May 17, 1945, Mysore, India
Teams: Karnataka (1963–64 to 1979–80)
First-class: 246 matches; 600 runs, average 4.61; 1,063 wickets, average 24.03
Tests (1963–64 to 1979): 58 matches; 167 runs, average 4.07; 242 wickets, average 29.74

Chandrasekhar bowled his leg-breaks at a brisk pace, and he proved to be a match-winner in Test cricket when leg-break bowling seemed to be a dying art. He made an immediate impression when he made his Test debut against England 1963–64, and he bowled India to victory over Australia in Bombay a year later. By 1966–67, he was one of a trio of spinners who began to make India a formidable force in world cricket, and he took 18 wickets in three Tests against the West Indies. He bowled well in England in 1967, but the home side won the series. Four years later, he took six for 38 in the second innings at the Oval, and India beat England in England for the first time. His eight for 72 in the first innings at Delhi, 1972–73, was still unable to prevent England winning by six wickets, but he ended the rubber with a record 35 wickets and India took the series. He also bowled India to victory over Australia in Australia for the first time, 1977–78, taking 12 for 104 in the match and claiming his 200th Test wicket in the process. Thereafter he was handicapped by injury and lost form. He played his last Test in England, 1979, and retired the following year.

CHANDRASEKHAR *Quick leg-breaks brought more wickets than he scored runs.*

Greg Chappell

Born: August 7, 1948, Unley, Adelaide, South Australia
Teams: South Australia (1966–67 to 1972–73); Somerset (1968–69); Queensland (1973–74 to 1983–84)
First-class: 321 matches; 24,535 runs, average 52.20; 291 wickets, average 29.95
Tests (1970–71 to 1983–84): 87 matches; 7,110 runs, average 53.86; 47 wickets, average 40.70

Grandson of one Test captain, Victor Richardson, and brother of another, Ian, Greg Chappell was a tall, slim, elegant batsman who sharpened his technique with Somerset, hit the first century in the Sunday League and 18 months later scored a hundred on his Test debut against England in Perth. Now an integral part of the Australian side and of his brother's plans to revive Australian cricket, he hit centuries at Lord's and the Oval in the 1972 Ashes series and made 247 not out against New Zealand at Wellington, 1973–74. He made 133 in the second innings.

His brother groomed him to take over as captain of Australia, and in his first Test as captain, against the West Indies at Brisbane, 1975–76, he created a record by scoring a century in each innings. In 1972, he and Ian had provided the first instance of brothers scoring centuries in the same innings of a Test, against England at the Oval.

The Packer affair sapped the strength of the Australian side in 1977, but when it was resolved Greg Chappell was reinstated as captain, leading Australia for the last time against Sri Lanka, 1983. He seemed to select when he would play and this attitude, and his notorious tactics in a one-day international against New Zealand when he told his brother Trevor to bowl under-arm, brought him much criticism, but he had a dignified air and a desire to win, and he was a fine cricketer.

Ian Chappell

Born: September 26, 1943, Unley, Adelaide, South Australia
Teams: South Australia (1961–62 to 1979–80); Lancashire (1963)
First-class: 262 matches; 19,680 runs, average 48.35; 176 wickets, average 37.57
Tests (1964–65 to 1979–80): 75 matches; 5,345 runs, average 42.42; 20 wickets, average 65.80

The eldest of three brothers, all of whom played for Australia, Ian Chappell was a determined, gritty batsman, a brilliant slip fielder and an occasional leg-break bowler. Greg, too, turned to leg-breaks with some success after beginning as a medium-pacer. Ian made his Test debut against Pakistan in 1964, but he did not win a regular place in the Australian side until three years later. His first Test hundred came against India, 1967–68, and he did well in England the following summer. This was a low period in Australian cricket history, however, and when Illingworth's side got the upper hand in Australia, 1970–71, Lawry was dropped for the last Test and Ian Chappell appointed captain. Chappell immediately set about reshaping the Australian side, and they became a formidable, ruthless team. In 1972, he and his brother Greg scored centuries in the last Test at The Oval to win the match and draw the series against England. Wins over Pakistan, the West Indies and, in 1975, England followed. Ian Chappell then handed over the captaincy to Greg, while he himself set about establishing Packer's World Series, and in all that followed he proved a very tough negotiator.

His success as batsman and captain are undeniable, but he was abrasive to opponents and authority. His colourful language and tendency to run his side as a self-contained unit answerable to no one did cause controversy.

Brian Close

Born: February 24, 1931, Rawdon, Leeds, Yorkshire
Teams: Yorkshire (1949–70); Somerset (1971–77)
First-class: 786 matches; 34,994 runs, average 33.26; 1,171 wickets, average 26.42
Tests (1949–76): 22 matches; 887 runs, average 25.34; 18 wickets, average 29.55

Brian Close did the "double" in his first season in first-class cricket and played for England against New Zealand. He was a left-handed batsman who suited his mood to the occasion, a medium-pace or off-break bowler and a brave and brilliant close-to-the-wicket fielder. He was the youngest to gain a Yorkshire cap, but never quite lived up to that early promise, and his 22 Test caps were spread over a period of 27 years.

He was something of a cricketing eccentric, very popular with his players, and he captained Yorkshire from 1963 to 1970. With England outplayed by the West Indies, Close was appointed captain for the last Test, 1966, and England won. Honest, brave, and an astute tactician, he led England to more successes over India and Pakistan, but the tactics he adopted in a county match against Warwickshire caused an outcry, and his invitation to lead England in the Caribbean was withdrawn. At Tony Greig's insistence, he was recalled to the England side in 1976 at the age of 45 because he was such a tough fighter.

A brush with the Yorkshire committee caused him to move to Somerset whom he captained from 1972 until his retirement. He led England seven times, and won six and drew one of the matches in which he was captain.

Denis Compton

Born: May 23, 1918, Hendon, Middlesex
Died: April 23, 1997, Windsor, Berkshire
Teams: Middlesex (1936–58); Holkar (1944–45); Europeans (1944–45 to 1945–46)
First-class: 515 matches; 38,942 runs, average 51.85; 622 wickets, average 32.27
Tests (1937 to 1956–57): 78 matches; 5,807 runs, average 50.06; 25 wickets, average 56.40

DENIS COMPTON *A great entertainer.*

In the entire history of cricket, no player gave more pleasure nor entertained a crowd more fully than Denis Compton. By any standards he was a pure genius, and his delight in what he was doing, his passion for the game, was as transparent as it was infectious. The sun always seemed to shine when he played cricket. He was first picked for Middlesex as a slow left-arm bowler and was effective, if eccentric, in this area to the end of his career. He batted number eleven in his first match, but within weeks he was number four, and he completed 1,000 runs by the end of the season, a feat he accomplished 14 times in England and three times overseas. The following season, he was in the England side against New Zealand at the Oval, run out 65, and he scored a century in his first Test against Australia, 1938. He was unable to tour at this time, because he was under contract to Arsenal FC, winning an FA Cup winners' medal in 1950, a League Championship medal in 1948 and being capped for England in wartime internationals.

He went to Australia, 1946–47, and scored a century in each innings of the Adelaide Test. The following summer he broke all records. He made 3,816 runs, average 90.85, and hit 18 centuries. It seems likely that these records will never be beaten.

In five Tests against the South Africans, he hit 753 runs, average 94.12. That season he also took 73 wickets in all first-class matches.

In 1948, against the might of Bradman's Australians, he hit 184 at Trent Bridge and an unbeaten 145 at Old Trafford after he had been forced to retire hurt early in his innings. In South Africa, 1948–49, he hit 300 in 181 minutes for MCC against NE Transvaal. It remains the fastest triple-century ever recorded. By now, he was being troubled by an old knee injury sustained while playing football. It was to prove a severe handicap and to shorten his career. He had a kneecap removed, scored 278 against Pakistan, 1954, and two years later, minus his kneecap, hit 94 in his last Test against Australia at the Oval.

He worked as a PR consultant and as a journalist, and continued to charm all who met him. His one piece of advice to young cricketers was: "Enjoy it. It is over all too soon."

Learie Constantine

Born: September 21, 1901, Petit Valley, Diego Martin, Trinidad
Died: July 1, 1971, Brondesbury, Hampstead, London
Teams: Trinidad (1921–22 to 1934–35); Freelooters, India (1934–5); Barbados (1938–39)
First-class: 119 matches; 4,475 runs, average 24.05; 439 wickets, average 20.48
Tests (1928–39): 18 matches; 635 runs, average 19.24; 58 wickets, average 30.10

The game has known no more dynamic cricketer than Learie Constantine. His fielding was spectacular, his bowling fast and his batting violent. He was capable of turning the course of any match by a sensational act in one of these areas. He performed the "double" in 1928, and spent most of the 1930s playing in the Lancashire League where he was a tremendous favourite. He might even have qualified for Lancashire but for the colour prejudice which existed at the time.

He took 103 wickets on the 1939 tour of England, and, in the final Test at the Oval, the last before the outbreak of war, he hit 79 in an hour and took five for 75 in the first innings.

Constantine did welfare work among black people in Britain during the Second World War. Refused admission to a London hotel on one occasion, he took successful legal action over the matter. In the memorable words of C.L.R. James, Constantine "revolted against the revolting contrast between his first-class status as a cricketer and his third-class status as a man". His greatest joy came at the end of the war when England met the Dominions at Lord's. Constantine was the only black man in the side, but the rest of the team insisted that he should captain them. It was his last first-class match.

A barrister, a writer and an MP in the Trinidad parliament, he came back to London as High Commissioner for Trinidad and Tobago. He was awarded the MBE, knighted and finally created a Life Peer, Baron of Maraval and Nelson. He was posthumously awarded Trinidad's highest honour, the Trinity Cross.

Colin Cowdrey

Born: December 24, 1932, Bangalore, India
Teams: Kent (1950–76); Oxford University (1952–54)
First-class: 692 matches; 42,719 runs, average 42.89; 65 wickets, average 51.21
Tests (1954–55 to 1974–75): 114 matches; 7,624 runs, average 44.06; no wickets for 104 runs

One of the very finest and most accomplished of post-war batsmen, Cowdrey was a prolific scorer who hit 107 centuries in first-class cricket and created a record by playing 114 times for England whom he captained on 27 occasions. He was a brilliant slip fielder, and, as a batsman, was a stylist who sought perfection. Had he been arrogant or ruthless, he would have scored many more runs.

He made his Test debut on Hutton's 1954–55 tour of Australia. He had been a surprise choice, but was an instant success, and his innings of 102 out of 191 in the third Test at Melbourne saved England from disaster in a match that they went on to win.

In 1957, at Edgbaston, he and Peter May shared a record partnership of 411 for the fourth wicket against the West Indies and ended the threat of Ramadhin. It seemed inevitable that he would succeed May as England captain, but he was forced to give way to Dexter and M.J.K. Smith as the selectors believed his approach to be too benign. In 1966, he took over from Smith and then was replaced by Close. He was reinstated when Close was dropped for his misdemeanours, and he took England to the Caribbean, winning the series against all expectations.

An injury in a Sunday League game was to cost him the England captaincy again in 1969, and he could not be called the luckiest of players. In 1963 at Lord's he had his left arm broken by a ball from Wes Hall, but he went out to bat with his arm in plaster to save the day. Fortunately, he did not have to face a delivery. In 1974–75, he was called to Australia at the age of 42. It was an emergency, and he was needed to help combat the fast bowlers. It was his sixth tour of the country where he was very popular.

He was a surprisingly revolutionary President of the MCC and an active Chairman of the ICC. He was knighted for his services to cricket in the New Year's Honours List, 1992.

Martin Crowe

Born: September 22, 1962, Henderson, Auckland, New Zealand
Teams: Auckland (1979–80 to 1982–83); Central Districts (1983–84 to 1989–90); Somerset (1984–88); Wellington (1990–91 to 1994–95)
First-class: 247 matches; 19,608 runs, average 56.02; 119 wickets, average 33.70
Tests (1981–82 to 1995–96): 77 matches; 5,444 runs, average 45.36; 14 wickets, average 48.28

Not only one of the greatest batsmen of his generation, but one of the finest of all New Zealand batsmen, Martin Crowe made his Test debut in the rain-ruined match against Australia at Wellington in February 1982, when he was still seven months short of his 20th birthday. Tall, orthodox in style, elegant and powerful in execution, sound in temperament, he made his first Test century against England at Wellington, 1983–84, saving a match which had looked lost. By the end of his Test career, he had 17 hundreds to his credit and had scored more Test runs than any other New Zealand batsman.

MARTIN CROWE *Elegant stylist.*

Initially, he bowled at a brisk medium pace, but a back injury, one of several which marred his career, effectively brought an end to his capacity as a bowler.

He made a great impact in his years with Somerset, encouraging young uncapped players and doing much for team spirit, but there was also controversy in that by offering him a new contract in 1987, Somerset brought to an end their association with Viv Richards and Joel Garner.

There was a reluctance to burden him with the captaincy of New Zealand too early in his career, but the decline in form of his elder brother Jeff and John Wright's unwillingness to do the job led to Martin Crowe being asked to take a young and inexperienced side to Pakistan, 1990–91. He battled bravely against the odds, and when he led New Zealand in New Zealand for the first time, he hit 299 against Sri Lanka at Wellington. This is the highest score ever made by a New Zealander in Test history, and he and Andrew Jones established a world record when they added 467 for the third wicket. Crowe scored centuries against all Test-playing nations with the exception of South Africa.

He developed a knee problem which necessitated an operation and caused him to play with a splint. He scored runs even though he was in pain, but following the tour of India, 1995–96, when he was in obvious trouble, he was asked to prove his fitness. Reluctantly, he was forced to retire, and a great player passed from the game.

D

Joseph Darling

Born: November 21, 1870, Glen Osmond, Adelaide, South Australia
Died: January 2, 1946, Hobart, Tasmania
Teams: South Australia (1893–94 to 1907–08)
First-class: 202 matches; 10,635 runs, average 34.52; 1 wicket, average 55.00
Tests (1894–95 to 1905): 34 matches; 1,657 runs, average 28.56

Son of a member of the Legislative Council who was responsible for introducing the bill which granted the lease on land that became Adelaide Oval, Joe Darling excelled as a left-handed batsman at college. First he worked in banking and then in wheat farming, so that it seemed he was lost to sport. But in 1893–94, he returned to Adelaide to open a sports store, and a year later, thickset with face burned by the sun, he was in the Australian side. He first toured England in 1896 and became an opening batsman. On his next three tours, 1899, 1902, and 1905, he captained the side.

Against MacLaren's side, 1897–98, he became the first batsman to hit three centuries in a Test rubber and the first to aggregate 500 runs in a series. In the third Test, at Adelaide, he made 178 and reached his century with the first six ever hit in Test cricket. To score six a batsman had to hit the ball out of the ground at that time. In the final Test, he hit 160 in 175 minutes.

A man of the utmost integrity, Darling was elected to the captaincy by his fellow players who revered him, and he worked hard on their behalf while maintaining strict discipline. He retired to help his wife raise their 15 children. He settled in Tasmania, reared merino sheep and became a successful politician.

He was President of the New South Wales Cricket Association for many years and was also Director of Rothman's National Sports Foundation.

Alan Davidson

Born: June 14, 1929, Lisarow, Gosford, New South Wales
Teams: New South Wales (1949–50 to 1962–63)
First-class: 193 matches; 6,804 runs, average 32.86; 672 wickets, average 20.90
Tests (1953 to 1962–63): 44 matches; 1,328 runs, average 24.59; 186 wickets, average 20.53

A left-handed fast bowler and a left-handed batsman who could hit the ball very hard, Alan Davidson made his Test debut in 1953, playing in all five matches. In 1958–59, he took 24 wickets against England, and two years later, he took 33 wickets and scored 212 runs against the West Indies. In the first match of that series, at Brisbane, he became the first player to score 100 runs and take 10 wickets in a Test.

In 25 Tests against England, he made 750 runs and took 84 wickets. He also held 23 catches to complete a fine record.

ARAVINDA DE SILVA *Wristy strength.*

Aravinda de Silva

Born: October 17, 1965, Colombo, Ceylon
Teams: Nondescripts (1988–89 to 1996–97); Kent (1995)
First-class: 154 matches; 10,225 runs, average 46.90; 72 wickets, average 33.84
Tests (1984 to 1996–97): 53 matches; 3,176 runs, average 35.68; 17 wickets, average 35.58

Arguably, Aravinda de Silva is the most exciting batsman in world cricket. Right-handed, wristy, quick-footed, he might even have scored more Test runs had he not been so eager to score quickly. As it is, he has a host of records to his credit. His 267 against New Zealand at Wellington, 1990–91, is a national record. The previous year he had hit a brilliant 167 against Australia at Brisbane. Twice he has reached a Test century with a six, and he became the first batsman to score an unbeaten century in each innings of a Test match, against Pakistan, 1997.

A useful off-break bowler, he played for Kent in 1995, scoring 1,781 runs, average 59.36, and in the Benson & Hedges Cup Final made 112 against Lancashire, one of the most thrilling and greatest innings ever seen at Lord's.

When Sri Lanka won the World Cup in 1986, de Silva took the Man of the Match award in the semi-final and in the final in which he scored an unbeaten century.

Ted Dexter

Born: May 15, 1935, Milan, Italy
Teams: Cambridge University (1956–58); Sussex (1957–68)
First-class: 327 matches, 21,150 runs, average 40.75; 419 wickets, average 29.92
Tests (1958–68): 62 matches; 4,502 runs, average 47.89; 66 wickets, average 34.93

DONALD *One of the fastest bowlers of the 1990s.*

An exciting attacking batsman, classical in style, and a most capable medium-pace bowler, Ted Dexter made an immediate impact at Cambridge and played for England against New Zealand at Old Trafford in 1958. The following winter he was flown to Australia to boost a sagging England side. He was a right-handed batsman of regal splendour, authority and immense power. Imperious of manner, he earned the nickname of "Lord Ted". He captained Sussex from 1960 to 1965, and he first led England in Pakistan and India, 1961–62, scoring 205, the highest innings of his career, against Pakistan in Karachi. He continued as England captain until the end of 1964, giving way to Cowdrey for just one "trial" Test in 1962.

For such an enterprising cricketer, he was a rather disappointing captain, being a great theorist and seemingly prone to lose interest. He was not the best handler of men, probably because he was so multi-talented. He was a very fine golfer.

He missed the tour of India, 1963–64, and stood as Conservative candidate against the future Labour Prime Minister, James Callaghan, in the autumn of 1964. He was unsuccessful and joined the England side in South Africa where he played under M.J.K. Smith. In 1965, he broke a leg and retired, but he continued to make infrequent appearances for Sussex and last played for England in 1968.

He was appointed chairman of the England committee in 1989 and held the job for four years. He did much good, intelligent work behind the scenes, but England's lack of success brought him unfair criticism. His contribution to the re-ordering of the game has never been fully appreciated.

Allan Donald

Born: October 20, 1966, Bloemfontein, South Africa
Teams: Orange Free State (1985–86 to 1996–97); Warwickshire (1987–88)
First-class: 221 matches; 1,872 runs, average 12.23; 837 wickets, average 23.14
Tests (1991–92 to 1996–97): 25 matches; 233 runs, average 15.53; 114 wickets, average 24.87

A fast bowler of genuine pace, Allan Donald had proved his quality before South Africa's re-admission to Test cricket. His arrival at Warwickshire brought about a revival in the county's fortunes. He claimed 86 wickets in 1989, 83 in 1991 and 89 in 1995. Although his entry into Test cricket was late, he quickly became the fourth South African to take 100 Test wickets, and now only Hugh Tayfield with 170 wickets stands ahead of him.

He bowls with dedication and passion at all times, but he keeps a fuller length than most fast bowlers of his generation. He demolished Zimbabwe with eight for 71 and three for 42 at Harare, 1995–96, and his best bowling in domestic cricket is his eight for 37 for Free State against Transvaal at Johannesburg, 1986–87. He holds a coaching position with Warwickshire.

Martin Donnelly

Born: October 17, 1917, Ngaruawahia, Auckland, New Zealand
Teams: Wellington (1936–37 to 1940–41) Canterbury (1938–39 to 1939–40); Middlesex (1946); Oxford University (1946–1947);Warwickshire (1948–1950)
First-class: 131 matches; 9,250 runs, average 47.43; 43 wickets, average 39.13
Tests (1937–1949): 7 matches; 582 runs, average 52.90; no wickets for 20 runs

A left-handed batsman of immense power and beauty, Martin Donnelly was a natural athlete who represented Oxford University and England at rugby. His Test matches were for New Zealand against England, in England and, when he made his debut at Lord's in 1937, he was the second-youngest cricketer ever to represent New Zealand. He did little in his first three Tests, but he scored 1,414 runs on the tour and was recognized as a batsman of outstanding quality.

He lost valuable years to the war in which he served as major in the Egyptian and Italian campaigns, but he was seen in cricket at Lord's and delighted all.

A graduate of University College, Canterbury, he went up to Oxford in 1946 and captained the eleven in 1947. He was a prolific run-scorer and hit 162 not out in three hours for the Gentlemen against the Players.

He played for Middlesex against the Indian tourists in 1946, but he went into business when he came down from Oxford and appeared for Warwickshire in 20 matches during the next three seasons.

In 1949 when New Zealand toured England, he excelled with 2,287 runs, average 61.81, which included 462 runs, average 77.00, in the Tests. At Lord's, he made 206, the first double-century in Test cricket by a New Zealand batsman.

His work took him to Australia and he settled in Sydney, leaving lovers of the game with a memory of charm and graciousness.

Jeffrey Dujon

Born: May 28, 1956, Kingston, Jamaica
Teams: Jamaica (1974–75 to 1991–92)
First-class: 194 matches; 9,308 runs, average 38.14; 1 wicket, average 45.00; caught 434, stumped 19;
Tests (1981–82 to 1991): 81 matches; 3,322 runs, average 31.94; caught 267, stumped 5

An elegant right-handed batsman and graceful, acrobatic wicket-keeper, Jeff Dujon established himself in the West Indian side on the tour of Australia, 1982–83, and the following season in the Caribbean hit his first Test century, against India in Antigua. He and Clive Lloyd put on 207 for the sixth wicket, and the West Indies won the series. Indeed, Dujon never played in a Test side which lost a series, and he was a member of the West Indian team which won a record 11 Tests in succession, 1984–85. He hit hundreds against England and Australia and claimed five Test centuries in all, a fine feat considering that he was invariably batting at number seven.

He had no serious rival for the position of West Indian keeper, and there was an outcry when he was finally omitted after an indifferent display against England in 1991.

E

John Edrich

Born: June 21, 1937, Blofield, Norfolk
Teams: Surrey (1958–78)
First-class: 564 matches; 39,790 runs, average 45.47; no wickets for 53 runs
Tests (1963–76): 77 matches; 5,138 runs, average 43.54; no wickets for 23 runs

A member of a famous Norfolk cricketing family, John Edrich was a solid, chunky, tough and dependable left-hand opening batsman who reached 1,000 runs in a season 21 times, including twice overseas. On six of those occasions he reached 2,000. He captained Surrey from 1973 to 1977, and led England in Sydney, 1974–75, when Denness dropped himself through lack of form. He had his ribs broken by the first ball he received from Lillee in the second innings and was forced to retire. Typically of Edrich, he returned to bat two and a half hours for an unbeaten 33.

He was one of that select group of batsmen who have scored a hundred hundreds, the highest of which was 310 not out against New Zealand at Headingley, 1965. He hit five sixes and 52 fours, the most boundaries ever hit in a Test innings.

Dogged by personal tragedies, he served as a Test selector and, more recently, as England batting coach.

Bill Edrich

Born: March 26, 1916, Lingwood, Norfolk
Died: April 24, 1986, Whitehill Court, Chesham, Buckinghamshire
Teams: Middlesex (1937–58)
First-class: 571 matches; 36,965 runs, average 42.39; 479 wickets, average 33.31

BILL EDRICH *Success in the ninth Test.*

Tests (1938 to 54–55): 39 matches; 2,440 runs, average 40.00; 41 wickets, average 41.29

Bill Edrich had three brothers and a cousin (John) who played county cricket, and there was a time when the Edriches could field a full eleven. Bill Edrich played for Norfolk from 1932 to 1936 when he should have made his debut for Middlesex, but his registration was delayed and he had to wait another year. He hit 2,154 runs in 1937, and the following season he scored 1,000 runs before the end of May and played for England against Australia. His first eight Tests were disastrous for him, but the ninth, against South Africa at Durban, 1938–39, saw him score 219.

A determined and aggressive batsman who finally settled at number three and a quick bowler off a shortish run who opened the England attack immediately after the Second World War, Edrich lived life to the full. He served in the RAF and was awarded the DFC and, pre-war, he played soccer for Tottenham Hotspur. He was a late selection for the England tour of Australia, 1946–47, but was named as senior professional. He turned amateur the following summer, probably hoping for the England captaincy, but his lust for living was not always in accord with the ideals of England selectors – which perhaps explains why he was often omitted from sides that he should have been in.

In 1947, he and his great friend Denis Compton rewrote the record books. The Middlesex "twins" excited a nation with their exploits as Edrich scored 3,539 runs, an aggregate beaten only by Compton that same summer, and hit 12 centuries, including his career-best 267 not out against Northamptonshire. The following season, he and Compton shared a Middlesex third-wicket record stand of 424 undefeated against Somerset. He captained Middlesex and, on retirement, returned to play for Norfolk. He was a man of intelligence and charm, and always good company.

Godfrey Evans

Born: August 18, 1920, Finchley, Middlesex
Teams: Kent (1939–67)
First-class: 465 matches; 14,882 runs, average 21.22; 2 wickets, average 122.50; caught 816, stumped 250
Tests (1946–59): 91 matches; 2,439 runs, average 20.49; caught 173, stumped 46

One of the very greatest of wicket-keepers and an entertainer much loved by the crowd, Godfrey Evans appeared for Kent in a handful of matches in 1939 before succeeding Les Ames in 1946. Within a year he was England's first-choice keeper. He was an extrovert and he was spectacular, but he was eminently dependable, and his keeping standing up to Alec Bedser became one of the features of immediate post-war cricket. He was also a capable batsman who reached 1,000 runs in a season four times, and he hit seven centuries, two of them in Tests. Against India at Lord's, 1952, he made 105, and 98 of these runs came before lunch, yet in Adelaide, 1946–47, he created a world record when he batted 97 minutes before scoring his first run in the second innings. He could bat as the occasion demanded, but perhaps he never treated batting quite seriously enough in county matches.

He made four tours to Australia and two to South Africa and the West Indies, and he was popular everywhere. On his retirement, he was employed by Ladbrokes for many years.

F

Aubrey Faulkner

Born: December 17, 1881, Port Elizabeth, South Africa
Died: September 10, 1930, Walham Green, London
Teams: Transvaal (1902–03 to 1909–10); MCC (1912–20)
First-class: 118 matches; 6,366 runs, average 36.58; 449 wickets, average 17.42
Tests (1905–06 to 1924): 25 matches; 1,754 runs, average 40.79; 82 wickets, average 26.58

Aubrey Faulkner was one of the earliest exponents of the googly when he delivered at a medium pace. He was also a very fine right-handed middle-order batsman. His Test debut came against England, 1905–06, and he played a significant part in South Africa winning four of the five Tests. He enjoyed a fine tour of England, 1907, and took nine wickets in the Headingley Test. When South Africa again beat England in a Test series in South Africa, 1909–10, he captured 29 wickets in the five Tests. In the first, he scored 78 and 123 and had match figures of eight for 160. He hit 99 in the last Test.

In Australia the following year, he made South Africa's first double-century in a Test match, 204 at Melbourne, and followed this with 115 at Adelaide when South Africa beat Australia for the first time. He did the "double" on the tour of England, 1912, and a year later settled in England. He had a fine war record, being awarded the DSO, and he opened an indoor cricket school in London which benefited many cricketers and became world-famous. He was one of the heroes of MacLaren's side which overcame the mighty Australian side of 1921. He scored 153 and took six wickets.

Given to fits of melancholia, he died tragically by his own hand.

Fazal Mahmood

Born: February 18, 1927, Lahore, India
Teams: Northern India (1943–44 to 1946–47); Punjab (1951–52 to 1956–57); Lahore (1958–59)
First-class: 111 matches; 2,602 runs, average 23.02; 460 wickets, average 19.11
Tests (1952–53 to 1962): 34 matches; 620 runs, average 14.09; 139 wickets, average 24.70

Fazal Mahmood was a right-arm fast medium-pace bowler whose style was akin to Alec Bedser's. He was selected for India's tour of Australia, 1947–48, but stood down on the announcement of the Partition and waited for his international debut until 1952–53 when Pakistan entered Test cricket. In his country's second Test, against India at Lucknow, he took five for 52 and seven for 42 to bring Pakistan an historic victory. He had proved himself particularly devastating on matting, but he was equally effective in England in 1954. He captured four wickets at Lord's and Old Trafford, and at the Oval he took six for 53 and six for 46 to take Pakistan to victory over England.

A national hero, happy and popular, he was chosen to lead Pakistan when Kardar stepped down, but Fazal did not have Kardar's social status. With the added responsibility of being the main strike bowler, his captaincy suffered. It had begun sensationally when he put the West Indies in at Karachi and took seven wickets to bowl his side to a 10-wicket victory. Thereafter, his bowling declined and his captaincy was criticized as factions developed. When he left Test cricket, he had a Pakistan record of 139 wickets to his credit.

R. E. Foster

Born: April 16, 1878, Malvern, Worcestershire
Died: May 13, 1914, Brompton, Kensington, London
Teams: Oxford University (1897–1900); Worcestershire (1899–1912)
First-class: 139 matches; 9,076 runs, average 41.82; 25 wickets, average 46.12
Tests (1903–04 to 1907): 8 matches; 602 runs, average 46.30

"Tip" Foster was a typical Edwardian sportsman of immense talent who was unable to give much time to cricket because of business commitments. The third of seven sons of a clergyman, all of whom played for Malvern and Worcestershire, he was in the Oxford side for four seasons, leading the side in inspiring fashion in the last year. He hit a record 171 in the Varsity match and a fortnight later became the first batsman to hit a century in each innings of a Gentlemen v Players match. He played only one regular season of county cricket, in 1901, when he captained Worcestershire and hit 2,128 runs. He accepted an invitation to tour Australia in 1903–04 and hit 287 in the first Test at Sydney, a record for a player on his Test debut and a record for Test cricket until 1929–30. He shared a fifth of 192 with Braund and a last-wicket stand of 130 in 66 minutes with Rhodes, which remains a record.

He led England against South Africa in 1907, the first time the Springboks had played Test cricket outside their own country, but he was able to give no more time after that. He won blues for golf, soccer and rackets and played soccer for Corinthians and England. He died of diabetes at the age of 36.

Tich Freeman

Born: May 17, 1888, Lewisham, London
Died: January 28, 1965, Bearsted, Kent
Teams: Kent (1914–36)
First-class: 592 matches; 4,961 runs, average 9.50; 3,776 wickets, average 18.42
Tests (1924–25 to 1929): 12 matches; 154 runs, average 14.00; 66 wickets, average 25.86

His height earning him the nickname "Tich", Freeman took more wickets in county cricket than any other bowler in the history of the game, and only Wilfred Rhodes took more wickets in all first-class cricket. In 1928, he became the only bowler to capture 300 wickets in a season, 304 at 18.05 runs each, and in the seven seasons that followed he took more than 200 wickets each season, so that between 1928 and 1935 he took 2,090 wickets. In 1936, he captured "only" 108 wickets for Kent and was not re-engaged.

Standing 5ft 2in, "Tich" Freeman was a leg-break and googly bowler who had immaculate control and posed difficulties with his flight which, because of his height, often had a low trajectory. That he played only 12 times for England and never against Australia in England is one of the unsolved mysteries of the game. In 1928, he took 22 wickets in three Tests against the West Indies, but he did not appear in a single Test on the tour of Australia that followed. Against South Africa, 1929, he captured 22 wickets in two matches, yet he did not play for England after that series.

He became a record wicket-taker in the Birmingham League after he left first-class cricket.

Charles Fry

Born: April 25, 1872, West Croydon, Surrey
Died: September 7, 1956, Child's Hill, Hampstead, London
Teams: Oxford University (1892–95); Sussex (1894–1908); London County (1900–1902); Hampshire (1909–1921); Europeans (1921–22)
First-class: 394 matches; 30,886 runs, average 50.22; 166 wickets, average 29.34
Tests (1895–96 to 1912): 26 matches; 1,223 runs, average 32.18; no wickets for 3 runs

Charles Fry made only one tour abroad with an England side, to South Africa, 1895–96, shortly after coming down from Oxford. He played in the first two Tests of the series, and his remaining 24 Test matches were all played in England. He would have been a regular choice for his country had he been able to spare the time. A first-class honours graduate in Classical Moderations, he won his blue in all four years at Oxford and also won blues for soccer and athletics. He would also have won a blue for rugby but for injury. He held the world long-jump record for 21 years, was capped for England against Ireland at soccer in 1901 and played for Southampton in the FA Cup Final the following year. He was an author, journalist, broadcaster, fought three unsuccessful campaigns as a Liberal candidate, represented India at the League of Nations, captained Sussex from 1904 to 1908, edited a magazine and founded and directed the training ship *Mercury*. After the First World War, it was alleged that he was offered and declined the throne of Albania.

A correct batsman and great thinker on the game, he hit six centuries in succession in 1901 and made 3,147 runs, average 78.67, in the season. His list of activities and achievements gives ample reason why he did not play more for England. He captained England in the 1912 Triangular Tournament, winning four and drawing two of the six matches, but he was frequently the "kingmaker". He maintained that he was asked to replace Douglas as England captain in 1921, but could not spare the time and suggested Tennyson.

G

Joel Garner

Born: December 16, 1952, Enterprise, Christ Church, Barbados
Teams: Barbados (1975–76 to 1987–88); Somerset (1977–86)
First-class: 214 matches; 2,964 runs, average 16.74; 881 wickets, average 18.53
Tests (1976–77 to 1986–87): 58 matches; 672 runs, average 12.44; 259 wickets, average 20.97

6ft 8in tall, Joel Garner, "Big Bird", was a giant of a fast bowler. He used his height to the full, generated considerable pace off a comparatively short run and swung and cut the ball both ways. His first Test series was against Pakistan, 1976–77, and he took 25 wickets in five matches. He took 13 wickets in the first two Tests against Australia the following season, but missed the rest of the series because of his association with World Series Cricket. In the World Cup Final at Lord's, 1979, he took five for 38 to ensure the West Indies' victory over England, and he was a major factor in Somerset winning both the Sunday League and the NatWest Trophy the same year. The county had won no trophies before this time.

GARNER *Speed from a great height.*

A shoulder injury handicapped him for a while, but he played a significant part in the West Indies' record 11 consecutive Test victories. He was not the least of a formidable quartet of fast bowlers. He captained Barbados when they won the Shell Shield, and, amidst controversy, was released by Somerset after the 1986 season. A genial man, he was popular wherever he went.

Mike Gatting

Born: June 6, 1957, Kingsbury, Middlesex
Teams: Middlesex (1975–97)
First-class: 515 matches, 34,357 runs, average 50.15; 156 wickets, average 29.79
Tests (1977–78 to 1994–95): 79 matches, 4,409 runs, average 35.55; 4 wickets, average 79.25

A stocky, belligerent batsman capable of taking apart any attack, and a medium-pace bowler, Mike Gatting is a dedicated professional who succeeded Mike Brearley as captain of Middlesex in 1983 and led them to every honour before standing down in 1997. A prolific scorer in county cricket, he made his Test debut in Pakistan, 1977–78, but did not score a Test hundred until his 54th innings at Bombay, 1984–85. He hit a double-century later in the same series, and thereafter runs flowed from his bat.

When Gower fell out of favour after losing the first Test to India, 1986, Gatting was named as England captain. He could not reverse the trend against India and lost to New Zealand the same summer, but he led a harmonious side to a totally surprising victory in Australia the following winter. There was unease about his captaincy when Pakistan won in England in 1987 although Gatting himself hit two centuries in the series. A dreadful reverse sweep cost him his wicket in the World Cup Final later the same year so that he took much of the blame for England losing a match that they had seemed to be winning. When the team went to Pakistan he had a notorious confrontation with umpire Shakoor Rana, and the following summer he was the subject of allegations in a newspaper regarding his social life. He was relieved of the captaincy and stood down after the third Test. He played against Australia in 1989, but it was revealed that he was to lead a side to South Africa, and he was automatically banned from Test cricket. He resumed his Test career in India, 1992–93, and was a controversial choice to tour Australia, 1994–95. He hit his 10th and last Test century at Adelaide, but he did not enjoy a successful tour.

Tough, rugged and honest, he became a Test selector in 1997.

Sunny Gavaskar

See Legends (pages 98–99)

George Geary

Born: July 9, 1893, Barwell, Leicestershire
Died: March 6, 1981, Leicester
Teams: Leicestershire (1912–38)
First-class: 549 matches; 13,504 runs, average 19.80; 2,063 wickets, average 20.03
Tests (1924–34): 14 matches; 249 runs, average 15.56; 46 wickets, average 29.41

George Geary bowled right-arm fast medium and was a good enough batsman in the lower order to score eight first-class centuries. He was the mainstay of Leicestershire for many years, taking 100 or more wickets in a season 11 times. He played an important part in England regaining the Ashes, 1926, and he played in four Tests on the Australian tour of 1928–29. He captured 19 wickets and, in the first innings of the final Test at Melbourne, took five for 105 in 81 overs, 36 of which were maidens, an astonishing feat in hot weather.

In 1929, playing for Leicestershire against Glamorgan, he captured all 10 wickets for 18 runs, which was, at the time, a world record. He later coached at Charterhouse where he was a guiding light to Peter May.

Lance Gibbs

Born: September 29, 1934, Queenstown, Georgetown, British Guiana
Teams: British Guiana/Guyana (1953–54 to 1974–75); Warwickshire (1967–73; South Australia (1969–70)
First-class: 330 matches; 1,729 runs, average 8.55; 1,024 wickets, average 22.72
Tests (1957–58 to 1975–76): 79 matches; 488 runs, average 6.97; 309 wickets, average 29.09

With his long fingers, Lance Gibbs was one of the greatest of off-spin bowlers and a very fine fielder in the gully. In his first Test series, against Pakistan, 1957–58, he took 17 wickets in four Tests, and in Australia he took 19 wickets in three Tests. At Sydney, he took three wickets in four balls, and in the next Test, at Adelaide, he

GIBBS *309 Test wickets with off-breaks.*

performed the hat-trick. A year later, in Barbados, he bowled the West Indies to victory over India with eight for 38 in the second innings. In fact, he took eight for six in 15.3 overs, 14 of which were maidens. His success continued unabated and when he retired his 309 Test wickets was a record.

He enjoyed much success with Warwickshire and captured 131 wickets in first-class matches in 1971. He settled in the United States, played for the USA. against Canada, 1983, and managed the West Indies in England, 1991.

Graham Gooch

Born: July 23, 1953, Whipps Cross, Leytonstone, Essex
Teams: Essex (1973–97): Western Province (1982–83 to 1983–84)
First-class: 570 matches; 44,472 runs, average 49.57; 246 wickets, average 34.36
Tests (1975 to 1994–95): 118 matches; 8,900 runs, average 42.58; 23 wickets, average 46.47

By the end of 1993, Graham Gooch stood surveying the game of cricket like an Alexander with no more worlds to conquer. He had scored more than a hundred hundreds, scored more runs in Test cricket than any other English batsman, more centuries for Essex than any other cricketer, played in more than 100 Tests, had captained England in victory and defeat, had made 333, the highest score by an England captain, and 123 against India at Lord's, 1990, had scored more runs in the Sunday League, Benson & Hedges Cup and sixty-over competition than any other batsman, had scored more runs in a season and more runs in a career than any other Essex batsman, and had captained his county to success in the championship as well as being an integral part of the side who had enjoyed a golden period in which they had won every honour in the game.

His career, though, has not been without its upsets. His Test career had begun with a "pair" against Australia in 1975, and he would have played more for England had he not excommunicated himself by joining a rebel tour in South Africa. He stands at the wicket suggesting a brooding melancholy, but he is a batsman of tremendous power, and he has been the scourge of attacks all over the world as 20 Test hundreds would testify. He is also a medium-pace bowler and a very fine slip fielder.

A fitness fanatic, he captained England in 34 Tests and went to Australia, 1994–95, under Mike Atherton, his successor, for his last Test series.

He became a Test selector in 1997.

GOOCH *456 runs in one Test.*

David Gower

Born: April 1, 1957, Tunbridge Wells, Kent
Teams: Leicestershire (1975–89); Hampshire (1990–93)
First-class: 448 matches; 26,339 runs, average 40.08; 4 wickets, average 56.75
Tests (1978–92): 117 matches; 8,231 runs, average 44.25; 1 wicket, average 20.00

GOWER *Carefree elegance of a former age.*

An effortless left-hander who timed the ball with a sweetness that few have been able to match, David Gower made his Test debut against Pakistan at Edgbaston in 1978. The first ball he received in Test cricket he hit for four, and by the time his Test career finished 14 years later he had scored more runs in Test cricket than any other batsman. Tall and blond, he had a languid eloquence with the bat and so delicate was his timing that his batting always had a suggestion of human frailty which but added to its attraction. He had the style of the carefree amateur of the Golden Age, and with his looks and grace, he might have been better playing in that age as the mood took him and expenses allowed. He would have graced the Golden Age as he would have any era in which he batted.

He abandoned his degree studies at London University to become a cricketer with Leicestershire in 1975, and if he took some time to prove himself statistically, his class was ever apparent. His first Test hundred came at the Oval in the second half of the 1978 summer. It was made against New Zealand, and it was followed by a century in Australia and 200 not out against India, 1979.

Gower first captained England against Pakistan, 1982–83, when he hit two centuries. He was unfortunate in being handed the poisoned chalice of captaining England against the powerful West Indies side, 1984, and England lost 5–0. The following winter, in India, he led with tact, shrewdness and calm, and England won the series which was played against the most tragic of backgrounds.

In 1985, his side regained the Ashes from a weakened Australian team, and he hit three centuries in the series, including 215 at Edgbaston. Then, in the winter, England lost 5–0 to the West Indies for the second time, and he took much blame for what many saw as his diffident approach. He was replaced when England lost to India, restored when England entertained Australia in 1989 and were soundly beaten, and not selected in the party to tour the West Indies the following winter. Back in the side in 1990 and chosen for the trip to Australia, he made two centuries, but he upset skipper Gooch and others with a flying exploit. When he was not selected for the tour of India, 1992–93, members of the MCC forced a special General Meeting to voice dissatisfaction at the way in which the game was being run.

Gower decided to retire and he became successful on television as a commentator.

W. G. Grace

See Legends (pages 100–101)

Tom Graveney

Born: June 16, 1927, Riding Mill, Northumberland
Teams: Gloucestershire (1948–60); Worcestershire (1961–70); Queensland (1969–70 to 1971–72)
First-class: 732 matches; 47,793 runs, average 44.91; 80 wickets, average 37.96
Tests (1951 to 69): 79 matches; 4,882 runs, average 44.38; 1 wicket, average 167.00

Tom Graveney scored 122 first-class centuries and reached 1,000 runs in an English season 20 times. He was one of the most attractive batsmen to have appeared since the war, full of grace and elegance. But, in spite of his complete command of stylish strokes and his consistency, he spent more than half his career unable to hold a regular place in the England side.

GRAVENEY *Style and grace.*

He began as the pride of Gloucestershire, whom he captained in 1959 and 1960, but he left the county following a disagreement over the captaincy and joined Worcestershire, whom he captained 1968–70. He first played for England against South Africa in 1951, and the following winter he hit the first of his 11 Test centuries, 175 against India at Bombay. His highest Test score was his 258 against the West Indies at Trent Bridge in 1957 when he and Peter Richardson added a record 266 for the second wicket. Graveney had an outstanding record against West Indies and played a major part in the series victory in the Caribbean, 1967–68, hitting 118 in Trinidad. He made 75 against the West Indies at Old Trafford, 1969, but was banned for appearing in a benefit game on the Sunday and never played Test cricket again.

Later, he was variously a coach in Australia, a landlord of a pub near Cheltenham and a commentator.

Gordon Greenidge

Born: May 1, 1951, Black Bess, St Peter, Barbados
Teams: Hampshire (1970–87); Barbados (1972–73 to 1990–91)
First-class: 523 matches; 37,354 runs, average 45.88; 18 wickets, average 26.61
Tests (1974–75 to 1990–91): 108 matches; 7,558 runs, average 44.72; no wicket for 4 runs

A brilliantly aggressive right-handed opening batsman, Gordon Greenidge was brought to England at the age of 12 and lived and was educated in Reading. He could have played for England but chose the West Indies instead, and with Desmond Haynes formed one of the most successful opening partnerships Test cricket has known. They shared 16 century partnerships in 89 Tests together. In county cricket, he had another formidable

GREENIDGE *Power and aggression.*

opening partnership with the South African Barry Richards. Greenidge was prolific in all forms of cricket, and at one time he held the record for the highest score in all three one-day competitions in England.

He hit double-centuries against England, Australia and New Zealand and made 19 Test centuries in all. Perhaps his most memorable innings came at Lord's in 1984 when the West Indies were set to score 342 runs in just over five hours. Greenidge made 214 not out off 241 balls with two sixes and 29 fours, and the West Indies won by nine wickets.

Greenidge captained the West Indies on one occasion when Richards was unfit.

Jack Gregory

Born: August 14, 1895, North Sydney, New South Wales, Australia
Died: August 7, 1973, Bega, New South Wales, Australia
Teams: New South Wales (1920–21 to 1928–29)
First-class: 129 matches; 5,659 runs, average 36.50; 504 wickets, average 20.99
Tests (1920–21 to 1928–29): 24 matches; 1,146 runs, average 36.96; 85 wickets, average 31.15

A bronzed, tall, powerful man, Jack Gregory was a fast right-arm bowler and a dynamic left-handed batsman. In the years immediately after the First World War, he formed one of the great fast bowling partnerships with Ted McDonald. He was first noted playing for the Australian Imperial Forces in 1919, and a year later he was in the Australian Test side. In his first series he took 23 wickets and scored 442 runs, including a century at number nine. England were routed 5–0 and, in England a few months later, Gregory and McDonald continued to cause havoc. Gregory took 19 wickets in the Tests and did the "double" on the tour. At Johannesburg, 1921–22, he hit a century in 70 minutes against South Africa. It was the fastest in Test cricket. He also took seven for 139 in the match.

He took two wickets against England, 1924–25, but, no longer paired with McDonald, his powers seemed on the wane, and he broke down physically on the tour of England, 1926. He played in the first Test against England, 1928–29, and sent down 41 overs for three wickets before retiring from the match and from Test cricket with a knee injury.

His wife was "Miss Australia".

Syd Gregory

Born: April 14, 1870, Moore Park, Randwick, Sydney, New South Wales, Australia
Died: August 1, 1929, Moore Park, Randwick, Sydney, New South Wales, Australia
Teams: New South Wales (1889–90 to 1911–12)
First-class: 369 matches; 15,190 runs, average 28.25; 2 wickets, average 195.00
Tests (1890–1912): 58 matches; 2,282 runs, average 24.53; no wickets for 33 runs

Known as "Little Tich" because he was only 5ft 4in tall, Syd Gregory was a quick-scoring, middle-order, right-handed batsman whose consistency and, above all, brilliant fielding at cover kept him in the Australian side for 22 years. He made the first of his eight tours to England in 1890, and on four of his tours he exceeded 1,000 runs. The first of his four Test hundreds came at Sydney in December 1894, when he hit 201 in 244 minutes. This was the first double century to be scored in a Test in Australia. He made a century at Lord's, 1896, and at the Oval three years later.

When Clem Hill and five other leading players refused to play in the Triangular Tournament in England, 1912, Syd Gregory was recalled to captain the side after an absence of three years from Test cricket. The side was woefully weak and ill-disciplined and, at 42, Gregory was past his best.

Tony Greig

Born: October 6, 1946, Queenstown, South Africa
Teams: Border (1965–66 to 1969–70); Sussex (1966–78); Eastern Province (1970–71 to 1971–72)
First-class: 350 matches; 16,660 runs, average 31.19; 856 wickets, average 28.85
Tests (1972–77): 58 matches; 3,599 runs, average 40.43; 141 wickets, average 32.20

Son of a Scottish RAF officer with a distinguished war record who was posted to South Africa at the end of the war, Tony Greig excites the same conflicting passions as Jardine. Standing 6ft 7in tall, with blond hair and an engaging smile, he was a brave, attacking batsman and a right-arm medium pace bowler who also bowled off-breaks to good effect. A dominant and attractive personality, he qualified for Sussex and made an impact with 156 against Lancashire in his first championship match, 1967. He played for England against Rest of the World, 1970, and two years later made his Test debut, hitting 57 and 62 and taking one for 21 and four for 53 against Australia at Old Trafford. It was the first of an unbroken sequence of 58 Tests.

GREIG *Over-charismatic, under-rated.*

The first of his eight Test centuries came against India the following winter, and a year later, as vice-captain on the tour of the Caribbean, he hit a century in the third Test and bowled England to a sensational victory and a draw in the series in the last Test when he took eight for 86 and five for 70 with his off-breaks. His match analysis in this game remains a record for England against the West Indies.

He was also involved in a controversial incident with Kallicharan in this series and deprived of the vice-captaincy in Australia. Having led Sussex since 1973, when Denness was sacked in 1975 he became captain of England. Immensely popular, he instilled self-belief and a fighting spirit into a flagging England side. He would smile even when beaten, but there were always those ready to remind him he was South African.

He inspired England to a memorable series victory in England, 1976–77, and English cricket was respectful and joyful, but in the Centenary Test in Melbourne, it was learned that he had been recruiting players for Packer's World Series. Regarded by some as a traitor, he was sacked as captain and did not play Test cricket after 1977. He had been the first man to score 3,000 runs and to take 100 Test wickets for England, and his record stands comparison with anyone's.

He settled in Australia and worked as a commentator and in insurance. His actions brought sponsorship and more money into cricket, and he shook the establishment out of complacency. It would be difficult to find a professional cricketer who has anything but praise and affection for him. It was revealed that he suffered from a mild form of epilepsy.

Clarrie Grimmett

Born: December 25, 1891, Caversham, Dunedin, New Zealand
Died: May 2, 1980, Kensington Park, Adelaide, South Australia
Teams: Wellington (1911–12 to 1913–14); Victoria (1918–19 to 1923–24); South Australia (1924–25 to 1940–41)
First-class: 248 matches; 4,720 runs, average 17.67; 1,424 wickets, average 22.28
Tests (1924–25 to 1935–36): 37 matches; 557 runs, average 13.92; 216 wickets, average 24.21

Clarrie Grimmett was the first bowler to take 200 Test wickets. He was a leg-break and googly bowler who was born in New Zealand and moved to Australia at the start of the First World War. A sign-writer by trade, he worked hard at his bowling and became a prolific wicket-taker in the Sheffield Shield, but he was 33 before he made his Test debut against England at Sydney, 1924–25. He took five for 45 and six for 37. On the tour of England, 1926, he took over 100 wickets, and he and fellow leg-spinner Arthur Mailey were the main Test wicket-takers.

Mailey had departed by 1928–29, and Grimmett bore the burden of the Australian attack, capturing 23 wickets but sending down nearly 400 overs in the Tests. In 1930, when he again captured more than 100 wickets in England, including all 10 for 37 in an innings against Yorkshire, he took 29 Test wickets, and the following winter he mesmerized the West Indies in Australia, claiming 33 wickets in the series. He repeated this feat in only four Tests against South Africa the following season. He was again successful in England, 1934, and in South Africa, 1935–36, he broke all records with 44 wickets, average 14.59, in five Tests. Astonishingly, he never played Test cricket again although many thought he should have come to England in 1938 even at the age of 46.

George Gunn

Born: June 13, 1879, Hucknall Torkard, Nottinghamshire
Died: June 29, 1958, Tylers Green, Cuckfield, Sussex
Teams: Nottinghamshire (1902–32)
First-class: 643 matches; 35,208 runs, average 35.96; 66 wickets, average 35.68
Tests (1907–08 to 1929–30): 15 matches; 1,120 runs, average 40.00; no wickets for 8 runs

A small, slim right-handed opening batsman, George Gunn was one of a cricketing family, and for a period he and his son played alongside each other in the Nottinghamshire side. George Gunn was a batsman in the classical mould, but he was an eccentric and played as the mood took him, which is probably why his only Test in England was against Australia at Lord's in 1909. The previous series, 1907–08, he had been in Australia and was called into the England side in an emergency. He made 119 and 74 in his first Test, hit another century in the last Test and headed the batting averages for the series. He reached 1,000 runs in a season 20 times and had a fine opening partnership with W.W. Whysall. His last Test was against the West Indies in Jamaica, April, 1930. He scored 85 and 47 run out. He was just short of his 51st birthday.

H

Richard Hadlee

See Legends (pages 102–103)

Wes Hall

Born: September 12, 1937, St Michael, Barbados, West Indies
Teams: Barbados (1955–56 to 1970–71); Trinidad (1966–67 to 1969–70); Queensland 1961–62 to 1962–63)
First-class: 170 matches; 2,673 runs, average 15.10; 546 wickets, average 26.14
Tests (1958–59 to 1968–69): 48 matches; 818 runs, average 15.73; 192 wickets, average 26.38

After beginning his career as a

HALL *Speed and stamina.*

wicket-keeper/batsman, the 6ft 2in Wes Hall developed into one of the great fast bowlers of the early 1960s. He took a very long run and brought the ball down from a great height, his smooth run-up foreshadowing that of Michael Holding in its athleticism and grace. He made his Test debut for the West Indies on a tour of India and Pakistan in 1958–59, taking 46 wickets in the eight Tests at a cost of less than 18 runs. He took 22 wickets against the English tourists the following year, and 21 in the great tour of Australia in 1960–61, nine of them in the famous tied Test. With Charlie Griffith as his partner, he was formidable when the West Indies beat England 3–1 in 1963 and bowled throughout the 200 minutes of the last day at Lord's, including the last over when England drew needing six to win with the last pair together, and Cowdrey batting with a broken arm in plaster. He was a slogging tail-ender, although at Trinidad in 1967–68 he batted throughout the last two hours with Sobers to save the match against England. On retiring he went into politics and became Sports Minister in Barbados.

Walter Hammond

Born: June 19, 1903, Dover, Kent
Died: July 1, 1965, Kloof, South Africa
Teams: Gloucestershire (1920–51); South African Air Force (1942–43)
First-class: 634 matches; 50,551 runs, average 56.10; 732 wickets, average 30.58
Tests (1927–28 to 1946–47): 85 matches; 7,249 runs, average 58.45; 83 wickets, average 37.80

Hammond was the outstanding English cricketer of the 1930s, topping the batting averages for each of the eight seasons between 1933 and 1946. No English batsman has beaten his total of 36 double-centuries, and his highest score of 336 not out, made for England against New Zealand in 1932–33, was at the time a Test match record. His average for the two-match series was 563. His county championship debut was delayed because of objections about his qualification and he returned from a tour of the

HAMMOND *with rival Bradman.*

West Indies in 1925–26 with a mystery illness which made him miss the 1926 season altogether. He came back so well in 1927 that he made his Test debut in South Africa the following winter.

He was a majestic batsman, whose off-drive was regarded as one of the classic shots of cricket, a more than useful fast-medium bowler and a brilliant fielder at slip, where for Gloucestershire against Surrey in 1928 he held a world record 10 catches. Against Australia, in the 1928–29 series, he made 905 runs, then a record, averaging 113.12.

Hammond turned amateur in 1938 and was immediately given the England captaincy, which he retained until the first tour after the war, in 1946–47, when his powers at last began to decline. He was a strange, aloof man, not popular as a captain, and played rarely after his Test career ended, finally going to live in South Africa. Of his many records his total of 7,249 runs in Tests stood for nearly 25 years.

Hanif Mohammad

Born: December 21, 1934, Junagadh, India
Teams: Bahawalpur (1953–54); Karachi (1954–55 to 1968–69); PIA (1960–61 to 1975–76)
First-class: 238 matches; 17,059 runs, average 52.32; 53 wickets, average 28.47
Tests (1952–53 to 1969–70): 55 matches; 3,915 runs, average 43.98; 1 wicket, average 95.00

Hanif Mohammad was a small batsman with an immaculate defence and limitless concentration. He was called "The Little Master". He made his first-class debut for Karachi and Bahawalpur in 1951–52 when only 16 years old, and after the partition of India made his Test debut for Pakistan against India in 1952–53, in Pakistan's first-ever Test. At 17 years 300 days, he was the world's youngest Test wicket-keeper. He also opened the batting, scoring 51 in his first innings, and he soon dropped wicket-keeping to become a specialist batsman. His Test career comprised 55 of Pakistan's first 57 Tests. In the first Test against the West Indies in Bridgetown in 1957–58, when Pakistan followed on 473 behind, he made the then second-highest Test score of 337 to save the match, batting for 16 hours, 10 minutes, the longest Test innings. In 1958–59, batting for Karachi against Bahawalpur at Karachi, he was run out off the last ball of the day for 499, the highest score in first-class cricket until Brian Lara beat it in 1994. He captained Pakistan in 11 Tests from 1964–65 to 1967. He is the brother of Wazir, Mushtaq and Sadiq, and the father of Shoaib, all Pakistani Test players.

Joe Hardstaff (jun.)

Born: July 3, 1911, Nuncargate, Nottinghamshire
Died: January 1, 1990, Worksop, Nottinghamshire
Teams: Nottinghamshire (1930–55); Services in India (1943–44 to 1944–45); Europeans (1944–45); Auckland (1948–49 to 1949–50)
First-class: 517 matches; 32,847 runs, average 44.35; 36 wickets, average 59.47
Tests (1935–48): 23 matches; 1,636 runs, average 46.74;

Joe Hardstaff was the son of Joe Hardstaff (sen.), who also played for Nottinghamshire and England, and who was a Test umpire until prevented from participating because of his son's selection for England. The younger Hardstaff was regarded in the 1930s as the most elegant batsman in England, making his Test debut in 1935. His career was badly hampered by the Second World War, but he played in England's first post-war Test, against India at Lord's, when he made 205 not out. However, he failed to establish himself in the side and made his last appearance in 1948, despite topping the first-class averages in 1949 with 2,251 runs, average 72.61.

Neil Harvey

Born: October 8, 1928, Fitzroy, Melbourne, Victoria, Australia
Teams: Victoria (1946–47 to 1956–57); New South Wales (1958–59 to 1962–63)
First-class: 306 matches; 21,699 runs, average 50.93; 30 wickets, average 36.86
Tests (1947–48 to 1962–63): 79 matches; 6,149 runs, average 48.41; 3 wickets, average 40.00

Neil Harvey was a brilliant left-handed middle-order batsman, an occasional off-break bowler and an outstanding fielder at cover point or slip. He was particularly good on difficult pitches. He had just turned 18 when he first played for Victoria and a year later made his Test debut against India. In his second Test be became the youngest Australian to score a century, at 19 years 121 days. He came to England with Bradman's great side in 1948, and scored a century in the fourth Test at Headingley, the first Aussie left-hander to make 100 on his debut against England. He was at the wicket in the second innings with Bradman as Australia scored 404 for three on the last day to win. For the next 15 years Harvey was Australia's leading batsman. In 1949–50 in South Africa, he hit four centuries and averaged 132.00, including a magnificent 152 not out to win on a crumbling pitch after Australia had made 75 in the first innings and were 59 for three in the second. He made four centuries against South Africa in 1952–53 (average 92.66) and three in the West Indies in 1954–55 (average 108.33). He captained Australia once, in Benaud's absence at Lord's in 1961, and Australia won. Twenty-one of his 67 centuries were in Tests, the highest, 205, against South Africa in Melbourne in 1952–53, and his Test aggregate was at the time second only to Bradman for Australia.

Lindsay Hassett

Born: August 28, 1913, Geelong, Victoria, Australia
Died: June 16, 1993, Batcman's Bay, New South Wales, Australia
Teams: Victoria (1932–33 to 1952–53)
First-class: 216 matches; 16,890 runs, average 58.24; 18 wickets, average 39.05
Tests (1938–53): 43 matches; 3,073 runs, average 46.56; no wicket for 78

HASSETT *Dapper batsman.*

The 17-year-old Lindsay Hassett made 147 not out against the touring West Indians two years before he made his first-class debut for Victoria. Only 5ft 6in, he was a neat, quick-footed batsman with all the strokes, and a polished fielder. In 1938 he toured England, making his debut in the first Test. After the war, he captained the Australian Services team in the unofficial Victory Tests in England and India. He was vice-captain to Bradman on the tour of England in 1948 and took over the captaincy of Australia for the tour of South Africa in 1949–50. He was an excellent captain with a well-known sense of humour – perhaps his most public joke coming after he had twice dropped Washbrook on the boundary from hooks in a Test at Old Trafford, when he borrowed a policeman's helmet in preparation for the next one. He retired after Australia lost the series in England in 1953. He made eight double-centuries, but the highest of his 10 Test centuries was 198 not out against India at Adelaide in 1947–48.

Desmond Haynes

Born: February 15, 1956, St James, Barbados, West Indies
Teams: Barbados (1976–77 to 1994–95); Middlesex (1989–94)
First-class: 360 matches; 25,027 runs, average 46.17; 7 wickets, average 28.71
Tests (1977–78 to 1993–94): 116 matches; 7,487 runs, average 42.29; 1 wicket, average 8.00

Desmond Haynes was a sound but aggressive opening batsman who made over 100 Test appearances for the West Indies, 89 in a prolific partnership with Gordon Greenidge, with whom he shared a record 16 century opening partnerships. Including World Cups, he made seven tours to England and eight to Australia, as well as tours to Pakistan, India, New Zealand and Zimbabwe. His first tour to England as a Test player, in 1980, was his most successful, when he averaged 51.33 in the Tests. In 1984 his 125 at the Oval in the fifth Test guaranteed the West Indies' "blackwash" – the first side to win all five in a rubber in England. A hamstring injury in 1988 ended a run of 78 consecutive Tests. He captained the West Indies in four Tests in 1990. He played county cricket for Middlesex from 1989 and in 1990 he hit 2,346 runs, average 69.00, including his career highest of 255 not out against Sussex at Lord's. His highest in Tests was also at Lord's, 184 against England in 1980. He was immensely successful in international one-day cricket, with a record number of runs, 8,649 (average 41.38) and centuries, 17.

Tom Hayward

Born: March 29, 1871, Cambridge
Died: July 19, 1939, Cambridge
Teams: Surrey (1893–1914)
First-class: 712 matches; 43,551 runs, average 41.79; 481 wickets, average 22.95
Tests (1895–96 to 1909): 35 matches; 1,999 runs, average 34.46; 14 wickets, average 38.64

One of a famous cricketing family, Tom Hayward was a most reliable right-handed opening batsman, who, in 1906, scored 3,518 runs in an English season, which stood as a record until 1947. In 1913, he became the first professional to score 100 hundreds in first-class cricket, and he reached 1,000 or more runs in a season for 20 consecutive seasons beginning in 1895. In 1900, he scored 1,000 runs before the end of May. He was also a useful medium-pace bowler, and in 1897 he completed the "double". The following year, he scored an unbeaten 315 against Lancashire at the Oval.

His Test debut came against South Africa, 1895–96, and he hit 122 at Johannesburg in his second match. He was a tremendous influence on Jack Hobbs who followed him from Cambridge to the Oval, and he was Hobbs's first great opening partner, the pair sharing 40 partnerships of 100 or more. Hayward was also involved in six century first-wicket stands for England.

He was coach at Oxford after his retirement.

Vijay Hazare

Born: March 11, 1915, Sangli, Maharashtra, India
Teams: Maharashtra (1934–35 to 1940–41); Central India (1935–36 to 1938–39); Baroda (1941–42)
First-class: 238 matches; 18,740 runs, average 58.38; 595 wickets, average 24.61
Tests (1946 to 1952–53): 30 matches; 2,192 runs, average 47.65; 20 wickets, average 61.00

A small, right-handed batsman with the full complement of wristy strokes and a medium-pace bowler, Vijay Hazare made two scores of over 300 in his career, and he and Gul Mahomed created a world record when they put on 577 for Baroda's fourth wicket against Holkar in 1946–47. In 1939–40, he had established himself with 316 not out for Maharashtra against Baroda and had hit another triple-century the same season. Duleepsinhji apart, who played his cricket in England, Hazare was the first Indian to hit a triple-century, and certainly the first to hit two. Coached by Clarrie Grimmett, he made his Test debut in England in 1946, and, at Adelaide, 1947–48, he became the first batsman to score a century in each innings of a Test for India. He was to go on to score centuries against each of the four countries against whom he played.

He was named captain of the side to tour England, 1952. His team was weak, and in spite of his consistent batting, the tour was a disaster. He was deposed as captain for the inaugural series against Pakistan, but he still managed a century in Bombay. He was reinstated for the tour of the West Indies, 1952–53, but India lost and that marked the end of his inter-

HAYNES *Reliable opener.*

national career. He can proudly boast that he scored two centuries against England, 1951–52, and captained his country to their first-ever Test victory in the same series.

George Headley

Born: May 30, 1909, Colon, Panama
Died: November 30, 1983, Meadowbridge, Kingston, Jamaica
Teams: Jamaica (1927–28 to 1953–54)
First-class: 103 matches; 9,921 runs, average 69.86; 51 wickets, average 36.11
Tests (1929–30 to 1953–54): 22 matches; 2,190 runs, average 60.83; no wickets for 230 runs

In the 1930s George Headley was nicknamed the "Black Bradman", and his Test record still shows him to have been one of the greatest batsmen in the history of the game. He announced his quality in his first Test match, hitting 176 against England in the second innings at Bridgetown. In the third Test, in Georgetown, he became the first West Indian to score a century in each innings, and this feat was followed by 223 in the fourth and final Test in Kingston. He remains the only batsman to score four Test hundreds before the age of 21, and, until the record was beaten by Javed Miandad, he was the youngest batsman to score a double-century in Test cricket.

The West Indies toured Australia, 1930–31, and lost the Test series by four to one, but Headley hit two centuries. He scored 169 against England at Old Trafford, 1933, and headed the first-class averages, and he took an unbeaten 270 off the England bowlers at Kingston in 1935. He headed the batting averages in England in 1939 and became the first man to score a century in each innings in a Test match at Lord's.

Nimble, with a natural instinct for the game, Headley had a fine cricket brain, but he was denied the West Indian captaincy until 1948, and then led the side for only one Test. He was the first black man to captain the West Indies, and he established a standard of batting by which all subsequent Caribbean batsmen have been measured.

He was a professional in the Lancashire League and both his son and grandson became Test cricketers, his grandson for England.

Patsy Hendren

Born: February 5, 1889, Turnham Green, Middlesex
Died: October 4, 1962, Tooting Bec, London
Teams: Middlesex (1907–37)
First-class: 833 matches; 57,611 runs, average 50.80; 47 wickets, average 54.76
Tests (1920–21 to 1934–35): 51 matches; 3,525 runs, average 47.63; 1 wicket, average 31.00

"Patsy" Hendren was not only a right-handed batsman of such talent that it brought him 170 first-class hundreds, he was a great entertainer and one of the most loved characters the game has known. For a decade after the First World War, he was an integral part of England's middle order, and he was a fine outfielder as befitted a professional soccer player. He did not have the easiest of Test baptisms against Armstrong's Australians, and it was not until Headingley, 1924, that he scored the first of his seven Test centuries, 132 against South Africa. He hit his second in the same series. He was part of Chapman's side which regained the Ashes in 1926, and he thrived in the West Indies, 1929–30, when he hit four double-centuries during the tour. His aggregate for the tour was 1,765 runs, average 135.76, which remains a record, and it included his highest Test innings, 205 not out in Trinidad. He hit 301 not out for Middlesex against Worcestershire in 1933, and three times he exceeded 3,000 runs in a season.

He coached Sussex and at Harrow following his retirement, and he was the Middlesex scorer, 1953–59.

Graeme Hick

Born: May 23, 1966, Salisbury, Rhodesia
Teams: Zimbabwe (1983–84 to 1985–86); Worcestershire (1984–97); Northern Districts (1987–88 to 1988–89); Queensland (1990–91)
First-class: 327 matches; 26,895 runs, average 55.79; 195 wickets, average 43.65
Tests (1991–96): 46 matches; 2,672, average 36.10; 22 wickets, average 56.68

Before they attained Test status, Zimbabwe invested much money and hope in Graeme Hick, a right-handed batsman of phenomenal potential and great power. He is also a capable off-break bowler and fine slip fielder. Hick decided to play league cricket, to qualify for Worcestershire and, ultimately, for England. Tall, confident, Hick appeared to be realizing the potential all had recognized during the seven years of county cricket he played prior to qualifying for England. He was the youngest cricketer to score 2,000 runs in a season; in 1986, he scored 1,000 runs before the end of May 1988, and became the youngest player to reach 50 first-class centuries. While reaching his thousand before the end of May he hit an astonishing 405 against Somerset. He was equally effective in New Zealand, and, after a slow start, scored well for Queensland although the Australians were never so enthusiastic about him as the English press.

Able to play Test cricket in 1991, he was looked upon as England's saviour, but he found international cricket a tough proposition. In his 22nd Test innings, he scored 178 against India in Bombay, and there was a century against South Africa at Leeds, 1994, but in 1996 he was vulnerable to both the guile of Mushtaq and the speed of Waqar. He was dropped and not selected for England's winter tour although, inevitably, he continues to prosper at county level.

Clem Hill

Born: March 18, 1877, Hindmarsh, Adelaide, South Australia
Died: September 5, 1945, Parkville, Melbourne, Victoria, Australia
Teams: South Australia (1892–93 to 1922–23)
First-class: 252 matches; 17,213 runs, average 43.57; 10 wickets, average 32.30
Tests (1896 to 1911–12): 49 matches; 3,412 runs, average 39.21

A short, powerful left-handed batsman with a crouched stance, Clem Hill delighted crowds with his sound defence and explosive attack. He had the right temperament for the big occasion and rarely failed although he was always at his best on the hard wickets in Australia. He was a magnificent fielder in the deep where he took some memorable catches, notably one to dismiss Lilley in the Old Trafford Test of 1902 which Australia won by three runs.

Not included in the side to tour England in 1896, he scored a double-century against New South Wales, and a public outcry caused him to be added to the party. His first Test century came at Melbourne, 1897–98, when he hit 188, the highest score made by an under-21 in an Ashes Test. In 1900–01, he made an unbeaten 365 for South Australia against New South Wales. In three successive Test innings the following season he scored 99, 98, and 97. In 1902, he hit 119 in the only Test match ever to be played at Bramall Lane, Sheffield.

His relations with the Australian Board were uneasy, and he twice refused to tour England. He captained Australia to success against South Africa, 1910–11, but lost heavily to Douglas's side the following season, and that defeat by England ended his Test career. It was alleged that he was involved in a fight with a selector.

George Hirst

Born: September 7, 1871, Kirkheaton, Yorkshire
Died: May 10, 1954, Lindley, Huddersfield, Yorkshire
Teams: Yorkshire (1891–1929); Europeans (1921–22)
First-class: 826 matches; 36,356 runs, average 34.13; 2,742 wickets, average 18.73
Tests (1897–98 to 1909): 24 matches; 790 runs, average 22.57; 59 wickets, average 30.00

In the years before the First World War, there were those who believed that if you needed a man to die for you on the cricket field, you would choose George Hirst. He was loyal, tough and kind, and he lived and breathed Yorkshire and the game itself. He bowled medium-fast left-arm, and he batted right-handed with skill and aggression. He performed the "double" 14 times, and he is the only man in the history of the game to have taken 200 wickets and scored 2,000 runs in the same season – 2,385 runs and 208 wickets, 1906. The previous year he had made 341 against Leicestershire, which remains a Yorkshire record.

Hirst's achievements for his native county are legion, yet his Test record was surprisingly moderate. Perhaps his most famous exploit was when he and Rhodes brought England victory over Australia at the Oval in 1902 by scoring the 15 runs needed in a tense last-wicket stand. Hirst, who had match figures of six for 84, was unbeaten on 58.

He coached at Eton for many years on his retirement.

Jack Hobbs

See Legends (pages 104–105)

Michael Holding

Born: February 16, 1954, Half Way Tree, Kingston, Jamaica
Teams: Jamaica (1972–73 to 1988–89); Lancashire (1981); Tasmania (1982–83); Derbyshire (1983–89); Canterbury (1987–88);
First-class: 222 matches; 3,600 runs, average 15.00; 778 wickets, average 23.43
Tests (1975–76 to 1986–87): 60 matches; 910 runs, average 13.78; 249 wickets, average 23.68

A right-arm fast bowler, Michael Holding made the art look easy, and it is not hard to understand why batsmen referred to him as "Whispering Death". Initially, he lacked control, but soon his considerable pace was allied with accuracy and remarkable stamina, and by 1976 he was the most formidable of the West Indies' pace quartet. At Old Trafford that year, he took five for 17 as England were hurried out for 71. In the final Test, at the Oval, he produced an astonishing display of fast bowling. On a benign pitch on which Amiss made a double-century and England scored 435, he took eight for 92, the best figures by a West Indian bowler against England, and when he took six for 57 in the second innings to win the game he became the first West Indian to take more than two wickets in a Test.

A man of education and charm, he fell from grace when he reacted angrily against an umpire's decision in New Zealand by kicking over the stumps. This was not characteristic. He performed well for Derbyshire and for Tasmania. He is now a popular commentator.

HOLDING *Silent, gliding menace.*

Conrad Hunte

Born: May 9, 1932, Shorey's Village, St Andrew, Barbados
Teams: Barbados (1950–51 to 1966–67)
First-class: 132 matches; 8,916 runs, average 43.92; 17 wickets, average 37.88
Tests (1957–58 to 1966–67): 44 matches; 3,245 runs, average 45.06; 2 wickets, average 55.00

Conrad Hunte was a most reliable and sound opening batsman and an excellent fielder. He scored 142 on his Test debut against Pakistan, 1957–58, and in the third Test of the same series he made 260, sharing a second-wicket stand of 446 with Sobers. A third century came in the fourth Test, and he had a different kind of record in the last when he became the first West Indian to be out to the first ball of a Test match. In England, 1966, he began the series with a flourishing 135, but three years earlier he had done even better with 182 followed by an unbeaten 108 in the final Test.

Hunte was a natural batsman who liked to attack, but who played to the needs of his side, and consistency was his trade mark. Following his retirement, he worked for the Moral Rearmament movement and coached in South African townships.

Len Hutton

Born: June 23, 1916, Fulneck, Pudsey, Yorkshire
Died: September 6, 1990, Norbiton, Kingston-upon-Thames, Surrey
Teams: Yorkshire (1934–55)
First-class: 513 matches; 40,140 runs, average 55.51; 170 wickets, average 29.51
Tests (1937 to 1954–55): 79 matches; 6,971 runs, average 56.67; 3 wickets, average 77.33

Len Hutton was one of the greatest opening batsmen that cricket has seen, and, in the opinion of many, England has never had a better captain. He batted in the classical mould. There was time to spare, and he had the mastery of every shot without resorting to brutality. In the years before the war, he was also a useful leg-break bowler. He was reared in the hard and eminently successful Yorkshire side of the 1930s and gained early guidance from his opening partner Herbert Sutcliffe. Chosen for England against New Zealand in 1937, he was out for 0 and 1 on his T but he made the first of his 19 Test hundreds in the next match. The following season, he scored a century in his first Test against Australia, and, at the Oval, he made history by batting 13 hours 17 minutes to score 364, which was to remain the highest score in Test cricket for nearly 20 years. He was 22 years old. Against the West Indies in 1939, he played innings of 196 and 165 not out to bring his aggregate to 1,109 runs in his last eight Tests before the outbreak of war.

An injury sustained in an accident early in the war led to him being invalided out of the army in 1942, and his left arm was now two inches shorter than his right. If, in the post-war years, he was not quite the batsman he had been in 1939, he was still as good as anyone in the world. He had his bad periods, but when England faced a crisis of captaincy they turned to Hutton. When he led England against India at Leeds in 1952 he was the first professional to captain England. He scored two centuries in the series which England won resoundingly. Traditionalists were still opposed to his appointment, but he regained the Ashes, 1953, led England to a draw in the Caribbean after they had been two Tests down and retained the Ashes in Australia, 1954–55. His own form did not falter, but a back problem and, one feels, weariness caused him to retire. He was, and remains, a national hero, knighted in 1956 for his services to cricket. He had led England out of the wilderness.

I

Raymond Illingworth

Born: June 8, 1932, Pudsey, Yorkshire
Teams: Yorkshire (1951–83); Leicestershire (1969–78)
First-class: 787 matches; 24,134 runs, average 28.06; 2,072 wickets, average 20.28
Tests (1958–73): 61 matches; 1,836 runs, average 23.24; 122 wickets, average 31.20

Ray Illingworth had a most eventful career, during and after his playing days. A right-handed, solid middle-order batsman and off-break bowler, he completed the "double" six times and won a place in the England side between 1958 and 1969, experiencing modest success. He had been a vital member of the Yorkshire side, but a contractual dispute led him to leave his native county and become captain of Leicestershire. His success with his new county was phenomenal, for they won all the domestic competitions bar the Gillette Cup during the period when he was their captain. But he had led the side in only eight first-class matches when he was called upon to lead England in place of the injured Colin Cowdrey in 1969. There was immediate success over the West Indies, and he both regained and defended the Ashes. He did not suffer defeat in a Test match until his twentieth game in charge, and there are those who say that he was the best captain they ever played under. The defeat by India followed by heavy defeats at the hands of the West Indies, 1973, ended his Test career.

In 1979, he retired from first-class cricket and became manager of Yorkshire, but problems at the club forced him to assume the captaincy in 1982 at the age of 50. He finally stood down in 1983.

In 1993, he became chairman of selectors, but his three years in charge were neither happy nor good for the game.

Imran Khan

See Legends (pages 106–107)

Intikhab Alam

Born: December 28, 1941, Hoshiarpur, India
Teams: Karachi (1957–58 to 1970–71); PIA (1960–61 to 1974–75); PWD (1967–68 to 1969–70); Surrey (1969–81); Sind (1973–74)
First-class: 489 matches; 14,331 runs, average 22.14; 1,571 wickets, average 27.67
Tests (1959–60 to 1976–77): 47 matches; 1,493 runs, average 22.28; 125 wickets, average 35.95

A burly, cheerful all-rounder, Intikhab Alam was the first Pakistani cricketer to complete the "double" in Test matches. He was a gloriously attacking batsman and a leg-break and googly bowler of quality in an age when that type of bowling was a rarity. He was a highly entertaining cricketer and a great favourite at Surrey for many years. He captured 104 wickets in 1971.

He took a wicket with his first ball in Test cricket, but his career with Pakistan had its ups and downs. He led his country in 17 Tests in a time of dissension and unease, and he had a difficult time although he was a most able captain. In New Zealand, 1972–73, he was outstanding, taking 18 wickets in three Tests and leading Pakistan to their first series victory abroad.

As a manager, he did much to forge unity in Pakistan cricket and to make possible the team's most successful period in international cricket.

J

Archie Jackson

Born: September 5, 1909, Rutherglen, Lanark, Scotland
Died: February 16, 1933, Clayfields, Brisbane, Queensland, Australia
Teams: New South Wales (1926–27 to 1930–31)
First-class: 70 matches; 4,383 runs, average 45.65
Tests (1928–29 to 1930–31): 8 matches; 474 runs, average 47.40

Archie Jackson was a right-handed batsman of grace and beauty who seemed destined for greatness, but who was the stuff of tragedy. He played his first Test match against England at Adelaide in February, 1929, and made 164, becoming the youngest player to score a century in an Ashes series. He arrived in England in 1930 with a reputation higher than Bradman's. He scored a thousand runs, but he appeared in only two Tests. He played four times against the West Indies the following winter, but his health was failing. He moved to Brisbane to be near his girlfriend and in the hope that a better climate would improve matters, but he died at the age of 23.

F. S. Jackson

Born: November 21, 1870, Allerton Hall, Chapel Allerton, Leeds, Yorkshire
Died: March 9, 1947, Knightsbridge, London
Teams: Cambridge University (1890–93); Yorkshire (1890–1907)
First-class: 309 matches; 15,901 runs, average 33.83; 774 wickets, average 20.37
Tests (1893–1905): 20 matches; uns, average 48.79; 24 wickets, average 33.29

Educated at Harrow and Cambridge where he won his blue all four years and was captain for two seasons, Sir Stanley Jackson was rarely able to play regularly although he was an all-rounder of outstanding ability, a right-handed stylish batsman and fast medium-pace bowler, who did the "double" in 1898. He had made his Test debut at Lord's in 1893, scoring 91 and 5. At the Oval, he made 103, but he was unable to play in the third and final Test. All his Test matches were in England against Australia.

He served in the Boer War, was invalided home with enteric fever and was persuaded to play for the Gentlemen against the Players at Scarborough while convalescing. He hit 13 and 42 against an attack which included Hirst and Rhodes, and then he went back to the Boer War.

He was an MP for 11 years, was Financial Secretary to the War Office and Party Chairman, but as soon as Baldwin became Prime Minister, Jackson was sent to India as Governor of Bengal where he narrowly escaped assassination.

Jackson was chosen for England whenever available and captained the side in 1905 when two Tests were won and three drawn. Jackson topped both the England batting and bowling averages for the series.

He was president of the MCC, a Test selector and president of Yorkshire CCC from 1939 until his death.

Douglas Jardine

Born: October 23, 1900, Malabar Hill, Bombay, India
Died: June 18, 1958, Montreux, Switzerland
Teams: Oxford University (1920–23); Surrey (1921–33)
First-class: 262 matches; 14,848 runs, average 46.83; 48 wickets, average 31.10
Tests (1928 to 1933–34): 22 matches; 1,296 runs, average 48.00; no wickets for 10 runs

Few captains of England have excited as much passion and controversy as Douglas Jardine; none has been more successful. His father, Malcolm, captained Oxford in 1891 and scored a century in the Varsity match the following year before embarking on a highly successful legal career in India. Douglas returned to Britain at the age of nine and was sent to Winchester. He played in three Varsity matches in his four years at Oxford where he was regarded as a rather cool intellectual and a batsman of outstanding ability with great powers of concentration and immense courage. He never bowed to pain.

He played for Surrey while still at Oxford and won his first Test caps against the West Indies in 1928. He went with Chapman's side to Australia, 1928–29, played in all five Tests and averaged 46.62. He also raised the passions of the Australian crowd who saw him as cold and aloof. He batted in a brightly coloured Harlequin cap and was regarded as symbolic of the Imperial order, the British establishment.

Jardine could well have captained England against Australia in 1930, but he had no independent means and had to give his time to business. He took no part in the series. But he led England against New Zealand in 1931 and against India in 1932, and was the obvious choice to take the side to Australia, 1932–33. There were those among the hierarchy who were worried about what they saw as his arrogance, but he prepared for the tour meticulously and, though amateur in status, he was professional in approach. He asserted that all things being equal he would select a Northerner before a Southerner because the Northerner's attitude and determination were akin to his own.

Jardine discussed tactics with Arthur Carr, the Nottinghamshire and former England skipper, and he evolved leg-theory, fast bowling on the leg side to a leg side field. It was later dubbed "bodyline". In Larwood, and to a lesser extent Voce, he had the bowlers to make the theory effective. England won the series four to one. He was the subject of fierce criticism, but he was worshipped by his men.

In 1933, he captained England against the West Indies – who employed leg-theory at Jardine. He countered with a century. He took the side to India the following winter, but announced that he would not play against Australia in 1934. There were those who believed that he had been let down by the administration. He was only 33 years old when he retired from cricket and was, arguably, the best number five in the world. In 15 Tests as captain, he won nine and lost only once. He averaged 50 with the bat.

Javed Miandad

Born: June 12, 1957, Karachi, Pakistan
Teams: Karachi (1973–74 to 1975–76); Sind (1973–74 to 1975–76); Sussex (1976–79); Habib Bank (1976–77 to 1995–96); Glamorgan (1980–85)
First-class: 402 matches; 28,647 runs, average 53.44; 191 wickets, average 33.48
Tests (1976–77 to 1994–95): 124

matches; 8,832 runs, average 52.57; 17 wickets, average 40.11

One of the most exciting batsman of his day, Javed Miandad towers over other Pakistani batsman in his achievements. He has 23 Test centuries to his credit, and he is 3,000 runs ahead of the field. His 280 not out against India at Hyderabad, 1982–83, is second only to Hanif Mohammad's triple-century in the Caribbean, but Javed has also hit 271 against New Zealand at Auckland, 1988–89, and 260 against England at the Oval, 1987. A strong aggressive right-handed batsman with every shot at his command and a useful leg-break bowler, Javed has captained Pakistan with distinction although he has never been far from controversy, and he has retired, been replaced and reinstated. He was highly successful in county cricket, but tended to be a law unto himself, and eventually he failed to report for duty at Glamorgan in 1986.

Certainly his exploits helped to take Pakistan to an eminence in world cricket, and he played a major part in the winning of the World Cup, 1992. He was persuaded to return to play in the World Cup, 1996, but that was not a success, and it is probable that cricket has now seen the last of him. He remains Pakistan's most capped player.

JAVED MIANDAD *Controversial run-getter.*

S. T. Jayasuriya

Born: June 30, 1969, Matara, Ceylon
Teams: Colombo (1988–89 to 1996–97)
First-class: 100 matches; 4,708 runs, average 38.59; 47 wickets, average 38.12
Tests (1990–91 to 1996–97): 17 matches; 771 runs, average 35.04; 4 wickets, average 96.50

Jayasuriya made a tremendous impact when he scored prolifically on Sri Lanka B's tour of Pakistan, 1988–89, and he won his first Test cap for Sri Lanka in New Zealand, 1990–91. A forceful, broad-shouldered, left-handed batsman and slow left-arm bowler, he was slow to establish himself in the Sri Lankan side. It was in the 1996 World Cup that he sprang to prominence. Used as an opener and in his all-round capacity, he was voted the most valuable man of the tournament, and he devastated England in the quarter-final with 82 off 44 balls, a brilliant innings. In August 1997 he made the fourth highest Test score when making 340 against India at Colombo, sharing in a record Test stand for any wicket of 576 with Roshan Mahanama.

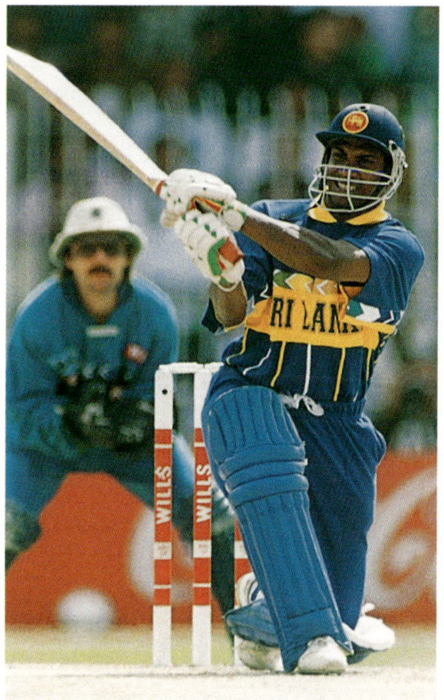

JAYASURIYA *World Cup hero.*

Gilbert Jessop

Born: May 19, 1874, Cheltenham, Gloucestershire
Died: May 11, 1955, Fordington, Dorset
Teams: Gloucestershire (1894–1914); Cambridge University (1896–99); London County (1900–03)
First-class: 493 matches; 26,698 runs, average 32.63; 873 wickets, average 22.79
Tests (1899–1912): 18 matches; 569 runs, average 21.88; 10 wickets, average 35.40

Gilbert Jessop was the stuff of legend. Known as "The Croucher" because of his stance at the wicket, he was the most consistent fast scorer the game has known, capable of hitting all round the wicket, and a most exciting figure. He batted right-handed and was a fast right-arm bowler who opened the attack on his Test debut against Australia, Lord's, 1899. He went to Australia, 1901–02, but he was too adventurous a player to be a total success in Test cricket. One of his 53 centuries came in 40 minutes, another in 42. He twice performed the "double", and he scored 1,000 runs in a season on 14 occasions, twice going on to 2,000. He captained both Cambridge University and Gloucestershire, and he was a secretary of that county for five years.

He was a very fine fielder, but his name is most remembered for his 104 for England against Australia at the Oval, 1902. Going in at 48 for five, he reached his century in 75 minutes, the fastest century in Test history at that time, and England went on to win by one wicket.

Ian Johnson

Born: December 8, 1917, North Melbourne, Victoria, Australia
Teams: Victoria (1935–36 to 1955–56)
First-class: 189 matches; 4,905 runs, average 22.92; 619 wickets, average 23.30
Tests (1945–46 to 1956–57): 45 matches; 1,000 runs, average 18.51; 109 wickets, average 29.19

Ian Johnson was a rare product for Australia, an off-break bowler. He relied more on variations in flight than in vicious turn, and he was a good lower-order batsman. He first played Test cricket in New Zealand, 1945–46, but he did not bowl. Indeed, he did not bowl until his third Test match, against England at Sydney, 1946–47, when he took six for 42 and two for 92. He did well against India, 1947–48, and he had a good tour of England, 1948, but had little effect in the Tests. He was not selected for the 1953 tour so it was very surprising when he was named as captain of Australia in succession to Hassett.

Victory in the first Test was followed by destruction at the hands of Tyson and Statham. There was surprising success in the West Indies where Johnson took seven for 44 to bring victory in Georgetown. In England, 1956, on pitches which aided spin, Johnson failed. When Laker took 19 wickets at Old Trafford Johnson had four for 151, which disappointed him bitterly. He took the side to India, but it was the magic of Benaud which won the series. In his last match, Johnson completed the "double" in Test cricket. He later became secretary of Melbourne CC.

Bill Johnston

Born: February 26, 1922, Beeac, Victoria, Australia
Teams: Victoria (1945–46 to 1954–55)
First-class: 142 matches; 1,129 runs, average 12.68; 554 wickets, average 23.35
Tests (1947–48 to 1954–55): 40 matches; 273 runs, average 11.37

Bill Johnston was a tall, strongly built left-arm fast medium-pace bowler who swung and cut the ball appreciably. He was quietly effective against India, 1947–48, but he took England by storm a few months later. He took nine for 183 in the first Test, and he shared the new ball with Lindwall when Miller was injured. He finished the series with 27 wickets in the five Tests, and he took 102 on the tour. His first Test against South Africa, 1949–50, brought his best figures, six for 44, in the second innings. His total for the series was 23 wickets as Australia won four of the five Tests, drawing in Johannesburg.

In successive home series, he scourged England with 22 wickets and West Indies with 23. At the time, he had reached 100 Test wickets faster than any other bowler in history. In 1952–53, he took 21 wickets against South Africa, but there were signs of wear and tear, and he had a persistent knee injury which hampered him on the 1953 tour of England when, being dismissed only once, he had the experience of averaging 102 with the bat, top score 28. He did well in four Tests against England, 1954–55, while all about him fell, but that marked the end of his career. His son played for South Australia.

Andrew Jones

Born: May 9, 1959, Wellington, New Zealand
Teams: Otago (1979–80 to 1984–85); Wellington (1985–86 to 1993–94); Central Districts (1994–95 to 1995–96)
First-class: 145 matches; 9,180 runs, average 41.53; 34 wickets, average 42.32
Tests (1986–87 to 1994–95): 39 matches; 2,922 runs, average 44.27; 1 wicket, average 194.00

A brave and patient batsman, Andrew Jones could never be termed stylish. He tended to move about at the crease particularly in defence, and was unorthodox in execution, but he was extremely effective and served New Zealand well. He worked hard at his game and proved himself by his results. His first Test tour, to Sri Lanka, was cut short by terrorist activities, and only the first match at the Colombo CC ground was played. Jones made 38. In 1987–88, he went to Australia and made a rather tedious 45 in the second innings of the first Test. His innings was not well received, but in the next Test, at Adelaide, he hit 150 and 64 and his position as New Zealand's number three was cemented.

He toured England in 1990 with moderate success, but against Sri Lanka the following winter he hit 186 at Wellington and shared a record third-wicket partnership of 467 with Martin Crowe.

He retired from Test cricket before New Zealand toured England in 1994, but he reversed his decision in the next home season. Sadly, his return to the Test arena was not successful.

K

Alvin Kallicharran

Born: March 21, 1949, Paidama, British Guiana
Teams: Guyana (1966–67 to 1980–81); Warwickshire (1971–90); Queensland (1977–78); Transvaal (1981–82 to 1983–84); Orange Free State (1984–85 to 1987–88)
First-class: 505 matches; 32,650 runs, average 43.64; 84 wickets, average 47.97
Tests (1971–72 to 1980–81): 66 matches; 4,399 runs, average 44.43; 4 wickets, average 39.50

KALLICHARRAN *Neat Test batsman.*

A most attractive left-handed batsman and a useful right-arm leg-break bowler, Alvin Kallicharran graced county cricket for several seasons, eventually being registered as an English qualified player. He hit 1,000 runs in an English season 12 times, and he scored 100 not out on his Test debut for the West Indies against New Zealand in Georgetown. This was followed by 101 in his next match in Trinidad. He was the second West Indian to accomplish this feat. He batted consistently against Australia and on his first tour of England, 1973, and in the Caribbean, 1973–74, he scored 158, 21, 93, and 119 in the first three Tests against England. He was equally successful in India the following year.

With the rest of the West Indian side, he signed to join Packer's World Series but withdrew when he found he was in breach of contract with a Queensland radio station. Left as senior player, he captained the West Indies against Australia and India, making centuries in both series, but this was not a happy time for him. When Clive Lloyd returned, Kallicharran's form declined, and he elected to play in South Africa so exiling himself from Test cricket.

Vinod Kambli

Born: January 18, 1972, Bombay, India
Teams: Bombay (1989–90 to 1996–97)
First-class: 60 matches; 5,347 runs, average 71.29; 4 wickets, average 51.75
Tests (1992–93 to 1996–97): 17 matches; 1,084 runs, average 54.20

A highly gifted left-handed batsman who hit the first ball he received in the Ranji Trophy for six, he won a place in India's limited-over side and scored heavily and quickly. He had been controversially omitted from the side that toured South Africa, but he made his Test debut against England, 1992–93, topped the batting averages for the series and hit 224 at Bombay. He followed this with 227 against Zimbabwe in his next Test, in Delhi. With two centuries against Sri Lanka in his next series, he became the fastest Indian to reach 1,000 Test runs. He struggled against the West Indies, did well in the World Cup, 1996, but was omitted from the side that toured England for "disciplinary reasons". Recalled for one-day games in 1996–97, he was faced with rebuilding his career.

Rohan Kanhai

Born: December 26, 1935, Port Mourant, British Guiana
Teams: British Guiana–Guyana (1954–55 to 1973–74); Western Australia (1961–62); Trinidad (1964–65); Warwickshire (1968–77); Tasmania (1969–70)
First-class: 416 matches; 28,774 runs, average 49.01; 18 wickets, average 56.05
Tests (1957 to 1973–74): 79 matches; 6,227 runs, average 47.53; no wickets for 85 runs

Rohan Kanhai believed in the power of bat over ball, and he would have been at home in the Golden Age, for he was a master in all he did. One of the most thrilling sights of the 1960s was that of Kanhai on his backside as the ball thundered over the boundary at square-leg after a pull so vicious that it had swept the batsman off his feet.

He made his Test debut in the first Test of the West Indies' tour of England in 1957. Unwisely, he was asked to keep wicket in the first three Tests, but thereafter he was allowed to concentrate on his batting. His maiden Test hundred came against India, at Calcutta, 1958-59, when he scored 256. He was to make 15 more Test centuries.

Kanhai played in many parts of the globe, and his contribution to Warwickshire cricket was immense. In 1974, at Edgbaston, he and John Jameson shared an unbroken second-wicket stand of 465 against Gloucestershire, which was, at the time, a world record.

In 1972–73, with Sobers recovering from an operation, Kanhai captained the West Indies against Australia. He was then 37 years old. He led West Indies in two series against England, both of which were tinged with controversy. In 1973, at Edgbaston, umpire Fagg refused to take the field at the start of the third day because of Kanhai's reaction to one of his decisions while the following winter, in Port of Spain, he was captain when Tony Greig ran out Kallicharran "after the close of play". Kallicharran was reinstated. In spite of these incidents, Kanhai was respected for having brought a sense of discipline to a West Indies side which had become very laxin the last years of Sobers' captaincy.

KAPIL DEV *Leading Test wicket-taker.*

Kapil Dev

Born: January 6, 1959, Chandigarh, India
Teams: Haryana (1975–76 to 1994–95); Northamptonshire (1981–1983); Worcestershire (1984–1985)
First-class: 275 matches; 11,356 runs, average 32.91; 835 wickets, average 27.09
Tests (1978–79 to 1993–94): 131 matches; 5,248 runs, average 31.05; 434 wickets, average 29.64

The greatest all-round cricketer that India has ever produced, Kapil Dev appeared in more Test matches than any other Indian. Only three Indian batsmen scored more Test runs, and, with 434 Test wickets, he holds a world record which is likely to stand for many years. He made his Test debut against Pakistan in October 1978, and in his 25th Test, with Pakistan again the opponents, he completed 1,000 runs and 100 wickets. At 21 years 27 days, he was the youngest cricketer to perform the "double" in Test matches.

In his first Test as India's captain, 1982–83, he completed 2,000 Test runs, and in the next match he became the youngest player to complete the double of 2,000 Test runs and 200 Test wickets. He led India to victory over England in England and, memorably, to triumph in the World Cup, 1983. In that competition, with India 17 for five and then 78 for seven against Zimbabwe at Tunbridge Wells, Kapil Dev played one of the most astonishing innings ever seen in international cricket, an unbeaten 175.

Some months later, he took nine for 83 in the West Indies' second innings of the Test in Ahmedabad, but India lost. He overtook Hadlee's record number of wickets in his last series, against Sri Lanka, 1993–94.

Alan Knott

Born: April 9, 1946, Belvedere, Kent
Teams: Kent (1964–85)
First-class: 511 matches; 18,105 runs, average 29.63; 2 wickets, average 43.50; caught 1,211, stumped 133
Tests (1967–81): 95 matches; 4,389 runs, average 32.75; caught 250, stumped 19

KNOTT *Dedicated wicket-keeper.*

A truly great wicket-keeper, Alan Knott was recognized as outstanding from the moment he first played for Kent and forced his way into the England side within three years. In his first two Tests, against Pakistan, he held 12 catches and made a stumping, and an illustrious career was launched. Meticulous and fastidious to the point of eccentricity, he maintained a strict diet and a disciplined programme of exercise. Through constant application, he made himself into a batsman capable of scoring five Test centuries and defying any attack. His batting was unorthodox, but it was a style he evolved to suit his needs and abilities.

In both Test and county cricket, he fashioned a wonderful partnership with the left-arm spinner Derek Underwood, and they became a telling combination.

Knott's involvement with World Series Cricket and with a tour of South Africa curtailed his Test career. He has aided in England coaching and selection, and his son James keeps wicket for Surrey.

C. J. Kortright

Born: January 9, 1871, Furze Hall, Fryerning, Ingatestone, Essex
Died: December 12, 1952, Brook Street, South Weald, Essex
Teams: Essex (1894–1907)
First-class: 170 matches; 4,404 runs, average 17.61; 489 wickets, average 21.05

Although he never appeared in Test cricket, Kortright is regarded by many as the fastest bowler ever to play county cricket. He first played for Essex before the county attained first-class status, and his best season was 1895 when he claimed 76 wickets at under 16 runs each. He was an amateur with a good private income, and he captained Essex in 1903, but by then his bowling had declined, and he played as a batsman.

Anil Kumble

Born: October 17, 1970, Bangalore, India
Teams: Karnataka (1989–90 to 1996–97); Northamptonshire (1995)
First-class: 92 matches; 2,331 runs, average 26.79; 416 wickets, average 23.09
Tests (1990 to 1996–97): 26 matches; 293 runs, average 12.73; 114 wickets, average 26.28

A leg-break and googly bowler, Anil Kumble was one of the three spinners who destroyed England in India, 1992–93. He had made little impact when he had toured England in 1990, playing in one Test and capturing three expensive wickets, but as he matured, he became a potent force in any attack. He bowls at a brisker pace than most spinners and is relentlessly accurate. Bespectacled and gentle, he is a most effective bowler in limited-over internationals as well as Test cricket.

He played for Northamptonshire in 1995 and, with 105 wickets in 17 games, he came close to taking them to the championship. In 1996, he failed to find form on India's tour of England, but he remains a vital part of India's attack.

L

Jim Laker

Born: February 9, 1922, Frizinghall, Bradford, Yorkshire
Died: April 23, 1986, Putney, London
Teams: Surrey (1946–59); Essex (1962–64); Auckland (1951–52)
First-class: 450 matches; 7,304 runs, average 16.60; 1,944 wickets, average 18.41
Tests (1947–48 to 1958–59): 46 matches; 676 runs, average 14.08; 193 wickets, average 21.24

The world of cricket has not seen a better off-spinner than Jim Laker, and his achievements stand as

LAKER *19 wickets in a Test.*

testimony to his greatness. A Yorkshireman who came south to follow his career with Surrey, for whom he made his debut shortly after the Second World War, he toured the West Indies, 1947–48, and was a success in a series that was mostly disastrous for England. Indeed, on his Test debut, he took seven for 103 and two for 95. He took four wickets in his first Test against Australia a few months later, but it was some time before he could claim a regular place in the England side.

He was a vital member of the Surrey side which won the county championship seven years in succession, and when Australia toured England in 1956 he took all 10 of their wickets for 88 runs at the Oval. More sensational events were to follow. He took 11 for 113 in the Headingley Test, and in the next encounter, at Old Trafford, he performed the greatest bowling feat in cricket by taking nine for 37 and 10 for 53. He finished the rubber with a record 46 wickets to his credit. His last Test was on the tour of Australia, 1958–59, when a great England side finally began to disintegrate. He wrote a book which caused him to part from Surrey in acrimony although wounds were later healed and he served on the cricket committee. He played for Essex as an amateur, helping to bring on young bowlers, and he earned fame as a commentator and journalist.

Allan Lamb

Born: June 20, 1954, Langebaanweg, Cape Province, South Africa
Teams: Western Province (1972–73 to 1982–82); Northamptonshire (1978–1995); Orange Free State (1987–88)
First-class: 467 matches; 32,502 runs, average 48.94; 8 wickets, average 24.87
Tests (1982–92): 79 matches; 4,656 runs, average 36.09; 1 wicket, average 23.0

Allan Lamb learned his cricket in South Africa and played for Western Province before coming to England to assist Northamptonshire. His English parentage and residence allowed him to qualify for England in 1982, and he was immediately selected to play against India. He scored the first of his 14 Test hundreds in his third match.

A stocky, belligerent batsman, he took three centuries off the West Indian attack in 1984, and he played 45 successive Tests for England before being dropped after failures against India, 1986. He bounced back with a brave century against the West Indies, 1988, and he scored heavily for Northamptonshire whom he captained from 1989 until 1995, taking them to success in the NatWest Trophy, 1992, and coming close to claiming the championship three years later.

A witty man and a joyful companion, he was an excellent batsman in limited-over matches, and he and his friend Ian Botham toured venues with their "Lamb and Beef" show.

Brian Lara

See Legends (pages 108–109)

Harold Larwood

Born: November 14, 1904, Nuncargate, Nottinghamshire
Died: July 22, 1995, Sydney, Australia
Teams: Nottinghamshire (1924–38); Europeans (1936–37)
First-class: 361 matches; 7,289 runs, average 19.91; 1,427 wickets, average 17.51
Tests (1926 to 1932–33): 21 matches; 485 runs, average 19.40; 78 wickets, average 28.35

Harold Larwood's name will for ever be linked with the term "bodyline", and for all too brief a period he was regarded as the fastest and the best bowler in the world. He was right-arm, bowled off an 18-yard run and, although of only medium height, leapt into a high, classical, explosive delivery. He made his England debut during his first full season, 1926, toured Australia in 1928–29 and played against them in 1930, but it was the tour of Australia, 1932–33, that is best remembered. Bowling very fast and with unerring accuracy, he often attacked the line of the leg stump to a packed leg side field. He took 33 wickets in the series which England won 4–0, but he and Jardine were accused of intimidation and deliberately attacking the batsman's body. Larwood never played Test cricket again, and he retired from county cricket owing to injury in 1938. He emigrated to Australia in 1949.

LARWOOD *"Bodyline" scapegoat.*

Bill Lawry

Born: February 11, 1937, Thornbury, Melbourne, Victoria, Australia
Teams: Victoria (1955–56 to 1971–72)
First-class: 249 matches; 18,734 runs, average 50.90; 5 wickets, average 37.60
Tests (1961 to 1970–71): 67 matches; 5,234 runs, average 47.15; no wickets for 6 runs

A tall, lean, left-handed opening batsman with immense powers of concentration and infinite patience, Bill Lawry enjoyed an excellent first Test series in England, 1961, when he hit two centuries and topped the batting averages in both the Test series and all first-class matches. His was not the style, however, to win over spectators at a time when cricket was in crisis and accused of dullness. He was not well treated by the press who continued to hound him when, as senior player, he automatically succeeded Simpson as captain, 1967–68. He won a series against India, drew with England and won a crushing victory in the West Indies after losing the first Test. In the second, he and Ian Chappell added 298 in 310 minutes for the second wicket, and Lawry made 205. He also hit 151 in the last Test. He led Australia to victory over India, but they were crushed in South Africa and when things began to go wrong against Illingworth's side, 1970–71, he was relieved of the captaincy and dropped for the final Test. He has since worked as a commentator.

LAWRY *Concentration and patience.*

Maurice Leyland

Born: July 20, 1900, New Park, Harrogate, Yorkshire
Died: January 1, 1967, Scotton Banks, Harrogate, Yorkshire
Teams: Yorkshire (1920–1947); Patiala (1926–27)
First-class: 686 matches; 33,660 runs, average 40.50; 466 wickets, average 29.31
Tests (1928–1938): 41 matches; 2,764 runs, average 46.06; 6 wickets, average 97.50

A tough left-hander whose fighting qualities epitomized Yorkshire cricket during the county's period of dominance in the 1930s, Leyland was also a fine outfielder and a very useful left-arm bowler who specialized in "Chinamen", the slow left-armer's off-break.

He was eight seasons in the Yorkshire side before winning his first Test cap, against the West Indies, 1928. He failed to score, but he was a controversial choice ahead of Woolley for the tour of Australia the following winter. He played only in the last Test, scoring 137 and 53 not out. He was now a virtual regular in the England side and was invaluable to Jardine on the "bodyline" tour, providing what the captain wanted, "concrete" in the middle of the order.

His last Test was at the Oval against Australia in 1938 when he and Hutton put on a record 382 for the second wicket and Leyland made his highest Test score, 187.

He was 46 when cricket resumed after the war, but he played for two seasons and later coached Yorkshire.

Dennis Lillee

See Legends (pages 110–111)

Ray Lindwall

Born: October 3, 1921, Mascot, Sydney, New South Wales, Australia
Died: June 23, 1996
Teams: New South Wales (1941–42 to 1953–54); Queensland (1954–55 to 1959–60)
First-class: 228 matches; 5,042 runs, average 21.82; 794 wickets, average 21.35
Tests (1945–46 to 1959–60): 61 matches; 1502 runs, average 21.15; 228 wickets, average 23.03

Ray Lindwall had a beautiful fast bowler's action, and he had no peer in the decade immediately following the Second World War. His Test debut was against New Zealand, 1945–46, and in the last two Tests against England the following season, he took 15 wickets. Against India, at Adelaide, 1947–48, he took seven for 38 in the second innings, which were to remain his best figures in Test cricket, but it was in England weeks later that he was to prove most devastating, taking 27 wickets in the series, which included six for 20 at the Oval as England were bowled out for 52. He continued to dominate batsmen, and he played Test cricket until he was 38, finishing with what was then a record number of wickets for an Australian.

He was a very useful, hard-hitting lower-order batsman and hit centuries against both England and the West Indies. He captained Australia once when Ian Johnson was unfit against India in Bombay, 1956–57.

Clive Lloyd

Born: August 31, 1944, Queenstown, Georgetown, British Guiana
Teams: British Guiana/Guyana (1963–64 to 1982–83); Lancashire (1968–86)
First-class: 490 matches; 31,232 runs, average 49.26; 114 wickets, average 36.00
Tests (1966–67 to 1984–85): 110 matches; 7,515 runs, average 46.67; 10 wickets, average 62.20

LLOYD *outstanding skipper.*

A hard-hitting, left-handed batsman, fine fielder and medium-pace bowler, Clive Lloyd captained the West Indies in 74 Tests and won 36 of them; both figures are records. He moved with the silkiness of a cat and began his long Test career with innings of 82 and 78 not out in the West Indies victory over India in Bombay, 1966–67. In his next series, he hit two centuries against England.

In 1974–75, he took over as captain of the West Indies for the tour of India. In his first match in charge, he reached 100 off 85 balls and finished with 163. In the fifth Test, he hit a career-best 242 not out. As well as his successes in Test matches, he took the West Indies to World Cup triumphs in 1975 and 1979.

He was criticized in that he simply rotated his four fast bowlers, and there were times when his sides appeared to lack discipline, but he won a record 11 Tests in a row between 1984 and 1985, and when he lost his last match as captain, in Sydney, January 1985, it was his first defeat in 26 matches.

He gave magnificent support to Lancashire, particularly when they dominated the one-day game, and he was immensely popular. He settled there on retirement although he has continued to manage West Indian sides.

George Lohmann

Born: June 2, 1865, Campden Hill, Kensington, London
Died: December 1, 1901, Worcester, Cape Province, South Africa
Teams: Surrey (1884–96); Western Province (1894–95 to 1896–97)
First-class: 293 matches; 7,247 runs, average 18.67; 1,841 wickets, average 13.73
Tests (1886–96): 18 matches; 213 runs, average 8.87; 112 wickets, average 10.75

George Lohmann's career figures in Test and county cricket are phenomenal. He bowled right-arm medium-fast, was a useful lower-order batsman and a good slip fielder. His bowling helped raise Surrey to the heights in the 1880s. Fair, handsome, blue-eyed, he shot to prominence, and Grace believed he had no superiors as a bowler. He knew his worth, was not an easy man and pressed hard with regard to contracts, but he threw himself into every game. In 1886, England won all three Tests against Australia, and in the third Lohmann took 12 for 104 at the Oval. He and Briggs bowled unchanged in the first innings. Lohmann took seven for 36, and Australia were out for 68. The following winter, he established a record with eight for 35 in the first innings at Sydney, and his first six tests coincided with England beating Australia six times. There was eight for 58 at Sydney, 1891–92, and when he went to South Africa, 1895–96, he wrought havoc. He took nine for 28 in the first innings at Johannesburg and finished the three-match series with 35 wickets at 5.8 runs each. Already ill, he emigrated to South Africa in hope of recovery. He was assistant manager of the South African side in England, 1901, but died of tuberculosis later that year.

M

Charles Macartney

Born: June 27, 1886, West Maitland, New South Wales, Australia
Died: September 9, 1958, Little Bay, Sydney, New South Wales, Australia
Teams: New South Wales (1905–06 to 1926–27)
First-class: 249 matches; 15,019 runs, average 45.78; 419 wickets, average 20.95
Tests (1907–08 to 1926): 35 matches; 2,131 runs, average 41.78; 45 wickets, average 27.55

Known as the "Governor General", Charles Macartney was a dominant batsman, never afraid to improvise and ever on the lookout for runs. There was artistry in his right-handed batting, but when he first came to England in 1909 he was primarily a slow left-arm bowler. His seven for 58 and four for 27 won the Headingley Test on that first tour, but against South Africa, 1910–11, it was his batting that flourished. In the fifth Test, he opened the innings for the first time and made 137 and 56. In the second innings, he reached 50 in 35 minutes.

In 1920–21, at Sydney, he scored 170, his highest Test score, in 244 minutes against England, and when Australia came to England in 1921 he hit the only Australian century of the rubber. It happened to be his fourth century in consecutive innings and followed his 345 in a day against Nottinghamshire.

In 1926, in England, he scored three hundreds in successive Test innings, becoming the first man to score three hundreds in a rubber in England. He retired from Test cricket after this tour.

Archie MacLaren

Born: December 1, 1871, Whalley Range, Manchester
Died: November 17, 1944, Warfield Park, Bracknell, Berkshire
Teams: Lancashire (1890–1914)
First-class: 424 matches; 22,236 runs, average 34.15; 1 wicket, average 267.00
Tests (1894–95 to 1909): 35 matches; 1,931 runs, average 33.87

As a batsman, Archie MacLaren was one of the brightest jewels of the Golden Age, but as captain of England in 22 Tests against Australia and of Lancashire for 12 seasons his credentials are less impressive. A majestic right-handed batsman, rich in classical strokes, he came into the Lancashire side in 1890 straight from Harrow and made 108 against Sussex at Hove in his first match. He hit 424 against Somerset at Taunton, 1895, the highest score in first-class cricket in England until 1994. He went to Australia, 1894–95, and scored 120 in the fifth Test; all of his Tests were against Australia. Four of his five Test hundreds were made in Australia where the warmer climate was kinder to his lumbago. In his second tour of Australia, 1897–98, he became the first English batsman to hit two centuries in a rubber. The five Test series in which he captained England all ended in defeat, but he was a reluctant skipper in 1909 when, at 37, he felt that he was no longer up to standard. In 1921, he fielded an all-amateur side against the conquering Australians and beat them in a match which has passed into legend. He took a side to New Zealand, 1922–23, and hit 200 not out in his last first-class match. He was 53 years old.

Stan McCabe

Born: July 16, 1910, Grenfell, New South Wales, Australia
Died: August 25, 1968, Beauty Point, Mosman, Sydney, New South Wales, Australia
Teams: New South Wales (1928–29 to 1941–42)
First-class: 182 matches; 11,951 runs, average 49.38; 159 wickets, average 33.72
Tests (1930–38): 39 matches; 2,748 runs, average 48.21; 36 wickets, average 42.86

Short, stocky and strongly built, Stan McCabe was an attacking middle-order batsman and medium-pace bowler who played one of Test cricket's great innings when he hit 232 out of 300 at Trent Bridge in 1938. He batted heroically against Larwood and Voce at Sydney, 1932–33, to make an unbeaten 187, and he was consistently successful on his three tours of England, 1930, 1934 and 1938.

He made his first-class debut at the age of 18 and was the "baby " of the side on his first tour of England. He did not return to cricket after the Second World War, setting up a successful sporting equipment business.

Craig McDermott

Born: April 14, 1965, Ipswich, Queensland, Australia
Teams: Queensland (1983–84 to 1995–96)
First-class: 174 matches; 2,856 runs, average 16.32; 677 wickets, average 28.10
Tests (1984–85 to 1995–96): 71 matches; 940 runs, average 12.20; 291 wickets, average 28.62

Craig McDermott was forced to retire in 1997 because of persistent injury problems, but he could point to the fact that only Dennis Lillee had taken more wickets in Test cricket for Australia than he had. A red-headed, right-arm fast bowler, he took 10 wickets in his first two Tests, against the West Indies, and in England, 1985, he claimed 30 wickets in the series to give him a sensational start to his Test career. At Old Trafford, he took eight for 141 to become the youngest Australian ever to take eight wickets in a Test innings.

There were troughs as well as heights in his career, but he destroyed India, 1991–92, with 31 wickets, average 12.83, in five Tests. He had agreed to play for Yorkshire the following summer but he was in need of an operation and was forced to withdraw. His tour of England, 1993, was blighted by the need for another operation, this time for an intestinal complaint. In spite of this, he returned in 1994–95 to take 32 English wickets and be the major force in the Ashes series.

His last Test matches were against Sri Lanka. Capable of hitting hard and often, he was sometimes sent in early in one-day internationals to help lift the scoring-rate.

Ted McDonald

Born: January 6, 1891, Launceston, Tasmania, Australia
Died: July 22, 1937, Blackrod, Bolton, Lancashire
Teams: Tasmania (1909–10 to 1910–11); Victoria (1911–12 to 1921–22); Lancashire (1924–31)
First-class: 281 matches; 2,663 runs, average 10.44; 1,395 wickets, average 20.76
Tests (1920–21 to 1921–22): 11 matches; 116 runs, average 16.57; 43 wickets, average 33.27

Tall and strong, "Ted" McDonald was a natural athlete whose fast bowling was rhythmical and graceful. He had exceptional pace and could move the ball either way. He played in the last three Tests against England, 1920–21, making little impact, but the following summer, he and Jack Gregory destroyed England. McDonald finished the series with 27 wickets in the three-Test rubber in South Africa, 1921–22. He then joined Nelson in the Lancashire League and qualified for the Red Rose county. He was a vital reason for Lancashire winning the championship four times in five seasons, beginning in 1926. He took 205 wickets in 1925 and 190 in 1928. He had no standing as a batsman, but he made a century in 100 minutes against Middlesex at Old Trafford, 1926.

He was killed in the aftermath of a road accident. Signalling for help, he was knocked down by another car.

Jackie McGlew

Born: March 11, 1929, Pietermaritzburg, South Africa
Teams: Natal (1947–48 to 1966–67)
First-class: 190 matches; 12,170 runs, average 45.92; 35 wickets, average 26.62
Tests (1951 to 1961–62): 34 matches; 2,440 runs, average 42.06; no wickets for 23 runs

An obdurate opening batsman with infinite patience, Jackie McGlew was an outstanding cover fielder and a respected and successful captain of Natal for several seasons. He first toured England in 1951 and made his Test debut at Trent Bridge. He was dropped after the second Test and accomplished little in four Tests in Australia, 1952–53, but when the team moved on to New Zealand he hit 255 not out at Wellington. This was then the highest score for South Africa in Test cricket, and he became only the second player to be on the field for the whole of a Test match.

Vice-captain for the tour of England in 1955, he led the side in the third and fourth Tests when Cheetham was injured, scored centuries in both and took South Africa to two victories. Appointed captain for the home series against England, 1956–57, he was able to play only in the second Test because of a shoulder injury. His replacement, van Ryneveld, did well and kept the job for the tour of Australia. McGlew, captain in the first Test when van Ryneveld was unavailable, hit two centuries in the series and was reinstated as captain when van Ryneveld retired.

McGlew led South Africa to England in 1960, but the series was painfully dull and he drew much of the criticism. In 1961–62, New Zealand surprisingly drew the series in South Africa. McGlew's last match ended in defeat, and he finished with a thumb in splints and a shoulder in plaster.

He continued to play for Natal, and he never lost the reputation or nickname of being "Sticky".

Graham McKenzie

Born: June 24, 1941, Cottesloe, Perth, Western Australia
Teams: Western Australia (1959–60 to 1973–74); Leicestershire (1969–75)
First-class: 383 matches; 5,662 runs, average 15.64; 1,219 wickets, average 26.96
Tests: (1961 to 1970–71): 60 matches; 945 runs, average 12.27; 246 wickets, average 29.78

"Garth" McKenzie had a superb physique and bowled fast with a smoothness and economy of style that were a model for younger players. At the time, he was the youngest cricketer to reach 100, 150 and 200 runs in Test cricket, and he was Australia's main strike bowler for a decade. His Test debut came at Lord's in 1961, and his five for 37 in the second innings set up Australia's victory. He captured 20 wickets when the Ashes were retained against Dexter's side, 1962–63, and he had 29 in England in 1964, which equalled Grimmett's record at that time. In the Old Trafford Test, he gave a remarkable performance, taking seven for 153 as England scored 611. His final Test came at Sydney, 1970–71, when he took his 246th wicket, just two short of Benaud's record, and was forced to retire hurt when struck in the mouth by a ball from Snow.

He gave fine service to Leicestershire for seven seasons, and they won the championship for the first time in his last season with them.

Roy McLean

Born: July 9, 1930, Pietermaritzburg, South Africa

Teams: Natal (1949–50 to 1965–66)
First-class: 200 matches; 10,969 runs, average 36.88; 2 wickets, average 61.00
Tests (1951 to 1964–65): 40 matches; 2,120 runs, average 30.28; no wickets for 1 run

A delightfully aggressive right-handed stroke-maker, Roy McLean was also a brilliant out-fielder. His eagerness to score and to entertain was not always to the liking of the South African selectors, and his 11 "ducks" in his Test career was a sign of his impetuosity. He first played Test cricket during the 1951 tour of England, making 67 run out at Headingley. He topped 1,000 runs in 1955 and 1960, and he scored 142 in the Lord's Test on the first of those tours, hitting a brisk 50 at Old Trafford as South Africa successfully chased a target of 145 in 135 minutes.

Not unnaturally, he was an immense favourite with crowds who warmed to his fielding.

Brian McMillan

Born: December 22, 1963, Welkom, Orange Free State, South Africa
Teams: Transvaal (1984–85 to 1988–89); Warwickshire (1986); Western Province (1989–90 to 1996–97)
First-class: 112 matches; 5,867 runs, average 39.91; 270 wickets, average 27.34
Tests (1992–93 to 1996–97): 23 matches; 1,226 runs, average 42.27; 60 wickets, average 29.81

Brian McMillan was engaged by Warwickshire in 1986 as a fast medium-pace right-arm bowler, but he disappointed with the ball and delighted with the bat, scoring 999 runs, average 58.76, in 12 matches before returning home with a back problem which had handicapped his bowling. When South Africa were re-admitted to international competition, he emerged as a top-class all-rounder. He is a tough competitor who can bat anywhere in the order, and to complement his bowling which, at times, can be genuinely quick, he is an excellent slip fielder. He notched his first Test hundred against Pakistan at Johannesburg in January 1995, and his second came against England in December of the same year.

Majid Khan

Born: September 28, 1946, Ludhiana, India
Teams: Lahore (1961–62 to 1982–83); Punjab (1964–65 to 1967–68); PIA (1968–69 to 1980–81); Glamorgan (1968–76); Cambridge University (1970–72)
First-class: 410 matches; 27,444 runs, average 43.01; 223 wickets, average 32.14
Tests (1964–65 to 1982–83): 63 matches; 3,931 runs, average 38.92; 27 wickets, average 53.92

Son of Jahangir Khan who played cricket for India with distinction, Majid was born in the year before Partition, but his cricket has been played in Pakistan. A highly gifted all-rounder, Majid was an attacking right-handed batsman, confident, calm and cultured, and a medium-pace or off-break bowler. His Test debut came against Australia in Karachi when he was out for 0 and opened the Pakistan bowling, claiming Bill Lawry as his first Test victim. He toured England in 1967 and, although he did little in the series, he hit an astonishing 147 not out in 89 minutes against Glamorgan. His innings included five sixes in an over off Roger Davis, and Glamorgan were prompted to engage him. He was a fine acquisition for the county and captained them for three years before finally leaving in acrimony and discord. He was a highly successful captain of Cambridge University.

His highest score against England was 99, but he hit eight Test centuries, three of them against Australia and two, including his highest, 167, against the West Indies. He was something of an amateur spirit, not totally at home in the new commercialism that was sweeping the game, and, as a captain, he was shabbily treated by authorities in Pakistan and at Glamorgan. He now has the most powerful position in cricket administration in Pakistan.

Vinoo Mankad

Born: April 12, 1917, Jamnagar, India
Died: August 21, 1978, Bombay, India
Teams: Western India (1935–36); Nawanagar (1936–37 to 1941–42); Hindus (1936–37 to 104–46); Maharashtra (1943–44); Gujarat (1944–45 to 1950–51); Bengal (1948–49); Bombay (1951–52 to 1955–56); Rajasthan (1956–57 to 1961–62)
First-class: 233 matches; 11,591 runs, average 34.70; 782 wickets, average 24.53
Tests (1946 to 1958–59): 44 matches; 2,109 runs, average 31.47; 162 wickets, average 32.32

"Vinoo" Mankad began his career with aspirations of becoming a fast bowler, but under the tutelage of the Sussex all-rounder A. F. Wensley, he became a left-arm spinner and a tenacious right-handed batsman who often opened the innings. He was India's first great spin bowler and the best all-rounder of his generation. His Test debut did not come until 1946 when he performed admirably in all three Tests and completed the "double" in all matches. He hit two centuries against Australia, 1947–48, and remained an automatic choice for India for the next decade. His first great moment came against England at Madras, 1951–52, when he took eight for 55 and four for 53 to bowl India to an innings victory, their first win in Test cricket. He captured 34 wickets in the series, a record at that time.

He received an offer to play in the Lancashire League, but said that he would not accept if the Indian Board assured him he would be picked to tour England, 1952. Insanely, they refused to give that assurance, but the side was so overwhelmed that Haslingden, his club, released him to play in three of the four Tests. He responded heroically. At Lord's, he hit 72 and then bowled 73 overs to take five for 196 as England made 537. Mankad then scored 184 out of 378 before sending down another 24 overs.

In 1952–53, India won their first rubber, beating Pakistan. Mankad was again the hero with 25 wickets in four Tests. In all, he hit five Test centuries, his highest being 231 against New Zealand at Madras, 1955–56, when he and Pankaj Roy scored 413 for the first wicket which remains a world Test record.

Rodney Marsh

Born: November 11, 1947, Armadale, Perth, Western Australia
Teams: Western Australia (1968–69 to 1983–84)
First-class: 257 matches; 11,067, average 31.17; 1 wicket, average 84.00; caught 803, stumped 66
Tests (1970–71 to 1983–84): 96 matches; 3,633 runs, average 26.51; no wickets for 54 runs; caught 343, stumped 12

MARSH *Threw off "iron gloves" to be the most successful Test 'keeper.*

No wicket-keeper has accounted for more batsmen in Test cricket than Rodney Marsh. Had he not spent a period with World Series cricket, his record would have been even greater for he had no rival during the time that he was Australia's keeper. He first appeared on the Test scene in 1970–71 when Illingworth's side regained the Ashes, and he was treated with contempt by English critics who dubbed him "iron gloves", but he made three stumpings during the series and scored an unbeaten 92 in his fourth match. His wicket-keeping improved dramatically and, when he hit 118 against Pakistan at Adelaide, 1972–73, he became the first Australian wicket-keeper to score a hundred in Test cricket. Two more were to follow before the end of his career, and he had made a century on his first-class debut.

Marsh became a folk hero, epitomizing the aggressive and determined cricket of the conquering Australians of the Chappell brothers' era, and, off the field, he was a great favourite as he mingled warmly with people at social events. He was a blunt broadcaster and became director of Australia's Cricket Academy.

Malcolm Marshall

See Legends (pages 113–114)

Peter May

Born: December 31, 1929, Reading, Berkshire
Died: December 21, 1994, Liphook, Hampshire
Teams: Surrey (1950–63); Cambridge University (1950–52)
First-class: 388 matches; 27,592 runs, average 51.00; no wickets for 49 runs
Tests (1951–61): 66 matches; 4,537 runs, average 46.77

The finest English batsman of the post-war era, Peter May first appeared for Surrey during his first year at Cambridge, and his England debut came the following season, against South Africa at Headingley. He made 158. He had a successful series against India, 1952, but a failure in the first Test of the Ashes series, 1953, led to his being dropped until the final Test when he returned to play a part in England's victory. From that point on, he was an automatic choice for England.

MAY *Classic batsman whose career was cut short by ill-health.*

A tall, elegant batsman with the full range of classical stroke-play, he was immediately recognized as the natural successor to Hutton as England's captain. He learned the art of captaincy under the two outstanding leaders of his time, Hutton and Surridge, whom he succeeded as Surrey's captain during the period of that county's greatest glory. Gentle and well-mannered as he was, and greatly admired and respected by his men, May had a ruthless, professional streak which served him well in Test cricket. He became captain of England in 1955 and led the side on a record 41 occasions with a record 20 victories to his credit. In 1957, he ended the West Indian supremacy over England when he and Colin Cowdrey defied Ramadhin in a fourth-wicket stand of 411, a record. May made 285 not out in that innings.

The disappointment came in Australia, 1958–59, when a great England side broke up and was surprisingly and heavily defeated. A year later, May was forced home from the Caribbean for medical treatment and, although he returned briefly in 1961, he announced his retirement. Illness and pressure had taken their toll. He was still short of his 32nd birthday.

He later held every high office in the game, but his period as chairman of selectors was not a happy one. He was dealing with players who no longer spoke his language. Values had changed.

Philip Mead

Born: March 9, 1887, Battersea, London
Died: March 26, 1958, Boscombe, Hampshire
Teams: Hampshire (1905–36)
First-class: 814 matches; 55,061 runs, average 47.67; 277 wickets, average 34.70
Tests (1911–12 to 1928–29): 17 matches; 1,185 runs, average 49.37

Philip Mead was the backbone of Hampshire cricket for 30 years. He scored 48,892 runs for the county, which is more than any batsman has scored for any other county. He was solidly left-handed with a defence which seemed impenetrable, and he hit 153 centuries in his career. He also bowled slow left-arm but never in a Test match. He first played for England in Australia, 1911–12, and he scored two centuries against South Africa, 1913–14, but he never claimed a regular place in the England side in spite of his consistency at county level. He reached 1,000 runs in a season 27 times, going on to 2,000 nine times and 3,000 twice.

His best season was 1921 when England were suffering badly against Australia. He was not chosen until the fourth Test when the series was already lost. He made 47, and in the next Test he scored 182 not out, which included 109 before lunch on the second day. His score remained a record for England against Australia at home until Hutton's 364 in 1938.

Alan Melville

Born: May 19, 1910, Carnavon, Cape Province, South Africa
Died: April 18, 1983, Sabie, Transvaal, South Africa
Teams: Natal (1928–29 to 1929–30); Oxford University (1930–33); Sussex (1932–36); Transvaal (1936–37 to 1948–49)
First-class: 190 matches; 10,598 runs, average 37.85; 132 wickets, average 29.99
Tests (1938–39 to 1948–49): 11 matches; 894 runs, average 52.58

Tall and elegant, Alan Melville was a batsman of great charm. He first played for Natal at the age of 17 and was chosen to tour England with the South African side in 1929. He declined as he was preparing to go to Oxford where he won his blue all four years, being captain in his last two. He captained Sussex in 1934 and 1935 and proved himself to be an inspiring captain, a man of dignity and a natural leader who was tactically persuasive.

He returned to South Africa and became captain of Transvaal. He led his country against England in 1938–39 and again in 1947. He scored a century in the "timeless" Test at Durban in 1939 and a century in each innings of the first Test at Trent Bridge, 1947. This was followed by a hundred in the first innings of the Lord's Test so that he became the first batsman to score four Test centuries in consecutive innings against England.

Immensely popular, he had suffered a back injury in his youth and a recurrence of the injury prompted his retirement at the end of the tour. He was persuaded to appear in one Test against England, 1948–49, his only Test in which he was not captain.

Vijay Merchant

Born: October 12, 1911, Bombay, India
Died: October 27, 1987, Bombay, India
Teams: Hindus (1929–30 to 1945–46); Bombay (1933–34 to 1950–51)
First-class: 150 matches; 13,470 runs, average 71.64; 65 wickets, average 32.12
Tests (1933–34 to 1951–52): 10 matches; 859 runs, average 47.72; no wickets for 40 runs

Merchant was small and compact, and there was a delicacy in his movement as he built an innings. A right-handed opener, he was India's first great batsman, and he gave evidence of his greatness on his two tours to England, scoring 1,745 runs in 1936 and 2,385 runs in 1946. His Test career began against Jardine's side, 1933–34, when he batted in the middle order, but he opened on the 1936 tour and scored 114 in the second innings at Old Trafford when he and Mushtaq Ali put on 203 for the first wicket and saved the Test. In 1946, he scored 128 at the Oval. His third Test hundred was his highest, 154 against England in Delhi, 1951–52, when he and Hazare established an Indian record for the series by scoring 211 for the third wicket. This was Merchant's last Test, for he sustained a shoulder injury which ended his career. He held high office in the administration of Indian cricket after his retirement.

In domestic cricket he bowled medium-pace and hit 359 not out for Bombay against Maharashtra, 1933–34.

Keith Miller

Born: November 28, 1919, Sunshine, Melbourne, Victoria, Australia
Teams: Victoria (1937–38 to 1946–47); New South Wales (1947–48 to 1955–56); Nottinghamshire (1959)
First-class: 226 matches; 14,183 runs, average 48.90; 497 wickets, average 22.30
Tests (1945–46 to 1956–57): 55 matches; 2,958 runs, average 36.97; 170 wickets, average 22.97

Keith Miller was a glorious all-round cricketer. He was a tremendous hitter of the ball, powerful and brilliant in his stroke-play, and a magnificent fielder and a fast bowler whose partnership with Ray Lindwall became legendary. His lust for life was transmitted into his cricket, and he thrilled crowds with all that he did on the field.

He served in England during the war, played for the Australian Services, was outstanding in the Victory Tests and scored a memorable 185 in 165 minutes for the Dominions against England in 1945, an innings that was studded with gigantic sixes. He made his Test debut against New Zealand, 1945–46, and in his first Test against England a year later he took seven for 60 in the first innings. In the fourth Test of the series he made 141 not out. In 1948, in England, he and Lindwall swept all before them initially, but injury prevented Miller from bowling for much of the time. His batting was still integral to Bradman's great side.

Tall and physically strong, Miller was a beautiful athlete, but he was a man of moods and he never found fun in destroying weak opposition. He relished a contest, and in the Caribbean, 1954–55, he hit three Test centuries and took 20 wickets in the series.

He never captained Australia but he led New South Wales with a characteristic casual air that gave rise to many amusing stories. He retired in 1956, but he appeared for Nottinghamshire against Cambridge University in 1959 and scored 62 and 102 not out. An author, journalist, commentator and bon viveur, he has never lost his desire to live life to the full.

Bruce Mitchell

Born: January 8, 1909, Ferrierer Deep Gold Mine, Johannesburg, South Africa
Died: July 2, 1995, Johannesburg, South Africa
Teams: Transvaal (1925–26 to 1949–50)
First-class: 173 matches; 11,395 runs, average 45.39; 249 wickets, average 25.63
Tests (1929 to 1948–49): 42 matches; 3,471 runs, average 48.88; 27 wickets, average 51.11

Bruce Mitchell retains the record of having scored more runs in Test cricket than any other South African batsman. He was a stylish, right-handed opening batsman of infinite patience, a leg-break bowler and an outstanding slip fielder. He came to England in 1929, scored 88 and 61 not out on his Test debut at Edgbaston, and played in all five matches in the series. Against Chapman's team, 1930–31, he hit 123 at Cape Town and shared a record opening stand of 260 with Siedle. The following season, in New Zealand, he shared an opening partnership of 196 with Christy which remains a record for the series. Mitchell made 113. When South Africa beat England in England for the first time, 1935, Mitchell hit two centuries, one of which was an unbeaten 164 in the Lord's Test where South Africa gained their famous victory.

He remained a dominant force, and when South Africa came to England in 1947, he hit 120 and 189 not out at the Oval and was on the field for the entire match bar eight minutes – 12 balls. There was a century and 99 against England, 1949–50, but, astonishingly, he was omitted when Australia went to South Africa a year later and so he retired.

Arthur Morris

Born: January 19, 1922, Bondi, New South Wales, Australia
Teams: New South Wales (1940–41 to 1954–55)
First-class: 162 matches; 12,614 runs, average 53.67; 12 wickets, average 49.33
Tests (1946–47 to 1954–55): 46 matches; 3,533 runs, average 46.48; 2 wickets, average 25.00

A century in each innings on the occasion of his first-class debut for New South Wales against Queensland heralded the career of Arthur Morris, one of the most graceful of left-handed opening batsman to have charmed the Test arena. In his first series against England, 1946–47, he scored three centuries in succession, including one in each innings at Adelaide. In England, 1948, he had an outstanding tour and topped the Test matches' batting averages. His three centuries in the series included a match-winning 182 at Headingley where he and Bradman put on 301 in 217 minutes for the second wicket. He followed this with 196 run out at the Oval. He hit centuries in successive innings against South Africa in South Africa, 1949–50 and made 206 against Freddie Brown's side at Adelaide the following season.

He had a poor series in England, 1953, and his last series was against Hutton's side, 1954–55, when he hit 153 in the first Test.

A delightful man, he captained Australia on two occasions.

Mushtaq Ahmed

Born: June 28, 1970, Sahiwal, Pakistan
Teams: Multan (1986–87 to 1990–91; United Bank (1987–88 to 1996–97); Somerset (1993–97)
First-class: 130 matches; 1,972 runs, average 13.60; 579 wickets, average 25.37
Tests (1989–90 to 1996–97): 24 matches; 246 runs, average 8.20; 89 wickets, average 29.29

A leg-spin and googly bowler of the very highest quality, Mushtaq Ahmed was 19 when he made his Test debut, and was seen as the natural successor to Abdul Qadir. Leg-spinning is a difficult art, and he fell out of favour for a time but he returned, to devastating effect, in 1995. He consistently bettered his previous best Test performances, culminating with seven for 56 for Pakistan against New Zealand at Christchurch. He played a major part in Pakistan's victory over England, 1996, taking five for 57 in the second innings at Lord's and six for 78 in the second innings at the Oval. Pakistan won both matches, and he took 17 wickets in three Tests to top the averages. He was even more devastating against New Zealand some months later when, returning after injury, he took 18 wickets in two Tests.

He has proved to be an inspiration to Somerset as their overseas player.

N

Monty Noble

Born: January 28, 1873, Sydney, New South Wales, Australia
Died: 22 June, 1940, Randwick, Sydney, New South Wales, Australia
Teams: New South Wales (1893–94 to 1919–20)
First-class: 248 matches, 13,975 runs, average 40.74; 624 wickets, average 23.14
Tests (1897–98 to 1909): 42 matches, 1,997 runs, average 30.25; 121 wickets, average 25.00

Banker, dentist, manufacturer's agent, writer, broadcaster, right-handed batsman with a sound defence and an ability to hit hard when necessary, a medium pace off-break bowler and a brilliant fielder, Monty Noble stood over 6ft tall and was a master of many trades, especially cricket. He took six for 49 on his Test debut against England, 1897–98, and he followed this with eight wickets in his next Test. He first captained Australia in the 1903–04 series and hit his only Test century in his first match as captain. He also led the side in 1907–08 and 1909.

He scored 1,000 runs on all of his four visits to England, making more than 2,000 in 1905. His highest score was 284 against Sussex at Hove, 1986.

A strong disciplinarian, he rebuked his players for talking to spectators and urged abstinence during a Test match. Dedicated to the ethics of the game, he was deeply respected by his opponents.

Dudley Nourse

Born: November 12, 1910, Durban, South Africa
Died: August 14, 1981, Durban, South Africa
Teams: Natal (1931–32 to 1952–53)
First-class: 175 matches; 12,472 runs, average 51.53; no wickets for 124 runs

DUDLEY NOURSE *Equally famous father.*

Tests (1935–1951): 34 matches; 2,960 runs, average 53.81; no wickets for 9 runs

Son of "Dave" Nourse, a Test player of the Edwardian era, Dudley Nourse was a sound right-handed batsman who must rank among the most gifted produced by South Africa. In the years either side of the Second World War, he could lay claim to a place in a World XI. He came to England in 1935 and was in the side that won at Lord's – South Africa's first win in England– but it was against Australia the following winter that he truly revealed his international class. He hit 91 in the first Test and 231 in 289 minutes in the second at Johannesburg. Two centuries followed against England, 1938–39, and he was vice-captain to Melville on the 1947 tour when he hit centuries at Trent Bridge and Old Trafford. He led South Africa against England and Australia, scoring two hundreds in the first series and one in the second.

He captained the party to England, 1951, and, batting with a broken thumb and in considerable pain, he hit 208 in 550 minutes at Trent Bridge to equal the record of seven centuries against England. He was 41 years old.

O

Bert Oldfield

Born: September 9, 1894, Alexandra, Sydney, New South Wales, Australia
Died: August 10, 1976, Killara, Sydney, New South Wales, Australia
Teams: New South Wales (1919–20 to 1937–38)
First-class: 245 matches; 6,135 runs, average 23.77; caught 400, stumped 262
Tests (1920–21 to 1936–37): 54 matches; 1,427 runs, average 22.65; caught 78, stumped 52

A quick, stylish, quietly effective wicket-keeper who has had few superiors, Bert Oldfield's career was confined to the inter-war years. He came to England as reserve keeper in 1920–21 and appeared in only one Test, but thereafter he was Australia's number one. He was particularly adept at taking spin bowlers like Mailey and Grimmett, and he was an inspiration to his fielders with his lightning stumpings.

He was a very useful batsman who hit six first-class hundreds and was consistently valuable in Tests. He was knocked unconscious when he was hit on the head by a ball from Larwood during the "bodyline" series, but he insisted the fault was his and not Larwood's, so preventing any recriminations. He was a most popular man.

Norm O'Neill

Born: February 19, 1937, Carlton, New South Wales, Sydney, Australia
Teams: New South Wales (1955–56 to 1966–70)
First-class: 188 matches; 13,859 runs, average 50.95; 99 wickets, average 41.01
Tests (1958–59 to 1964–65): 42 matches; 2,779 runs, average 45.55; 17 wickets, average 39.23

Norman O'Neill was an unlucky cricketer in that he suffered from being dubbed "the new Bradman" when he first broke upon the scene. In spite of having only a moderate time in the Ashes series, 1958–59, he arrived in England two years later with an immense reputation. He had scored a century against Pakistan and two against India, 1959–60, and had made 181 against the West Indies in the famous tied Test of December, 1960, but he found English conditions difficult in 1961 and did not score a century until the final Test, at the Oval. On the tour as a whole, though, he did well.

O'Neill was a highly entertaining right-handed batsman, rich in strokes, a useful leg-break bowler and brilliant fielder. He was a warm and generous man but he was a rather nervous starter and, although he hit six Test centuries, never quite accomplished all that had been expected of him. It should be said, though, that he was hampered by recurring knee trouble which eventually caused his retirement.

He appeared to become less enamoured of the game, and at the end of the series against the West Indies in the Caribbean, 1964–65, articles appeared under his name criticizing the action of Griffith, the West Indian fast bowler. His Test career was at an end, but he continued to score heavily in domestic cricket.

Bill O'Reilly

Born: December 20, 1905, White Cliffs, New South Wales, Australia
Died: October 6, 1992, Sutherland, Sydney, New South Wales
Teams: New South Wales (1927–28 to 1945–46)
First-class: 135 matches; 1,655 runs, average 13.13; 774 wickets, average 16.60
Tests (1931–32 to 1945–46): 27 matches; 410 runs, average 12.81; 144 wickets, average 22.59

In the years immediately before the Second World War, "Tiger" O'Reilly was described as one of the greatest bowlers of all time. He bowled leg-breaks and googlies and had the ability to vary his pace and to make the ball rear awkwardly.

His Test debut came against South Africa, 1931–32. In the "bodyline" series a year later, he captured 27 wickets, including 10 for 129 at Melbourne where Australia gained their only victory of the rubber. In England, 1934, he was a huge success, heading the first-class averages and topping the Test averages with 28 wickets at 24.92 runs each. In his first Test in England, at Trent Bridge, he had four for 75 and seven for 54, his best in Test cricket. He claimed 28 wickets in South Africa, 1935–36, and 25 against Allen's side the following year. In a full Test series, he never failed to take at least 20 wickets, and, in four Tests in England, 1938, he captured 22 wickets at 27.72, a remarkable performance considering England's 903 for seven at the Oval where he sent down 85 overs to take three for 178. At Headingley, he bowled Australia to victory with his third 10-wicket haul in Test cricket. His last Test was in New Zealand shortly after the war, with match figures of eight for 33.

He became a well-respected cricket writer.

P

Eddie Paynter

Born: November 5, 1901, Oswaldtwistle, Lancashire
Died: February 5, 1979, Keighley, Yorkshire
Teams: Lancashire (1926–45)
First-class: 352 matches; 20,075 runs, average 42.46; 30 wickets, average 45.70
Tests (1931–39): 20 matches; 1,540 runs, average 59.23

Eddie Paynter scored 322 for Lancashire at Hove in 1937, and was a most loyal servant to the Red Rose county. An attacking left-handed batsman and brilliant fielder, he made his Test debut against New Zealand, 1931, and went to Australia with Jardine's team, 1932–33. He did not play until the third Test when he scored 77 as England staged a recovery, and, in the next Test, became the stuff of legend when he rose from his sickbed to hit 83 at number eight when England were in some trouble. He scored a century in each innings of the first Test in South Africa, 1938–39, and made his highest Test score, 243, in the third match.

He had not gained a regular place in the Lancashire side until 1931, and his career was effectively ended by the outbreak of the Second World War.

Robert Peel

Born: February 12, 1857, Churwell, Leeds, Yorkshire
Died: August 12, 1941, Morley, Leeds, Yorkshire
Teams: Yorkshire (1882–98)
First-class: 436 matches; 12,191 runs, average 19.44; 1,775 wickets, average 16.20
Tests (1884–85 to 1896): 20 matches; 427 runs, average 14.72; 101 wickets, average 16.98

In the great Yorkshire tradition of slow left-arm bowlers, Bobby Peel maintained the principles of line and, especially, length. He was a most capable, punishing left-arm batsman who scored 210 not out against Warwickshire in 1896, the year he did the "double". He took 100 wickets in a season on seven other occasions. He was regarded as the best bowler of his type in England and made three trips to Australia. In his first Test, 1884–85, he took eight wickets at Sydney and finished the series with 21 to his credit. He was triumphant at Sydney again three years later when he had match figures of 10 for 58, and he and Lohmann bowled Australia out for 42 in the first innings.

Peel took 24 wickets in three Tests against Australia, 1888, including seven for 31 and four for 37 in the final match at Old Trafford. Rarely, if ever, did he fail, and in his last Test, against Australia at the Oval, 1896, he took two for 30 and six for 23 to bowl England to victory. Australia were all out for 44 in their second innings.

The following year he took the field for Yorkshire in an inebriated state and, according to some reports, urinated against the sightscreen. Lord Hawke dismissed him immediately from the Yorkshire XI.

Graeme Pollock

See Legends (pages 114–115)

Peter Pollock

Born: June 30, 1941, Pietermaritzburg, Natal, South Africa
Teams: Eastern Province (1958–59 to 1971–72)
First-class: 127 matches; 3,028 runs, average 22.59; 485 wickets, average 21.89
Tests (1961–62 to 1969–70): 28 matches; 607 runs, average 21.67; 116 wickets, average 24.18

Tall, fair-haired and a bowler of genuine pace, Peter Pollock comes from a cricketing family. His younger brother Graeme was one of the world's great left-handers while his son Shaun has followed his father and uncle into the South African side. On his Test debut, 20 years old, he took three for 61 and six for 38, his best Test figures, against New Zealand, and he finished the series with 17 wickets from three matches.

When South Africa drew the rubber in Australia, 1963–64, he confirmed his standing as a leading strike bowler with 25 wickets in the series. In 1965, in the three-match series in England, he claimed 20 wickets, and his 10 for 87 in 47.5 overs in the match at Trent Bridge brought South Africa victory and clinched the rubber.

In 1969–70, Australia were trounced in all four Tests in South Africa. The South African opening attack of Procter and Peter Pollock was lethal. Pollock had 15 wickets in the series, but he pulled a hamstring and could bowl only seven balls in the last innings of what was to be his final Test, for South Africa's exile from international cricket followed. When the exile ended in 1992, Pollock was chairman of selectors.

Bill Ponsford

Born: October 19, 1900, North Fitzroy, Melbourne, Victoria, Australia
Died: April 6, 1991, Kyneton, Victoria, Australia
Teams: Victoria (1920–21 to 1933–34)
First-class: 162 matches; 13,819 runs, average 65.18; no wickets for 41 runs
Tests (1924–25 to 1934): 29 matches; 2,122 runs, average 48.22

Before the arrival of Don Bradman, Bill Ponsford threatened to become the greatest run-accumulator the game had known. He made 429 against Tasmania at Melbourne, 1922–23, and five years later, on the same ground, he hit 437 against Queensland. He was a right-handed opening batsman whose defence looked impenetrable and who had a wide range of shots. He hit 110 on his Test debut, against England, 1924–25, and when he hit 128 at Melbourne he became the first batsman to score centuries in his first two Tests. He was hampered by illness in England in 1926 and appeared only in the last two Tests. In Australia, 1928–29, he had his hand broken by a ball from Larwood in the second Test and did not play again in the series.

By 1930, his opening partnership with Woodfull was established, and the pair set up Australia's victory at the Oval with a stand of 159. Ponsford scored 110, and he followed this with two centuries against the West Indies a few months later. Two unsuccessful home series cast doubts on his ability at the top level, but, at Headingley, 1934, he made 181, and in the next match, at the Oval, he and Bradman scored 451 in 316 minutes for a world-record partnership for the second wicket – Ponsford hit 266. His Test career ended with that Test.

Mike Procter

Born: September 15, 1946, Durban, South Africa
Teams: Gloucestershire (1965–81); Natal (1965–66 to 1988–89); Western Province (1969–70); Rhodesia (1970–71 to 1975–76); Orange Free State (1987–88)
First-class: 401 matches; 21,936 runs, average 36.01; 1,417 wickets, average 19.53
Tests (1966–67 to 1969–70): 7 matches; 226 runs, average 25.11; 41 wickets, average 15.02

One of the most dynamic performers the game has known, Mike Procter played only seven Test matches because his career began to flower just as South Africa were excluded from international cricket. He made his Test debut against Australia in South Africa, 1966–67, and took 15 wickets in three matches. Three years later, against the same opposition, he took 26 wickets in four Tests, finishing with his best, six for 73, at Port Elizabeth. In seven Test matches, he was never on a losing side, and South Africa won six of them.

His energies then had to be concentrated on domestic cricket. In 1970–71, he hit six hundreds in consecutive innings for Rhodesia, and he will ever be remembered for his achievements with Gloucestershire and the influence

MIKE PROCTER *Great all-rounder whose Test career was sadly short.*

he had on that county. He was a ferocious batsman, a fielder of brilliance, and a fast bowler who occasionally turned to off-breaks. Gloucestershire won trophies when he was in the side, for he always seemed to be scoring runs, taking wickets or making a catch. He captained the county from 1977 to 1981. He hit 1,000 runs in a season nine times and took 100 wickets in a season twice. He was cricket manager at Northamptonshire, 1990–91, and held a similar position with the South African national side from 1992 to 1994.

R

Sonny Ramadhin

Born: May 1, 1929, Esperance Village, Trinidad
Teams: Trinidad (1949–50 to 1952–53); Lancashire (1964–65)
First-class: 184 matches; 1,092 runs, average 8.66; 758 wickets, average 20.24
Tests (1950 to 1960–61): 43 matches; 361 runs, average 8.20; 158 wickets, average 28.98

RAMADHIN *An instant sensation.*

Sonny Ramadhin came to England in 1950 with a handful of first-class matches behind him and nothing known of him save that he was a spin bowler. Within months he had become the talk of the cricket world. Having been beaten in cold weather at Old Trafford, the West Indies won the remaining three Tests of the series, and Ramadhin took 26 wickets. He headed the first-class averages for the tour with 135 wickets, average 14.88. It was at Lord's that he and his spin partner Valentine bowled the West Indies to their first win in England. Ramadhin took five for 66 and six for 86. He had a perfect control of length, flighted the ball well, and bowled both off-breaks and leg-breaks – he was truly a "mystery" bowler. He was less successful in Australia but he devastated the New Zealand batsmen.

He continued to trouble England in the Caribbean with 23 wickets, 1953–54, and when he arrived in England in 1957 and took a Test-best seven for 49 in the first encounter at Edgbaston it seemed that England would again fall under his spell, but he was destroyed by May and Cowdrey in the second innings. He sent down 98 overs and took two for 179, and he was never quite the same again.

He played Lancashire League cricket, but his venture into county cricket came late in his career and was not a success. He is now a publican.

Arjuna Ranatunga

Born: December 1, 1963, Colombo, Ceylon
Teams: Sinhalese SC (1988–89 to 1996–97)
First-class: 146 matches; 7,941 runs, average 42.33; 90 wickets, average 32.65
Tests (1981–82 to 1996–97): 61 matches; 3,471 runs, average 35.41; 14 wickets, average 67.28

A chunky, aggressive, left-handed batsman and a right-arm medium-pace bowler, Arjuna Ranatunga played in Sri Lanka's inaugural Test against England, February 1982. He was 18 years 78 days old and still attending Anada College. He hit 54, Sri Lanka's first 50 in Test cricket. A year later, he made 90 against Australia, and, at Lord's, August 1984, hit a splendidly entertaining 84. He revealed himself as a joyous and enthusiastic cricketer, and his love of the game was infectious.

He hit centuries against India and Pakistan, and remains a consistent scorer. He first captained Sri Lanka in Australia, 1989–90 – it was not an easy time, but he battled on happily. Greatness awaited him, though. Sri Lanka became most adept at the one-day game, and, in 1996, Ranatunga led them to victory in the World Cup. His own contribution was immense – he averaged 120.50 from the six matches and topped the batting averages for the competition.

Derek Randall

Born: February 24, 1951, Retford, Nottinghamshire
Teams: Nottinghamshire (1972–93)
First-class: 488 matches; 28,456 runs, average 38.14; 13 wickets, average 31.76
Tests (1976–77 to 1984): 47 matches; 2,470 runs, average 33.37; no wickets for 3 runs

For the purist, Derek Randall was too fidgety at the crease to be accepted as a batsman of real Test class; for the general spectator in the 1980s, no man was more popular nor gave so much joy. He was a highly entertaining right-handed batsman, good enough to score seven Test hundreds, one of which was a famous 174 in the Centenary match in Melbourne, 1976–77, and to hit 1,000 runs in a season 13 times.

The batting record is good enough, but it reveals nothing of the contribution he made to a side in the field. His love of the game was transparent and it was reflected in his fielding, which was electric. He earned the nickname "Arkle", after the great steeplechaser, because of his speed in training runs with his county, and the followers of the game, with whom he had a magical rapport, accepted it as apt.

He was an audacious, brave cricketer, never willing to surrender. He almost stole the NatWest cup for Nottinghamshire in 1985. They looked well beaten by Essex and needed 18 off the last over. Randall hit 16 off the first five balls but was caught off the sixth. Perhaps the lasting memory of him will be taking the catch to dismiss Marsh which regained the Ashes for England at Leeds, 1977. He turned a somersault in celebration.

K. S. Ranjitsinhji

Born: September 10, 1872, Sarodar, Kathiawar, India
Died: April 2, 1933, Jamnagar, India
Teams: Cambridge University (1893–94); Sussex (1895–1920); London County (1901–04)
First-class: 307 matches; 24,692 runs, average 56.37; 133 wickets, average 34.59
Tests (1896–1902): 15 matches; 989 runs, average 44.95; 1 wicket, average 39.00

A batsman of feline grace and Eastern mystery, "Ranji" was a cricket legend. With exceptionally keen eyesight and supple and powerful wrists, he played shots that others could only imagine, and his leg-glance was breathtaking in audacity, beauty and execution. He had moderate success at Cambridge, but from 1899 to 1904 he was supreme among batsmen in England. He hit 3,159 runs in 1899, and followed this with 3,065 runs, average 87.57 in 1900. In three other seasons he reached 2,000 runs and in six more 1,000. He also reached 1,000 runs on a tour of Australia, 1897–98.

He was the first Indian to play Test cricket and the second batsman, after Grace, to hit a century on his Test debut. He was also the first batsman to score a hundred before lunch in a Test. He made 62 and 154 not out at Old Trafford, 1896, and he went from 41 to 154 in 130 minutes before lunch on the third day. In 1897–98, he hit 175 in his first Test in Australia.

Ranjitsinhji captained Sussex from 1899 to 1903 and then returned to India. He made infrequent appearances thereafter. As the Maharaja Jam Sahib of Nawanagar, he became involved in administration of his state and was a delegate to the League of Nations.

John Reid

Born: June 3, 1928, Auckland, New Zealand
Teams: Wellington (1947–48 to 1964–65); Otago (1956–57 to 1957–58)
First-class: 246 matches; 16,128 runs, average 41.35; 466 wickets, average 22.60
Tests (1949–1965): 58 matches; 3,428 runs, average 33.28; 85 wickets, average 33.35

JOHN REID *A good all-rounder and inspiring captain of New Zealand.*

John Reid was a complete all-round cricketer, a hard-hitting middle-order batsman, a brisk bowler of off-cutters and a wicket-keeper of no mean ability. He made 50 and 25 on his Test debut at Old Trafford, 1949, and in his next match, at the Oval, he kept wicket and scored 93. He did not really blossom until the 1953–54 series in South Africa when, at Cape Town, he hit his maiden Test century.

New Zealand cricket had reached a low ebb by the mid-1950s, and, following a crushing defeat by the West Indies at Dunedin, 1955–56, Reid was appointed captain. In the last match of the series, he top-scored with 84 and New Zealand won a famous victory. His side suffered badly in England, 1958, but in South Africa, 1961–62, against all expectations, New Zealand drew the series, each side winning two Tests. It was the first time New Zealand had won two Tests in a rubber, and Reid topped the batting and bowling averages, hitting 142 in Johannesburg.

He led New Zealand in 34 consecutive Tests, but retired after the disappointing 1965 tour of England, feeling his side had made no real advance. In all, he hit six Test centuries.

Wilfred Rhodes

Born: October 29, 1877, Kirkheaton, Yorkshire
Died: July 8, 1973, Branksome Park, Dorset
Teams: Yorkshire (1898–1930); Patiala (1926–27); Europeans (1921–22 to 1922–23)
First-class: 1,110 matches; 39,969 runs, average 30.81; 4,204 wickets, average 16.72
Tests (1899 to 1929–30): 58 matches; 2,325 runs, average 30.19; 127 wickets, average 26.96

When Lord Hawke dismissed Robert Peel from the Yorkshire team in 1897 the county were left in need of a slow left-arm bowler. The vacancy was filled by Wilfred Rhodes who took six for 63 in the first match of the 1898 season and, by the end of the season, he had claimed 154 wickets. So began one of the most illustrious and record-breaking careers in cricket. He was to take 100 or more wickets 23 times, and in three of those seasons he exceeded 200 wickets. He achieved the "double" in 16 seasons, a record that is never likely to be beaten, and, in all, he reached 1,000 runs 20 times. His total of 4,024 wickets is a world record.

He made his Test debut at Trent Bridge in 1899. It was the first Test to be played at the ground, and it also marked the end of W.G. Grace's Test career. Rhodes had match figures of seven Australian wickets for 118. He also played in the first Test staged at Edgbaston, 1902, when Australia were bowled out for 36 – Rhodes took seven for 17. Better was to come. On his first tour of Australia, 1903–04, he took seven for 56 and eight for 68 to bowl England to victory in the Melbourne Test. When he went to Australia eight years later, he was Hobbs's opening partner, and the pair established an Ashes record at Melbourne in the fourth Test when they put on 323, Rhodes making 179. The record stood for 77 years.

Barry Richards

Born: July 21, 1945, Morningside, Durban, South Africa
Teams: Natal (1964–65 to 1982–83); Gloucestershire (1965); Hampshire (1968–78); South Australia (1970–71); Transvaal (1970–71)
First-class: 339 matches; 28,358 runs, average 54.74; 77 wickets, average 37.48
Tests (1969–70): 4 matches; 508 runs, average 75.57; 1 wicket, average 26.00

In the opinion of many, Barry Richards was unquestionably the finest batsman of his generation. An aggressive right-handed opening batsman with total command of every shot, he adorned county cricket for a decade, and his first-wicket partnership with Gordon Greenidge was largely instrumental in bringing Hampshire the county championship and two Sunday League titles.

BARRY RICHARDS *Careless genius.*

If he had a fault, it was that it all seemed to come so easily to him that at times he appeared lackadaisical. A thrilling batsman, he hit 325 on the opening day of the match between South Australia and Western Australia at Perth, 1970–71. He finally made 356. He scored 1,000 runs in a season five times in South Africa and nine times in England. He was also a useful off-break bowler.

His Test debut in 1969–70 saw him score two centuries in seven innings against Australia and average 75.57 for the series. That was to be both the beginning and end of his Test career, for these were South Africa's last Tests before their exclusion.

Richards was very successful in Packer's World Series cricket.

Viv Richards

Born: March 7, 1952, St John's, Antigua
Teams: Leeward Islands (1971–72 to 1990–91); Somerset (1974–86); Queensland (1976–77); Glamorgan (1990–93)
First-class: 507 matches; 36,212 runs, average 49.33; 223 wickets, average 45.15
Tests (1974–75 to 1991): 121 matches; 8,540 runs, average 50.23; 32 wickets, average 61.37

Viv Richards scored more runs and played in more Test matches than any other West Indian cricketer. A brilliant, natural right-handed attacking batsman and a right-arm bowler of medium pace or spin, he was capable of destroying any attack in the world in all forms of cricket. Apart from his mighty Test record, he scored 6,721 runs in limited-over internationals, including 11 centuries.

He first played for Somerset in 1974 and made his Test debut in India the following winter, scoring 192 not out in his second match, the first of 24 Test centuries. A fine natural athlete who played World Cup soccer as well as World Cup cricket, he led a violent assault on the England bowling in the World Cup Final 1979, and the following year he captained the West Indies for the first time. He already had a host of records behind him.

VIV RICHARDS *Dismissive arrogance of a master batsman.*

In 1976, he appeared in only four Tests in the series against England but hit 232, 63, 4, 135, 66, 38 and 291 to give him 829 runs, average 118.42. It brought his aggregate of Test runs for the calendar year to a record 1,710. His second tour of England was an equal triumph, and when he came for his fourth tour, 1988, he was captain. He retired from Test cricket after the 1991 series, having led the West Indies 50 times.

The first West Indian to score a hundred hundreds, he dominated in county cricket although he lived excitingly and dangerously. He was associated with Somerset in their glory years when they won all the one-day trophies. His highest innings for Somerset was 322 against Warwickshire, 1985. He left Somerset with some acrimony, but returned to county cricket with Glamorgan and showed great emotion when he helped them to win the Sunday League in his last season in the game.

Richie Richardson

Born: January 2, 1962, Five Islands Village, Antigua
Teams: Leeward Islands (1981–82 to 1995–96); Yorkshire (1994)
First-class: 217 matches; 13,950 runs, average 42.40; 6 wickets, average 39.66
Tests (1983–84 to 1995–96): 86 matches; 5,949 runs, average 44.39; no wickets for 18 runs

A shy, modest and courteous man, Richie Richardson succeeded Viv Richards as captain of Leeward Islands and of the West Indies. A right-handed batsman of immense talent and great eagerness to hit the ball, he took some time to prove himself at Test level. He hit two centuries against Australia, 1983–84, but he failed to do himself justice in England the following summer although his ability was apparent. When he made his third trip to England, 1991, he showed that he had mastered the slower wickets and topped theTest batting averages. He now began to thrive, and hit his eighth Test hundred against Australia, 1992–93, and led the West Indies to victory in the series. In all, he now has 16 Test hundreds to his credit.

He was hugely successful in one-day internationals, but the pressures began to tell on him. He left Yorkshire because he was exhausted and ordered to rest for six months. He was reinstated as the West Indies' captain far too quickly and failure in the World Cup, 1996, led to him relinquishing the captaincy and leaving Test cricket. He played in South Africa, 1996–97, but he failed to live up to his reputation as a great batsman.

Andy Roberts

Born: January 29, 1951, Urlings Village, Antigua
Teams: Leeward Islands (1969–70 to 1983–84); Hampshire (1973–78); New South Wales (1976–77); Leicestershire (1981–84)
First-class: 228 matches; 3,516 runs, average 15.69; 889 wickets, average 21.01
Tests (1973–74 to 1983–84): 47 matches; 762 runs, average 14.94; 202 wickets, average 25.61

Andy Roberts was the third West Indian to claim 200 Test wickets and, at his peak, he was considered to be one of the two or three best fast bowlers in the world. He reached 100 Test wickets more quickly than any bowler had done before, although his record was later beaten by Botham. He was a great favourite with Hampshire, and he played a major part in their Sunday League triumphs. In 1974, he took 119 wickets, average 13.62, in 21 matches for the county in first-class cricket and was the most feared bowler in the land.

His Test debut had come against England the previous winter, but it was in India, 1974–75, that he really established himself as an international cricketer. He captured 32 wickets in the series, and at Madras he had match figures of 12 for 121. His best bowling came in Perth a year later when he took seven for 54 in the second innings to give the West Indies their only victory of the series.

He joined Packer's World Series along with the other West Indian cricketers, and he was never quite the same afterwards. He assisted Leicestershire on a part-time basis, appearing in 36 matches, and later coached the West Indian team.

Lawrence Rowe

Born: January 8, 1949, Kingston, Jamaica
Teams: Jamaica (1968–69 to 1981–82); Derbyshire (1974)
First-class: 149 matches; 8,755 runs, average 37.57; 2 wickets, average 112.0

ROBERTS *One of the West Indian fast bowlers who dominated the 1980s.*

Tests (1971–72 to 1979–80): 30 matches; 2,047 runs, average 43.55; no wickets for 44 runs

Lawrence Rowe will forever remain one of the great "lost " batsmen of cricket history. He was an attacking right-handed batsman who, in the opinion of many in the Caribbean, was destined to be a better player than Viv Richards and would have emulated Garfield Sobers.

Making his Test debut against New Zealand at Kingston, January, 1972, he became the first player ever to score hundreds in both innings of his first Test. He made 214 and 100 not out, and had scored a double-century for Jamaica in his last innings before this Test. He began to be dogged by injury and did not appear in a Test in England in 1973. The following winter, however, he made 120 against England at Kingston and followed this with 302 in Barbados and 123 in Trinidad.

Injury haunted his season with Derbyshire, and, following a century against Australia at Brisbane, his Test career began to fall away due to problems with eyesight, injury and allergies. He joined World Series Cricket, and later took a side to South Africa, passing permanently into the wilderness.

Jack Russell

Born: August 15, 1963, Stroud, Gloucestershire
Teams: Gloucestershire (1981–97)
First-class: 347 matches; 11,824 runs, average 30.01; 1 wicket, average 53.00; caught 838, stumped 104
Tests (1988–96): 49 matches; 1,807 runs, average 29.14; caught 141, stumped 11

A most accomplished wicket-keeper, neat and balanced, and a tenacious left-handed batsman who has two Test centuries to his credit, Robert "Jack" Russell follows his mentor Alan Knott in his fastidiousness over diet and training. He made his Test debut against Sri Lanka at Lord's, 1988, and, coming in as night-watchman, hit 94 which was, at the time, his highest score in first-class cricket.

He was always most effective as England's keeper, but he was often omitted because of the need for England to bolster their batting. Incomprehensibly, he was left out of the party to tour India and Sri Lanka, 1992–93, but he had an outstanding tour of South Africa, 1995–96. In the second Test, at Johannesburg, he claimed the Test record with 11 catches, and then batted for 277 minutes to score 29 not out and help Atherton to save the match.

In Zimbabwe and New Zealand a year later, he was again omitted so that Stewart could keep wicket and another batsman could be brought in. Russell is also noted for his drawings and paintings, and often exhibits at Gloucestershire grounds.

S

Salim Malik

Born: April 16, 1963, Lahore, Pakistan
Teams: Lahore (1978–79 to 1985–86); Habib Bank (1982–83 to 1994–95)
First-class: 239 matches; 14,871 runs, average 47.35; 84 wickets, average 34.25
Tests (1981–82 to 1996–97): 90 matches; 5,101 runs, average 45.14; 5 wickets, average 49.40

An exquisite stroke-maker, Salim Malik is a right-handed batsman and leg-break bowler who caught the eye as soon as he appeared in international cricket. He became the youngest player to score a hundred in his first Test, 100 not out against Sri Lanka, March 1982. He did not play in any of the Tests in England the following summer, but on his second trip to England, 1987, scoring 99 at Headingley and 102 at the Oval, he was a huge success and was the linchpin of the side. He was even more successful five years later.

He assisted Essex for two seasons and scored heavily in 1991, sharing in a fourth-wicket record stand of 314 with Hussain at the Oval and ending the season with 1,972 runs to his credit. He was less prolific in 1993, but remained highly entertaining.

Salim's career has had its troughs, and, having been made captain of Pakistan in South Africa and Zimbabwe, he faced allegations of bribery which led to his suspension for some time. He was deemed innocent and regained his place in the Pakistan side where he showed that he had lost none of his ability to play as his side required.

Sarfraz Nawaz

Born: December 1, 1948, Lahore, Pakistan
Teams: Lahore (1967–68 to 1984–85); Punjab University (1968–69 to 1971–72); Northamptonshire (1969–1982); Punjab (1974–75); Railways (1975–75); United Bank (1976–77 to 1977–78)
First-class: 299 matches; 5,709 runs, average 19.35; 1,005 wickets, average 24.62
Tests (1968–69 to 1983–84): 55 matches; 1,045 runs, average 17.71; 177 wickets, average 32.75

Sarfraz Nawaz was a high-class, fast medium-pace bowler who was only the third Pakistani cricketer to take 100 Test wickets and score 1,000 Test runs. He had an impressive Test career, but it was punctuated by injury and arguments with the Pakistan Board of Control. He was never far from controversy, and the last such incident was when he refuted Allan Lamb's assertion that he was the bowler who taught others how to scratch one side of the surface of the ball. Sarfraz took legal action but did not pursue the case to the full.

In March 1979, at Melbourne, Pakistan celebrated their 100th Test by beating Australia. It was a most unlikely victory, for Australia needed 77 to win and had seven wickets in hand with time to spare. Sarfraz then produced one of the greatest spells of bowling in Test history taking those seven wickets in 33 balls while he conceded one run. He finished with nine for 86, and Pakistan won by 71 runs. In the next Test, he caused a furore when he successfully appealed for "handled ball" against Hilditch when the batsman picked up the ball and tossed it back to him.

He helped Northamptonshire during a successful period although he was once not re-engaged. He went into politics when he left cricket.

Ravi Shastri

Born: May 27, 1962, Bombay, India
Teams: Bombay (1979–80 to 1993–94); Glamorgan (1987–91)
First-class: 245 matches; 13,202 runs, average 44.00; 509 wickets, average 32.89
Tests (1980–81 to 1992–93): 80 matches; 3,830 runs, average 35.79; 151 wickets, average 40.96

Ravi Shastri is the only batsman other than Gary Sobers who has hit six sixes in one over. He scored 200 not out for Bombay against Baroda, 1984–85, and hit 13 sixes, six of them in one over. It was the fastest double-century on record, 113 minutes, and the runs came off 123 balls.

A tall, calm and composed right-handed batsman, he won his first Test cap as a slow left-arm bowler. He was flown to New Zealand as a replacement in February 1981, and just short of his 19th birthday, took six wickets in the match including three with his last four balls in the second innings. In spite of these achievements, he never quite reached the peak expected of him. His bowling lacked variety and subtlety in flight, but he became a reliable opening batsman. He was seen as captain-elect of India, but, in the event, led his country in only one Test. He played a fine innings of 187 against England at the Oval, 1990, and made 206 against Australia at Sydney, 1991–92.

He did well with Glamorgan and was immensely successful in one-day internationals.

Alfred Shaw

Born: August 29, 1842, Burton Joyce, Nottinghamshire
Died: January 16, 1907, Gedling, Nottinghamshire
Teams: Nottinghamshire (1864–1897); Sussex (1894–95)
First-class: 404 matches; 6,585 runs, average 12.44; 2,026 wickets, average 12.13
Tests (1876–77 to 1881–82): 7 matches; 111 runs, average 10.09; 12 wickets, average 23.75

Alfred Shaw sent down the first ball to be bowled in Test cricket and appeared in seven of the first eight Test matches. He made two tours to North America and was involved with four tours of Australia, captaining the 1881–82 side. For a long period during his career he was, without question, supreme among slow bowlers, so relentlessly accurate that he bowled more overs in his career than he conceded runs.

A natural leader of men, with a strong personality, Shaw captained Nottinghamshire to four successive championship titles, 1883 to 1886, after which his connection with his native county virtually ended and he was employed to coach young Sussex cricketers. After six years' absence from county cricket, he reappeared for Sussex in 1894 at the age of 50.

He was a strong upholder of the rights of the professional cricketer and did much to help his fellow men. He refused to tour Australia with Grace's side in 1875 because the professionals were to be allowed only second-class facilities, and he led a strike of Nottinghamshire professionals six years later. His faction demanded a formal contract of employment which would guarantee an automatic benefit at the end of an agreed span of years. This was seen as anarchy by the Nottinghamshire committee who dropped the offenders, confirmed in their belief that it would be better to have an amateur captain. There was a reconciliation eventually, but Shaw's team-mates pointed out that the county went into rapid decline when he was no longer at the helm.

Shoaib Mohammad

Born: January 8, 1961, Karachi, Pakistan
Teams: PIA (1976–77 to 1996–97); Karachi (1983–84 to 1996–97)
First-class: 178 matches; 10,712 runs, average 41.20; 23 wickets, average 44.69
Tests (1983–84 to 1995–96): 45 matches; 2,705 runs, average 44.34; 5 wickets, average 34.00

Shoaib has not found the burden of being the son of the great Hanif easy to carry. He also has had the added weight of being a member of the most distinguished of cricketing families.

Initially, there was an impetuosity in his batting. He was a pugnacious, right-handed opener, but in later years he adopted a more cautious approach to the game, and he was never quite sure of his place in the Pakistan side. He made a century on his debut in first-class cricket and won his first Test cap against Pakistan in Jullundur, 1983–84. In his first match against England some months later, he scored 84, but his appearances have tended to be sporadic.

His first Test hundred came against India in Madras, 1986–87, but it was a painstaking affair. His greatest successes have come against New Zealand. He hit 163 and 112 in successive innings, 1988–89, and, in 1990–91, he scored an unbeaten 203 against them at Karachi. He followed this with two more centuries.

Arthur Shrewsbury

Born: April 11, 1856, New Lenton, Nottinghamshire
Died: May 19, 1903, Gedling, Nottinghamshire
Teams: Nottinghamshire (1875–1902)
First-class: 498 matches; 26,505 runs, average 36.65; no wickets for 2 runs
Tests (1881–82 to 1893): 23 matches; 1,277 runs, average 35.47

When asked to name the contemporary batsman he rated above all others, W.G. Grace replied "Give me Arthur", and unquestionably, in the period covered by his Test career, Arthur Shrewsbury was the finest professional batsman in England. He topped the first-class batting averages five times between 1886 and 1892 and again in 1902, his last season. In 1887, he scored 1,653 runs, average 78.71, which, at that time, was the highest average ever recorded by a batsman playing regular first-class cricket. He scored 1,000 runs in a season on 13 occasions.

He joined Lillywhite and Shaw in organizing four trips to Australia, and made his Test debut on the first, 1881–82. He captained the sides of 1884–85 and 1886–87, and in the fifth Test of the first of those series he hit 105 not out, so becoming the first England captain to score a century in a Test match. He was the first England batsman to reach 1,000 Test runs and the first to score three Test hundreds.

Admired and respected as a man and as a player, Shrewsbury won both series in which he was captain. He last led England at Sydney in 1887, and it was to be another 65 years before a professional again captained England.

He did much to raise the status of the professional cricketer, but he himself was to have the saddest of ends. Believing that ill-health and failing sight would prevent him from playing the game he loved and had served so well, he shot himself within a year of his last first-class match.

Bobby Simpson

Born: February 3, 1936, Marrickville, New South Wales, Australia
Teams: New South Wales (1952–53 to 1977–78); Western Australia (1956–57 to 1960–61)
First-class: 257 matches; 21,029 runs, average 56.22; 349 wickets, average 38.07
Tests (1957–58 to 1977–78): 62 matches; 4,869 runs, average 46.81; 71 wickets, average 42.26

A most dependable and attractive right-handed opening batsman, useful leg-break and googly bowler and one of the finest slip fielders the game has known, Bobby Simpson had a Test career that was divided into two distinct parts. When he became captain of Australia, 1963–64, he had not recorded a Test match century, and it was not until his second tour of England, 1964, in the fourth Test at Old Trafford, that Simpson reached three figures; it was his 52nd Test innings. He and Lawry put on 201 for the first wicket, and Simpson went on to score 311, the highest score by an Australian Test captain and the longest innings played against England, 762 minutes. He followed this with a century in each innings against Pakistan at Karachi, 1964–65. Three years later, he announced that he would retire at the end of the season. He scored hundreds in the first two Tests against India and stood down. Recalled for the fourth Test as a farewell gesture, he had match figures of eight for 97.

He became director of a successful public relations business, and it was believed his career was over. In 1977–78, however, Australian cricket was ravaged by the Packer affair and the defection of the leading players. Simpson came out of retirement to lead Australia against India. Superbly fit in his forties, he hit two Test centuries and won the series. He was less successful in the Caribbean, and with the war with Packer resolved, the Australian Board no longer had need of him.

He held strict, traditional values in attitude, fitness, dress and behaviour, and he became coach to Allan Border's side of the late 1980s. He also coached Leicestershire for two seasons.

John Snow

Born: October 13, 1941, Peopleton, Worcester
Teams: Sussex (1961–77)
First-class: 346 matches; 4,832 runs, average 14.17; 1,174 wickets, average 22.72
Tests (1965–76): 49 matches; 772 runs, average 13.54; 202 wickets, average 26.66

SNOW *Poet who destroyed Australia with fast bowling in 1970–71.*

Among the greatest of English post-war fast bowlers, John Snow was also among the most moody and most prone to brushes with authority. While not possessing a classical action, he was rhythmical and intelligent. He was raw when he first played for England in 1965, and did not go to Australia the following winter. He took 12 wickets in three Tests against the West Indies, 1966, and played a major part in England's victory in the final Test, not least because he scored his maiden first-class fifty and shared a last-wicket stand of 128 in 140 minutes with Higgs.

In the West Indies, 1967–68, he was outstanding, taking seven for 79 at Kingston, 10 for 142 in the match at Georgetown, and finishing the series with 27 wickets in four Tests. Yet perhaps his greatest performance was in Australia with Illingworth's side, 1970–71, when England regained the Ashes and he took 31 wickets, including a Test-best seven for 40 at Sydney. Controversy struck the following summer when he barged into Gavaskar in the Lord's Test and was banned for one match. He lost his appetite for county cricket, joined World Series Cricket, published two volumes of poetry and an autobiography called *Cricket Rebel*. He played Sunday League cricket for Warwickshire in 1980.

Gary Sobers

See Legends (pages 116–117)

F.R. Spofforth

Born: September 9, 1853, Balmain, Sydney, New South Wales, Australia
Died: June 4, 1926, Ditton Hill Lodge, Long Ditton, Surrey
Teams: New South Wales (1874–75 to 1884–85); Victoria (1885–86 to 1887–88)
First-class: 155 matches; 1,928 runs, average 9.88; 853 wickets, average 14.95
Tests (1876–77 to 1886–87): 18 matches; 217 runs, average 9.43; 94 wickets, average 18.41

Tall, intelligent, able to vary speed, cut and swerve, Spofforth was basically a fast medium-pace bowler. He refused to play in the first Test match of all in 1876–77 because his wicket-keeper Murdoch was not chosen, but he appeared in the second. It was in the third Test, January 1879, at Melbourne that he really made his mark, taking six for 48 and seven for 62 as Australia won by 10 wickets. This came as no surprise, for "The Demon" had routed the MCC at Lord's in 1878, taking six for 4 and five for 16 as the Australians won in a day. His record in England was phenomenal, and in 1884 he took 207 wickets, average 12.82.

He had lost some of his demon by 1887 and emigrated to England the following year. He played for Derbyshire from 1889 to 1891, captaining the side in 1890, but the county did not have first-class status at that time.

Brian Statham

Born: June 17, 1930, Gorton, Manchester, Lancashire
Teams: Lancashire (1950–68)
First-class: 559 matches; 5,424 runs, average 19.80; 2,260 wickets, average 16.37
Tests (1950–51 to 1965): 70 matches; 675 runs, average 11.44; 252 wickets, average 24.84

For a period of more than 10 years, Statham was one of England's great opening bowlers, forming lethal partnerships with both Trueman and Tyson. He bowled right-arm with a fluid, easy action and was relentlessly accurate. He was honest, loyal and reliable, a great teamman who, reluctantly, captained Lancashire from 1965 to 1967.

Flown to Australia as a reinforcement, 1950–51, he made his Test debut in New Zealand and claimed Bert Sutcliffe as his first Test wicket. He did not really establish a regular place in the England side until the tour of the Caribbean, 1953–54, and it was in Australia a year later that he and Tyson bowled England to victory. A few months later, he showed the English public his prowess with a Test-best seven for 39 against South Africa at Lord's. He played for England until the Oval Test against South Africa, 1965, and in this last match took five for 40 and two for 105.

A left-handed batsman, he was capable of useful tail-end innings, and was a fine fielder in the deep. He took 100 wickets in a season 13 times and performed the hat-trick on three occasions.

Bert Sutcliffe

Born: November 17, 1923, Ponsonby, Auckland, New Zealand
Teams: Auckland (1941–42 to 1948–79); Otago (1946–47 to 1961–62); Northern Districts (1962–63 to 1965–66)
First-class: 233 matches; 17,447 runs, average 47.41; 86 wickets, average 38.05
Tests (1946–47 to 1965): 42 matches; 2,727 runs, average 40.10; 4 wickets, average 86.00

Bert Sutcliffe was the finest New Zealand cricketer of his generation and must rank as one of the best left-handed batsmen of the period. He had a cheerful disposition, and was a thing of beauty with a bat in his hands. He was stylish, correct and joyful. He made his Test debut in March 1947, when he shared an opening stand of 133 with Walter Hadlee against England. Sutcliffe made 58, and his class was obvious. He was an outstanding success in England in 1949, scoring 2,627 runs on the tour and averaging 60.42 in the Tests with a century at Old Trafford. In 1952–53 he hit 385 for Otago against Canterbury, and three years earlier had hit 355 for Otago against Auckland. These remain the two highest individual scores to be made in New Zealand.

He captained New Zealand in four Tests between 1951 and 1954, but captaincy was not a job he relished, and it is significant that his best Test score, 230 not out against India in Delhi, 1955–56, came after he had relinquished the leadership.

Sutcliffe retired from Test cricket in 1958–59, but was persuaded to return in 1967. He made 151 against India in Calcutta, but was 42 years old. He proved to be a fine coach.

Herbert Sutcliffe

Born: November 24, 1894, Summerbridge, Harrogate, Yorkshire
Died: January 22, 1978, Cross Hills, Yorkshire
Teams: Yorkshire (1919–45)
First-class: 754 matches; 50,670 runs, average 52.02; 14 wickets, average 41.21
Tests (1924–35): 54 matches; 4,555 runs, average 60.73

HERBERT SUTCLIFFE *Imperturbable.*

Herbert Sutcliffe's career fits neatly into the period between the two wars, and he averaged 1,000 runs in a season every year from 1919 to 1939. He made only a brief appearance in 1945. He was unquestionably one of the greatest opening batsman of all time with an outstanding Test record. Technically sound, neat, determined and totally unflappable, he batted right-handed, was at home on any wicket and shaped his game to the occasion. His opening partnership with Hobbs in the England side is legendary, and his county partnership with Holmes was equally famous. He was mentor to the young Len Hutton.

The first of his 15 three-figure Test opening partnerships with Hobbs came in his debut Test against South Africa, in 1924. In the next match, they put on 268, and Sutcliffe made 122, the first of his 16 Test centuries. He scored a century in his first match against Australia, a century in each innings in his second, and in the fourth match of the series became the first batsman to hit four centuries in a rubber. Most famously, at the Oval, 1926, when England regained the Ashes, Hobbs and Sutcliffe made 172 on a sticky wicket. Sutcliffe ended with 161.

In 1930, at Leyton, Sutcliffe and Holmes scored a world-record 555 for the first wicked against Essex. Sutcliffe made 313. His last Test was against South Africa at Lord's in 1935, although many felt he should have been retained longer. Once offered the captaincy of Yorkshire, he refused, unwilling to break the amateur tradition.

T

Maurice Tate

Born: May 30, 1895, Brighton, Sussex
Died: May 18, 1956, Wadhurst, Sussex
Teams: Sussex (1912–1937)
First-class: 679 matches; 21,717 runs, average 25.04; 2,784 wickets, average 18.16
Tests (1924–35): 39 matches; 1,198 runs, average 25.48; 155 wickets, average 26.16

Son of a Sussex cricketer who played one match for England, Maurice Tate was a great medium-pace right-arm bowler and a great character. He began as an off-break bowler, but became a seam bowler of brisk pace after the Second World War. Some insisted his deliveries gathered pace off the wicket. Few bowlers have used the seam to such good effect; very few have been as popular. He was also a most capable lower middle-order batsman, good enough, in fact, to score 100 not out against South Africa at Lord's in 1929.

Tate's Test debut was sensational. At Edgbaston, 1924, he and Arthur Gilligan bowled South Africa out for 30 in 12.3 overs. Tate took four for 12 and had five for 83 in the second innings. He took 30 wickets in the series, and created a record with 38 wickets in Australia the following winter. He was England's leading bowler of the time before the pace of Larwood.

He completed the "double" eight times, and in three of those seasons his 1,000 runs were coupled with 200 wickets. He was held in great affection by the public.

Hugh Tayfield

Born: January 30, 1929, Durban, South Africa
Died: February 25, 1994, Pietermaritzburg, South Africa
Teams: Natal (1945–46 to 1946–47); Rhodesia (1947–48 to 1948–49); Transvaal (1956–57 to 1962–63)
First-class: 187 matches; 3,668 runs, average 17.30; 864 wickets, average 21.86
Tests (1949–50 to 1960): 37 matches; 862 runs, average 16.90; 170 wickets, average 25.91

Hugh Tayfield was a very fine off-break bowler whose 170 wickets in Test cricket remains a South African record. He played in all five Tests against Australia 1949–50, and took seven for 23 at Durban when he and Mann bowled the opposition out for 75. Surprisingly not chosen for the tour of England in 1951, he was flown out as a replacement but did not play in a Test. In Australia in 1952–53 he thrived with a record 30 wickets, and at Melbourne he bowled South Africa to victory with 13 for 165 in the match.

Success continued unabated, and when South Africa came to England in 1955 he became the first bowler from that country to take 100 Test wickets. He took 26 wickets in the series and had astonishing figures in the second innings at the Oval when he took five for 60 in 53.4 overs of which 29 were maidens. England suffered more at his hands in South Africa, 1956–57, when he established a record with 37 wickets in the rubber, including his career-best nine for 113 in Johannesburg. That marked the peak of his achievements.

Mark Taylor

Born: October 27, 1964, Leeton, New South Wales, Australia
Teams: New South Wales (1985–86 to 1996–97)
First-class: 192 matches; 13,951 runs, average 44.14; 2 wickets, average 34.00
Tests (1988–89 to 1996–97): 72 matches; 5,502 runs, average 45.85; 1 wicket, average 26.00

A left-handed opening batsman and brilliant slip fielder, he forced his way into the Australian side against the West Indies in 1988–89, and scored 136 in his first Test against England the following summer. He and Geoff Marsh became a formidable opening pair and, at Trent Bridge, they established a record with a stand of 329. Taylor hit 219. He finished the series with 839 runs, an aggregate exceeded only by Bradman and Hammond in rubbers between England and Australia.

When Marsh retired, Taylor continued to flourish with Slater as his partner, and he succeeded Border as Australia's captain. He helped maintain Australia's supremacy in world cricket with home and away series victories against the West Indies and triumph over Atherton's side, 1994–95.

Unfortunately, he lost form. He failed to average 20 in Tests or domestic cricket in Australia, 1996–97, and laboured in South Africa. In spite of this, he was appointed captain for the tour of England, 1997, a decision that was strongly criticized.

Sachin Tendulkar

Born: April 24, 1973, Bombay, India
Teams: Bombay (1988–89 to 1996–97); Yorkshire (1992)
First-class: 112 matches; 8,824 runs, average 59.22; 25 wickets, average 68.00
Tests (1989–90 to 1996–97): 41 matches; 2,911 runs, average 54.92; 4 wickets, average 55.00

Sachin Tendulkar scored an unbeaten century on the occasion of his first-class debut when he was 15 years old. A year later, he became the youngest player to represent India, and in his second match against Pakistan he became the youngest to hit a Test 50. In England, 1990, he hit a century in the Old Trafford Test, at 17 years, 112 days, the youngest to score a Test hundred in England. Two Test hundreds in Australia were next of the list. In 1992, he became Yorkshire's first overseas signing and coped remarkably well with the pressure, making 1,070 runs.

Runs have flowed from his bat in all forms of cricket, and his eagerness to score freely and his majestic execution of every shot make him a favourite throughout the world. Short and powerful, he has no superior as a right-handed batsman in world cricket, and his career has just begun. He is capable of re-writing all the record

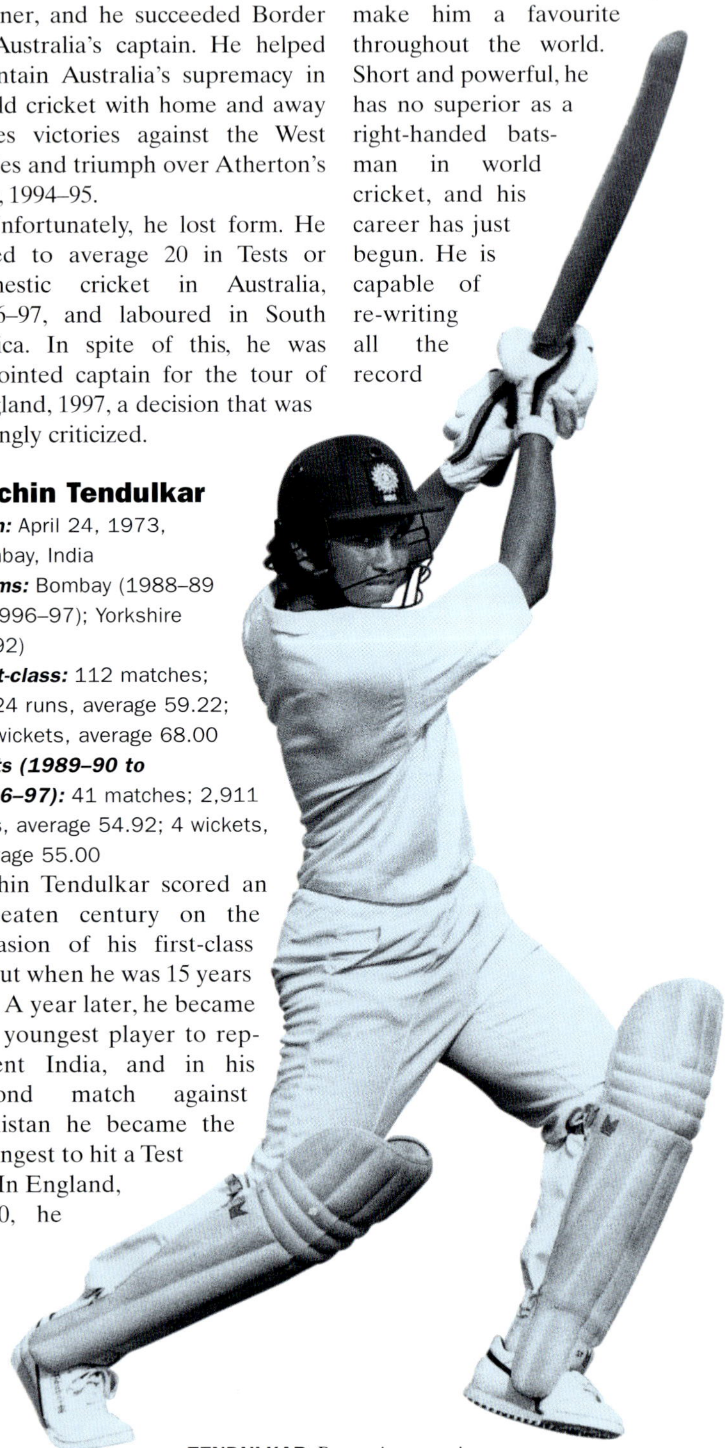

TENDULKAR *Precocious genius.*

books in Tests and one-day internationals. In 1996, aged 23, he was appointed captain of India.

His intelligence is not restricted to his command of cricket, and he supplements his regal batting with gentle medium-pace bowling and brilliant fielding.

Jeff Thomson

Born: August 16, 1950, Greenacre, Sydney, New South Wales, Australia
Teams: New South Wales (1972–74); Queensland (1974–75 to 1985–86); Middlesex (1981)
First-class: 187 matches; 2,065 runs, average 13.58; 675 wickets, average 26.46
Tests (1972–73 to 1985): 51 matches; 679 runs, average 12.81; 200 wickets, average 28.00

Jeff Thomson made an inauspicious start in Test cricket when he played against Pakistan, 1972–73, but two years later, after he had moved to Queensland, the selectors recalled him. The result was devastating as he and Lillee, with whom his name was to be permanently associated, demolished England. Thomson, bowling at a great pace, took three for 59 and six for 46. He finished the series with 33 wickets in nine innings. A few weeks later he was in England for the World Cup and a four-match series, and, if not quite so potent as in Australia, he and Lillee again destroyed England. Back in Australia the following winter, 1975–76, he and Lillee outbowled their West Indian counterparts and swept Australia to a 5–1 series victory.

Thomson joined World Series Cricket, then retracted, and then rejoined. He played for Middlesex in 1981, but injury restricted him to eight matches. He was recalled to the Test scene in 1985 after three years' absence, but the old bite had gone.

JEFF THOMSON *With Lillee he formed a devastating partnership.*

Graham Thorpe

Born: August 1, 1969, Farnham, Surrey
Teams: Surrey (1988–97)
First-class: 192 matches; 12,377 runs, average 44.04; 24 wickets, average 50.41
Tests (1993–1997): 32 matches; 2,194 runs, average 40.62; no wickets for 37 runs

A left-handed batsman and right-arm medium-pace bowler who has repaid the faith shown in him initially by chairman of selectors, Ted Dexter, and county captain, Ian Greig, Graham Thorpe made his Test debut against Australia, 1993, and hit 114 not out.

He was the veteran of several "A" tours before winning his first Test cap, and held his place in the Surrey side because his bowling was considered useful even when he was not scoring runs. Once in the Test side, he displayed admirable temperament and confirmed that he was the most reliable of batsmen. He hit 123 against Australia at Perth, 1994–95, and was England's leading run-scorer against the West Indies the following summer. An indifferent run throughout 1996 was ended with centuries in successive Tests in New Zealand early in 1997.

Frederick Trueman

Born: February 6, 1931, Stainton, Yorkshire
Teams: Yorkshire (1949–68)
First-class: 603 matches; 9,231 runs, average 15.56; 2,304 wickets, average 18.29
Tests (1952–65): 67 matches; 981 runs, average 13.81; 307 wickets, average 21.57

A genuine, whole-hearted fast bowler whose belligerence made him feared by batsmen and whose outspokenness and reputation caused him to clash with authority more than once and to miss tours and Tests he might have played in, Freddie Trueman was one of the game's great bowlers, fit to rank alongside Hadlee, Lillee and the rest.

TRUEMAN *First to 300 Test wickets.*

Initial raw pace was augmented by subtlety, and he made a dramatic entry into Test cricket, 1952. He took three Indian wickets for 89 in the first innings and four for 27 in the second. Three of these came in eight balls and left India 0 for 4. This was on his home ground of Headingley, and there were eight wickets at Lord's and nine at Old Trafford where his first-innings eight for 31 remains the best analysis against India and was the best of Trueman's Test career. Another five wickets in a rain-ruined final Test gave 29 for the series.

Thereafter things did not go so smoothly. He helped England regain the Ashes, 1953, with four for 86 in the deciding match of the series, but it was the only Test in which he appeared. He fared poorly in the Caribbean and gained adverse publicity, with the result that he missed the tour of Australia, 1954–55, and it was not until 1957 that he re-established himself and was a permanent fixture in the England side.

For Yorkshire, Trueman was a leading force throughout his career. He took 100 wickets in a season 12 times and did the hat-trick four times. He was in seven championship-winning sides, and Yorkshire have not taken the title since his departure. He was a very useful aggressive batsman and a brilliant close-to-the-wicket fielder.

At the Oval, 1964, Neil Hawke, the Australian, was caught at slip by Cowdrey off Trueman who thereby became the first bowler in Test history to take 300 wickets. His international career ended the following season.

Trueman played Sunday League matches for Derbyshire, 1972, and became a noted commentator and much in demand as an after-dinner speaker.

Hugh Trumble

Born: May 12, 1867, Abbotsford, Melbourne, Victoria, Australia
Died: August 14, 1938, Hawthorn, Melbourne, Victoria, Australia
Teams: Victoria (1887–88 to 1903–04)
First-class: 213 matches; 5,395 runs, average 19.47; 929 wickets, average 18.44
Tests (1890 to 1903–04): 32 matches; 851 runs, average 19.79; 141 wickets, average 21.78

Hugh Trumble was a right-arm medium-pace off-break bowler and sound middle-order batsman. He had prominent ears and a large nose, and he usually wore a large stetson. Grace said that he was the best bowler Australia have ever sent to England, and Fry believed him to be not only one of the greatest bowlers but a master of field-placing and a wonderful judge of the game. The first of his five tours to England was in 1890 when he did little, but thereafter he was immensely successful. In 1901–02, he performed the hat-trick at Melbourne against England, and two years later, on the same ground, he again did the hat-trick when he took seven English wickets for 28 in what proved to be his last first-class match.

At the Oval, 1902, he took eight for 65 and four for 108, and scored 64 not out and 7 not out to become the first Australian to take 10 wickets and score 50 runs in a Test. He captained Australia in two Tests.

Victor Trumper

Born: November 2, 1877, Darlinghurst, Sydney, New South Wales, Australia
Died: June 28, 1915, Darlinghurst, Sydney, New South Wales, Australia
Teams: New South Wales (1894–95 to 1913–14)
First-class: 255 matches; 16,939 runs, average 44.57; 64 wickets, average 31.37
Tests (1899 to 1911–12): 48 matches; 3,163 runs, average 39.04; 8 wickets, average 39.62

Trumper's figures cannot compare with those of Bradman, yet there is a unanimity of opinion that he was the greatest batsman Australia produced before the arrival of Don. Right-handed, effortless, perfectly balanced, supple, he moved into his shots with a grace that bewitched all who saw him. He was modest, kindly and immensely popular. Arthur Mailey described the effect that Trumper had on people when he recalled, as a junior, bowling the great man and feeling he that he had killed a dove. He scored 0 and 11 in his first Test, and in his second, at Lord's, he made a chanceless unbeaten 135. He was 21.

By the end of that tour, he was opening the innings, and when Australia arrived in England in 1902 he was supreme. At Old Trafford, he reached his century in 108 minutes before lunch on the first day.

In 1903–04, at Sydney, he reached his century in 94 minutes and, batting number five, he got 185 not out. He made another century in the same series. Seven years later, South Africa visited Australia, and Trumper scored 159 at Melbourne and 214 not out, a Test record for Australia at the time, at Adelaide. He died of Bright's disease in 1915, and a country mourned.

Charles Turner

Born: November 16, 1862, Bathurst, New South Wales, Australia
Died: January 1, 1944, Manly, Sydney, New South Wales, Australia
Teams: New South Wales (1882–83 to 1909–10)
First-class: 155 matches; 3,856 runs, average 15.54; 993 wickets, average 14.25
Tests (1886–87 to 1894–95): 17 matches; 323 runs, average 11.53; 101 wickets, average 16.53

Short and thick-set, Turner bowled fast-medium and shot to fame when he took 17 wickets against Alfred Shaw's England side in 1881–82. This feat was for Twenty-two of Bathurst, and by the following season he was in the state side. On the occasion of his Test debut at Sydney, 1887, he took six for 15 as England were bowled out for 45, their lowest-ever score against Australia. From this moment, the legend of "Turner the Terror" was born. In his next two Tests against England, he took nine wickets and 12 wickets, and his first three Tests in England, 1888, brought him 21 wickets in four innings. Yet England won the series.

He formed a lethal partnership with Ferris, and on that 1888 tour they took 534 wickets between them in all matches. In 1887–88, Turner had become the first bowler to take 100 wickets in an Australian season.

In 1894–95, having taken 11 wickets in two Tests against England, he was dropped. Reinstated for the fourth Test, he took seven wickets as Australia won by an innings, but he was dropped again. Belatedly receiving an invitation to tour England, 1896, he declined through pressure of business and passed from Test cricket.

Glenn Turner

Born: May 26, 1947, Dunedin, New Zealand
Teams: Otago (1964–65 to 1982–83); Northern Districts (1976–77); Worcestershire (1967–82)
First-class: 455 matches; 34,346 runs, average 49.70; 5 wickets, average 37.80
Tests (1968–69 to 1982–83): 41 matches; 2.991 runs, average 44.64; no wickets for 5 runs

Glenn Turner is the only New Zealand batsman to have scored more than 30,000 runs in his career and the only New Zealand batsman to have scored a hundred centuries (103). His 100th hundred came in his last season with Worcestershire, 1982, when he hit the highest score of his career, 311 not out against Warwickshire at Worcester.

Turner was the total professional cricketer. He dedicated himself to cricket, working tirelessly to earn his fare to England and joining Worcestershire to learn the game in the hard round of county cricket. He never forgot a lesson, and he developed from the "strokeless wonder" of his early days to a free-scoring opening batsman capable of making runs as quickly as anybody.

He began his Test career with a "duck" against the West Indies, 1968–69, but in his second Test he hit 74, and New Zealand won. His first Test century came in Pakistan in November 1969, when he batted over seven hours for 110.

It was in the 1971–72 series in the Caribbean that Turner established himself as one of the most accomplished batsmen in world cricket. He hit 672 runs in the series, including two double-centuries, average 96.

On the tour of England, 1973, he reached a thousand runs by the end of May, the only New Zealander to have achieved the feat, but he disappointed in the Test series. He led New Zealand in the World Cup, 1975, and in the series against India which followed.

In 1978, he decided to give all his efforts to Worcestershire, and the first rift occurred between Turner and the New Zealand authorities. He did return to Test cricket, but his relationship with the New Zealand Board was never an easy one. He saw them as amateurs in a professional world.

He subsequently managed and coached New Zealand sides, but he was replaced in 1997, mainly because many considered him too authoritarian and too demanding while stinting with praise. Whatever the case, Glenn Turner remains one of the most dedicated, most professional and most successful cricketers that New Zealand has ever produced, and it is unlikely that his records will ever be beaten.

Frank Tyson

Born: June 6, 1930, Farnworth, Lancashire
Teams: Northamptonshire (1952–60)
First-class: 244 matches; 4,103 runs, average 17.09; 767 wickets, average 20.89
Tests (1954 to 1958–59): 17 matches; 230 runs, average 10.95; 76 wickets, average 18.56

Tall and strong, "Typhoon" Tyson was, for all too brief a period, the most aggressive and lethal fast bowler in the world. His exceptional speed was recognized from the start of his career, but his run-up was excessive and his accuracy was not always to be relied upon. He was chosen to tour Australia in 1954–55 ahead of Freddie Trueman, and made his Test debut against Pakistan shortly before the party left for the southern hemisphere. He took four wickets in the first innings, but England lost.

In the first Test, at Brisbane, he took one for 160, and England lost by an innings, but, in the second match, at Sydney, he had four for 45 and six for 85. He bowled with amazing stamina and great speed, and England won a remarkable victory. He took seven for 27 and his place in history was assured when England went on to win their first rubber in Australia for 22 years and so retain the Ashes. He bowled with considerable success against South Africa the following summer, but wear and tear and injuries took their toll, and he played in only a handful of Tests before his retirement.

An English graduate from Durham University, he settled in Australia where he taught, coached, wrote and commentated.

U

Polly Umrigar

Born: March 28, 1926, Sholapur, Maharashtra, India
Teams: Parsees (1944–45 to 1945–46); Bombay (1946–47 to 1962–63); Gujarat (1950–51 to 1951–52)
First-class: 243 matches; 16,155 runs, average 52.28; 325 wickets, average 25.68
Tests (1948–49 to 1961–62): 59 matches; 3,631 runs, average 42.22; 35 wickets, average 42.08

A tall, forceful batsman, medium-pace bowler and splendid fielder, "Polly" Umrigar was a dashing cricketer who led Bombay to five successive Ranji Trophy triumphs at the beginning of their period of dominance in the competition. He was the leading Indian batsman of his generation and made his Test debut in 1948, but he had to wait until the last match of the series against England, 1951–52, for his second cap. He hit 130 not out, India won by an innings and Umrigar's international career was launched.

He had a wretched time in England, 1952, as did other Indian batsmen, but he topped the averages in the inaugural series with Pakistan, 1952–53. In the first Test against New Zealand at Hyderabad, 1955–56, he made India's first double-century in Test cricket, 223. He later took over the captaincy and won the series. He led India in eight Tests, and hit 12 Test centuries.

Derek Underwood

Born: June 8, 1945, Bromley, Kent
Teams: Kent (1963–87)
First-class: 676 matches; 5,165 runs, average 10.12; 2,465 wickets, average 20.28
Tests (1966 to 1981–82): 86 matches; 937 runs, average 11.56; 297 wickets, average 25.83

Derek Underwood was the leading spin bowler in England for nearly 20 years. Left-arm, he bowled at a pace quicker than most spinners, but he combined accuracy with variety and was a danger to batsmen on any wicket. His career began sensationally for he was the youngest player to take 100 wickets in his debut season, but he was wicketless on his Test debut, against the West Indies, three years later. The following year, 1967, he had his first five-wicket Test haul, against Pakistan, and in the final match of the Ashes series, 1968, bowled England to victory at the Oval with seven for 50 in the second innings. He continued to thrive, and on a damp wicket he was unplayable. He established records against New Zealand, and at Lord's, 1974, became the only English bowler to take 13 wickets in a Test against Pakistan. His eight for 51 in the second innings was a record.

His partnership with wicket-keeper Knott was vital and, but for the fact that Underwood became involved with World Series Cricket and a rebel tour to South Africa, he might well have become the leading wicket-taker in Test cricket.

UNDERWOOD *Sometimes unplayable spinner whose pace approached medium.*

V

Alf Valentine

Born: April 28, 1930, Kingston, Jamaica
Teams: Jamaica (1949–50 to 1964–65)
First-class: 125 matches; 470 runs, average 5.00; 475 wickets, average 26.21
Tests (1950 to 1961–62): 36 matches; 141 runs, average 4.70; 139 wickets, average 30.32

Tall and slim, Alf Valentine was a slow left-arm spinner who arrived in England in 1950 with little experience of first-class cricket. He was to take 123 wickets on the tour, 33 of them in Tests. He began with eight for 104 and three for 100 at Old Trafford, but the West Indies lost. The sensation came at Lord's when he and Ramadhin bowled the West Indies to a famous victory and were celebrated in a calypso.

VALENTINE *11 wickets on Test debut.*

He showed his real quality with 24 wickets in a difficult series in Australia, 1951–52, when his six for 102 in the second innings of the Adelaide Test gave the West Indies their sole victory in the series. He was equally successful against India, 1952–53, but he had declined by the time England went to the Caribbean the following year, and he was ineffective in England in 1957 and 1963.

Dilip Vengsarkar

Born: April 6, 1956, Rajapur, Bombay, India
Teams: Bombay (1975–76 to 1991–92)
First-class: 260 matches; 17,868 runs, average 52.86; 1 wicket, average 126.00
Tests (1975–76 to 1991–92): 116 matches; 6,868 runs, average 42.13; no wickets for 36 runs.

Only Gavaskar stands ahead of Vengsarkar as the most prolific run-scorer in Indian Test history, and only Gavaskar has scored more Test centuries for India than Vengsarkar's 17. He was a batsman of true quality, an artist and fluent stroke-maker who was rushed into the Test side as an opener before his 20th birthday, but who settled to become India's regular number three. In 1976–77, he had his hand broken by a ball from Bob Willis, but he established himself in Australia the following season. In

VENGSARKAR *The only overseas cricketer to make three Test 100s at Lords.*

1978–79, he scored two Test centuries against the West Indies, and, in Calcutta, where he made an unbeaten 157, he and Gavaskar shared a record unbroken stand of 344 for the second wicket.

In 1979, he made a century in the Lord's Test, and was to repeat this feat in 1982 and 1986 to establish a record. India won the Lord's Test in 1986, and Vengsarkar followed his century with 61 and 102 not out in difficult conditions at Headingley to help India clinch the series. He captained India in 10 Tests and scored centuries against all nations he faced, with the exception of New Zealand.

S. Venkataraghavan

Born: April 21, 1945, Madras, India
Teams: Madras/Tamil Nadu (1963–64 to 1984–85); Derbyshire (1973–75)
First-class: 341 matches; 6,617 runs, average 17.73; 1,390 wickets, average 24.14
Tests (1964–65 to 1983–84): 57 matches; 748 runs, average 11.68; 156 wickets, average 36.11

An intelligent off-break and fine close-to-the-wicket fielder, Venkataraghavan made his Test debut against New Zealand, 1964–65, and in the fourth and final Test of the series he produced his best performance in international cricket, taking eight for 72 and four for 80 to bowl India to victory. For much of his Test career he vied with Prasanna for the off-spinner's spot in the Indian side, but Venkataraghavan bowled well on the 1971 tour of England and played an important role in India's victory in the series. He captained India in the World Cup, 1975, and on the tour of England, 1979.

He had productive years with Derbyshire, taking 68 wickets in 1975. He is now recognized as one of the world's leading umpires.

Hedley Verity

Born: May 18, 1905, Headingley, Leeds, Yorkshire
Died: July 31, 1943, Caserta, Italy
Teams: Yorkshire (1930–39)
First-class: 378 matches; 5,605 runs, average 18.08; 1,956 wickets, average 14.90
Tests (1931–1939): 40 matches; 669 runs, average 20.90; 144 wickets, average 24.37

The strength of Yorkshire cricket was founded on sound batting and on great slow left-arm bowlers – Peate, Peel, Rhodes and, in the 1930s, Hedley Verity. Quicker than many of his type, Verity was relentlessly accurate and could spin the ball viciously. He was an intelligent cricketer, dignified and equable of temperament, who took 100 wickets in a season nine times. In 1935, 1936 and 1937, he exceeded 200 wickets.

On a damp pitch at Lord's in 1934, he took 14 Australian wickets in a day, 15 for 104 in the match, and bowled England to an innings victory. He was a key member of the England side for seven years.

At Headingley, in 1932, he took all 10 Nottinghamshire wickets for 10 runs, a world record which remains unequalled. He had taken all ten Warwickshire wickets on the same ground the previous season.

On September 1, 1939, he took seven for 9 as Yorkshire beat Sussex at Hove. On the outbreak of war, he was commissioned in the Green Howards and was wounded leading his men in an 8th Army attack in Sicily during the invasion of Italy in 1943. He died of his wounds some days later.

Gundappa Viswanath

Born: February 12, 1949, Bhadravati, Mysore, India
Teams: Mysore/Karnataka (1967–68 to 1987–88)
First-class: 308 matches; 17,970 runs, average 40.93; 15 wickets, average 48.60
Tests (1969–70 to 1982–83): 91 matches; 6,080 runs, average 41.93; 1 wicket, average 46.00

Brother-in-law to Sunil Gavaskar, Viswanath was a most attractive and attacking middle-order batsman who hit 230 in 340 minutes on the occasion of his first-class debut for Mysore against Andhra. In 1969–70, he made his Test debut for India against Australia at Kanpur. He was out for 0 in the first innings and made 137 in the second. It was the first of 14 Test hundreds, and only against Sri Lanka did he fail to score a century. He played in a record 87 consecutive Tests for India and captained them on two occasions.

A kind and gentle man, characteristics reflected in his delightful batting, he toured England four times and played in all the Tests on those tours, but his highest Test score came at Madras, 1981–82, when he hit 316 with Yashpal Sharma. His 222 was, at the time, the highest score made by an Indian batsman against England, and Viswanath ranks behind Gavaskar and Vengsarkar as India's most prolific scorer in Test cricket.

He is now chairman of the Indian selectors.

Bill Voce

Born: August 8, 1909, Annesley Woodhouse, Nottinghamshire
Died: June 6, 1984, Nottingham
Teams: Nottinghamshire (1927–52)
First-class: 426 matches; 7,590 runs, average 19.21; 1,558 wickets, average 23.08

VISWANATH *87 consecutive Tests and over 6,000 Test runs.*

Tests (1929–30 to 1946–47): 27 matches; 308 runs, average 13.39; 98 wickets, average 27.88

Bill Voce is always remembered as Larwood's partner in the "bodyline" series. He bowled fast left-arm and was a hard-hitting lower-order right-handed batsman. He formed a fine combination with Larwood at Nottinghamshire and won his first Test cap against the West Indies, 1929–30, taking 11 for 149, including his Test-best seven for 70, in his second match. He did not play against Australia until the 1932–33 when he played in four of the Tests and took 15 wickets. In the wake of the bodyline controversy, he did not play for England again until the final Test of the 1936 series against India. He went to Australia the following winter and was England's leading bowler with 26 wickets. He played once against New Zealand in 1937. He was recalled for the tour of Australia, 1946–47, but he had served in the army, was well beyond his best, not fully fit and overweight. He found in 1952 that he could no longer continue county cricket and became Nottinghamshire's coach.

W

Clyde Walcott

Born: January 17, 1926, New Orleans, St Michael, Barbados
Teams: Barbados (1941–42 to 1955–56); British Guiana (1954–55 to 1963–64)
First-class: 146 matches; 11,820 runs, average 56.55; 35 wickets, average 36.25; caught 174, stumped 33
Tests (1947–48 to 1959–60): 44 matches; 3,798 runs, average 56.68; 11 wickets, average 37.00; caught 53, stumped 11

In the years immediately after the Second World War, the West Indies were powered by three great batsmen: the Three Ws, Worrell, Weekes, and Walcott. In 1945–46, Walcott and Worrell added an unbroken 574 for Barbados's fourth wicket against Trinidad. It was just a sample of what was to come. Walcott was a giant of a man who could hit with

WALCOTT *Powerful and prolific.*

tremendous power and could play all the shots. He was also a capable wicket-keeper who kept to Ramadhin and Valentine, an excellent slip and a useful medium-pace bowler.

At Lord's, 1950, he scored 168 not out in the second Test and shared a record stand of 211 with Gomez for the sixth wicket. He also dominated the series against England, 1953–54, and against Australia, 1954–55. He made three centuries against England, the highest being 220 at Bridgetown, and against Australia he hit five centuries in the series, scoring a century in each innings of the second and fifth Tests, even though Australia took the rubber by three matches to nil. In all, he hit 15 Test centuries, and his highest score in first-class cricket was the 314 not out he scored during his record partnership with Worrell, 1945–46, when he was 20 years old.

He played in the Lancashire League in the 1950s, managed several West Indian sides after his retirement and was awarded the OBE for his services to the game. He coached and commentated and was President of the West Indian Board for some years. He became Chairman of the International Cricket Council and was knighted in 1994.

Courtney Walsh

Born: October 30, 1962, Kingston, Jamaica
Teams: Jamaica (1981–82 to 1996–97); Gloucestershire (1984–96)
First-class: 339 matches; 4,020 runs, average 12.40; 1,404 wickets, average 22.09
Tests (1984–85 to 1996–97): 82 matches; 712 runs, average 9.36; 309 wickets, average 25.04

A right-arm fast bowler with a high-action and economic style, Courtney Walsh has enhanced his talent as a bowler by remaining consistent and durable over a number of years, and he is now in reach of overtaking Malcolm Marshall as the West Indies' leading wicket-taker in Test cricket. Deeply respected as a player, he has become, in turn, captain of Jamaica, Gloucestershire and the West Indies. He toured England in 1984 without playing in a Test, but appeared in all five matches in Australia the following winter. With the West Indies having such a battery of fast bowlers at their disposal, it was hard for Walsh to maintain a regular place in the side, but he had an outstanding tour of India, 1987–88, with 26 wickets in four Tests. Initially, he rarely had use of the new ball, but he took wickets regularly.

When Richardson stood down in 1996, Walsh was appointed captain of the West Indies and has done much to draw together the various factions in the side. He did an equally fine job during his time as captain of Gloucestershire for three seasons.

Doug Walters

Born: December 21, 1945, Marshdale, Dungog, New South Wales, Australia
Teams: New South Wales (1962–63 to 1980–81)
First-class: 258 matches; 16,180 runs, average 43.84; 190 wickets, average 35.69
Tests (1965–77 to 1980–81): 74 matches; 5,357 runs, average 48.26; 49 wickets, average 29.08

Doug Walters was an attacking right-handed batsman who delighted with his stroke-play and his sense of adventure. He was also a successful medium-pace bowler. He triumphed in Australia, but crowds in England and South Africa never saw the best of him. He burst upon the scene with 155 on his debut against England at Brisbane,

WALSH *Fine fast bowler and captain.*

DOUG WALTERS *Exciting stroke-maker.*

1965–77, and made 115 in his second Test, at Melbourne. On leave from national service, 1967–68, he made 93, 62 not out, 94 and run out 5 against India. Released for the tour of England, 1968, he was not a success, and he was to make three more trips without doing himself justice. He tended to be impetuous and bowlers exploited this weakness by attacking his off-stump. Elsewhere he thrived.

Against the West Indies in Australia, 1968–69, he scored 118, 110, 50, 242 and 103 in successive Test innings to become the first to score four centuries in a rubber against the West Indies. At Christchurch, 1976–77, he made 250 against New Zealand, his highest Test score. In all, he made 15 Test hundreds.

Waqar Younis

Born: November 16, 1971, Vehari, Pakistan
Teams: Multan (1987–88 to 1990–91); United Bank (1988–89 to 1996–97); Surrey (1990–93); Glamorgan (1997)
First-class: 132 matches; 1,368 runs, average 12.78; 609 wickets, average 20.78
Tests (1989–90 to 1996–97): 41 matches; 403 runs, average 9.59; 216 wickets, average 21.07

In the opinion of many people, Waqar Younis is the best fast bowler to have appeared in Test cricket since the Second World War. He is able to move the ball late both ways at great pace and possesses a deadly yorker. In 1991, playing for Surrey on the unresponsive wickets at the Oval, he was the leading bowler in England with 113 wickets. His Test debut against India at Karachi, 1989–90, had seen him take four for 80, and by the time he had played 10 Tests he had 50 victims to his credit. With Wasim Akram, he formed a lethal partnership for Pakistan which is now accepted as one of the great fast-bowling duos of all time. Waqar took a record 29 wickets in a three-match series against New Zealand, 1990–91, and his 100th victim came in his 20th Test. He routed England with a record 22 wickets, 1992, and was devastating again in 1996. Records continue to tumble to him even though he missed many months with a back injury. There seems to be no reason why he should not continue to break records and to keep Pakistan at the top in world cricket.

WAQAR YOUNIS *Master of swing and reverse-swing at great pace.*

Johnny Wardle

Born: January 8, 1923, Ardsley, Yorkshire
Died: July 23, 1985, Hatfield, Doncaster, Yorkshire
Teams: Yorkshire (1946–58)
First-class: 412 matches; 7,333 runs, average 16.08; 1,846 wickets, average 18.97
Tests (1947–48 to 1957): 28 matches; 653 runs, average 19.78; 102 wickets, average 20.39

Johnny Wardle was the best left-arm wrist spinner of his generation, one in a long line of great Yorkshire slow left-arm bowlers. He had an infinite variety of deliveries in his armoury and was a wicket-taker on any surface. He was a hard-hitting later-order batsman and a keen fielder. He made his Test debut on the 1947–48 tour of the West Indies, but was poorly used by G.O. Allen, and his Test appearances were to remain intermittent for some seasons as he vied first with Jack Young and then with Tony Lock. He played in the first three Tests in 1953 when England regained the Ashes and captured 13 wickets, but he gave way to Lock for the last two Tests.

He was outstanding in South Africa, 1956–57, taking 23 wickets in four Tests, and he played in one Test against the West Indies the following summer, but that marked the end of his international career. He put his name to newspaper articles criticizing the Yorkshire captain and some of his colleagues. He was sacked by his county, and the MCC withdrew the invitation he had been sent to tour Australia in 1958–59. To the crowd he had seemed a jolly prankster; many of his team-mates saw a different character. It was a sad end to a fine career.

Shane Warne

Born: September 13, 1969, Ferntree Gully, Victoria, Australia
Teams: Victoria (1990–91 to 1996–97)
First-class: 85 matches; 1,321 runs, average 15.18; 371 wickets, average 24.70
Tests (1991–92 to 1996–97): 44 matches; 669 runs, average 13.65; 207 wickets, average 23.52

Blond, strong, broad-shouldered, Shane Warne emerged in the early 1990s as a leg-spin and googly bowler whom many would now consider the greatest the game has seen. He made his Test debut against India at Sydney in 1991–92, his second season in first-class cricket. He took one for 150. There were three expensive wickets against Sri Lanka the following season, and then, at Melbourne, 1992–93, he took seven for 52 in the West Indies' second innings to give Australia victory, and a star was born.

In 1993, at Old Trafford, he bowled his first ball in a Test in England to Mike Gatting. It pitched outside his leg stump and hit off-stump. He finished the

WARNE *Prodigious leg-breaks.*

series with 34 wickets, and the England batsmen, like batsmen all over the world, could make nothing of him. He was the only spinner in Test cricket who was a positive match-winner. By the end of 1996, he had dismissed Gooch, Atherton, Stewart and Thorpe, England's leading batsmen, *six* times each in 11 Tests. Against England, 1994–95, he captured 27 wickets, including a hat-trick at Melbourne. He was then briefly hampered by a shoulder injury and by an operation on a spinning finger, but he returned as accurate and lethal as ever.

Cyril Washbrook

Born: December 6, 1914, Barrow, Clitheroe, Lancashire
Teams: Lancashire (1953–59)
First-class: 592 matches; 34,101 runs, average 42.67; 7 wickets, average 44.14
Tests (1937–56): 37 matches; 2,569 runs, average 42.81; 1 wicket, average 33.00

A right-handed opening batsman and brilliant cover fielder, Washbrook captained Lancashire from 1954 to 1959, the first professional to hold that post. He was later president of the club he served so well as a player. His Test debut came against New Zealand in 1937, but it was not until 1946 that he played his second match. In the years immediately after the Second World War, he formed a successful opening partnership with Hutton, and they shared three consecutive century partnerships in Australia, 1946–47, when Washbrook hit the first of his six Test hundreds. His second came against Australia at Leeds in 1948, but it was on the tour of South Africa the following winter that he excelled. He made 195 at Johannesburg, and he and Hutton put on 359 for the first wicket.

It was believed that his Test career had ended with the tour of Australia, 1950–51, but he was a Test selector in 1956, and his fellow selectors persuaded him to return to play against Australia at Leeds at the age of 41. He scored 98, and England won by an innings.

Wasim Akram

Born: June 3, 1966, Lahore, Pakistan
Teams: PACO (1984–85); Lahore (1985–86); Lancashire (1988–1997)
First-class: 193 matches; 5,043 runs, average 21.45; 300 wickets, average 22.91
Tests (1984–85 to 1996–97): 70 matches; 1,652 runs, average 19.20; 300 wickets, average 22.91

Wasim Akram has developed into one of the great all-rounders of world cricket. A left-arm fast bowler with a capacity to swing the ball late either way, in 1996 at the Oval he became the second Pakistani bowler to take 300 wickets in Test cricket. Two months later, against Zimbabwe in Sheikhupura, he hit 257 not out batting at number eight, a Test record, and shared a record eighth-wicket stand of 313 with Saqlain Mushtaq in the match against Zimbabwe. Left-handed, he is a ferocious hitter of the ball, unwinding like a spring.

With Waqar Younis, Akram has formed one of the most feared fast-bowling partnerships cricket has known, and he is now firmly established as Pakistan captain, a position which was confirmed by his side's decisive victory over England in 1996.

He has proved to be a wonderful acquisition for Lancashire, particularly effective in the one-day game, helping them to four limited-over trophies.

Willie Watson

Born: March 7, 1920, Bolton-on Dearne, Yorkshire
Teams: Yorkshire (1939–57); Leicestershire (1958–64)
First-class: 468 matches; 25,670 runs, average 39.86; no wickets for 127 runs
Tests (1950 to 1958–59): 23 matches; 879 runs, average 25.85

Willie Watson was a graceful and patient left-hander who represented England at both soccer and cricket. He hit 1,000 runs in a season 14 times and, leaving his native county, went on to captain Leicestershire 1958–1961. Watson made two Test centuries, the first and more famous being against Australia at Lord's, 1953. He batted for 346 minutes in the second innings and scored 109. He and Bailey added 163 and saved the match. It was one of the classic rearguard actions in Test cricket. It was Watson's first Test against Australia.

Watson's second Test hundred came when he opened the innings with Hutton in Jamaica, 1953–54, and made 116.

He emigrated to South Africa and was coach of the Wanderers, Johannesburg.

Mark Waugh

Born: June 2, 1965, Canterbury, Sydney, New South Wales, Australia
Teams: New South Wales (1985–86 to 1996–97); Essex (1988–90 and 1992)
First-class: 235 matches; 18,065 runs, average 55.24: 170 wickets, average 38.45
Tests (1990–91 to 1996–97): 54 matches; 3,627 runs, average 44.23; 38 wickets, average 35.31

When English crowds first saw Mark Waugh play for Essex they wondered how this majestic, delightful, quick-scoring strokemaker had not claimed a place in the Australian side alongside his twin brother. He was at last rewarded with a Test cap against England at Adelaide, 1990–91, and made an outstanding 138. Since that time, he has been a regular member of the Australian side and ranks among the leading Test batsmen of the day. He can also bowl medium-pace and off-breaks and is a magnificent fielder. He and his twin brother Steve established a world-record fifth-wicket partnership for New South Wales against Western Australia, 1990–91, with an unbroen stand of 464. Mark Waugh made 229 not out, his highest score.

If he has a fault, it is that he frustrates his public, sometimes giving his wicket away in a careless or languid manner when it seems he could bat for ever. No batsman in world cricket displays such total command over any attack.

Steve Waugh

Born: June 2, 1965, Canterbury, Sydney, New South Wales, Australia
Teams: New South Wales (1984–85 to 1996–97); Somerset (1987–88)
First-class: 210 matches; 13,537 runs, average 51.27; 229 wickets, average 30.88
Tests (1985–86 to 1996–97): 81 matches; 5,002 runs, average 50.52; 77 wickets, average 35.19

Steve Waugh won a place in the Australian side five years ahead of his twin brother with whom, in 1990–91, he shared a stand of 464, the highest recorded in Australia. A lean, clean hitter of the ball, with great determination and concentration, he has proved himself a top-class all-rounder with his medium-pace bowling. He was most impressive in two seasons with Somerset and quickly learned to master English conditions.

His Test debut came against India, 1985–86, but it was not until his 27th Test that he first notched a century. He had made two 90s against the West Indies, 1988–89, but in England the following summer he scored 177 not out at Leeds and 152 not out at Lord's. He was the player of the series, but there were doubts as to his ability against the fastest bowling. Briefly, he lost his place in the Australian side, but then returned to dismiss any doubts as to his courage and technique. Subjected to a barrage of short-pitched bowling, he scored 200 against the West Indies in Jamaica, 1994–95, when Australia won a famous series. He was

STEVE WAUGH *Outstanding Test twin.*

appointed Australia's vice-captain for the tour of England, 1997.

Everton Weekes

Born: February 26, 1925, Westbury, St Michael, Barbados
Teams: Barbados (1944–45 to 1963–64)
First-class: 152 matches; 12,010 runs, average 55.34; 17 wickets, average 43.00
Tests (1947–48 to 1957–58): 48 matches; 4,455 runs, average 58.61; 1 wicket, average 77.00

Short and thick-set, Everton Weekes was a brilliant, attacking right-handed batsman, glorious to watch, and one of the legendary Three Ws – Worrell, Weeks and Walcott. The first of his 15 Test centuries came in his fourth match, against England at Kingston, Jamaica. This was followed by centuries in his next four Test innings, against India a year later. These included a century in each innings in Calcutta. He was close to hitting six hundreds in successive Test innings but was run out for 90 in Madras. He established a record in the final Test when he made 56 in the first innings, so becoming the only batsman to hit seven consecutive 50s in Test cricket. He enjoyed a fine tour of England, 1950, hitting a century in the Trent Bridge Test. He made 206 against England, 1953–54, and had made 207, his highest Test score, a year earlier.

Troubled by sinus problems, he left the Test scene earlier than expected. He continued to play league cricket, coached and commentated.

Like the other two Ws, he was knighted for his services to the game.

Bob Willis

Born: May 30, 1949, Sunderland, County Durham
Teams: Surrey (1969–71); Warwickshire (1972–84); Northern Transvaal (1972–73)
First-class: 308 matches; 2,690 runs, average 14.30; 899 wickets, average 24.99
Tests (1970–71 to 1984): 90 matches; 840 runs, average 11.50; 325 wickets, average 25.20

Tall, with an unorthodox open-chested action, Bob Willis made himself one of England's greatest fast bowlers, and only Ian Botham has taken more wickets for England. He first played for Surrey in 1969 and within 18 months was on his way to Australia as replacement for the injured Alan Ward. Surrey's reluctance to give him his county cap persuaded him to join Warwickshire, whom he captained from 1980 to 1984. In truth, he was never a great performer in county cricket, but in Tests no man has given more for his country nor with greater passion. At Headingley in 1981, he took eight for 43 in Australia's second innings to give England victory by 18 runs. He operated with amazing concentration, as if he were a man possessed. There was fire in his heart and in his eyes. The Test arena has rarely seen a better or more passionate display of fast bowling.

He captained England from 1982 to 1984 having been vice-captain on several tours. He has since acted as a commentator and as head of the National Sporting Club.

Bill Woodfull

Born: August 22, 1897, Maldon, Victoria, Australia
Died: August 11, 1965, Tweed Heads South, New South Wales, Australia
Teams: Victoria (1921–22 to 1933–34)
First-class: 174 matches; 13,388 runs, average 64.99; 1 wicket, average 24.00
Tests (1926–34): 35 matches; 2,300 runs, average 46.00

Bill Woodfull was a right-handed opening batsman with so solid and stout a defence that he was deemed "unbowlable". His Test career began on the tour of England in 1926, and he scored centuries in his third and fourth Tests. He was a surprising and somewhat controversial choice to lead Australia to England in 1930, but he hit 155 at Lord's and Australia won the series. He was equally successful as captain against both the West Indies and South Africa, but against Jardine's side in the "bodyline" series the outcome was very different.

The son of a clergyman, a teacher and a man of dignity and calm, Woodfull was highly respected by his players, but he was a traditionalist in a changing world. His reaction to Jardine's tactics in 1932–33 was to accuse England of not playing the game, and his attitude virtually assured Australia that they would not be opposed by Jardine and Larwood in 1934. Australia duly regained the Ashes when confronted by a toothless attack and an ill-led side.

A true assessment of Woodfull as a captain is difficult to make, for the achievements of Bradman intrude, but apart from 1932–33 he was successful, and his record as a batsman is impressive.

Frank Woolley

Born: May 27, 1887, Tonbridge, Kent
Died: October 18, 1978, Halifax, Nova Scotia, Canada
Teams: Kent (1906–38)
First-class: 978 matches; 58,959 runs, average 40.77; 2,066 wickets, average 19.87
Tests (1909–34): 64 matches; 3,283 runs, average 36.07; 83 wickets, average 33.91

"There was all summer in a stroke by Woolley, and he batted as is sometimes shown in dreams." So said Robertson-Glasgow, and none who saw the great left-handed all-rounder would disagree with him. He was an exquisite batsman, a slow left-arm bowler and a brilliant slip fielder whose 1,018 catches remain a world record. He scored his runs quickly and gracefully, and he ended his career with 132 centuries to his credit, five of them in Tests. His bowling was a feature of the first part of his career, and he completed the "double" eight times. In four of those seasons, he took 100 wickets and scored 2,000 runs. No other cricketer has achieved this feat on four occasions. He reached 1,000 runs in a season 28 times and, in 1928 went on to reach 3,352. The substance of his Test career came between 1912 and 1926, although he played last against Australia in 1934 at the age of 47.

Frank Worrell

Born: August 1, 1924, Bank Hall, Bridgetown, Barbados
Died: March 13, 1967, Mona, Kingston, Jamaica
Teams: Barbados (1941–42 to 1946–47); Jamaica (1947–48 to 1963–64)
First-class: 208 matches; 15,025 runs, average 54.24; 349 wickets, average 28.98
Tests (1947–48 to 1963): 51 matches; 3,860 runs, average 49.48; 69 wickets, average 38.72

After years of discussion and controversy, Frank Worrell was, in 1960–61, the first black man to be appointed captain of the West Indies for more than a single match. He began his career regarded primarily as a left-arm bowler of great pace and movement. He quickly climbed the batting order, for his elegant right-handed batting was stamped with class. He made his maiden century in his second season and scored 131 in his second Test, against England, 1947–48. From that point, he was linked with two other great batsmen, Weekes and Walcott, as a triumvirate, the Three Ws. He and Walcott had already shared an unbroken stand of 574 for Barbados against Trinidad, and Worrell had made 308 not out for Barbados against Trinidad, 1943–44, when he and John Goddard put on 502 for the fourth wicket. Worrell was 19 years old.

Before he became captain of the West Indies, he had led a Commonwealth side in India, and was admired as a man of character and dignity, all grace and charm on and off the field. When he was appointed captain of the West Indies in Australia, 1960–61, the pressure upon him was immense for the campaign on his behalf had been strong and involved issues outside cricket. His response to the situation was heroic, and the outcome romantic.

The first Test was tied and, although the West Indies eventually lost the series, Worrell and his side left Australia amid tumultuous acclaim. He led the West Indies in two more series and won them both. He had united the side which had once been a group of individuals from different islands vying for supremacy. At the end of the 1963 tour of England, mission accomplished, he retired.

He became a senator in the Jamaican parliament, was knighted and continued as a cricket administrator. Three years after being knighted, he died of leukaemia at the age of 42 and was honoured by a memorial service in Westminster Abbey, the first sportsman to be so recognized.

Doug Wright

Born: August 21, 1914, Sidcup, Kent
Teams: Kent (1932–57)
First-class: 497 matches; 5,903 runs, average 12.34; 2,056 wickets, average 23.98
Tests (1938 to 1950–51): 34 matches; 289 runs, average 11.11; 108 wickets, average 39.11

Doug Wright bowled leg-breaks and googlies at medium pace. He had a kangaroo-like approach to the wicket, and he was unique among bowlers. He first played for England against Australia in 1938 and took five wickets on his debut, but he was woefully erratic. The selectors kept faith with him over a number of years because he was capable of producing the unexpected that could turn a match. He took 100 wickets in a season 10 times, with 177 in 1947 as his best, but a greater measure of his ability to change the course of a game is the fact that he performed the hat-trick on no fewer than seven occasions.

A professional cricketer and a man of warmth and honesty, he captained Kent from 1954 to 1956, a difficult time in the county's history.

John Wright

Born: July 5, 1954, Darfield, Christchurch, New Zealand
Teams: Northern Districts (1975–76 to 1983–84); Derbyshire (1977–88); Canterbury (1984–85 to 1988–89); Auckland (1989–90 to 1992–93)
First-class: 366 matches; 25,073 runs, average 42.35; 2 wickets, average 169.50
Tests (1977–78 to 1992–93): 82 matches; 5,334 runs, average 37.82; no wickets for 5 runs

A man of the utmost courtesy and charm, John Wright was a left-handed opening batsman who became the first New Zealander to pass 4,000 runs in Test cricket. Only Richard Hadlee played in more Test matches for the Kiwis, and only Martin Crowe scored more runs. Wright had great powers of concentration and was an elegant strokemaker, exceptionally strong off the back foot, ever popular and always a delight to watch.

He gave Derbyshire outstanding service for 12 seasons, and was a mainstay of the New Zealand side during the finest period of that country's cricketing history. When, in 1987–88, Jeff Crowe lost form and confidence, Wright took over the captaincy of New Zealand, but only on the understanding that Crowe should return as soon as he wished. In all, Wright led New Zealand in 14 tests, but, in truth, he was captaining a great side that was already in decline.

Wright's Test record was exemplary in that he scored centuries against all six countries against whom he played and maintained a consistent average.

A graduate of Otago University, he was appointed the coach and manager of Kent in 1997.

Bob Wyatt

Born: May 2, 1901, Milford, Surrey
Died: April 20, 1995, Truro, Cornwall
Teams: Warwickshire (1923–39); Worcestershire (1946–51)
First-class: 739 matches; 39,405 runs, average 40.04; 901 wickets, average 32.84
Tests (1927–28 to 1936–37): 40 matches; 1,839 runs, average 31.70; 18 wickets, average 35.66

A consistent and determined batsman and useful medium-pace bowler, Bob Wyatt captained Warwickshire from 1930 to 1937 and Worcestershire from 1949 until 1951. He also captained England in 16 Tests, but he was never fortunate as England's captain nor was his selection as captain a popular one.

He had made his Test debut in South Africa, 1927–28, and made the first of his two Test centuries against the same opposition in 1929. The following year he captained England against Australia in controversial circumstances. Percy Chapman, a national hero, the England captain who had brought back and retained the Ashes, was dropped for the Oval Test and Wyatt appointed in his place. It was not a popular move.

Wyatt served under Chapman in South Africa and was vice-captain to Jardine in Australia, 1932–33. When Jardine stood down, Wyatt was named as captain against Australia in 1934 but was unable to play in the first Test because of injury. England were heavily beaten in the final Test and surrendered the Ashes.

He led England to the West Indies, 1934–35, where he made some rather bizarre decisions which turned the tour into something of a disaster. The West Indies won a series for the first time and Wyatt had his jaw broken in the final Test.

In spite of this, he captained England against South Africa in 1935. The South Africans won a Test and a series in England for the first time, and Wyatt's unfortunate career as England skipper was at an end. He played under Allen against India in 1936 and was a late call-up for the Australian tour that followed, but, in 1938, he announced that he was contracted to write for the *Daily Mail* and was not available for Test cricket.

Never at ease with authority, he resigned the captaincy of Warwickshire when he disagreed with the committee. He became a Test selector for several years and was 56 when he played his last game of cricket. He died less than two weeks from his 94th birthday.

Z

Zaheer Abbas

Born: July 24, 1947, Sialkot, India
Teams: Karachi (1965–66 to 1975–76); PWD (1968–69); PIA (1969–70 to 1986–87); Gloucestershire (1972–85); Sind (1975–76 to 1976–77); Dawood Club (1975–76)
First-class: 459 matches; 34,843 runs, average 51.54; 30 wickets, average 38.20
Tests (1969–70 to 1985–86): 78 matches; 5,062 runs, average 44.79; 3 wickets, average 44.00

The first Pakistani batsman to hit 100 centuries in a first-class career, Zaheer Abbas was a player of rare quality with an infinite capacity to entertain with his vast repertoire of beautiful strokes. Initially, he batted in glasses, later changing to contact lenses, but this never handicapped his batting nor his fine slip fielding. He made a spectacular entrance into Test cricket, scoring 274 at Edgbaston in 1971, his first Test in England and only his second in all. He made 240 at the Oval in 1974 and 235 not out against India at Lahore in 1978. His fourth double-century in a Test match was the most historic, in that he emulated Boycott by scoring his 100th hundred in a Test, 215 against India, again at Lahore. In that series, he became the first Pakistani batsman to score centuries in three successive innings, and he was also the first Pakistani batsman to score 5,000 Test runs. Zaheer set two career records: eight times he scored a century in each innings of a match and four times he made 200 and 100 in a match.

A modest, gentle man, he was immensely popular in his years with Gloucestershire when the county enjoyed a successful time, particularly in limited-overs cricket.

Zaheer captained Pakistan in 14 Tests, taking over from Imran in 1983–84, acting as a buffer between Javed and his critics before relinquishing the job to Javed in 1984–85. He stood down from the national side after the second Test against Sri Lanka in 1985, intimating that he had been forced to retire by certain senior players. It was a sad end to an outstanding career.

THE CATHEDRALS OF CRICKET

Whilst Lord's Cricket Ground in London is considered the world headquarters of cricket, Test Matches were played at both The Oval and Old Trafford before such games took place at Lord's. Over 70 venues have now staged Test matches.

It is impossible to say with any certainty which is the oldest ground still used for cricket, if only because early references give such descriptions as Richmond Green, Kennington Common, Dartford Heath, Moulsey Hurst, Penhurst Park, Kew Green, Hyde Park and Clapham Common, but there is no information as to where exactly in these parks, commons or greens the matches took place.

The oldest ground where we have definite knowledge of a match being played approximately where cricket is still played is the Artillery Ground on City Road, Finsbury, London. The match in question was London v Surrey played on August 30, 1730. The following year the first definite reference to a specific match on a current ground is Mitcham v Ewell on Mitcham Green on October 2, 1731.

The Sevenoaks Vine Ground is first mentioned in July 1740, when Sevenoaks opposed London, but it is most probable that the ground had been used some years earlier when Kent played Sussex in Sevenoaks. Extracts from the diary of Thomas Marchant, written between 1717 and 1727, indicate that cricket was played regularly in the Henfield and Hurstpierpoint areas of Sussex between the various villages, and references in documents to matches in Kent and Surrey would seem to imply that similar inter-village matches were being played in those counties. It would therefore come as no surprise if evidence emerged proving that a number of village greens in the south-east of England, on which cricket is still played, were used for cricket prior to 1730.

THE CLASSIC *Lord's Cricket Ground*

TOTAL 89 for 5 Wkts
*RC Russell 5
RA Smith 13
Last wicket 84
GA Gooch 37
b Walsh
Overs 37 Extras 4
IBA Allen
CA Walsh
WEST INDIES 419 all out
3 Overs Remaining
Cornhill Insurance
FLY CATHAY PACIFIC
KIER
Britannic Assurance
Timberland
TESCO
British Steel
Walter Lawrence
TEXACO
Red Stripe
Rabbit
Hutchison Telecom
TOYOTA
LEXUS

ENGLISH GROUNDS

LORD'S

Of the cricket grounds in the British Isles in use today for first-class cricket, Lord's ground is the oldest. The first match on the ground was MCC v Hertfordshire on June 22, 1814 and the first first-class match was MCC v St John's Wood on July 13 to 15 the same year.

The present site was the third ground laid out by Thomas Lord. The first, which is now Dorset Square, London, was opened in 1787. Lord had laid out the ground at the behest of the Cricket Club, which met at the Star and Garter in Pall Mall and had in recent years played its matches on White Conduit Fields, Islington. The ground was used until 1810, by which time Lord had already set out an alternative ground at Lisson Grove not far away. However, the building of the Regent's Canal meant that within a few years Lord had to seek a third site off St John's Wood Road, a few hundred yards north-east of the second ground.

The Cricket Club of the Star and Garter adopted the name Marylebone Cricket Club from the district of London in which Lord's was situated and in 1866 the club bought the freehold of the ground. At this time, the ground was used by the MCC and for such set-piece matches as had traditionally been staged there – Eton v Harrow, Oxford v Cambridge, Gentlemen v Players and North v South. In 1877, the MCC agreed to allow Middlesex County Cricket Club to use the ground for their home fixtures. Immediately prior to 1877, the Middlesex Club had been located at Prince's Ground in Chelsea, but this was shortly to disappear under bricks and mortar.

The first Test match to take place there was staged on the ground on July 21 to 23, 1884, England beating Australia by an innings and five runs.

TRENT BRIDGE

This ground, situated in the Nottingham suburb of West Bridgford, was laid out in 1838 by William Clarke. Clarke was the landlord of the Trent Bridge Inn, the ground being in the field at the rear of the Inn; he was also the captain and effective manager of the Nottinghamshire county team. The first first-class match was played on the ground in 1840 when Nottinghamshire opposed Sussex.

The county had previously played their matches on the Nottingham racecourse, but as this was owned by the town council, no entrance money could be charged to spectators, hence the move to the new ground. In the nineteenth century, the ground was also used at various times by both Nottingham Forest Football Club and Notts County FC. The latter did not leave until 1910 and two England soccer internationals were staged at the venue in the 1890s.

The first Test Match staged on the ground was on June 1 to 3, 1899 when England drew with Australia. Tests were played in Nottingham intermittently until 1939, and since the Second World War Test matches have been held on the ground in most seasons.

THE OVAL *The Pavilion at Kensington Oval in 1997.*

THE OVAL

William Baker, treasurer of the Montpelier Cricket Club, took a lease on 10 acres of ground, then used as a market garden and situated at the Oval, Kennington. He converted the land to a cricket ground and the first match was played on the new ground on May 13, 1845. In August of the same year, the Gentlemen of Surrey opposed the Players of Surrey on the ground, and after the match a meeting was arranged, at which it was proposed to form a Surrey County Cricket Club. The formation duly took place and the Surrey Club played the first first-class match at the Oval on May 25 and 26, 1846. The Surrey Club created an organization for South London similar to the Marylebone Club at Lord's.

The Oval was to become a centre of more than just cricket. The first Association Football match played on the ground was England v Scotland on November 19, 1870. Within two years, the Oval was recognized as the major football ground in London and in 1872 the Football Association Cup Final, between Royal Engineers and Wanderers, took place there. To soccer were added regular rugby union matches, with the University Rugby Union match being played at the Oval from 1873. England met Ireland in a rugby union match in 1875, but in 1891 it was decided that the scrummages were damaging the turf too much and rugby ceased to be played there. Soccer ceased to be staged on the ground as a regular event after 1895.

The first Test match to be played in England was at the Oval on September 6 to 8, 1880, when England beat Australia by five wickets. It is still a tradition that the final Test in a five- or six-match series in England takes place at the Oval.

FENNER'S, CAMBRIDGE

F.P. Fenner, the Cambridge Town Club all-rounder, took the lease of a field in Cambridge and opened a cricket ground on the land in

EDGBASTON *with the scoreboard overshadowed by the replay screen.*

1846. In 1848, having created what was described as perhaps the smoothest ground in England – being in fact too easy, causing too much run-getting – he sublet the ground to Cambridge University Cricket Club and the first first-class match was staged on the ground on May 18 and 19, 1848, the university playing the MCC. It has remained the university ground ever since, the university buying the freehold in 1894. Prior to 1848, the university played on Parker's Piece, the first notable match there being against the town club in 1871. A cinder running track was laid out round Fenner's cricket area in the mid-1860s and was used by the University Athletics Club – athletics were staged there until the 1950s.

ST LAWRENCE GROUND, CANTERBURY

The headquarters of Kent County Cricket Club, the St Lawrence ground, was officially opened on May 16, 1847. Immediately prior to 1847, Kent had played on the Beverley Cricket Club ground in Canterbury, but for six years from 1835 the centre of the county club had been at West Malling. The Kent County Cricket Club, on its reformation in 1870, announced that the St Lawrence ground would in future be the official county ground. The club purchased the freehold of the ground in 1896. In 1876, W.G. Grace scored 344 for MCC v Kent at Canterbury, this being the highest individual first-class score at the time, and it remains the ground record. By coincidence, the bowling record for the ground is held by W.G.'s brother, E.M. Grace, who took 10 for 69 for the MCC in 1862.

More than anything else the ground was famous for the Canterbury Festival, which for many years involved an MCC-selected England team opposing Kent, followed by two more fixtures; apart from cricket, theatrical performances were an integral part of the festival.

Kent by no means confined their matches to Canterbury, though, and since the Second World War have staged matches on the following other grounds: Rectory Field, Blackheath; Hesketh Park, Dartford; Crabble ground, Dover; Cheriton Road, Folkestone; Garrison ground, Gillingham; Bat and Ball ground, Gravesend; Mote Park, Maidstone; Lloyds Bank ground, Beckenham; and the Nevill ground, Tunbridge Wells. In recent years, of these only Maidstone and Tunbridge Wells have still found favour.

OLD TRAFFORD, MANCHESTER

The ground was formed in 1857 as the home of Manchester Cricket Club; when the present Lancashire Club was formed in 1864, the county made Old Trafford its home. Until recent years the official name of the major club was the Lancashire County and Manchester CC.

The first major inter-county game on the Old Trafford ground was staged on July 20 to 22, 1865, when Lancashire played Middlesex. Old Trafford became the second ground in England to hold a Test match, when England played Australia in the first of a series of three Tests in 1884. The ground began to build its reputation for rain interruptions immediately – the first day of the first Test was completely washed out.

As the name implies, the ground was at one time owned by the de Trafford family, but was acquired by the Manchester Club in 1898.

It was the one major English cricket ground to be badly affected by bombing in the Second World War, but repairs were quickly undertaken when the war ended and it was possible to play one of the Victory Tests there in August 1945. Appropriately, the new press box, opened in 1987, was named after Neville Cardus, whose reputation had been made through the columns of the *Manchester Guardian*.

EDGBASTON, BIRMINGHAM

The present Warwickshire County Cricket Club was founded in 1882 and it soon became apparent that the club would not flourish until it established a good ground in the Birmingham area. William Ansell, the honorary secretary of the county club, was the driving force behind the search for and the acquisition of a suitable site in Edgbaston. The Warwickshire Cricket Ground Co. Ltd was founded in 1885 to raise the necessary capital, and the ground staged its first match on June 7, 1886, Warwickshire opposing the MCC. The first first-class game came late on in the same season when the Australian touring team played an England XI.

Warwickshire were promoted to first-class status in 1894 and the ground has been the headquarters of the County Championship playing side since it commenced in the competition in 1895.

The first Test match to be played at Edgbaston was on May 29 to 31, 1902, England opposing Australia in a remarkable match which saw the touring side all out for 36, their lowest total ever – this in reply to England's 376 for 9 declared. Rain on the last day prevented an England victory. The next Test was in 1909 – again Australia failed badly, being all out for 74. Edgbaston, however, was rarely used for international matches after that until 1957 when the West Indies played England. Since that date, it has been one of the six Test grounds in regular use.

HEADINGLEY, LEEDS

In 1887, a group of sports enthusiasts set up the Leeds Cricket, Football and Athletic Co. Ltd, chaired by Lord Hawke, in order to buy land in the Leeds area for use as a sports field. A 22-acre site was purchased and divided into portions for a variety of sports. The cricket area was officially opened on May 27, 1890 when the local Leeds Cricket Club used the grounds; the first first-class match was in September 1890, a North-of-England side playing the Australians. In 1891, Yorkshire County Cricket Club played its first first-class game at Headingley and the first Test was on June 29 and 30, 1899, England opposing Australia.

At that time, the headquarters of Yorkshire County Cricket Club were in Sheffield. In fact Sheffield had always been considered the centre of Yorkshire cricket – two grounds had been laid out, one following the other in Darnall, then another appeared in Hyde Park. It was on Sheffield Hyde Park ground that Yorkshire opposed Norfolk in 1833. In the 1840s, the Hyde Park ground became run down and M.J. Ellison, a keen supporter of Sheffield cricket, organized a meeting to discuss the foundation of a new ground. This materialized in April 1855 as Bramall Lane Cricket Ground. Some eight years later Ellison was instrumental in founding Yorkshire County Cricket Club and naturally Sheffield and Bramall Lane were the headquarters of the new club. In 1862, the first soccer match was played at Bramall Lane, which led to the foundation of Sheffield United, and the ground was shared by the cricket and football clubs. The first first-class match at Bramall Lane was Yorkshire v Sussex in August 1855. The first, and only, Test match was played on July 3 to 5, 1902 when England played Australia. Bramall Lane continued to stage county matches with success through to 1939, but after the Second World War the football club became more and more dominant and the last county match was Yorkshire v Lancashire, August 4 to 7, 1973.

Headingley, like Bramall Lane, has suffered because of its football connections, but its Test-match status has been maintained to the present day. However, Yorkshire County Cricket Club, at the time of writing, have passed a resolution deciding to leave Headingley and in its place build a completely new stadium on the outskirts of Wakefield.

Yorkshire have had, and indeed do have, a number of other famous grounds. Scarborough has been staging an important cricket festival for more than 100 years at its North Marine Road ground. The first first-class match was on September 7 to 9, 1874: Yorkshire v Middlesex. For many years, the September Festival comprised a Gentlemen v Players match and a match involving the current touring side.

Another major cricketing centre is Bradford. The Park Avenue ground was opened in July 1880. The football club which shared the venue fell on hard times in the 1950s and left the Football League, as a result of which the accommodation became increasingly dilapidated. In 1980, the grandstand had to be demolished and in 1985 the pavilion followed suit. Friends of Park Avenue formed an association to restore the ground and first-class cricket returned in 1992 after a gap of some years. Other grounds which were used by Yorkshire for first-class cricket in 1996 were Acklam Park, Middlesbrough (first used in 1956), Abbeydale Park, Sheffield (first used in 1946, by Derbyshire) and St George's Road, Harrogate (first used in 1882).

COUNTY GROUND, HOVE

The cricket ground in Eaton Road, Hove has been the headquarters of Sussex County Cricket Club since 1872. The first match by Sussex on the ground was, appropriately, against Kent, the home county's oldest rivals, commencing June 6, 1872.

Sussex have been as unfortunate as Thomas Lord in their battle with building development. Their original ground had been set out at the behest of the Prince of Wales in the 1790s, when he made Brighton a fashionable resort. This ground was taken over in the 1820s by a Brighton businessman, James Ireland, and he was responsible for organizing what is now considered the first match to decide the Champion County of England, in 1825 against Kent. The Prince's ground then became known as Ireland's Gardens. The builders took over the site in the 1840s and it is now Park Crescent, Brighton. Sussex then moved to a new

BATTING

NOTABLE BATTING RECORDS ON SOME CURRENT ENGLISH FIRST-CLASS GROUNDS

Ground	Score	Record
Edgbaston	**501***	B.C. Lara, Warwickshire v Durham, 1994
Taunton	**424**	A.C. MacLaren, Lancashire v Somerset, 1895
The Oval	**366**	N.H. Fairbrother, Lancashire v Surrey, 1990
Trent Bridge	**345**	C.G. MacCartney, Australians v Nottinghamshire, 1921
Canterbury	**344**	W.G. Grace, MCC v Kent, 1876
Chesterfield	**343***	P.A. Perrin, Essex v Derbyshire, 1904
Headingley	**334**	D.G. Bradman, Australia v England, 1930
Hove	**333**	K.S. Duleepsinjhi, Sussex v Northamptonshire, 1930
Lord's	**333**	G.A. Gooch, England v India, 1990
Worcester	**331***	J.D.B. Robertson, Middlesex v Worcestershire, 1949
Cheltenham College	**318***	W.G. Grace, Gloucestershire v Yorkshire, 1876
Gloucester	**317**	W.R. Hammond, Gloucestershire v Nottinghamshire, 1936
Scarborough	**317**	K.R. Rutherford, New Zealand v D.B. Close's XI, 1986
Cardiff	**313***	S.J. Cook, Somerset v Glamorgan, 1990
Old Trafford	**312**	J.E.R. Gallian, Lancashire v Derbyshire, 1996
Eastbourne	**310**	H. Gimblett, Somerset v Sussex, 1948
Fenner's	**304***	E. de C. Weekes, West Indies v Cambridge University, 1950
Bristol	**302***	W.R. Hammond, Gloucestershire v Glamorgan, 1934

BOWLING

NOTABLE BOWLING RECORDS ON SOME CURRENT ENGLISH FIRST-CLASS GROUNDS

Ground	Figures	Record
Headingley	**10–10**	H. Verity, Yorkshire v Nottinghamshire, 1932
The Oval	**10–28**	W.P. Howell, Australians v Surrey, 1899
Lord's	**10–38**	S.E. Butler, Oxford University v Cambridge University, 1871
Bristol	**10–40**	E.G. Dennett, Gloucestershire v Essex, 1906
Taunton	**10–42**	A.E. Trott, Middlesex v Somerset, 1900
Edgbaston	**10–51**	H. Howell, Warwickshire v Yorkshire, 1923
Worcester	**10–51**	J. Mercer, Glamorgan v Worcestershire, 1936
Old Trafford	**10–53**	J.C. Laker, England v Australia, 1956
Cheltenham College	**10–66**	A.A. Mailey, Australians v Gloucestershire, 1921
Chesterfield	**10–66**	J.K. Graveney, Gloucestershire v Derbyshire, 1949
Fenner's	**10–69**	S.M.J. Woods, Cambridge University v C.I. Thornton's XI, 1890
Canterbury	**10–129**	Jas. Lillywhite, South v North, 1872
Trent Bridge	**9–19**	J. Grundy, Nottinghamshire v Kent, 1864
Scarborough	**9–28**	J.M. Preston, Yorkshire v MCC, 1888
Hove	**9–35**	J.E.B.B.P.Q.C. Dwyer, Sussex v Derbyshire, 1906
Gloucester	**9–44**	C.W.L. Parker, Gloucestershire v Essex, 1925
Cardiff	**9–57**	P.I. Pocock, Surrey v Glamorgan, 1979
Eastbourne	**9–62**	A.G. Nicholson, Yorkshire v Sussex, 1967

ground in Hove, close to the sea front and known as the Brunswick ground. This opened in 1848, but in 1871 the builders took over and the site of this ground is Third and Fourth Avenues, Hove. The county's next move was to their present ground, but to further complicate the story another ground was in operation between 1834 and 1844 which was generally known as Lillywhite's ground and situated where Montpelier Crescent now stands.

Sussex have also played on various other grounds in the county, but by 1996 only two of the old established county venues remained in use for first-class cricket: Horsham (the current ground there has been used by the county since 1908) and Eastbourne (The Saffrons, which Sussex have used since 1897). In addition, the county has been playing matches at Arundel Castle since 1975, when a Sunday League game was staged there. More recently, championship games have come to Arundel.

COUNTY GROUND, BRISTOL

Gloucestershire County Cricket Club have used the ground at Ashley Down since 1899. It has, however, had a somewhat chequered history – in 1916 the county club had to sell the ground to Fry's, the chocolate manufacturers, in order to pay off the club's debts. The club regained ownership of the ground in 1932.

In its earliest days, the county club played many of its matches on two school grounds. The one at Clifton College was used from 1871 to 1932, whilst the one at Cheltenham College, which came into county use the year after Clifton College, has long been established as a ground for an annual cricket festival. In 1882, the County staged its first match on the Spa ground at Gloucester, but this has not been used for county matches since 1923. After that year, the majority of county matches played in the city have been at what is still known, though incorrectly, as the Wagon Works ground.

AUSTRALIAN GROUNDS

MCG, VICTORIA

The first home inter-colonial match played by Victoria was staged at Emerald Hill on the south side of the Yarra River on March 29 and 30, 1852, in the district now known as South Melbourne, and Victoria's opponents were Tasmania. Within a few years of this game, the ground had disappeared, with a railway line through its centre.

SYDNEY CRICKET GROUND *under lights during the 1992 World Cup.*

When Victoria faced New South Wales for the first time at home on March 26 and 27, 1856, the match was staged on what is still Melbourne Cricket Ground. It was on March 15, 1877 that what is now considered to be the first Test match was commenced. The English touring team, under James Lillywhite, opposed Australia. Australia won this historic first match by 45 runs and a return match was immediately arranged on the same ground; this time England won by four wickets. Some spectators accused the England team of deliberately losing the initial match in order to raise the odds on England winning the second so that, with betting a major feature of cricket, the England players could make a killing!

SCG, NSW

The first first-class match to be played in Sydney took place on January 14 and 15, 1857, when New South Wales played Victoria. This game was played on the Domain, the ground having been used for the first time in the previous month. In 1870–71, the New South Wales v Victoria fixture was moved to the much better ground of the Albert Club. Here spectators had to pay, whereas previously the inter-colonial matches in Sydney could be viewed free of charge.

However, in the 1870s, the New South Wales Cricket Association wished to find a new ground and, after various discussions and some objections from the Albert Cricket Ground Company, took over the Garrison ground in Sydney, whose name was then changed to the Association ground. The first first-class match on the Association ground was New South Wales v Victoria on February 22 to 25, 1878. The Albert ground itself was sold off as a building site. The Association ground, now known as Sydney Cricket Ground, is still the major ground in New South Wales. The first Test match to be staged there took place on February 17 to 21, 1882, when Australia beat England by five wickets.

ADELAIDE OVAL, SOUTH AUSTRALIA

The Adelaide Oval has been the principal cricket ground in South Australia since the introduction of first-class cricket to the colony. In 1871, the South Australian Cricket Club had set about finding suitable land to create a ground for inter-colonial matches and a South Australian Cricket Association was set up to pursue that aim. Land was found in North Park, Adelaide, and the first game was played there on November 11, 1872. It was between British-born and Colonial-born. The first first-class match was against Tasmania in November 1877 – the first time that South Australia opposed another colony on even terms. It was not until 1881 that Victoria played South Australia even-handed at Adelaide and the first Test match on the ground commenced on December 12, 1884, when England beat Australia by eight wickets.

GABBA, QUEENSLAND

Queensland was created as a separate colony in 1859 and played its first first-class match on April 1 to 4, 1893 when the home team defeated New South Wales by 14 runs. The match was played on the Exhibition ground in Brisbane which was situated in Bowen Hills. The ground had first been used for a match when the 1887–88 English team had visited Brisbane.

However, in 1896 a new ground was opened at Woolloongabba (more commonly known as Gabba). The first first-class match was played there on February 19 to 22,

1898, when A.E. Stoddart's team opposed a combined Queensland and Victoria XI. Queensland played its first Shield match there against South Australia in 1898–99 and the Gabba, as it is familiarly called, remains the principal cricket venue in Queensland. The first Test match in the state was not staged at the Gabba, but on the Exhibition ground on November 30 to December 5, 1928, when England beat Australia by 675 runs. The first Test at the Gabba was Australia v South Africa, commencing November 27, 1931, and every subsequent Brisbane Test has been played on that ground.

WACA, WEST AUSTRALIA

The Western Australian Cricket Association was formed by the leading clubs of Perth specifically to create a good-quality ground within the city. A suitable site was secured in East Perth in 1899, but it took several years to form a practical cricketing surface and the first match on the ground did not take place until the 1893–94 season. The first first-class match was on April 3 to 6, 1899, when South Australia beat Western Australia by four wickets.

In addition to cricket, football was played on the ground and a cycle track was laid round the perimeter.

Western Australia did not join the Sheffield Shield until 1947–48. It was not until December 1970 that the first Test match was played in Perth, Australia opposing England.

TASMANIAN GROUNDS

The two major cricket centres on the island are at Hobart and Launceston. The first first-class match in Australia was staged at Launceston on February 11 and 12, 1851, Tasmania playing Victoria – the game was billed at the time as XI of Port Philip against XI of Van Diemen's Land. The cricket ground used was part of the local racecourse at the time and the Northern Tasmanian Cricket Association, on its formation, took over the ground in 1886–87 – adjacent to the ground cycling, tennis and bowling also took place. A limited-overs international was staged at Launceston in 1985–86 but, since the Second World War, the ground has generally taken second place to the one at Hobart.

The first first-class match in Hobart was played on March 4 and 5, 1858: Tasmania v Victoria. The match was staged on the Lower Domain ground which was taken over by the Southern Tasmanian Cricket Association in 1869. However, because of the building of a railway, cricket ended on the ground in 1873 and the STCA opened a new ground in 1881–82. The first first-class game on the new ground was on January 8 and 9, 1890, Tasmania v Victoria. This ground is usually referred to as the Upper Domain ground or TCA ground.

A limited-overs international match was played on the ground in 1984–85, but the State Government were trying to bring Test cricket to Tasmania and decided that the best prospective venue was the Bellerive Oval. Cricket had been played in Bellerive Park from the 1880s, but the cricket area did not become enclosed until 1947. Major redevelopment of the ground began in 1985 and the first first-class game took place from January 23 to 25, 1987, Tasmania playing the West Indies. Continued improvements to the ground led to the first Test match at Bellerive and in Tasmania in December 1989, when Australia opposed Sri Lanka.

BELLERIVE GROUND *in Tasmania.*

WACA *the home of Western Australia.*

BATTING

NOTABLE BATTING FEATS ON AUSTRALIA'S MAJOR GROUNDS

Ground	Score	Details
Sydney	**452***	D.G. Bradman, NSW v Queensland, 1929–30
Melbourne	**437**	W.H. Ponsford, Victoria v Queensland, 1927–28
Brisbane	**383**	C.W. Gregory, NSW v Queensland, 1906–07
Adelaide	**369**	D.G. Bradman, S Australia v Tasmania, 1935–36
Perth	**356**	B.A. Richards, S Australia v W Australia, 1970–71
Hobart	**305***	F.E. Woolley, MCC v Tasmania, 1911–12

* not out

BOWLING

NOTABLE BOWLING FEATS ON AUSTRALIA'S MAJOR GROUNDS

Ground	Figures	Details
Perth	**10–44**	I.J. Brayshaw, W Australia v Victoria, 1967–68
Melbourne	**10–61**	P.J. Allan, Queensland v Victoria, 1965–66
Sydney	**10–66**	G.Giffen, Australia v The Rest, 1883–84
Launceston	**9–2**	G. Elliott, Victoria v Tasmania, 1857–58
Adelaide	**9–41**	W.J. OReilly, NSW v South Australia, 1937–38
Brisbane	**9–45**	G.E. Tribe, Queensland v Victoria, 1945–46

SOUTH AFRICAN GROUNDS

The first Test matches played in South Africa both occurred in March 1889, the first being on St George's Park, Port Elizabeth, and the second on the Newlands ground, Cape Town. These two matches are also considered to be the first two first-class matches played in South Africa. Both of the grounds used are still venues for Test and first-class cricket.

Port Elizabeth Cricket Club has played at St George's Park from its earliest days and in 1876 the first major South African cricket competition – the Champion Bat Tournament – was staged in St George's Park, between Kingwilliamstown, Grahamstown, Capetown and Port Elizabeth. Eastern Province, whose base is Port Elizabeth, played in the Currie Cup for the first time in 1893–94, but the first Currie Cup game at St George's Park was not until 1902–03.

The Newlands ground is the base for Western Province. WPCC was formed in 1864 and originally played on Southey's Field, now part of Plumstead, due to city expansion. They moved to Newlands in 1888, the first match being Mother Country v Colonial-Born on January 2, 1888.

Western Province entered the Currie Cup in 1892–93 and the first Currie Cup games were played at Newlands in 1893–94, when Western Province, who had won the trophy in 1892–93, retained the title.

NEWLANDS GROUND *in Cape Town, South Africa,under floodlights.*

Johannesburg was the third South African city to stage a Test match, commencing on March 2, 1896 – with South Africa playing England on what is now termed the Old Wanderers ground. The Old Wanderers ground was required for an expansion of the railway and in 1948–49 Test cricket was transferred to the rugby stadium at Ellis Park, Johannesburg. In 1956–57, the present Wanderers Stadium at Kent Park, Johannesburg, saw its first Test match, South Africa playing England. The ground is also the headquarters of the Transvaal side.

The first first-class match staged in Durban took place in April 1885, when Transvaal played Western Province on the Oval, Albert Park. The second first-class match in the city was on the Lord's ground in March 1898, and on this ground Durban saw its first Test in January 1910 when South Africa played England. The Lord's ground is now long gone and since 1923 Test matches in Durban have been played on the Kingsmead ground.

In 1995–96, South Africa played for the first time at Centurion, formerly Verwoerdburg. Centurion Park is the headquarters of Northern Transvaal Cricket Union.

BATTING

NOTABLE BATTING FEATS ON SOUTH AFRICA'S MAJOR GROUNDS

Johannesburg

337* D.J. Cullinan, Transvaal v N Transvaal, 1993–94

306* E.A.B. Rowan, Transvaal v Natal, 1939–40

304* A.W. Nourse, Natal v Transvaal, 1919–20

(No 300s scored on South Africa's other Test grounds)

BOWLING

NOTABLE BOWLING FEATS ON SOUTH AFRICA'S MAJOR GROUNDS

Johannesburg

10–26 A.E.E. Vogler, E Province v Griqualand West, 1906–07

Cape Town

10–59 S.T. Jefferies, W Province v OFS, 1987–88

WEST INDIAN GROUNDS

The first first-class match in the West Indies was played on the Garrison Savannah ground in Bridgetown, Barbados, on February 15 and 16, 1865, when the island opposed Demerara. It was not until 1883–84 that a second first-class match took place in

SABINA PARK *in Kingston, Jamaica.*

Barbados, and this time the venue was the Wanderers CC ground at Bay Pasture, Bridgetown. The Pickwick CC ground at Kensington Oval saw first-class cricket in 1894–95, when R.S. Lucas's Team visited Barbados. It is appropriate that the first Test in the West Indies should have taken place in Barbados on the Kensington Oval ground against England in January 1930. Test matches and first-class cricket have been staged regularly on the ground since then.

Georgetown, Guyana, saw its first first-class game on the Eve Leary Parade ground in 1865–66. The present ground, Bourda, was first used for first-class matches in September 1887–88 and the first Test played there was in February 1930, West Indies v England. This remains the principal ground in what was British Guiana, now Guyana.

The Queen's Park Oval in Port of Spain is the major Trinidad ground, whilst Sabina Park is the main venue in Kingston, Jamaica. Both these grounds were first used for Test cricket during the 1929–30 series against England.

The fifth ground in the West Indies to hold a Test match was the Recreation Ground in St John's, Antigua.

NOTABLE BATTING FEATS ON MAJOR WEST INDIES GROUNDS

BATTING

St John's
375 B.C. Lara, West Indies v England, 1993–94

Kingston
365* G.St A. Sobers, West Indies v Pakistan, 1957–58

Bridgetown
337 Hanif Mohammad, Pakistan v West Indies, 1957–58
308* F.M.M. Worrell, Barbados v Trinidad, 1943–44

Port of Spain
324 J. B. Stollmeyer, Trinidad v British Guiana, 1946–47

* not out

NOTABLE BOWLING FEATS ON MAJOR WEST INDIES GROUNDS

BOWLING

Port of Spain
10–36 D.C.S. Hinds, A.B. St Hills XI v Trinidad, 1900–01

Kingston
10–175 E.E. Hemmings, International XI v West Indies, 1982–83

NEW ZEALAND GROUNDS

New Zealand first-class cricket commenced in Dunedin on January 27, 1864, when Otago played Canterbury. The venue was the South Dunedin recreation ground. In 1879–80, the Caledonian ground in Dunedin was used by Otago, but in 1883–84 the Province played on the Carisbrook ground. It was not, however, until March 1955 that a Test match was played at Carisbrook, when New Zealand played England. This ground remains the main venue in Otago.

The ground at Hagley Park, Christchurch, has staged first-class matches, commencing February 1865, but the present main Christchurch ground for Test and for Canterbury first-class games is Lancaster Park. The reason for the switch from Hagley Park to Lancaster Park was that no admission charges could be levied at the former ground. Lancaster Park saw its first first-class match in 1882–83 and its first Test in 1929–30, when New Zealand played England.

The first first-class match at Wellington was Wellington v Auckland on November 28 and 29, 1873. The principal ground is the Basin Reserve which has staged Test matches since January 1930.

The Domain was the major ground in Auckland from 1853, but in the season 1912–13 Eden Park superseded the Domain as the principal first-class venue. The first Test at Eden Park was in February 1930. The ground is used for both cricket and rugby.

McLean Park, Napier, where Central Districts play some of their first-class matches, staged its first Test in February 1979, when New Zealand played Pakistan.

NOTABLE BATTING FEATS ON MAJOR NEW ZEALAND GROUNDS

BATTING

Christchurch
385 B. Sutcliffe, Otago v Canterbury, 1952–53

Dunedin
355 B. Sutcliffe, Otago v Auckland, 1949–50

Auckland
336* W. R. Hammond, England v New Zealand, 193233

* not out

NOTABLE BOWLING FEATS ON MAJOR NEW ZEALAND GROUNDS

BOWLING

Christchurch
10–28 A.E. Moss, Canterbury v Wellington, 1889–90

Auckland
9–36 A.F. Wensley, Auckland v Otago, 1929–30

Wellington
9–43 T. Eden, Nelson v Wellington, 1875–76

Napier
9–47 T.H. Dent, Hawkes Bay v Wellington, 1900–01

Dunedin
9–50 A.H. Fisher, Otago v Queensland, 1896–97

BASIN RESERVE *in Wellington, New Zealand.*

INDIAN GROUNDS

Something in the region of 300 separate grounds have staged first-class cricket in India, but in a number of towns and cities it is not totally clear which ground was used, mainly because the names of grounds have changed in many cases.

This brief piece on Indian grounds is therefore confined to the major Test match grounds – there have been 19 Test venues so far. The oldest and senior ground for Test cricket is Eden Gardens, Calcutta, where India played England in 1933–34. The Gymkhana ground in Bombay and the Chepauk ground in Madras were also used for Test matches that same season. When the West Indies toured India in 1948–49, the Feroz Shah Kotla ground in Delhi and the Brabourne Stadium in Bombay hosted Tests for the first time. Neither of the two Bombay grounds mentioned is now used for Tests, the current ground being the Wankhede Stadium, first used in 1974–75. The two grounds not so far mentioned which have seen most Test cricket are Green Park, Kanpur (first match played 1951–52) and Karnataka CA ground, Bangalore (first match 1974–75).

NOTABLE BATTING FEATS ON INDIAN GROUNDS

BATTING

Poona (Pune)
443* B.B. Nimbalkar, Maharashtra v Kathiawar, 1948–49

Bombay
377 S.V. Manjrekar, Bombay v Hyderabad, 1990–91

Secunderabad
366 M.V. Sridhar, Hyderabad v Andhra, 1993–94

* not out

NOTABLE BOWLING FEATS ON INDIAN GROUNDS

BOWLING

Jorhat
10–20 P.M. Chatterjee, Bengal v Assam, 1956–57

Bombay
10–78 S.P. Gupte, President's XI v Combined XI, 1954–55

Jodhpur
10–78 P. Sunderam, Rajasthan v Vidarbha, 1985–86

PAKISTANI GROUNDS

The first home Test match by Pakistan was played at the Dacca Stadium in 1954–55 – but Dacca is now in Bangladesh. Four other venues were used in the same season for Tests: Dring Stadium, Bahawalpur; Lawrence Gardens, Lahore; Services ground, Peshawar; and National Stadium, Karachi. Only the last has remained a regular Test venue. Lawrence Gardens in Lahore was superseded by the Gaddafi Stadium. The other venue that has regularly seen Test cricket is the Iqbal Stadium, Faisalabad.

Since 1980, other cities which have hosted Tests are Rawalpindi, Gujranwala, Sialkot and Multan. The Services Ground at Peshawar has been superseded by the Arbab Niaz Stadium. The Defence Stadium at Karachi was used in 1993.

NOTABLE BATTING FEATS ON PAKISTANI GROUNDS

BATTING

Karachi
499 Hanif Mohammad, Karachi v Bahawalpur, 1958–59

Karachi
428 Aftab Baloch, Sind v Baluchistan, 1973–74

Lahore
350 Rashid Israr, Habib Bank v National Bank, 1976–77

NOTABLE BOWLING FEATS ON PAKISTANI GROUNDS

BOWLING

Peshawar
10–28 Naeem Akhtar, Rawalpindi B v Peshawar, 1995–96

Karachi
10–58 Shahid Mahmood, Karachi Whites v Khairpur, 1969–70

Faisalabad
10–92 Imran Adil, Bahawalpur v Faisalabad, 1989–90

SRI LANKAN GROUNDS

Since Sri Lanka was raised to Test-match status in 1981–82, four different grounds in Colombo have been used for Test matches, namely Saravanamuttu Stadium, Sinhalese Sports CC, Colombo CC and Premadasa Stadium. Tests have also been played at Kandy and at Moratuwa.

The highest innings in Sri Lanka is 285 by F.M.M. Worrell for Commonwealth XI v Ceylon in 1950–51 and the best bowling feat is 10–41 by G.P. Wickramasinghe for Sinhalese SC in 1991–92.

ZIMBABWEAN GROUNDS

Three grounds have been used for Test matches in Zimbabwe: Harare Sports Club in Harare and two in Bulawayo, namely Bulawayo Athletic Club and the Queen's Sports Club. The highest score in Zimbabwe is 266 by D.L. Houghton in 1994–95 and the best bowling feat is 9–71 by M.J. Procter in 1972–73.

CHEPAUK GROUND *in Madras, India.*

ADMINISTRATION & BUSINESS

The administration of cricket is founded on tradition. The Cricket Club at the Star and Garter Tavern in London set out the Laws of the game, and the MCC has continued to revise and update them. Regulations concerning the qualification of players and teams for Test and first-class cricket have not been so adroitly handled. Much of the history of administration has been about trying to shut the door after the horse has bolted.

After several years of consultation and one false dawn, the controllers of English cricket created a new governing body, the England and Wales Cricket Board, which was officially established on January 1, 1997 and succeeded the Cricket Council, nominally the ruling body since 1969. The new board's objective is closer co-operation between the first-class professional game and the amateur game, and to this end each first-class county has a cricket board which includes representatives of the county club and the County Cricket Association.

TIM LAMB *Chief Executive of the EWCB.*

The England and Wales Cricket Board is run directly by a management board of 14 plus a non-voting chief executive. Its first chief executive is T.M. Lamb, former Middlesex and Northamptonshire bowler and, until his appointment, Cricket Secretary of the now disbanded Test and County Cricket Board. Its first chairman is Lord MacLaurin of Knebworth, former Chairman of the Tesco supermarket chain.

The reason behind the change is the poor performance of the England Test team during the last five or so years. It was felt that the old regime failed to develop enough cricketers of real international standard. It is clearly several years too early to assess the merits of the new set-up

MCC DOMINANT

The foundations for cricket administration seem to have been laid in the Star and Garter Tavern, Pall Mall, the dinner venue for the Cricket Club – akin to the Jockey Club, another sporting organization based at the Star and Garter. The Laws of cricket were made and revised on several occasions by this club, whose membership was drawn from the aristocracy and landed gentry of the day. In 1787, the club persuaded Thomas Lord to set out a private cricket ground in Marylebone for the use of the club's members, and the press dubbed the organization the Marylebone Cricket Club. Prior to this it had been known as the White Conduit Cricket Club, since it had played its matches on White Conduit Fields in Islington, and on occasion it was also referred to as the Star and Garter Cricket Club. But it is as the Marylebone Cricket Club that it has achieved worldwide fame.

Through the first half of the nineteenth century English cricket, apart from the Laws which were adjusted from time to time by the MCC Committee, was allowed to grow unchecked by any controlling body. In 1861, the secretary of Surrey, William Burrup, wrote to the MCC asking if a meeting of county officers and the MCC could be convened to sort out the qualifications for county players and the boundary between North and South – the match between North of England and the South being the major fixture of the day. The MCC ignored the request for a meeting and simply replied giving the definition the MCC used in both cases for matches at Lord's. Democracy didn't raise its ugly head.

Three years later, when the problems of legalizing over-arm bowling were being resolved by the MCC Committee, a meeting in London sparked discussion about a "cricket parliament". The MCC allowed the arguments for and against to run their course in the press and the idea drifted away.

COUNTIES CONVENE

In 1872, eight counties were represented at a meeting held in London to define the qualification of county cricketers. One of the regulations which it passed stated that, in case of a dispute regarding residential qualification, the MCC should make the final decision. The matter was then debated at the MCC Annual General Meeting in May 1873 and a final set of regulations agreed on July 1, 1873. Earlier in the same year, the MCC had attempted to offer a cricket Challenge Cup to be competed for by the counties. Five counties entered, but two then withdrew and only one match, Kent v Sussex, was actually played – the idea that all the matches be staged at Lord's did not seem attractive to some counties.

The next question which needed to be resolved was the arrangement of inter-county fixtures. Surrey took the initiative by inviting all the county clubs to a fixtures meeting in December 1875. The man who instigated this meeting, which was thereafter an annual event, though from 1877 at Lord's rather than at the Oval, was Charlie Alcock, the greatest of all sports administrators. One story about him recalls when he became secretary to Surrey in 1872 only to find an unbusiness-like organization paying its players haphazardly. Alcock told one of the senior pros that, in future, payment would be made on a set day each month, and was surprised that the player seemed not to like the arrangement. Apparently the previous year Mr Burrup (Alcock's predecessor) had paid him three times for the Lancashire match!

Because counties only played 10 or 12 matches a season in the 1870s, the professionals were paid by the match and usually had a summer engagement with a local club, with a clause releasing them if they were selected by the county. After 1895, when the County Championship expanded and increased fixtures to perhaps 20, the counties took to employing players for the season, seconding them to local league clubs when they were not needed.

Although the Australians toured England every other year throughout the 1880s, the top players were not greatly inconvenienced by England call-ups. The 1880 Test was not played until September 6, and the 1882 match in late August. Three Tests were arranged per season in 1884, 1886, 1888 and 1890, but each was scheduled for three days. There was no England selection committee – the committee which ran the home ground picked the England side.

BOARD OF CONTROL

Everything was rather casual until Lord Harris, the captain of Kent,

LORD HARRIS *Power at Lord's for 30 years.*

decided to put cricket's house in order. At the Secretaries' Meeting of December 1887, he proposed the setting-up of a committee to look at the feasibility of a County Cricket Council – the motion was passed by 14 votes to 9. The council was duly set up and held meetings in 1888. Unfortunately, Lord Harris, its first chairman, was appointed Governor of Bombay and, in his absence, the council effectively collapsed when in December 1890 A.J. Webbe (Middlesex) proposed and W.H.C. Oates seconded that this meeting of the County Cricket Council be suspended *sine die*.

It was a very sad end to a laudable venture. The problem was

MACLAREN *Outstanding captain.*

that the individual county committees had grown too strong and were wary of giving power to a central body.

Once Lord Harris's stint as Governor of Bombay was over he began moves to create an English Board of Control and finally succeeded in 1898. The board comprised six members of the MCC and six county representatives, all also members of the MCC. It agreed to stage five Tests in 1899 against the Australians (compared to three in the recent past) and, more importantly, to distribute the profits among all the county clubs.

The board would also appoint a selection committee and raise the fees paid to England players selected for the Tests. What the board did not decide to control were English Test teams going overseas. These touring parties remained private speculations, at least for the present.

In 1903, Archie MacLaren, with the backing of the Australians, was trying to gather an England team to tour Australia. He failed to get the players he wanted and gave up, but at the last minute the MCC offered to organize the tour. The professionals were to be paid £300 and the amateurs just their expenses. The pros would receive bonuses if the tour made a profit. Although England won the Test series, the venture lost £1,500. There would be more successful trips, however, in the future. The MCC also embarked on frequent tours to other countries, normally with the host country guaranteeing the MCC against loss.

AUSTRALIAN RULES

The principal Australian cricketing colonies – New South Wales, Victoria and South Australia – were an independent trio, and the first two were divided within themselves. New South Wales Cricket Association had to co-operate with the trustees of the Sydney Cricket Ground for the staging of New South Wales' representative games. Similarly Victoria Cricket Association needed Melbourne Cricket Club, because the latter controlled the Melbourne ground. The only English equivalent was the MCC, which, of course, controlled Lord's ground, and Middlesex County Cricket Club, but in this case the relationship was almost invariably amiable.

The NSWCA were very much the junior partner and had to do what the Sydney ground authorities wanted during the last years of the nineteenth century, but common sense later prevailed and both sides benefited. The Melbourne Cricket Club was the most powerful body in Australian cricket, responsible for organizing touring teams overseas, both to England under the Australia banner and to New Zealand under its own name. The Victorian Cricket Association staggered from one crisis to another and had very little financial clout.

From these divisions a central Australian body had to be formed to represent Australian interests in the growing arena of international cricket. The first attempt was the Australasian Cricket Council founded in March 1892, a feeble body which soon disappeared. The present Australian Board of Control first met in May 1905, despite the fact that South Australia, who were in the original discussions, withdrew. Queensland were admitted almost at once; South Australia came into the fold within two years; Tasmania joined in 1907; and Western Australia in 1914. From 1909, this representative board was responsible for all Test tours to and from Australia.

The Australian administration and its English counterpart were very different in approach. The Australian system involved virtually every active cricketer on a democratic basis. Each cricket club which belonged to a colony (now state) cricket association elected representatives to the association; in its turn the association elected members to the Board of Control. In England, local cricketers and local cricket clubs had no say in the government of the game. Even for paid-up members of a first-class county club the link with the Board of Control was tenuous. The only people with any real say were members of the MCC, and membership was not easy to obtain.

CRICKET CONFLICT *The Calcutta Club from India.*

SOUTH AFRICAN DEMOCRACY

The only other country to achieve by the turn of the century a similar standard of cricket administration to England and Australia was South Africa. The South African Cricket Association was formed in April 1890 and was run on the same lines as the Australian Board. South African local cricket was organized into a number of Provincial Unions. Each union was managed by delegates from local affiliated clubs and sent two representatives to the meetings of the South African CA.

South Africa sent its first team to England in 1894. It was a far-sighted South African who took it upon himself to complete the administrative pyramid by creating in 1909 the Imperial Cricket Conference, with delegates from England, Australia and South Africa. The architect was Sir Abe Bailey. Behind his plan was the idea of a Test Tournament, staged in England, between the three countries. After some problems raised by Australia, the scheme came off in 1912. Unfortunately for Sir Abe, the weather that summer was dreadful, and open war was being waged in Australia between the major cricketers and their Board of Control, leaving the 1912 Australian side without their stars. It would be many years before another triangular contest between the top cricketing nations would be tried.

On the first-class domestic front in England, the MCC had been embarrassed twice – in 1902 and 1903 – when suggested alterations to the Laws, which had been expected to be passed without controversy, provoked outcries. The MCC secretary realized that some sort of discussion with the world outside Lord's was needed if this type of awkwardness were to be avoided in the future. He therefore set up in 1904 the Advisory County Cricket Committee which included members of the first-class counties and could act as a sounding board before legislation was debated by the MCC Committee itself. By this odd arrangement, first-class county cricket was governed until 1969.

ICC EXPANSION

Between the two World Wars, the major change in administration came at the top. Lord Harris, almost single-handedly, decided to expand the Imperial Cricket Conference. At one fell swoop, he brought in New Zealand, the West Indies and India, despite the apparently insuperable problem that India did not have a governing body.

New Zealand had had such a body – the New Zealand Cricket Council – since December 1894. It was somewhat dominated by Christchurch, its base, but was a representative organization. West Indian cricket in the 1920s was very much under the thumb of H.B.G. Austin (later Sir Harold Austin) of Barbados. He had captained two West Indian sides to England and effectively created the West Indian Board of Control in 1926, with the help of R.H. Mallett. The Indian Board of Control was set up in December 1928.

In India there was a conflict of interest between the powerful Calcutta Club and the factions which ran the Bombay Quadrangular Tournaments. One of the thorny problems was whether Englishmen long resident in India should play Test cricket for India – there was already the precedent of Ranjitsinhji representing England rather than India and soon his path would be followed both by his nephew Duleepsinhji and by the Nawab of Pataudi. The other thorn was even sharper – who should be the leader of Indian cricket? In 1931, Lord Willingdon, a former Sussex cricketer, was appointed Viceroy. He was not in favour of the Maharaja of Patiala, an extremely enthusiastic patron of the game and on the surface an obvious choice. A second candidate was the Maharajkumar of Vizianagram. Considerable intrigue and machinations went on between the interested parties. Somehow Anthony De Mello, as secretary of the Cricket Board, kept the organization afloat and Test tours to and from India went ahead. Just as importantly, the Ranji Trophy was launched. To have achieved these things in a country as vast and diverse as India is an enormous tribute to De Mello's efforts.

With each Test country now having an established system of rules for its cricket and the ICC set on a firm base, the game continued with no major administrative problems until after the Second World War. The creation of Pakistan in 1947 established another strong cricketing entity. Having joined the ICC, Pakistan in 1952–53 became the seventh Test-playing country, their first series being against neighbouring India. The idea of Pakistan remaining as part of India for cricketing purposes had been suggested briefly, but this soon faded away.

In 1961 international cricket administration went awry when South Africa left the British Commonwealth. By the then rules of the Imperial Cricket Conference, South Africa were now automatically debarred from Test cricket. England, Australia and New Zealand simply ignored the ruling and Test matches by those countries continued against South Africa as if nothing had happened.

It was not a situation which could continue, and in 1965 the world body changed its name to the International Cricket Conference and created a new class of membership for non-Test-playing countries. Ceylon (now Sri Lanka), Fiji and the United States joined as associate members. The following year Bermuda, Denmark, East Africa and the Netherlands became members. More countries joined throughout the 1970s and in 1981 Sri Lanka was moved up to full membership and Test Match status. Zimbabwe became the ninth full member in 1992.

South Africa's Test Matches ceased in 1969–70 because of pressure from anti-apartheid campaigners, and did not resume until 1991, when South Africa's race laws were abolished.

In order to produce some competitive international cricket below Test level, John Gardiner devised the ICC Trophy. This limited-overs competition was first staged in 1979 in England and involved the following countries: Bermuda, East Africa, Papua New Guinea, Singapore, Argentina, Denmark, Canada, Bangladesh, Fiji, Malaysia, Sri Lanka, USA, Wales, the Netherlands and Israel. Wales only played because Gibraltar dropped out at the last minute. Sri Lanka beat Canada in the final.

In 1984, the ICC created a third category of membership for the very minor cricketing nations. Italy became the first affiliate. The world organization had a second change of title in 1989 and since then has been known as the International Cricket Council. From being little more than an annual talking shop, the ICC now has a chief executive and a permanent office based at Lord's.

Over the last few years, governing bodies in the countries belonging to the ICC have been radically overhauled and brought up to date, largely due to the revolution of televising matches and the advertising revenues this generates.

ENGLAND CATCHES UP

English cricket remained run by the MCC, in the guise of the MCC-dominated Board of Control and the MCC Advisory County Cricket Committee, until 1969, when a new governing body, the Cricket Council, was set up with two administrative bodies directly under it – the Test and County Cricket Board (dealing, as its name implies, with England Test teams and the County Championship), and the National Cricket Association, which ran amateur cricket below county level. The 1997 foundation of the England and Wales Cricket Board swept all this away. Scotland and Ireland have gone their own way and joined the ICC as associate members.

The last 30 years have also seen the financial side of English cricket transformed, as the table below shows.

ENGLISH COUNTY CLUB FINANCES: Comparison of revenue

1969	
Match receipts	17%
Membership	25%
Supporters' association	28%
Broadcasting, Test matches and sponsors	29%
1996	
Match receipts	01%
Membership	11%
Catering	06%
Broadcasting, Test matches and sponsors	81%

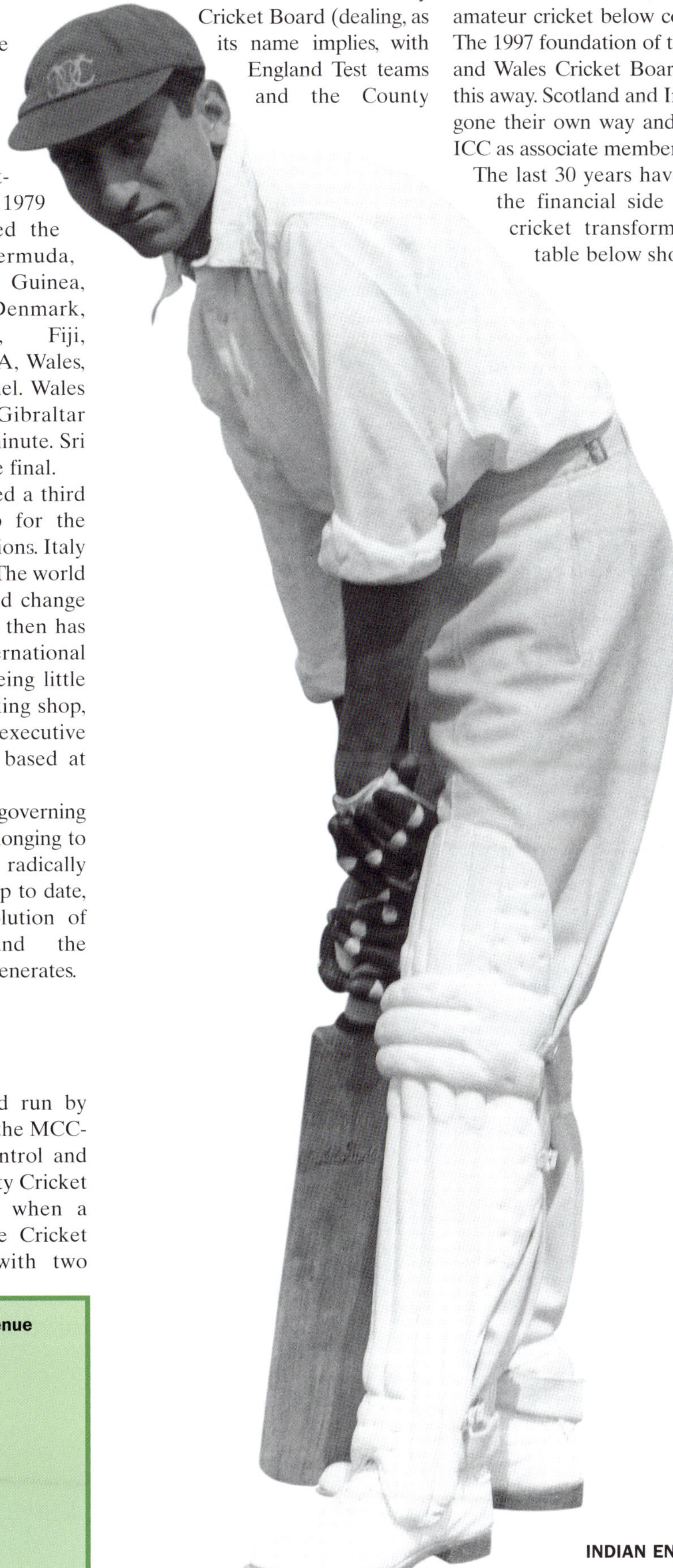

INDIAN ENGLISHMAN
The Nawab of Pataudi.

HISTORY OF THE LAWS OF CRICKET

No game can operate without a set of rules, written or unwritten. Cricket's earliest laws are apparently lost, but the code of 1744, which survives, contains the basic elements which are still in operation today.

The basic Laws of today are almost a book in their own right, yet it would be perfectly possible to stage a game using the simple laws of 1744 and scarcely notice the difference between a 1744 game and a game played under current laws.

The 1744 Laws were merely a revision of an earlier version, now apparently lost. This is not supposition because a document exists of 1727 which is entitled *Articles of Agreement between His Grace the Duke of Richmond and Mr Brodrick for two cricket Matches concluded the eleventh of July 1727*. These articles discuss points of possible controversy and not the basic rules for cricket and therefore constitute an agreed appendix laid down for the two specific matches – it was vital that disputes did not arise since large sums of money were wagered on the match result.

A study of the 1744 Laws does reveal some interesting detail. For instance, although the size of the wicket, the length of the pitch, the weight of the ball and the number of balls per over are all given, there is no mention of the number of players required for each team. The magical number of eleven which seems sacred to cricket therefore does not go back even as far as the earliest known laws. It is not until 1884 – after Test matches had been established for seven years and the County Championship for more than half a century – that a law is introduced: "A match is played between two sides of eleven players each, unless otherwise agreed to".

The one 1744 Law which has been repeatedly changed relates to the size of the wickets: in 1798 this was increased to 24 inches by 7 inches; around 1819 it was increased again to 26 inches by 7 inches; about four years later there was another increase, to 27 inches by 8 inches; and in 1931 the size became 28 inches by 9 inches. These changes were made because pitches improved and batsmen again and again came to dominate bowlers.

GENTLEMANLY CONDUCT *A game of cricket as played when the 1744 Laws were in force*

Many of the newer laws that are not in the original 1744 version have been added simply because players have tried to subvert the spirit of the game. The first of these attempts came in 1771. The 1744 Laws give no ruling on the size of a cricket bat. In September 1771, a certain Thomas White of Reigate arrived at the wicket with a bat which was the same width as the wicket. A law was passed there and then limiting the width of a bat to $4^{1}/_{4}$ inches, and the law specifying this dimension has remained in force to the present time.

In 1774, the first law specifically ruling that a batsman could be out leg before wicket was introduced. Again, this was made law because batsmen began to deliberately put their legs in front of the wicket to prevent themselves being bowled, though the 1744 code does include a note about umpires judging

Ye Laws of Ye Game of Cricket

Ye pitching of ye first Wicket is to be determined by ye cast of a piece of Money.

When ye first Wicket is pitched and ye popping Crease cut, which must be exactly 3 Foot 10 Inches from ye Wicket, ye other Wicket is to be pitched, directly opposite, at 22 Yards distance, and ye other popping Crease cut 3 Foot 10 Inches before it.

Ye bowling Creases must be cut, in a direct line, from each Stump.

Ye Stumps must be 22 inches long, and ye Bail 6 inches.

Ye Ball must weigh between 5 and 6 ounces.

When ye Wickets are both pitched and all ye Creases cut, ye Party that wins the toss up may order which Side shall go in first at his option.

Laws for ye Bowlers 4 Balls and Over

Ye bowler must deliver ye Ball with one foot behind ye Crease even with ye Wicket, and When he has bowled one ball or more shall bowl to ye number 4 before he changes wickets, and he shall change but one in ye same innings.

He may order ye Players that is in at his Wicket to stand on which side of it he pleases at a reasonable distance.

If he delivers ye Ball with his hinder foot over ye bowling Crease ye Umpire shall call No Ball, though she be struck, or ye Players bowled out, Which he shall do without being asked, and no Person shall have any right to ask him.

Laws for ye Strikers, or Those that are in

If ye Wicket is Bowled down, it's Out.

If he strokes, or treads down, or falls himself upon ye Wicket in striking, but not in over running, it's Out.

A stroke or nip over or under his Batt, or upon his hands, but not arms, if ye Ball be held before she touches ye ground, though she be hug'd to the body, it's Out.

If in striking both his feet over ye popping Crease and his Wicket put down, except his Batt is down within, it's Out.

If he runs out of his ground to hinder a Catch, it's Out.

If a Ball is nipp'd up and he strikes her again, wilfully, before she comes to ye Wicket, it's Out.

If ye Players have cross'd each other, he that runs for ye Wicket that is put down is out. If they are not cross'd, he that returns is out.

Batt Foot or Hand over Ye Crease

If in running a notch ye Wicket is struck down by a throw, before his foot hand or Batt is over ye popping Crease, or a stump hit by ye Ball though ye Bail was down, it's Out. But if ye Bail is down before, he that catches ye Ball must strike a Stump out of ye ground, Ball in hand, then it's Out.

If ye Stroker touches or takes up ye Ball before she is lain quite still, unless asked by ye Bowler or Wicket-keeper, it's Out.

When ye Ball has been in hand by one of ye Keepers or Stopers, and ye Player has been at home, He may go where he pleases till ye next ball is bowled.

If either of ye Strikers is cross'd in his running ground, designedly, which design must be determined by the Umpires, N. B. the umpire(s) may order that Notch to be scored.

When ye Ball is hit up, either of ye Strikers may hinder ye catch in his running ground, or if she's hit directly across ye wickets, ye other Player may place his body any where within ye swing of his Batt, so as to hinder ye Bowler from catching her, but he must neither strike at her nor touch her with his hands.

If a Striker nips a ball up just before him, he may fall before his Wicket, or pop down his Batt before she comes to it, to save it.

Ye Bail hanging on one Stump, though ye Ball hit ye Wicket, it's not Out.

Laws for Wicket Keepers

Ye Wicket Keepers shall stand at a reasonable distance behind ye Wicket, and shall not move till ye Ball is out of ye Bowler's hand, and shall not by any noise incommode ye Striker, and if his hands, knees, foot or head be over or before ye Wicket, though ye Ball hit it, it shall not be Out.

Laws for Ye Umpires

To allow 2 Minutes for each Man to come in when one is out, and 10 Minutes between each Hand.

To mark ye Ball that it may not be changed.

They are sole judge(s) of all Outs and Ins, of all fair and unfair play, of frivolous delays, of all hurts, whether real or pretended, and are discretionally to allow what time they think proper before ye Game goes on again.

In case of a real hurt to a Striker, they are to allow another to come in and ye Person hurt to come in again but are not to allow a fresh Man to play, on either Side, on any Account. They are sole judge(s) of all hindrances, crossing ye Players in running, and standing unfair to strike, and in case of hindrance may order a Notch to be scored.

They are not to order any Man out unless appealed to by (any) one of ye Players.

(These Laws are to ye Umpires Jointly)

Each Umpire is ye sole judge of all Nips and Catches, Ins and Outs, good or bad Runs, at his own wicket, and his determination shall be absolute, and he shall not be changed for another Umpire without ye consent of both Sides.

When ye 4 Balls are bowled he is to call Over.

(These Laws are Separately)

When both Umpire(s) (shall) call Play, 3 times, 'tis at ye peril of giving ye Game from them that refuse (to) Play.

THE CODE OF 1744
These laws of cricket were, in all probability, written to control the conduct of the players in the match between Kent and All England, which was staged on the Artillery Ground in 1744.

whether a batsman was standing unfair to strike. At that time batsmen were firm-footed, not moving their feet to the ball.

In 1788 came the law giving a penalty of five runs if the fieldsman stops the ball with his hat. It would seem that the information about the fielder who kept doing this and thus forced a change in the law is lost. A similar type of law is that relating to a lost ball – about 1805 a fielder was allowed to claim lost ball and the batting side would be credited with a given number of runs. One visualizes an important match sometime prior to this law being introduced, with a pair of batsmen scurrying forever between the wickets as the fieldsmen search a field of wheat for the ball.

The law stating that bowling must be under-arm was brought in during the early years of the nineteenth century when bowlers, frustrated that the batsmen had mastered their attack, raised their bowling arm above shoulder height in order to deliver the ball at a faster pace. The law to permit bowling with the hand up to shoulder height was finalized in 1835. In 1864, over-arm bowling was legalized.

It is worth noting that boundaries did not appear in the Laws until 1884. In the earliest days all runs were run out, but when pavilions began to be erected at the side of the grounds and tents became more common a given number of runs were agreed on each ground to account for these obstacles!

In historical terms, the Laws of 1744 were tinkered with as the years went by, but the first total revision was not undertaken until 1883–84, when the MCC set up a sub-committee whose task it was to revise the Laws by defining terms, supplying omissions, and better wording, but without altering the spirit of the game. The sub-committee did not simply closet itself at Lord's and then hand out new tablets of stone. They produced draft copies which were sent to all the major county clubs, to Oxford and Cambridge, to Victoria and New South Wales, and to New York and Philadelphia. No vast alterations were made in the course of this revision and it was a very good attempt to put the laws into a logical sequence, having regard to all the amendments that had crept in. The success of this new version can be judged by the fact that it was to last for over 60 years.

With regard to the pitch and its location, in the 1744 Laws the side which won the toss selected the piece of ground on which the wickets should be pitched. In 1774, the law stated that the visitors could select the ground for the pitch, but it had to be within 30 yards of the spot chosen by the home team. Thirty years later, the law stated that the umpires had the task of selecting the ground to be used for the pitch.

There was no mention in the earliest Laws of the way the pitch should be maintained during the match, but in the 1788 version rolling, watering, covering, mowing and beating of the pitch could take place by mutual consent. About 1823, a clause was added to say that the pitch could be changed after rain. In 1860, the side next to bat could order the pitch to be rolled, and in 1883 a clause was added to allow rolling for 10 minutes before the start of play. In 1931, this was reduced to seven minutes. The most controversial topic now concerning the pitch is the question of whether matches should be played on covered or uncovered pitches.

A period of three years was spent during the 1940s drafting a totally revised set of Laws, mainly to remove all the oddments of footnotes and ambiguities which had built up during the years. The man who rationalized the draft was Colonel R.S. Rait Kerr and the new code came into effect in April 1948.

Throughout the 1950s the chief concern of the officials in relation to the Laws was connected with bowling. The problem of drag caused by the fast bowler's back foot being over the bowling crease when the ball was delivered was highlighted by the increasing improvement in camera techniques. Therefore, a rule governing the front foot's position was eventually passed. There was also a spate of throwing whereby a number of bowlers no-balled in first-class cricket. The famous case of the South African, Geoff Griffin, who was no-balled in the 1960 Lord's Test brought matters to a head – the various countries agreed to clamp down on bowlers with dubious actions, in the same way as the county captains had done 60 years before. Bumpers also featured strongly and the law was changed to limit the number bowled in an over.

Over the years minor additions were required as players tried to bend the Laws – the appearance of a metal bat, for example, required a law stating that bats should be wooden – and the wearing of helmets required another change. In autumn 1974, Billy Griffith was asked to redraft the 1947 code and in 1980 the present Laws came into force.

INTIMIDATORY BOWLING

The Laws, however, are not set in concrete, and the regulations which govern the game are under constant review. The front-foot law which, as stated, is the present method of determining a no-ball is a case in point. This law is unpopular with bowlers and with many commentators, but the authorities have tried to ensure that a batsman has only to face a ball propelled at him from the full 22 yards. In a positive attempt to reduce the number of no-balls bowled, the Australian Board of Control began to penalize bowlers two runs for each no-ball in the 1990–91 season, and England adopted the same penalty in 1993, although these strictures have only applied in first-class domestic competitions not Test matches.

The punishment is heavy because some regard the no-ball as a form of intimidatory bowling. The war against intimidatory bowling, the direct attack on the batsman's body, was waged by MCC in 1935 in the wake of the "bodyline" tour. Umpires were instructed to take action against such bowling, and umpires remain the sole arbiters of what is fair and unfair play. It is the bowling of fast, short-pitched deliveries that is considered unfair if, in the opinion of the umpire at the bowler's end, such deliveries are an attempt to intimidate the batsman. The International Cricket Council has decreed that a bowler may not bowl more than two fast, short-pitched deliveries an over, but great responsibility has been placed upon the umpire and the way in which he interprets the law. Umpires and captains have certainly disagreed over its implementation, and West Indian sides under Clive Lloyd and Viv Richards opposed the restriction as a deliberate attempt to reduce the effectiveness of attacks which consisted of four bowlers of considerable pace.

Bowlers would argue that all laws and regulations which have been introduced in the past 20 years have been introduced in an attempt to reduce their potency and to give greater advantages to

AVOIDING A BOUNCER *Intimidatory bowling has led to several law changes.*

NO BALL *Griffin, the South African fast bowler, was no-balled for throwing in the 1960 Lord's Test.*

the batsman. The decision in the early 1980s to have complete, unconditional covering for all pitches meant that never again would a bowler operate on a pitch severely affected by the weather. The decision certainly took some romance from the game. Hobbs and Sutcliffe had become part of legend when, on a pitch made treacherous by overnight rain, they scored 172 for England's first wicket against Australia at the Oval in 1926, and, six years later, at Headingley, Hedley Verity exploited a drying wicket to take all 10 Nottinghamshire wickets for 10 runs to establish a record that is not likely to be beaten. On the reverse side, Morris Sievers took five for 21 as Australia bowled out England for 76 on a Melbourne "gluepot" in 1937, but he never played Test cricket again, for the Australian selectors decided that he was only a "bad wicket" bowler.

LBW

Certainly the complete covering of pitches has made life easier for the batsman and harder for the bowler, but the batsman would argue that the changes in the lbw law have been in favour of the bowler. Until 1935, a ball had to be pitched straight in line between wicket and wicket to obtain a leg before decision, but in 1935, a new law was introduced which embraced balls pitched outside the off-stump although the ball had to strike the batsman in line between wicket and wicket. In 1970, the law was amended again so that a batsman could be adjudged leg before if he offered no stroke to a ball which struck him outside the off stump and which, in the opinion of the umpire, would have hit the wicket. Mike Gatting was to be forgetful of this law at Lord's in 1984 when he succumbed twice to Malcom Marshall in the England-West Indies Test.

These changes in the law regarding lbw had tended to encourage the off-break or in-slant bowler while the leg-break bowler can gain no decision for a ball pitched outside leg stump which the batsman is still at liberty to pad away. This fact, and lush outfields which enable the ball to retain its shine longer, made leg-break bowling virtually extinct by the 1960s, but top performers like Abdul Qadir, Anil Kumble and Shane Warne have resurrected the art and became the most potent match-winners in Test cricket, not least because batsmen were at a loss as to how to play them.

Although several batsmen argued against the "new" lbw law in 1935 and again against its extension in 1970, none really saw a reduction in his run-getting powers, and the bowler would continue to argue that all legislation has been against him, especially in the restrictions set upon him in the limited-over game where the length of his run-up is often bounded by regulations and his allowed number of overs is invariably determined as a fifth of the innings quota.

ONE-DAY FIELDING

Following a pattern of defensive fields in the early days of one-day competitions which began domestically in England in 1963 and internationally in Australia in 1970–71, a circle was drawn some 30 yards from the pitch and fielders had to be within the circle at certain times during the innings. By the time of the 1996 World Cup, only two fieldsmen were permitted to be outside the circle during the first 15 overs of the innings, and for the remaining overs only five fieldsmen were permitted to be outside the circle. This ruling was brilliantly exploited by Sri Lanka whose opening batsmen, Jayasuriya and Kaluwitharana, were never afraid to hit over the heads of fielders and scored at a devastating rate.

Limited-over cricket became exceedingly popular when Kerry Packer introduced his break-away World Series Cricket in 1978–79. It was in this era that coloured clothing and floodlit games became the norm, and the limited-over game has proliferated to such an extent that, internationally, it outnumbers Test cricket by five to one. Coloured clothing has been adopted for Sunday League games in England and a white ball is also used although, until 1997, there were not even plans for a day/night game.

It could be said that the one-day game has transformed the attitude of both players and spectators, yet it moves at a pace and excites attention. The first-class game stands accused of reducing itself to a crawl. Where once 20 overs an hour was the expectation, the ICC now recognizes 15 overs an hour as being the requirement for a Test match, and few Test sides have been able to maintain the rate, so anxious are players to preserve their stamina. Even heavy fines have failed to solve the problem just as they have problems of behaviour.

SUBSTITUTES

It has now become a regular occurrence for bowlers to leave the field to change shirts or to receive some form of treatment after finishing a spell, and the substitute is increasingly in evidence. Indeed, South Africa has experimented with allowing sides to name 14 players and to use eleven of them in whatever capacity they wish during the course of a game while, in New Zealand, 1996–97, as many as 15 players appeared for one side in an inter-provincial game because four of the original 11 had to be released midway through the match to appear in an international fixture.

The truth is that cricket is ever in an evolutionary process and that laws and regulations will change as the conception of the game alters. A third umpire now judges run outs and stumpings. Who can say what his next duty will be?

EQUIPMENT

To play cricket requires a bat, a ball and a set of wickets – the three basic necessities since records began. The bat has changed only once, from a hockey-stick type to the present one. The ball has scarcely altered. The stumps have simply grown in size as the pitch has altered from rough meadow to billiard table. The one major change has been the armour demanded by the batsman.

The three essential elements of cricket are the bat, the ball and the wicket. Everyone is familiar with the appearance, size and material of these three pieces of cricket equipment as used in present-day cricket matches, but originally they must have been nothing more than a thick wooden stave to use as a bat, probably a rounded lump of wood as a ball and two thin sticks stuck in the ground as a wicket.

The first mention of the bat comes in a court case of 1613, when Nicholas Hockley assaulted Robert Hewett with a stick called a "cricket staffe" value one penny. In 1622, several youths were in court for playing at cricket in a churchyard because, for one reason, their ball might have broken the church windows. Unfortunately for the historian, the man presiding over the court didn't ask for a description of the ball, so we can only assume it was a hard object!

INDISTINGUISHABLE *In this cricket match, painted in about 1744, the batsman and the fielders are equally unprotected.*

The price of bats seems to have halved between 1613 and 1624, since in the latter year, in a court case there is a reference to a small staff called a "cricket batt", worth half a penny.

In 1658, the writer Edward Phillips, a nephew of Milton, states in a piece:

"Would my eyes had been beat out of my head with a cricket-ball, the day before I saw thee."

The cricket ball thus remains a hard and dangerous object, but its exact nature is still a mystery.

These lines written in a bible about 1680 are the first to refer to the wicket:

"All you that do delight
in Cricket
Come to Marden, Pitch
your wickets"

At the start of the eighteenth century there is no evidence as to the sizes of the bat, ball or wickets and there are no pictorial representations. No actual bats, balls or wickets from the seventeenth century are preserved in any museum or pavilion.

The first detailed description of a match, published in 1706, throws no further light on the matter. The Articles of Agreement for the two matches between the Duke of Richmond's side and Mr Brodrick's side say nothing on the subject, though they state that the pitch should be 23 yards long and that there should be 12 players per side.

The first dim light to be shed on the nature of bat, ball and wicket comes with a lithograph of 1739 showing young children, eight or nine years old, playing cricket. The bat is very much like a modern hockey stick; the wicket, two stumps and a cross-piece. The Laws of 1744 only help in two aspects: firstly that the stumps should be 22 inches high and six inches wide, and secondly that the ball should weigh between five and six ounces. The bat is not mentioned. However, in or about 1744, comes

LIKE A HOCKEY STICK *A bat of the type used in the 1760s.*

RECORD MAKER *The bat used by Gary Sobers to create a new Test record of 365 in 1957–58.*

TYPICAL BAT *used in County Cricket in the 1980s.*

Francis Hayman's *Cricket in Marylebone Fields* – an oil painting which clearly shows the leading players of the day. The two wooden stumps with a single bail are seen, and four bats are featured, one with each batsman and one with each umpire. The bats have a covered black handle and the blades are slightly curved. A red ball is in the bowler's hand. The players are dressed overall in white, with knee breeches and silk stockings, black buckled shoes and dark jockey caps. The batsmen and wicket-keepers do not wear any pads or gloves.

The change to a straight bat came in the 1770s and the law about the regulation size is noted in the section of this book devoted to the Laws. The bat at this stage is still made of a single piece of wood. As bats developed shoulders, there came the natural tendency for the handle to snap off at the shoulder. This led to the spliced bat which came into vogue about 1830, but bats made out of a single piece of wood went on being produced (because they were so much cheaper) until the last years of the nineteenth century. Thomas Nixon, the Nottingham professional, invented the idea of cane handles. From this development came the next step of inserting a sandwich of rubber, or one of canvas and rubber, held between slices of cane. Rubber handle covers were patented in 1880.

So far as cricket balls are concerned, Duke & Son of Penshurst in Kent were the first manufacturers of cricket balls, it is claimed, from 1760. The best early description of ball manufacture comes from Joseph Farington's diary of 1811, when he visited Duke's factory. Thread was wound round an octagonal piece of cork and then a leather case of bull hide put on the rounded core.

There were also various experiments with stumps. The wood was usually ash and a brass ferrule at the top was common to prevent damage. Several makes of stump also had iron or steel spikes so that it was easier to drive them into the ground. The idea of a stump which would automatically spring back into place when disturbed by the ball was tried out and a number of patents were lodged on the spring gadget required, but these were never used in major matches because of the law which

LITTLE CHANGE *Over the last 125 years there have been remarkably few modifications to the cricket ball.*

STUMPS *have changed in size several times during cricket's history. The topmost in this picture is a typical stump of the 1930s, with its brass ferrule. Below it are the smaller stumps used until 1931.*

entitles a fielder to pull the stump from the ground if the bails are missing. Bails were usually made of ash or boxwood, though in the 1860s iron bails were tried when a fierce wind was blowing.

SILENT WITNESS *This stump saw the cricketing action of the 1946 Tests.*

KEEPING SCORE

The first scoreboards were used in the 1840s, and consisted of a board with hooks on which metal number plates were hung. These boards simply gave the current total, the number of wickets which had fallen and the score of the last batsman. In 1884 came the addition of the scores of both the batsmen at the wicket, so figures on movable rollers replaced the individual tin scoring plates.

The Australian main grounds by 1890 had scoreboards which gave the names of all the batsmen and the score they made, and within 10 years the boards had, in some cases, been extended so that the bowler's name and analyses were displayed. This comprehensive scoreboard was only tried once in England on a permanent basis, at Trent Bridge, Nottingham from 1950 until the 1970s.

Electronic, computerized scoreboards have been gradually phased in during the last 20 years, the Packer World Series Cricket of the late 1970s hastening this process.

As regards the implements of the scorer, the notching of runs on a stick is clearly shown on Hayman's painting of 1744. The switch to written records must have occurred when it was thought necessary to record individual batsmen's runs, rather than simply the team total. The detailed score for the Kent v England match of 1744 is known, so someone must have written down the details at the time. A few books with scores written in them exist for the first half of the nineteenth century and by the mid-nineteenth century scorebooks were being printed with set grids for batsmen and bowlers in the type of pattern that is still in common use. More sophisticated methods of recording the score have been devised in the twentieth century – Bill Ferguson, for many years Australia's scorer, was foremost in this development.

DRESS CODE

The change in cricketing dress simply followed fashion as breeches gave way to trousers in about 1815. A tall hat replaced the jockey caps.

The first move in the direction of batsmen's pads came with the idea of stitching a lining inside the trouser and inserting rubber between the lining and outer cover, but this was a brief fad before leg-guards became common. Thomas Nixon, who had introduced cane handles, is credited with inventing cork pads in 1841 and open pads in 1853.

India-rubber padded gloves were advertised for sale in 1844. In 1846, Robert Dark of Lord's was the inventor and manufacturer of Tubular Indian Rubber Gloves, though another note states that Nicholas Felix, the famous batsman, invented gloves in 1835 with slips of india-rubber glued to each finger. So far as the wicket-keeper was concerned, in 1844 it was recommended that he wear a pair of ordinary gloves, but by 1851 new improved wicket-keeping gloves were being talked about. Lord

TOURING BLAZER *of the MCC. Until 1996, this style was worn by England cricketers overseas.*

TOURING ATTIRE *The MCC touring sleeveless sweater.*

Harris stated that in his early days (i.e. about 1868) wicket-keeping gloves were made of yellow leather, which used to get so hard that the gloves had to be soaked before being put on.

The use of white clothing during the eighteenth century had given way by the mid-nineteenth century to a bizarre variety which would surprise even today's multi-coloured teams. A description of a fictitious cricketer in 1858 makes interesting reading: "Captain Spangles was attired as follows: cap of harlequin pattern, red neck-cloth with a pin composed of gold stumps and cross bat, the British cricketer shirt, illustrated with portraits of favourite players in attitude, and grey and black zebra flannel trousers." The writer fails to mention the very likely elastic belt with a buckle incorporating a cricketing design and probably brown, or brown and white, boots.

The professional teams of the 1850s wore standard coloured shirts, the All-England shirt being white with red dots. Blazers were first used, it is believed, for the Lady Margaret Boat Club of St John's College, Cambridge, in 1862. The following year the Oxford cricket team wore blue blazers. Striped blazers were in vogue in the 1880s.

Head gear changed from top hats to pot hats and in the 1850s hats often had a club ribbon as a band. Public schools seem to have introduced caps to cricket, Eton, Rugby, Winchester and Harrow all having their own distinctive caps in the 1850s. The I Zingari had a striped forage cap with IZ on the front and elastic to hold the cap on the wearer's head.

The buckled belt gave way to a silk scarf round the waist in the 1880s and brown boots were replaced by white buckskin. The Australian Aborigines each wore a sash of a different colour when playing in England in 1868, which colour was marked on the score-card, thus enabling spectators to identify the players.

PROTECTING ONE'S PERSON

The first abdominal protectors were noted in 1851, but their design is not known. In 1880, they were known as person protectors and in 1890 as groin protectors.

The idea of an umpire wearing a white coat has an interesting beginning. In the days of under-arm and round-arm bowling, umpires wore ordinary black suits, but when over-arm bowling and the idea of bowling over the wicket began batsmen complained that they lost sight of the ball against the umpire's suit. It is believed that the first time an umpire wore a white overcoat was in 1861, when the United Eleven opposed the Free Foresters. At first, some spectators ridiculed white-coated umpires, but the innovation caught on and by the 1870s was common practice. The white coats in many cases reached almost to the ground, but they have gradually had their hems raised, first in Australia, then generally, to the present level.

Cricket pads were worn by most batsmen by the 1880s. Pads had been of brown leather, but white

EARLY PAD *Brown leather was often used in the construction of pads during the late nineteenth century.*

BREAKING WITH TRADITION *In the 1990s coloured pads were introduced in the Sunday League.*

canvas or leather ones were in use generally by the close of the nineteenth century. Some batsmen wore skeleton pads but they did not last.

In the Edwardian era, cricket dress became standardized, players being dressed uniformly in white shirt and flannels, white boots and white pads. Every club of any pretension had its own colours and these appeared on caps, blazers and as bands on sweaters – the wearing of sweaters had arrived in the late 1890s. In English county cricket, amateurs still appeared in their ordinary club caps, rather than the county cap, and often wore a neckerchief.

This standard dress remained almost unchanged until the 1970s – except that the Australians adopted a baggy cap, as opposed to the close-fitting English style of cap. In the late 1960s, floppy hats began to appear in first-class matches – Greg Chappell, playing for Somerset in 1968 and 1969, was one of the first to sport such a garment in county matches; it later became the trademark of the England wicket-keeper Bob Taylor. More recently, the West Indian players adopted broad-brimmed hats.

The major change in headgear, though, was the use of the protective helmet. Back in 1933, Patsy Hendren had devised a three-peak cap to guard the temples against the fast bowling of the time, but this did not catch on. Even earlier, in 1870, when the first and only fatality in English first-class cricket occurred through a batsman being hit on the head, the next batsman to come in wore a towel as a turban. So far as the modern helmet is concerned, Mike Brearley, the England captain, devised a sort of helmet which looked like dog flaps hanging out of his cap. Within a year or so Dennis Amiss, the Warwickshire and England batsman, adapted a motorcycle helmet and quite a number of designs developed with various grilles in front of the face and other protective pieces. By the middle of the 1980s, it was unusual to see a batsman come to the wicket in first-class cricket without a

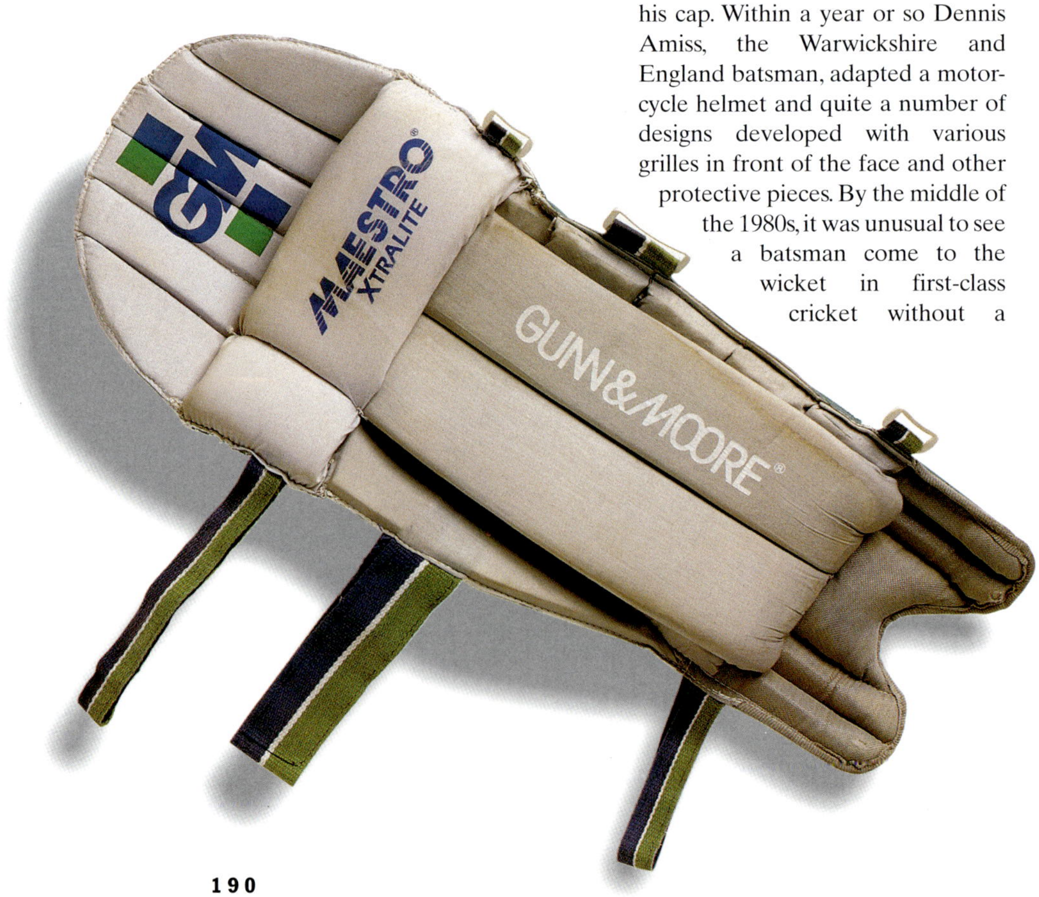

helmet. The practice of close-to-the-wicket fielders on the leg side also wearing a helmet followed. Other protection used by batsmen involved thigh pads and forearm protectors. Thigh pads were certainly being worn in first-class cricket in 1947.

The advent of coloured clothing has been an emotive subject among traditional English supporters. The Kerry Packer World Series players in the late 1970s wore different-coloured apparel. The English county players were instructed to wear coloured clothing for Sunday League matches for the first time in 1993; the players had their names on the back and the name of the team on the front of the shirt. Coloured pads were also used and a white ball with black sightscreens, although these games were all played in daylight, unlike overseas where night or day-night games were common practice.

The editor of *Wisden* was happy enough to accept the break with traditional white clothing, but he ended his statement on the matter with the following warning:

"If, however, the counties are planning to change their colours every year to exploit children and make them buy up-to-date gear at rip-off prices, which is what happens in football, then they are taking the road to hell." It need hardly be added that since 1993 the designs have all been changed!

The major grounds have a new design of sightscreen, which can not only be converted from black to white, but can also be switched to an advertising display. This option is used in alternate overs during televised matches. Also to accommodate television, the middle stump has been hollowed out and a television camera installed to give close-up pictures.

***above* SUN HAT** *worn by Clive Rice in the 1980s.*

***left* ENGLAND TOURING CAP** *worn during the the 1901–02 visit to Australia.*

***below* MCC** *England touring cap of the 1930s.*

***right* NOTTINGHAMSHIRE COUNTY CRICKET CLUB** *cap of the 1940s.*

THE CULTURE OF CRICKET

Whether on the field or off it, cricket exerts a powerful influence over the English way of life. The writings of Neville Cardus and John Arlott appeal to a wide audience, as does cricket coverage on radio and television. The sport has also inspired many talented artists, from G. F. Watts onwards.

Strenuous efforts are now being made to promote cricket as a worldwide game, mainly through television. Countries which possess fewer cricket players than any self-respecting Yorkshire town are being given membership of the International Cricket Council, in the belief that official recognition will inspire the inhabitants to adopt cricket wholesale. Test-playing countries are being asked to foster the game on their continent. The scheme is thoroughly commendable, but will nations that have steadfastly turned their backs on cricket, in some cases for as long as 200 years, now be persuaded that cricket is for them?

THE NEXT GENERATION *Children playing cricket in Pakistan.*

ENGLISH EXPORT

It is a historical fact, however, that cricket is peculiar to the English and to Anglophiles. Even such near neighbours as the Irish, Scots and Welsh have for the most part ignored the game. It was the English landlords with estates in the rest of the British Isles who played cricket in front of the "big house", usually with guests of the household and against such invited teams as Free Foresters, Incogniti and the like. The tenants and estate workers, for their part, made up annual teams, but rarely took the game back to their villages.

Although the villagers of the Weald can be said to have created the modern game, Wealden folk stayed very much between the North and South Downs and did little or nothing to promulgate the sport beyond their boundaries. Those responsible for spreading cricket were the landed gentry of Surrey, Sussex and Kent – or rather their sons, for those youths took the game to Eton, Harrow, Charterhouse, Westminster and Winchester. When they left those schools, they went to Oxford or Cambridge or to the army or navy. Cricket went with them.

It was an ideal occupation for soldiers with time on their hands. Thus the militia, mustered to ensure that the French Revolution did not spread across the English Channel, played cricket. Meanwhile, the boys at the great schools organized the first inter-schools matches and a little later the undergraduates fixed the first university match.

As early as 1676 there is a record of cricket being played outside Britain – in Aleppo (now in Syria) but then part of the sprawling Ottoman Empire. The players were visitors from a British naval vessel and English residents in Aleppo. No evidence exists, though, that the Turks or the Syrians were wielding cricket bats.

The first description of a cricket match was written, in 1706, by William Goldwin, educated at Eton and Cambridge. In 1721, sailors of the East India Company were reported to be playing cricket on the west coast of India and a few years later the English colonists in America organized games. In 1766, cricket was being played in Paris, but only by Englishmen and some upper-class Frenchmen.

The oldest cricket club outside mainland Britain and still existing today is the Calcutta Club, founded in or before 1792 and then intended exclusively for Europeans. When the first known century was scored in Ireland in 1800, the batsman was Ensign Beckett of the Coldstream Guards – the first hundred in India, in 1804, was by R. Vansittart of the Old Etonians. A match was recorded in Cape Town, between officers of the Artillery Mess and the Colony in 1808. The officers of the Brigade of Guards played cricket near Brussels on the eve of the Battle of Waterloo. As the British Empire expanded, cricket was played by the army, however outlandish the locale.

The middle of the nineteenth century saw the creation of the modern public school system, one of its tenets being muscular Christianity. Cricket was an integral part of this ethos. "It's not cricket" was a phrase which emanated from the schools – as was the importance of playing the game for the game's sake rather than for winning or losing.

This last point is of interest because in the late twentieth century winning has become all-important in many quarters and this conflicts with the Englishness of cricket. Lord Harris, at one time Governor of Bombay, and for much of his life the most important figure in cricket, expressed great concern that inter-county cricket in the nineteenth century was becoming a sport dominated by trophies, cups and money. He begged county cricketers not to follow such a path.

Until the 1960s, cricket clubs in the South of England stood firm against being forced into league systems, content to play just friendly fixtures. The greatest cricket club of all, the MCC, which played hundreds of fixtures each season, steered clear of competitive games.

In contrast to this, Australian cricket at club level has been organized into competitive leagues since the Victorian era. This is one reason why Australia, with a fraction of the number of active cricketers that could be found in England, has competed on an equal footing at Test level.

In two parts of what was the British Empire cricket has been taken up at a serious level – one being the West Indies, the other the Indian sub-continent. In both cases it was a long slow process – in contrast to the speed with which soccer spread.

As the twenty-first century approaches, the throbbing heartland of cricket can be found in Pakistan, India and Sri Lanka. In those three countries youths play cricket on odd pieces of land using home-made implements, just as used to happen in England. Rowland Bowen, the noted cricket historian, expressed the opinion about 30 years ago that cricket was dying; he was referring only to cricket in England. And though cricket as the cultural experience known to Englishmen is dying, a new variety is blossoming.

GENTLEMEN VERSUS PLAYERS

In the eighteenth century match scores were careful to distinguish between the paid players and the amateurs, the former being shown purely by the surname or sometimes their Christian name and surname, the latter being Mr Blank or Blank Esq.

According to Pycroft's *The Cricket Field*, the Gentlemen (i.e. the amateurs) first opposed the Players in 1798, but the first recognized match in the series between the two classes took place at Lord's in 1806. The Gentlemen won both the games played that year, though they had a professional or two as given men. The match became one of the showpieces of the year and, after the creation of Surrey's ground at the Oval, it was common practice to stage one fixture at each ground each season. A third venue, Scarborough, was used regularly for an end-of-season match from the 1880s onwards. Other venues occasionally staged the match.

The distinction between Gentlemen and Players was maintained even when a county side was made up of a mixture – the two classes having separate dressing rooms, even separate gates to enter the playing area. When playing away they stayed in separate hotels and travelled to their destination in separate compartments on the train, first-class and third.

The distinction in first-class county cricket did not cease until 1963. Since the Australians did not divide their cricketers into two classes, this caused some problems when they first toured England – the Australians were all paid players. The English authorities got around this, however, by making the Australians "honorary" amateurs!

LITERARY TRADITION

The earliest known publication on the game of cricket is a description of a match, issued in 1706 and written in Latin verse, called *In Certamen Pilae* by William Goldwin. The second, *Cricket: An Heroic Poem* by James Love, describes the Kent v All England match on the Artillery Ground, London, in 1744. Several more pieces of verse in the manner of Love's poem followed.

Aside from these "literary" efforts, cricket's appearances in print until the 1830s were confined to books of instruction, of scores, of the Laws and of regulations for various clubs. This rather staid diet was enlivened in 1833 when a volume entitled *The Young Cricketer's Tutor* made its appearance. The author was named as John Nyren, whose father had captained the famous Hambledon Club side in the 1770s, but the actual writer, described as the "editor", was Charles Cowden Clarke, a well-known literary figure of the day.

The book gives pen portraits of the Hambledon players and their most notable opponents, and the style in which it is written evokes the feel of Hambledon in its heyday. The book has been reprinted numerous times and is still issued at intervals to satisfy the demand of new generations of readers. Thirteen years after the Nyren-Clarke masterpiece, the journalist William Denison wrote *Cricket: Sketches of the Players*, which consisted of long essays on 37 contemporary cricketers. The year before, an amateur cricketer and Blackheath schoolmaster wrote a treatise on batsmanship entitled *Felix on the Bat*. (Felix was the cricketing name of Nicholas Wanostrocht.) An integral part of this well-written book are the illustrations derived from a series of sketches by G. F. Watts.

The end of the 1840s saw the start of the modern cricket annual. Fred Lillywhite, the scorecard printer at the Oval, published *The Young Cricketer's Guide*. This annual, which was made up of potted scores, averages and current players' biographies, ran until 1866 when Fred Lillywhite died – though not before he had also pioneered the cricket tour book. He accompanied George Parr's team to North America in 1859 and wrote and published a book on that first tour. The annual – known to cricket bibliophiles as "Fred's Guide" – had two rivals including John Wisden's *Cricketers' Almanack*. This last-named commenced publication in 1864 and through the 1870s had two more Lillywhite annuals to contend with – James Lillywhite's *Cricketers' Annual* and John Lillywhite's *Cricketers' Companion*. The final Lillywhite production came out in 1900; thereafter *Wisden* was out on its own and earning its sobriquet, the cricketer's bible.

The first worthwhile history of the game had appeared in 1851 – James Pycroft's *The Cricket Field*.

"FRED'S GUIDE" *title-page from 1859.*

Like Nyren's book, this history was to be reissued many times and remained the standard work on the game's early history until the 1890s, although such exhaustive tomes as Charles Box's history – gilt-edged and running to over 500 pages – arrived to fill bookcases.

The first weekly magazine devoted entirely to cricket, simply entitled *Cricket*, appeared in 1882 under the editorship of the most versatile of sporting polymaths, C.W. Alcock.

Cricket biographies, or ghosted autobiographies, commenced inevitably with W.G. Grace in 1890, closely followed by Richard Daft (from the same publisher) .

Arthur Haygarth, that diligent gatherer of scores and biographical notices, persuaded the Lillywhite organization to undertake publication of his life's work, namely the full score of every important cricket match in chronological order, with biographical notes on players, usually when they first appeared at Lord's. The project lost money for everyone connected with it, but the MCC were kind enough to publish 10 volumes even after the initial four had made a loss. They are now regarded as an essential part of a cricket historian's library.

The master of erudite cricket statistics, wrapped in a cloak of history, was F.S. Ashley-Cooper. He assisted Alcock on the weekly magazine and contributed to several of the annuals. He also wrote a goodly number of small cricket booklets.

The newspapers had from the 1830s devoted many column inches, relatively speaking, to cricket reports, but these were very pedestrian – a plodding account of the day's play, in the extreme cases almost over by over. This all changed after the First World War with the emergence of a new style of reporting in the pages of the *Manchester Guardian*. Their correspondent was Neville Cardus. He captured on paper the cricketer's characteristics and the atmosphere of the game, the subtle differences between the county teams and the ambience of the grounds they used.

Cardus never played cricket at a senior level, but one writer of distinction who did was R.C. Robertson–Glasgow. He followed Cardus's lead, but in his own inimitable way. The period between the wars also produced the best description of a fictitious village match – A.G. Macdonell's chapter entitled "The Cricket Match" in the book *England, their England*.

JOHN ARLOTT *Outstanding broadcaster.*

In Australia, the outstanding journalist of the 1930s was Ray Robinson, who wrote for the *Melbourne Star* and, in the 1940s, for the *Sydney Daily Telegraph* and later other Sydney papers. His first book did not appear until 1945, but was a great success and several more followed. Arthur Mailey, the leg-spinner, was, though in an entirely different vein, Australia's answer to Robertson-Glasgow. Mailey not only wrote but illustrated his pieces with cartoons.

The major West Indian writer whose career began in the inter-war period was C.L.R. James. He used cricket to mirror the political problems of the West Indies. *Beyond a Boundary*, which is still in print, is his best-known book.

After the Second World War, two former Test cricketers became noted journalists: Ian Peebles, the Scottish-born Middlesex bowler, and Jack Fingleton, the Australian opening bat. Fingleton wrote the book on the famous "bodyline" tour – *Cricket Crisis*.

The 1940s saw a deluge of tour books, some fairly dire, and the number of ghosted autobiographies rose until scarcely a cricketer of note lacked at least one. By now however the spoken word was vying with the written. Continuous radio commentary on Test Matches became available, and enthusiasts in England woke in the small hours to listen to their wireless sets where voices fought against atmospherics. One man successfully combined the written and spoken word, John Arlott. He was to wireless commentary what Cardus had been to journalism. His Hampshire burr epitomized cricket's roots – was Hambledon calling once more? His extensive vocabulary gave him a head start on most of his fellow commentators.

In total contrast to Arlott, it seemed, was Brian Johnson, a man of jolly wheezes, whose literary diet at Eton must have been mainly *The Magnet* and its contemporaries. His schoolboy humour, centred on cream cakes, made the BBC programme 'Test Match Special' so popular that people only moderately interested in the game switched on.

CRICKET AND THE BOX

Television, however, began to dominate the airwaves. At first TV merely provided commentary with pictures, but that all changed with the Packer Revolution. Kerry Packer, the Australian television mogul, tried to obtain the broadcasting rights for major matches in Australia, but the cricket officials stayed faithful to the national Australian Broadcasting Corporation. Packer reacted in 1977 by buying up almost the entire Australian Test team, the West Indian Test side and sundry Test players from the rest of the world. He then proceeded to stage "Super-Tests" in rivalry with the official games. To promote his venture he abandoned the traditional white clothing for cricketers and gave each side coloured clothing in the manner of soccer. He played matches under floodlight and tried such gimmicks as a camera hidden in the middle stump, logos painted on the turf and many other innovative ploys. Within two or three years, traditional cricket had fallen for his television-based ideas and the advertising firms who wanted exposure on television became more important than the ordinary spectator.

In a curious way all the television razzmatazz has affected one esoteric group who would normally shun such public exposure. Television requires winners – not only teams, but "Man of the Match", "Man of the Series", "Player of the Year". The idea that two or more players could possibly be judged equal appears to be anathema to advertisers and TV moguls, so peculiar statistical analyses have to be devised to ensure a single victor.

The cricket statisticians now come into their own. Cricketing records, which had been the ultra-introverted Ashley-Cooper's province, became important to the commercial cricketing world. Roy Webber, the scorer for BBC television, even had a telephone exchange named after him. The Association of Cricket Statisticians and Historians was formed in 1973 and has a membership of some 1,300. More to the point, it has published about 300 books on statistics over the last 25 years.

Rowland Bowen took it upon himself to investigate the origins of cricket, and indeed to research the "facts" published in many books which touched on cricket history. For eight years he published the findings of the researches made by himself and his coterie in a quarterly magazine. This culminated in his book *Cricket: A History of its Growth and Development Throughout the World*.

In Australia, the study of cricket's history has been pursued in much greater depth than elsewhere and has reached university level, with a number of books on the Australian people and cricket being published.

MEMORABILIA

Before the First World War only a handful of eccentrics collected "memorabilia" related to cricket. Foremost of this small band was Charles Pratt Green. Green wrote to all the famous batsmen of the day asking for one of their worn-out bats, preferably one which had been used to record a notable innings, and in return he bought the batsman a new bat of his own choice. In that way, he amassed over 100 bats.

A. J. Gaston, a Sussex cricket enthusiast, concentrated more on cricket books. Autographs were eagerly sought by schoolboys who in some cases took their hobby on into later life. Between the wars, the millionaire Sir Julien Cahn built up a valuable collection, not only buying Green's historic bats, but also acquiring the library of Ashley-Cooper.

The ultimate aim of cricket book collectors is a complete set of *Wisden*. Demand outstripped supply and prices reflected this. The first three editions of John Wisden's little almanack all command a price at auction exceeding £3,000 – in contrast with the original published price of one shilling (5p). Bookshops specializing in cricket have been founded to cater for the growing market. Dealers operating from their own homes issue lists of stock for sale.

The major auction houses in the UK hold sales of sports items, largely centred on cricket. A society has been established for some 10 years catering for memorabilia collectors. If a cricket motif is present on an otherwise unremarkable piece of pottery or bric-a-brac, the price rises considerably, the aesthetic value counting for little. Professional cricketers hold auctions at which they seem to sell their entire wardrobe – caps and blazers are particularly prized by collectors.

CIGARETTE AND TRADE CARDS

In the popular mind, cricketing cigarette cards will always be associated with John Player & Sons and in particular with the album that firm issued for the 50 cards in the 1938 *Cricketers* series. The cards depict 34 current English county cricketers – those likely to feature

CRICKETING CARDS *A major collectible.*

in the 1938 Tests – and the 16 Australians chosen to tour England that summer. In fact, the first cigarette cards depicting cricket personalities had been issued in the United States and in Australia in the 1880s. Complete sets devoted to cricketers, however, were first issued in the UK by Wills. Taddy & Co in 1908 produced the most extensive range ever attempted: 238 cards in all are believed to have been issued, Taddy having a card for virtually every county player of note.

The ill-fated Triangular Test Tournament of 1912, when England, Australia and South Africa competed during a rain-sodden English summer, produced another surge of cricket cards, a set of 70 being published by F & J Smith.

Some collectors specialize in cigarette and other cricketing trade cards. It is estimated that there are in excess of 12,000 such cards.

After the First World War, the cricket card rivalry did not return until 1923 when two firms, R & J Hill and Godfrey Phillips, launched sets. John Player produced their first *Ashes* set in 1926. The outbreak of the Second World War saw the end of cigarette cards, but firms such as those producing packets of tea and packets of sweets issued trade cards, some of which featured cricketers. Increasingly, though, soccer players took preference, the market for the latter being that much larger.

POSTAGE STAMPS

Unlike cigarette cards, postage stamps featuring cricketers are an entirely post-Second World War phenomenon. The first cricket stamps were issued in 1962 by the Cape Verde Islands, a Portuguese colony off the west coast of Africa. Later that year Pakistan followed suit.

English philatelists had for many years to be satisfied with a collection of Post Office cancellation marks on the standard British stamp – the major cricket grounds had at some time post offices on site. The first cricket-related British stamp was issued in 1973 and depicted W.G. Grace as drawn by Harry Furniss, the cartoonist. The GPO had intended to celebrate the centenary of the County Championship, but the issue was regarded by historians as a bizarre joke since most considered either 1864 or 1890 as the start of the championship.

Marcus Williams, who at one time wrote many articles on the subject, is considered the expert on cricketing postage stamps.

POSTCARDS

Over the last 10 years the interest in collecting postcards featuring cricket has increased considerably. This hobby of "deltiology" began soon after the legalization of picture postcards in 1894 and enjoyed its original heyday in the days prior to the First World War. Hawkins & Co., a firm of photographers based in Brighton, took photographs of most of the county teams which visited the County Ground at Hove, as well as individual pictures of many players. These are now eagerly sought by collectors.

CONTROVERSIES & SCANDALS

With the exception of apartheid, cricket's controversies have tended to centre on money. Gambling in the eighteenth century led to game rigging. Amateur 'earnings' have upset professionals. The higher rewards given to winning players and teams causes the laws to be bent. Cricket has never been quite the 'gentlemanly' game portrayed by idealists.

As soon as the latest scandal breaks, be it the allegations of bribery among certain Pakistani cricketers, or the suggestion that Mike Atherton tried to insert dirt into the seam of the ball, or Ed Giddins failing a drugs test, the pundits cry that cricket is going to the dogs. In the old days nothing like this, or that, ever occurred; all cricketers were as pure as the driven snow. Gentlemen would never stoop to such low conduct. All the rose-coloured-spectacle-wearers come out in force, and the petty squabbles of the past are lost in the glow.

The very first records of the game are mainly concerned with court cases of some sort. The seventeenth-century players who were brought before the ecclesiastical court for playing cricket on a Sunday no doubt besmirched the good name of cricket. In the civil court in 1718, a judge was asked to make a decision regarding a match. Kent were playing London for half a guinea a man, but when it seemed Kent would lose, three of the Kent team left in order to avoid defeat and thus having to pay. The judge ordered that the match had to be completed, which it duly was – the court costs were reported as £200.

"PUBLIC DISSIPATION" *Eighteenth-century commentators were cautious of cricket.*

By the 1760s the game had gained a grim reputation, as the following paragraph indicates:

"The game of cricket which requires the utmost exertion of strength and agility, was followed until of late years, for manly exercise, animated by a noble spirit of Emulation. This sport has too long been perverted from diversion and innocent pastime to excessive gaming and public dissipation: Cricket matches are now degenerated into business of importance."

The authorities at London's most celebrated cricket ground, the Artillery Ground, banned public matches from the ground because of the numbers of rogues and vagabonds attracted by the gambling and various criminal activities.

The early 1800s still saw bookmakers at major cricket matches and players being bribed to lose matches. In 1817, William Lambert, the leading professional of the time, was accused of selling a match and banned from Lord's for life. About the same time bookmakers were removed from Lord's. However, betting on matches still continued and was to cause some major problems when the England teams toured Australia.

AMATEURS v PROFESSIONALS

In the 1850s and 1860s, the major quarrels were between various groups of professionals. William Clarke was the manager and captain of the highly successful professional touring side which travelled the British Isles, playing anywhere provided the remuneration for Clarke was sufficient. After several years, about half the players employed by Clarke reckoned that they would do better by breaking away and forming a rival professional side. This was duly created and was financially viable, though Clarke ignored it and would not allow his players to play against the rival team.

After Clarke died in 1856, the

two XIs made up their differences and for some seasons the major showpiece match was between the two sides at Lord's. George Parr succeeded Clarke in managing the professional touring side, but in the 1860s he became embroiled in an argument with the authorities who ran the ground at the Oval. This meant that the professionals employed by Parr refused to play for their counties at the Oval and Nottinghamshire ceased temporarily to play Surrey.

The appearance of W.G. Grace on the cricket field and his incredible batting performances in the 1870s meant that he was the star attraction at any cricket match and added hundreds if not thousands to the numbers who paid to watch a game. The problem was that he played as an amateur, but did not belong to the landed gentry and thus could not afford to spend his summers playing cricket six days a week without payment. He therefore put in very heavy expenses claims for each match appearance. To aggravate the position, the whole of the county team for which Grace played – Gloucestershire – were amateurs, but when they played a county game their expenses were more than if the whole team had been professional. In fact, Grace himself put in expenses which were twice the top professionals' pay.

The Gloucestershire County Cricket Club Committee held a meeting and issued the following statement:

"That only actual expenses shall be paid to members playing for the county, EXCEPT where special arrangements are made, such arrangements to be made from time to time by the Committee."

This resolution seemed to cover all eventualities and helped everyone, but satisfied no one.

The cricket press were upset when the MCC announced that they never paid amateurs more than their bare expenses and asked how the club could reconcile their statement with the acknowledged fact that W.G. Grace made more money from cricket than any professional. The English professionals were upset when the 1878 Australians toured England, supposedly as amateurs, but were paid £20 each for a match appearance whereas the English pros opposing them were only offered £10 per man.

The position of the Australians as paid amateurs came to be accepted by the English pros as a fact of life, but the next problem to erupt came from the leading Nottinghamshire pros. Nottinghamshire at that time was the strongest county and the players felt that they were unfairly treated by the county committee. They put a set of demands to the club which included the guarantee of a benefit after 10 years and a permanent engagement for the season, rather than being paid on a match-by-match basis. The committee refused to budge and the seven principal players went on strike. The strike held solid until mid-July, when the players started to trickle back, though the two ringleaders, Arthur Shrewsbury and Alfred Shaw, did not make peace with the club until the following season.

THROWING ACTION

No sooner had Nottinghamshire settled its differences with its players than cricket encountered trouble from another direction. The actions of some of the current fast bowlers were considered illegal in some quarters – and that of Lancashire's Jack Crossland was particularly suspect. The captain of the 1882 Australian touring team, Billy Murdoch, stated that several English bowlers would be no-balled if they appeared in Australia. It was obvious that the English authorities paid heed to Murdoch for, when selecting the England team for the Test at the Oval, they pointedly ignored Crossland, although in terms of form he was the clear choice to fill a vacancy left when Fred Morley was unfit to take part.

Crossland nonetheless continued to play for Lancashire through 1882 and 1883, even though in the latter season he was no-balled for throwing in local cricket, but never in county games.

Lord Harris met the problem head on, as captain of Kent, when he announced that the county would not play against Lancashire until both Crossland and another Lancashire bowler, Nash, were withdrawn from the side. This hit Lancashire hard since Nottinghamshire had already refused fixtures with them on the grounds that Crossland was not qualified to play for Lancashire (he was Nottinghamshire-born). Middlesex also cancelled their Lancashire fixture. In the middle of 1885, the MCC ruled that

1909 AUSSIE TEAM *and Pete McAlister.*

Crossland was not qualified for Lancashire; that county therefore dropped him and at the end of the year also finished with Nash.

The throwing row died away for a while. However, 10 years later it surfaced once more. The Australians Jones and McKibbin were both singled out in the press as chuckers. Australian umpire James Phillips no-balled Jones for throwing and the famous Australian bowler of a previous generation, Spofforth, condemned McKibbin's action. In England, a number of bowlers were no-balled for throwing including the famous C.B. Fry, but the epidemic did not end until a list of doubtful bowlers was drawn up and the county captains came to a gentlemen's agreement not to use any of the bowlers on the list. This effectively ended the throwing problem for some 50 years.

AUSSIES BATTLE IT OUT

The next major controversy was entirely an Australian affair. It was a battle for control between the leading Australian players and the Australian Board of Control with regard to teams sent to tour England. The Board was formed in 1905, but not in time to organize the proposed 1905 Australian tour to England. This tour was run by the Melbourne Club in conjunction with the players themselves and Frank Laver of Victoria was appointed by the team as the player-manager. The tour went ahead and nothing untoward occurred. In 1906, however, disputes arose between anyone and everyone in Australian cricket, including the various state associations and their players, particularly in New South Wales. The best way to illustrate the muddle is to quote the cricket press from May 1906:

"It is simply impossible to say what is the latest development of the situation in Australia, for the cablegrams, press and private, differ to a degree which is unusual. Hence it is stated that several players have been suspended, disqualified, excommunicated by the New South Wales Cricketers' Association; that no players have been suspended etc; that time has been given to the recalcitrant players to repent of their misdeed; that the Melbourne Club has sent an invitation to the Marylebone Club to send out a team this autumn, and that the offer has been declined; that no such invitation was ever sent; that a rival Board of Control has been formed by clubs which would not join the original Board; that no rival Board has been formed; that the players who accepted the offer of the Melbourne Club, and were suspended, have gone down on their knees to apologise, and have thrown over the Melbourne Club."

This confusion continued so that, when in 1909 a team was organized to tour England again, the selection committee chosen by the Board was somewhat odd, for it included Peter McAlister rather than either Monty Noble or Victor Trumper, both of whom put their names forward and were far better qualified in terms of experience and expertise. To compound the error, the committee selected McAlister as vice-captain for the tour. McAlister was also appointed treasurer for the tourists, whilst the players independently picked Frank Laver to look after their financial interests. This produced a conflict of interest, and a great deal of mud-slinging when the Board tried to check the details on the team's return to Australia.

The ill-feeling generated bubbled through the next two years and finally blew up during a selectors' meeting convened to pick the players for the fourth Test of the 1911–12 Ashes series v England. McAlister accused Clem Hill, the current Australian captain, of being the worst leader Australia had ever had. Hill punched McAlister and the pair went into a clinch. They were saved from falling through a window to the street 30 feet below by the intervention of the Board's secretary. This was one dramatic incident in a catalogue of rows between the Board and the players and the end result was that most of the major players did not go to England on the 1912 tour. The First World War finally brought the quarrels to an end.

BODYLINE BOWLING

The great controversy between the two World Wars revolved round the 1932–33 bodyline series. In the late 1920s, pitches in Australia specifically were all in favour of the bat; allied to this, two batsmen of extraordinary talent, Don Bradman and Bill Ponsford, emerged. On two occasions, team totals topped 1,000 and both players had innings exceeding 400. When Australia toured England in 1930, Bradman proved almost invincible and among other feats created a new highest score in Test cricket. After the England side had been chosen for the 1932–33 tour to Australia, studies of Bradman's technique revealed that he appeared to be weakest playing fast bowling pitched on the leg stump. England possessed a battery of fine fast bowlers with Harold Larwood as the spearhead. Douglas Jardine, the England captain, decided to use Larwood to attack the leg stump with a half circle of close fielders on the leg side. The tactic proved successful, in that Bradman's batting average all but halved from around 100 to nearer 50. England went on to win the Ashes.

CLEM HILL *Australia's 1911–12 captain.*

However, in the process, several Australian batsmen were injured, hit by the ball whilst batting against Larwood, and the Australian press named the leg-theory method "bodyline". Larwood and Jardine, in particular, were accused of not playing cricket; the Australian Board threatened to cease playing the Test series and bitter telegrams were dispatched by the Board to the MCC at Lord's. The English authorities were adamant that the English bowlers were not bowling at the batsmen and that the only serious injury caused to an Australian happened when Bert Oldfield ducked into a ball that he thought would rise, was hit on the head and knocked out. This accident was not the result of "bodyline" bowling. The Australian crowds barracked Larwood and Jardine excessively in support of their team and this led to a counter-claim by the MCC that this volume of barracking was unsportsmanlike.

The arguments went on through the English summer of 1933 and, with the Australians touring England in 1934, something had to be done to placate both sides if the 1934 Ashes series was to proceed peacefully. Jardine led the England side in India in the winter of 1933–34, then from India announced he would not play in England in 1934. This removed the architect of leg-theory; the question at the start of the 1934 season, therefore, was whether Larwood and his principal bowling partner, the left-armer Bill Voce, would play for England. Injury had meant that Larwood had missed most of the 1933 summer, but he was now fully fit again. The MCC asked Larwood and Voce to make an apology for the way they had bowled in 1932–33 but both refused. They were of the opinion that they had simply bowled to the orders of the England captain and thus had nothing to apologize for. Several ghosted newspaper articles under Larwood's name put matters a little more forcibly. Larwood and Voce were both Nottinghamshire players and were supported by their county captain, Arthur Carr. Carr employed the bowlers using leg-theory tactics in some championship games. This not only made the situation worse but meant that two counties announced that they would not be playing Nottinghamshire again.

Despite tremendous clamour from the English press, the selectors did not pick Larwood and Voce for the 1934 Ashes series. Australia won the series. Arthur Carr was sacked by Nottinghamshire; Larwood never again played in Test cricket; but Voce returned and was the most successful bowler on the next trip to Australia in 1936–37. Larwood retired from first-class cricket in 1938 and in 1949 emigrated to Australia with his family.

"STOP THE TOUR"

The major cricketing problem of the period between 1960 and 1990 has been how to deal with the relationship between South Africa and the other Test-playing countries. The whole situation regarding the English cricket authorities and apartheid came to a head in 1968, when the English selectors decided to replace Tom Cartwright, who had reported unfit, with Basil D'Oliveira in the squad to tour South Africa during the winter of 1968–69.

D'Oliveira was born in Cape Town and had great success in local cricket in South Africa, but as a Cape coloured had no prospect of being chosen for first-class cricket or Test cricket in South Africa. He had emigrated to England and qualified by residence for Worcestershire and for England. In 1965, he began a successful career as a middle-order batsman and swing bowler, being chosen for England in 1966. However, he was not on the original list to tour South Africa in 1968–69. When he filled a vacancy that arose in mid-September, the South African Prime Minister, Mr Vorster, immediately accused the English authorities of picking D'Oliveira for political reasons and the tour was cancelled.

A special meeting of the MCC was called to discuss tours to and from South Africa, the Reverend David Sheppard and Mike Brearley being the major figures to suggest that tours should cease. However, those wishing to continue tours won the day, and South Africa were given the green light to visit England in 1970. A young white South African studying in London, Peter Hain, then organized a "Stop the Tour" campaign. After discussions with the British Government and a debate in the House of Commons, the tour was cancelled and the South African Cricket Association were informed that no further Test tours involving South Africa would take place until South African cricket was run on multi-racial lines.

Official Test matches involving South Africa therefore ceased, but the reaction from South Africa was to persuade Test-quality players to come to the country unofficially. Teams from England, Australia, the West Indies and Sri Lanka all toured South Africa in the 1980s. The players who went found themselves facing a variety of bans when, or if, they returned home – both the West Indian and Sri Lankan authorities put a life ban on their rebel players. The problems were not settled until 1991 when the South African Government changed its policy and introduced multi-racial elections.

PACKER'S CIRCUS

The Kerry Packer Affair occupied the cricket officials for several years in the late 1970s. Mr Packer, a media tycoon, put in a bid to broadcast Test matches from his station in 1976 and his bid was higher than that already accepted by the Australian Board. Despite discussions, the Board stayed with its original decision and Packer decided to set up rival super-Tests. In 1977, he signed up virtually the whole of the current Australian Test squad, almost all the notable West Indian Test players, plus a selection of English, South African, Pakistani and other players. The last group formed The Rest and Packer organized a full programme of Super-Tests and one-day games between the three sides, playing throughout Australia.

The reaction in England was to ban the English players who signed for Packer but, after a famous court case, the English authorities were found guilty of restraint of trade. The trial lasted nearly seven weeks and cost the TCCB dearly. Packer's Circus, as it was called, played two full seasons in Australia and toured the West Indies, after which Packer reached an agreement with the Australian Board and obtained exclusive rights to broadcast official Tests for 10 years. Packer's revolution changed the face of cricket, with the official bodies adopting many of the TV gimmicks used by Packer and the salaries paid to players being massively increased.

MIKE ATHERTON *Accused of cheating.*

BALL TAMPERING

The most recent scandal arose during the Lord's Test, England v South Africa, in 1994. Mike Atherton, the England captain, was accused of cheating, having been seen to apparently rub dirt into the seam of the ball. He initially denied his action, but was then fined £2,000 by the England manager for lying and for tampering with the ball. Such tampering by lifting the seam and altering the surface of the ball was done to help the bowler produce a reverse swing. The Pakistani bowlers had perfected the reverse swing two or three years earlier and the former Pakistani captain, Imran Khan, claimed that he had bowled such deliveries in the Lord's Test of 1982. The whole legitimacy of such bowling depended on whether the ball reached the right condition for this reverse swing by natural causes, or whether the bowlers tampered with the ball to achieve this condition.

CRICKET RECORDS

HIGHEST TEAM TOTALS

Only two totals over 1,000 have been scored in first-class cricket. In both cases, the batsman who led the run glut was W.H. Ponsford – 429 v Tasmania and 352 against New South Wales. The 10 highest team totals are:

1,107	Victoria v New South Wales, Melbourne	1926–27
1,059	Victoria v Tasmania, Melbourne	1922–23
952–6	Sri Lanka v India, Colombo	1997
951–7d	Sind v Baluchistan, Karachi	1973–74
944–6d	Hyderabad v Andhra, Secunderabad	1993–94
918	New South Wales v South Australia, Sydney	1900–01
912–8d	Holkar v Mysore, Indore	1945–46
912–6d	Tamil Nadu v Goa, Panjim	1988–89
910–6d	Railways v Dera Ismail Khan, Lahore	1964–65
903–7d	England v Australia, the Oval	1938
887	Yorkshire v Warwickshire, Edgbaston	1896

LOWEST TEAM TOTALS

The lowest total in any game of cricket is naturally enough 0. The first recorded example was in Norfolk in July 1815 – Fakenham, Walsingham and Hempton were all out 0 against Le cham, Dunham and Brisley. The 10 lowest totals in first-class cricket are:

6	Bs v England, Lord's	1810
12	Oxford University v MCC, Cowley Marsh	1877
12	Northamptonshire v Gloucestershire, Gloucester	1907
13	Auckland v Canterbury, Auckland	1877–78
13	Nottinghamshire v Yorkshire, Trent Bridge	1901
14	Surrey v Essex, Chelmsford	1983
15	MCC v Surrey, Lord's	1983
15	Victoria v MCC, Melbourne	1903–04
15	Northamptonshire v Yorkshire, Northampton	1908
15	Hampshire v Warwickshire, Edgbaston	1922

The last score on the above list is unique in that, batting a second time, Hampshire hit 521, then bowled out Warwickshire to win the game by 155 runs.

The lowest team total in Test cricket:

26	New Zealand v England, Auckland	1954–55

VICTORIES BY THE LARGEST MARGINS

The biggest victory of all occurred when Pakistan Railways – see highest team totals – hit 910–6d and their opponents only managed 59 in their two innings! The five biggest wins are:

Innings and 851 runs	Railways v Dera Ismail Khan, Lahore	1964–65
Innings and 666 runs	Victoria v Tasmania, Melbourne	1922–23
Innings and 656 runs	Victoria v New South Wales, Melbourne	1926–27
Innings and 605 runs	New South Wales v S Australia, Sydney	1900–01
Innings and 579 runs	England v Australia, the Oval	1938

HIGHEST INDIVIDUAL INNINGS

The first recorded innings above 100 was made by John Minshull who hit 107 for the Duke of Dorset's XI v Wrotham in 1769. William Ward hit the first double-century – 278 for MCC v Norfolk – in 1820. The present record score has stood for nearly 100 years. The top 10 highest innings in first-class cricket are:

501*	B.C. Lara, Warwickshire v Durham, Edgbaston	1994
499	Hanif Mohammad, Karachi v Bahawalpur, Karachi	1958–59
452*	D.G. Bradman, New South Wales v Queensland, Sydney	1929–30
443*	B.B. Nimbalkar, Maharashtra v Kathiswar, Poona	1948–49
437	W.H. Ponsford, Victoria v Queensland, Melbourne	1927–28
429	W.H. Ponsford, Victoria v Tasmania, Melbourne	1922–23
428	Aftab Baloch, Sind v Baluchistan, Karachi	1973–74
424	A.C. MacLaren, Lancashire v Somerset, Taunton	1895
405*	G.A. Hick, Worcestershire v Somerset, Taunton	1988
386	B. Sutcliffe, Otago v Canterbury, Christchurch	1952–53

*** not out**

The best innings in Test cricket are:

375	B.C. Lara, West Indies v England, St John's	1993–94
365*	G.St.A. Sobers, West Indies v Pakistan, Kingston	1957–58
364	L. Hutton, England v Australia, the Oval	1938
340	S.T. Jayasuriya, Sri Lanka v India, Colombo	1997
337	Hanif Mohammad, Pakistan v West Indies, Bridgetown	1957–58
336*	W.R. Hammond, England v New Zealand, Auckland	1932–33
334	D.G. Bradman, Australia v England, Headingley	1930

*** not out**

MOST RUNS IN A SEASON

When Denis Compton and Bill Edrich broke the record in 1947, they each played in 30 first-class matches. The most matches played by anyone in 1996 was 20, so though four-day games in theory might provide an opportunity to beat Compton's record, it is most unlikely – the highest aggregate in 1997 was 1,944 by Graham Gooch. The leading run-scorers in an English first-class season are:

		M	I	NO	Runs	HS	Avge	100s
D.C.S. Compton (Middx)	1947	30	50	8	3,816	246	90.85	18
W.J. Edrich (Middx)	1947	30	52	8	3,539	267*	80.43	12
T.W. Hayward (Surrey)	1906	37	61	8	3,518	219	66.37	13
L Hutton (Yorks)	1949	33	56	6	3,429	269*	68.58	12
F.E. Woolley (Kent)	1928	36	59	4	3,352	198	60.94	12
H. Sutcliffe (Yorks)	1932	35	52	7	3,336	313	74.13	14
W.R. Hammond (Gloucs)	1933	34	54	5	3,323	264	67.81	13
E.H. Hendren (Middx)	1928	35	54	7	3,311	209*	70.44	13
R. Abel (Surrey)	1901	38	68	8	3,309	247	55.15	7
W.R. Hammond (Gloucs)	1937	33	55	5	3,252	217	65.04	13

* not out

Outside England the most runs in the current Test-playing countries in a single season are:

		Runs	Avge	
Australia	D.G. Bradman	1,690	93.88	1928–29
South Africa	J.R. Reid	1,915	68.39	1961–62
West Indies	E.H. Hendren	1,765	135.76	1929–30
New Zealand	M.D. Crowe	1,676	93.11	1986–87
India	C.G. Borde	1,604	64.16	1964–65
Pakistan	Saadat Ali	1,649	63.42	1983–84
Sri Lanka	R.P. Arnold	1,475	70.23	1995–96
Zimbabwe	G.W. Flower	983	57.82	1994–95

MOST RUNS IN A FIRST-CLASS CAREER

As with the most runs in a season, the reduction in the number of first-class matches means that Hobbs' record is unlikely to be broken.

		M	I	NO	Runs	HS	Avge	100s
J.B. Hobbs	1905–34	834	1,325	107	61,760	316*	50.70	199
F.E. Woolley	1906–38	978	1,530	84	58,969	305*	40.77	145
E.H. Hendren	1907–38	833	1,300	166	57,611	301*	50.80	170
C.P. Mead	1905–36	814	1,340	185	55,061	280*	47.67	153
W.G. Grace	1865–08	869	1,478	104	54,211	344	39.45	124
W.R. Hammond	1920–51	634	1,005	104	50,551	336*	56.10	167
H. Sutcliffe	1919–45	754	1,098	124	50,670	313	52.02	151
G. Boycott	1962–86	609	1,014	162	48,426	261*	56.83	151

*** not out**

The highest career averages by a batsman who reached 10,000 runs are as follows:

D.G. Bradman	1927–48	234	338	43	28,067	452*	95.14	117
V.M. Merchant	1929–51	150	234	46	13,470	359*	71.64	45
W.H. Ponsford	1920–34	162	235	23	13,819	437	65.18	47
W.M. Woodfull	1921–34	174	245	39	13,388	284	64.99	49

*** not out**

MOST RUNS IN TEST CAREER FOR EACH COUNTRY

England	G.A. Gooch	118	215	6	8,900	333	42.58	20
Australia	A.R. Border	156	265	44	11,174	205	50.56	27
South Africa	B. Mitchell	42	80	9	3,471	189*	48.88	8
West Indies	I.V.A. Richards	121	182	12	8,540	291	50.23	24
New Zealand	M.D. Crowe	77	131	11	5,444	299	45.36	17
India	S.M. Gavaskar	125	214	16	10,122	236*	51.12	34
Pakistan	Javed Miandad	124	189	21	8,832	280*	52.57	23

* **not out**

HIGHEST WICKET PARTNERSHIP

FIRST

561	Waheed Mirza and Mansoor Akhtar, Karachi Whites v Quetts, Karachi	1976–77
413	V. Mankad and Pankaj Roy, India v New Zealand, Madras	1955

SECOND

576	S.T. Jayasuriya and R. Mahanama, Sri Lanka v India, Colombo	1997
475	Zahir Alam and L.S. Rajput, Assam v Tripura, Gahati	1991–92

THIRD

467	A.H. Jones and M.D. Crowe, New Zealand v Sri Lanka, Wellington	1990–91

FOURTH

577	V.S. Hazare and Gul Mahomed, Baroda v Holkar, Baroda	1946–47
411	P.B.H. May and M.C. Cowdrey, England v West Indies, Edgbaston	1957

FIFTH

464*	M.E. Waugh and S.R. Waugh, New South Wales v W Australia, Perth	1990–91
405	S.G. Barnes and D.G. Bradman, Australia v England, Sydney	1946–47

SIXTH

487*	G.A. Headley and C.C. Passailaigue, Jamaica v Lord Tennyson's XI, Kingston	1931–32
346	J.H.W. Fingleton and D.G. Bradman, Australia v England, Melbourne	1936–37

SEVENTH

460	Bhupinder Singh and P. Dharmani, Punjab v Delhi, Delhi	1994–95
308	Waqar Hassan and Imtiaz Ahmed, Pakistan v New Zealand, Lahore	1955–56

EIGHT

433	V.T. Trumper and A. Sims, A. Sims' XI v Canterbury, Christchurch	1913–14
246	L.E.G. Ames and G.O.B. Allen, England v New Zealand, Lord's	1931

NINTH

283	J. Chapman and A. Warren, Derbyshire v Warwickshire, Blackwell	1910
190	Asif Iqbal and Intikhab Alam, Pakistan v England, the Oval	1967

TENTH

307	A.F. Kippax and J.E.H. Hooker, New South Wales v Victoria, Melbourne	1928–29
151	B.F. Hastings and R.O. Collinge, New Zealand v Pakistan	1972–73

BEST BOWLING IN AN INNINGS

The best possible analysis for a bowler in an eleven-a-side match is to take all 10 wickets without allowing a single run. The top 10 analyses in first-class cricket are:

O	M	R	W		
19.4	16	10	10	H. Verity, Yorkshire v Nottinghamshire, Headingley	1932
19	11	20	10	P.M. Chatterjee, Bengal v Assam, Jorhat	1956–57
12	2	25	10	A.E.E. Vogler, E. Province v Griqualand West, Johannesburg	1906–07
21.3	10	28	10	Naeem Akhtar, Rawalpindi B v Peshawar	1995–96
16.2	8	18	10	G. Geary, Leicestershire v Glamorgan, Pontypridd	1929
23.2	14	28	10	W.P. Howell, Australians v Surrey, the Oval	1899
21.3	10	28	10	A.E. Moss, Canterbury v Wellington, Christchurch	1889–90
16	7	30	10	C. Blythe, Kent v Northamptonshire, Northampton	1907
8.5	0	35	10	A. Drake, Yorkshire v Somerset, Weston	1895
27	11	32	10	H. Picket, Essex v Leicestershire, Leyton	1895

The best analysis in Test cricket is:

51.2	23	53	10	J.C. Laker, England v Australia, Old Trafford	1956

BEST BOWLING IN A MATCH

A number of bowlers have taken all 20 wickets in a match, the first recorded instance being by the F.R. Spofforth, who took 20 for 48 in Bendigo, NSW in 1881–82.

The best records in first-class matches are (the first being the Test record):

19–90	J.C. Laker, England v Australia, Old Trafford	1956
17–48	C. Blythe, Kent v Northamptonshire, Northampton	1907
17–50	C.T.B. Turner, Australians v England XI, Hastings	1888
17–54	W.P. Howell, Australians v W. Province, Cape Town	1902–03
17–56	C.W.L. Parker, Gloucestershire v Essex, Colchester	1925
17–67	A.P. Freeman, Kent v Sussex, Hove	1922
17–89	W.G. Grace, Gloucestershire v Nottinghamshire, Cheltenham	1877
17–89	F.C.L. Matthews, Nottinghamshire v Northamptonshire, Trent Bridge	1923

MOST WICKETS IN ENGLAND IN A SEASON

The contraction in the number of first-class matches means that the records below are unlikely to be beaten. It is now rare for a bowler to reach 100 wickets in a season.

		O	M	R	W	Avge
A.P. Freeman	1928	1,976.1	423	5,489	304	18.05
A.P. Freeman	1933	2,039.0	651	4,549	298	15.26
T. Richardson	1895	1,690.1	463	4,170	290	14.37
C.T.B. Turner	1888	2,427.2	1,127	3,307	283	11.68
A.P. Freeman	1931	1,618.0	360	4,307	276	15.60
A.P. Freeman	1930	1,914.3	472	4,632	275	16.84

To take 100 wickets in a season outside England is most unusual. The following have achieved the feat:

Australia, C.T.B. Turner 106 in 1887–88
South Africa, R. Benaud 106 in 1957–58
India, M.W. Tate 116 in 1926–27
Pakistan, Ijaz Faqih 107 in 1985–86; Murtaza Hussain 105 in 1995–96; Abdul Qadir 103 in 1982–83
South Africa, S.F. Barnes 104 in 1913–14

MOST WICKETS IN A FIRST-CLASS CAREER

		R	W	Avge	5i	10m	BB
W. Rhodes	1898–30	70,322	4204	16.72	287	68	9–24
A.P. Freeman	1914–36	69,577	3776	18.42	386	140	10–53
C.W.L. Parker	1903–35	63,817	3278	19.46	277	91	10–79
J.T. Hearne	1888–23	54,352	3061	17.75	255	66	9–32
T.W.J. Goddard	1922–52	59,116	2979	19.84	251	86	10–113
A.S. Kennedy	1907–36	61,034	2874	21.23	225	45	10–37
D. Shackleton	1948–69	53,303	2857	18.65	194	38	9–30
G.A.R. Lock	1946–70	54,709	2844	19.23	196	50	10–54
F.J. Titmus	1949–82	63,313	2830	22.37	168	26	9–52
W.G. Grace	1865–08	50,980	2809	18.14	240	64	10–49

MOST WICKETS IN TEST CAREER FOR EACH COUNTRY

England	I.T. Botham	10,878	383	28.4	27	4	8–34
Australia	D.K. Lillee	8,493	355	23.92	23	7	7–83
South Africa	H.J. Tayfield	4,405	170	25.91	14	2	9–113
West Indies	M.D. Marshall	7,876	376	20.94	22	4	7–22
New Zealand	R.J. Hadlee	9,612	431	22.29	36	9	9–52
India	Kapil Dev	12,867	434	29.74	23	2	9–83
Pakistan	Imran Khan	8,258	362	22.81	23	6	8–58

ALL-ROUND RECORDS

Until the reduction of first-class matches in England, the standard measurement of an all-rounder was that he scored 1,000 runs in a season and took 100 wickets. The two outstanding all-round feats which go beyond this record are 2,000 runs and 200 wickets in a season – performed only once by G.H. Hirst of Yorkshire in 1906, and 3,000 runs and 100 wickets, again only achieved once, by J.H. Parks of Sussex in 1937. Since the reduction in matches, just two players have managed 1,000 runs and 100 wickets – R.J. Hadlee in 1984 and F.D. Stephenson in 1988 – and both played for Nottinghamshire.

The outstanding all-round career figures are as follows:

	M	R	Avge	W	Avge
W. Rhodes	1,110	39,969	30.81	4,204	16.72
W.G. Grace	869	54,211	39.45	2,809	18.14

The outstanding all-round career figures at Test level are:

I.T. Botham (Eng)	102	5,200	33.54	383	28.40
R. Benaud (Aus)	63	2,201	24.45	248	27.03
G.St.A. Sobers (WI)	93	8,032	57.78	235	34.03
R.J. Hadlee (NZ)	86	3,124	27.16	431	22.29
Kapil Dev (India)	131	5,248	31.05	434	29.64
Imran Khan (Pak)	88	3,807	37.69	362	22.81

Botham and Sobers also took more than 100 catches each.

WICKET-KEEPING

Most dismissals in an English season are 128 (79 ct, 49 st) by L.E.G. Ames for Kent in 1929; in a career, 1,649 (147 ct, 176 st) by R.W. Taylor of Derbyshire.

At Test level, both these records are held by R.W. Marsh of Australia; he took 28 (all ct) in a single series and 355 (343 ct, 12 st) in his career.

FIELDING

Most catches by a fielder in an English season are 78 by W.R. Hammond of Gloucestershire in 1928; the most in a career by F.E. Woolley of Kent with 1,018.
Most catches in a Test series are 15 by J.M. Gregory of Australia, and in a Test career 156 by A.R. Border of Australia.

CRICKET CHRONOLOGY

1598 First reference to the game – in a court case in Guildford, Surrey

1646 First recorded cricket match at Coxheath, Kent

1706 A poem in Latin by William Goldwin gives first description of a match

1709 Match between Kent and Surrey at Dartford – first inter-county game

1710 Cricket first mentioned at Cambridge University

1727 Cricket first mentioned at Oxford University

1739 Earliest known pictorial reference showing boys playing cricket.

1744 Kent v All England on the Artillery Ground, London, first major match whose detailed score is preserved

1744 Earliest extant Laws of Cricket

1751 New York oppose London in New York

1767 Charles Powlett takes over the Hambledon Club in Hampshire about this time

1769 First recorded century: John Minshull 107 for Duke of Dorset's XI

1787 Thomas Lord opens his first ground (now Dorset Square) in London

1792 Calcutta Club in India in existence

1794 First recorded public school match: Charterhouse v Westminster

1800 First instructional book published by T. Boxall

1803 First cricket in Australia – Sydney

1806 First Gentlemen v Players Match at Lord's

1814 Present Lord's cricket ground opened

1825 Sussex play Kent in the match from which the county championship originated

1827 First Oxford v Cambridge university match

1828 Round-arm bowling legalized

1835 Nottinghamshire oppose Sussex in the former's first quest for the title of Champion County

1844 United States play Canada for the first time – the oldest international contest in the world

1846 Surrey oppose Kent in the former's first quest for the title of Champion County

1850–51 Tasmania play Victoria at Launceston in the first Australian inter-colonial first-class match

1855–56 New South Wales play Victoria in the former's firstfirst-class match

1857 Cambridgeshire oppose Surrey in the former's first quest for the title Champion County

1859 George Parr leads first England team overseas – to North America

1859 Middlesex oppose Kent in the former's first quest for the title Champion County

1861 Yorkshire oppose Surrey in the former's first quest for the title Champion County

1863–64 Otago play Canterbury in the first first-class match in New Zealand

1864 *Wisden's Cricketers' Almanack* first published

1864–65 Barbados play Demerara (British Guiana) at Bridgetown in the first first-class match in the British West Indies

1864 Over-arm bowling legalized

1864 Hampshire join the County Championship (drop out in 1885 and rejoin in 1895)

1865 Lancashire join the County Championship

1868 Australian Aborigines tour England

1868–69 Trinidad play Demerara (Guyana) in the former's first first-class match

1870 Gloucestershire join the County Championship

1871 W.G. Grace becomes the first batsman to hit 2,000 first-class runs in a season

1871 Derbyshire join County Championship (drop out after 1887 and rejoin in 1895)

1873–74 Auckland and Wellington each play their first first-class match

1876 W.G. Grace becomes the first batsman to score 300 in first-class cricket: 344 for MCC at Canterbury

1876–77 First-ever Test match: England v Australia, Melbourne

1877–78 South Australia play Tasmania in the former's first first-class match

1878 First first-class match in the United States – Philadelphia v Australia at Nicetown

1878 First official Australian tour to England

1880 Kennington Oval stages its first Test, England v Australia

1881–82 Sydney cricket ground stages its first Test, England v Australia

1882 Somerset join County Championship (drop out after 1884 and rejoin in 1891)

1884 Lord's, London, stages its first Test, England v Australia
1884 Old Trafford, Manchester, stages its first Test, England v Australia
1888–89 South Africa's first Test v England at Port Elizabeth
1888–89 Newlands, Cape Town, stages its first Test, England v South Africa
1889–90 Natal, Western Province and Transvaal each play their first first-class match. Currie Cup inaugurated
1889–90 First English team tours India
1890–91 Eastern Province and Griqualand West play their first first-class match
1892–93 Sheffield Shield competition inaugurated this season
1892–93 Queensland play New South Wales in the former's first first-class match
1892–93 First first-class match in India: Parsees v Europeans in Bombay
1892–93 Western Australia play Victoria in the former's first first-class match
1894–95 Jamaica play their first first-class match
1895 Essex, Leicestershire and Warwickshire join the County Championship
1898 Board of Control set up to run Tests in England
1899 Worcestershire join the County Championship
1899 Trent Bridge, Nottingham, stages its first Test, England v Australia
1899 Headingley, Leeds, stages its first Test, England v Australia
1900 Six-ball over introduced into England
1902 Edgbaston, Birmingham, stages its first Test, England v Australia
1902–03 Borderplay their first first-class match
1903–04 Orange Free State play their first first-class match
1905 Australian Board of Control set up
1905–06 Hindus join the Bombay Tournament
1905 Northamptonshire join the County Championship
1906–07 Plunket Shield presented to Canterbury
1909 ICC (Imperial, now International, Cricket Conference) founded
1909–10 Rhodesia (Zimbabwe) play their first first-class match
1911–12 First first-class match in South America
1912–13 Muslims join the Bombay Tournament
1915–16 First first-class match in Madras Presidency Tournament
1921 Glamorgan join County Championship
1925–26 First first-class match in Ceylon (Sri Lanka): Dr J. Rockwood's Ceylon XI v W.E. Lucas's Bombay XI
1926 English Women's Cricket Association founded
1926 India, New Zealand and the West Indies join England, Australia and South Africa in the ICC
1926–27 Queensland join the Sheffield Shield
1928 West Indies' first Test v England at Lord's
1929–30 New Zealand's first Test v England at Christchurch
1929–30 Queen's Park Oval, Port of Spain, stages its first Test, England v West Indies
1929–30 Basin Reserve, Wellington, stages its first Test, England v New Zealand
1929–30 Kensington Oval, Bridgetown, stages its first Test, England v West Indies
1930–31 First first-class match in the Moin-ud-Dowlah Cup
1931–32 Woolloongabba, Brisbane, stages its first Test, Australia v South Africa
1932 India's first Test v England at Lord's
1932–33 England v Australia bodyline series
1933–34 Eden Gardens, Calcutta, stages its first Test, India v England
1934–35 Ranji Trophy Competition inaugurated
1937–38 Last first-class match in South America: Argentina v Sir T. Brinckman's XI at Belgrano
1947–48 Western Australia join the Sheffield Shield
1947–48 First first-class match in Pakistan: West Punjab Governor's XI v Punjab University
1947 D.C.S. Compton hits 3,816 first-class runs in season – new record and also 18 hundreds
1950–51 Central Districts join Plunket Shield
1952–53 Pakistan's first Test v India at Delhi
1952 Pakistan join the ICC
1953–54 Qaid-I-Azam Tournament for first-class cricket in Pakistan inaugurated
1956–57 Northern Districts join Plunket Shield
1958–59 Leeward Islands play their first first-class match
1959–60 Windward Islands play their first first-class match
1961–62 Duleep Trophy competition inaugurated
1963 Gillette (now NatWest) Cup inaugurated
1965–66 Shell Shield competition inaugurated in the West Indies
1965 Ceylon, Fiji and USA become first Associate ICC members
1968 TCCB replaces English Board of Control
1969–70 First one-day competition in Australia
1969 Players (now AXA Life) Sunday League inaugurated
1970 South African tour to England cancelled due to anti-apartheid campaign
1970–71 BCCP Trophy competition inaugurated (continued as Patron's Trophy)
1970–71 First one-day international, Australia v England, Melbourne
1971–72 NZ Motor Corp Tournament: first one-day competition of major standing in New Zealand inaugurated
1972 Benson & Hedges Cup inaugurated
1972 Prudential (now Texaco) One-Day Trophy inaugurated
1973–74 Deodhar Trophy inaugurated: first one-day competition of major standing in India
1975–76 Gillette Cup for one-day matches in the West Indies inaugurated (now Shell/Sandals Trophy)
1975 First World Cup
1977 Kerry Packer, Australian media magnate, signs up 51 Test players to create World Series Cricket
1977–78 Tasmania join the Sheffield Shield
1979–80 First Benson & Hedges World Series Cup
1980 Present Laws of Cricket published
1981–82 Benson & Hedges Night Series inaugurated in South Africa
1981–82 Sri Lanka's first Test v England in Colombo
1983–84 Asia Cup inaugurated
1988–89 Lakspray Trophy (later Sara Trophy) inaugurated as first first-class competition in Sri Lanka
1991–92 Zimbabwe's first Test v Indiain Harare
1992 Durham join the County Championship
1993 All County Championship matches arranged for four days
1993–94 Logan Cup raised to first-class status in Zimbabwe
1997 England and Wales Cricket Board established

INDEX

Bold page numbers refer to pictures

O

P

R

S

T

PICTURE CREDITS

The publishers would like to thank the following sources for their kind permission to reproduce the pictures in this book:

Allsport UK Ltd/Shaun Botterill, Simon Bruty, Graham Chadwick, Chris Cole, Stu Forster, John Gichigi, Laurence Griffiths, Mike Hewitt, Inpho, Ross Kinnaird, Joe Mann, Clive Mason, Adrian Murrell, Ben Radford, Mark Thompson; Allsport Historical/Hulton Getty; Alpha/Sport and General; Bridgeman Art Library, London/Marylebone Cricket Club, London, *Cricket in Marylebone Fields* by Francis Hayman; Colorsport; Patrick Eagar; Mary Evans Picture Library; Hulton Getty; Image Select/Ann Ronan; Ken Kelly; courtesy M.C.C., London; Popperfoto/BTH, Dave Joyner; Sporting Pictures (UK) Ltd.; Topham Picturepoint; Peter Wynne-Thomas

Every effort has been made to acknowledge correctly and contact the source and/copyright holder of each picture, and Carlton Books Limited apologises for any unintentional errors or omissions which will be corrected in future editions of this book.